Discovering Beautiful: On The Road To Somewhere
Published in 2009 by Capera Publishing

Second Edition

Check www.discoveringbeautiful.com for more info, short stories,
contact details, naked squirrel pictures, and cheese.

A massive thank you to Leah Welch, who read and re-read this book
several times, found loads of errors, and suggested all manner of
clever and useful edit. Without her, it would have been at least
fourteen and a half percent worse.

Also to David Ferguson who painted the lovely picture on the front.

Plus: those of you who have encouraged and supported me in my writing over the
years. In particular: Mr Peart, Mr Jones, Mr Witham, Annie the Scot, Beth Xeney,
Nancy Firedrake, Stevie Jay Savitt, Gus Mueller, Janette Dollar, Tim, Richard and Ben
(The Ears Boys), Shawn Boland, Patti Perkins, Julie Solari, Saram Singh, John Dunn
and family, Paul Haas, Matthew and Easterly, Patricia Debney, Susan Wicks,
Marasiller, Lynn Gabriel, Lizzie Hibbert, Mikey and Abi, Dave and Lorraine, Eve
Mignot, Carmen and Diego, Jo Kerr, Ana, Ana and José, Steve, Stuart and Anita,
Marie and Janet, Jessica Daeschner, David, Lucio, Mariela, Dalia and David, and
Mother Meera. Also thanks to everyone I ever met.

I once met a soul spinning through eternity trapped
   in a dirty yellow blanket
He was like the sun burning through the clouds
   yet thinking himself the shadow
He burned he burned he burned for that thing,
   the it, the all, the unknowable
He burned not knowing he was aflame like the phoenix
And I watched
   as he fell to the sand as ash
      And I watched, as he rose again
         recreated

- Shawn Boland

Prologue

So I've just been on my usual visit to see my gran and I'm walking down the hill in South Elmsall – *Emsul 'ill*, we call it – past the old stone cottages and the length of yellow sandstone wall, and just after the little church on the corner I run into Gavin, a guy I knew in high school.

"Rory," he says, "I haven't seen you in years. What you been up to?"

"I've been away," I say, "I've been travelling."

The questions begin and I'm eagerly feeding him my stories as we walk down the remainder of the hill: up over the hump of the railway bridge and the lines where I played as a boy, putting stones and milk-crates in front of high speed trains; past the scary, piss-stink steps and the burnt-out shell of a pub; and at the bottom, the steel and perspex bus station, red and green Yorkshire buses advertising destinations as diverse as South Kirby, Upton, and Grimethorpe.

We reach the clock tower outside the market – the clock that has told the same time for as long as anyone can remember – and come to the end of our journey. He's got his way to go and I've got mine.

"You should write a book," he says – and then he's gone, past the butcher's, past the one-restaurant-in-town, past the catalogue store and the line of shoppers stretching from the baker's door, where the same women sell the same tarts and scones I swapped my pennies for something like twelve years and several lifetimes ago. If he keeps walking in that direction he'll come to the red-brick of our old school, and then the field of our footballing youth, and after that the remnants of the colliery, once a complex of tunnels and mines and shafts, and now – thanks to Maggie Thatcher – a flat, weed-filled expanse. Nothing remains but the cracked concrete car park and the rolling black hills of the slag-heap, and the miners that fought so hard for their jobs in the eighties have gone elsewhere, into the factories or onto the dole, never to know the joys of emphysema and lungs filled with coal dust, and slow, staggering deaths.

Like my grandfather, and his father before him, it could have been my fate once. But, Insha'Allah, it wasn't meant to be.

"You should write a book," he'd said, as dozens have before him, on roads, in deserts, on beaches. I've thought about it for years but it never seemed the time. Even talking about it once, down in the canyon with my angel nurse and her husband, the words, "maybe you should wait; maybe something else will happen" – and they were right. But now...his words have struck me and I wonder, maybe the time has come.

I walk down the high street and into the library, and I write all this in an email to my California friend Christine – the one I shared that platonic Mexican bath with, the one with the pendulous breasts, twenty years older than I – and I end it all by asking, "but where should I start?"

Later, in her reply, she says, "start at the beginning; start in New York" – and with that I'm thrown into confusion, because, of all things, that's something I've never thought of. Why New York? Why there, when it could have been the madness of Charlottesville, or that first day walking down the highway towards the mountains and promises of the west? Why Manhattan when I have Mexico and Montana – adventures far greater than anything I did in my days and weeks there?

It's a question I've never been able to answer, and, like Gavin's suggestion, it's a question I've never been able to forget, not once, in the seven years that separate this paragraph and the last.

Part One

Chapter One

So let's go back. Let's go back to the thirty-first of May, nineteen ninety-six, and to a picture of a twenty year-old Yorkshireman sitting on a New York subway train as it zips its way from JFK and heads across Brooklyn and into Manhattan. And let's get a picture in our heads of this young man: slim; pale-skinned; moderately good-looking; a mop of brown hair, à la Hugh Grant, à la the Britpop fashion of the time; five feet eleven and a half – always that elusive centimetre shy of the magic height, the height of men – and clean-shaven, because that was the only option available to him. And his shoulders hunched up tense around his neck. And his arms clinging tightly to the small purple backpack that he hugs to his chest, that contains all he will have to survive for the next four weeks. Hugging and clinging and tense because he was scared. And scared because he was in New York.

And that hugging and clinging and scared young man was me.

I don't mind admitting I was scared: all that I'd heard of New York was that it was a mad, bad and dangerous place to be: stories of Central Park muggers and shifty black men that lure you down dark alleys and when their smiles fade and switchblade knives appear, glinting under rainy streetlights, and more of them surround you...I knew the score: I knew all about Times Square whores, bent Texan cops, Alabama bum-lovin' hicks; I'd seen the movies. A ride on the subway is tantamount to certain death. And everybody's carrying a gun. And New York City is hell on Earth. About three days before leaving Yorkshire I'd watched Kids – a film about AIDS-infected, drugged-up youths battering people to death with skateboards in places like Washington Square Park, places I wanted to go – and suddenly going to America didn't seem like such a good

3

idea – just as it didn't when I'd been chatting with Dave, my dad's business partner, a man who had actually been there several times.

"What you want to do," he says, "first thing, when you get off the plane, is buy yourself a gun. 'Specially if you're going to New York or Florida. Friend of mine knew a couple who went out there, got stopped by a guy in the middle of the swamps with a broken down car: shot them both, took their wallets, and then stuffed them in the car and pushed them into the swamps. Never find you out there." His grizzled and hairy voice is serious in its warning. "Get yourself a gun," he says, sucking hard and rueful on his cigarette, as if to prove the point, "get yourself some protection."

And now here I am, in the kingdom of New York, the Rome, the Paris, the London of the late twentieth century, moments away from a mugging, a stabbing, my death. I clutch and hug and wait for the inevitable attack. I look up and down the carriage to try and spot my assailant. And every stop, and every door that opens sends my heart a-beating just that little bit faster. It's perhaps a little ridiculous. Outside the world is bathed in the most brilliant blue sky I've ever seen and the only people in my carriage are a couple of kids swinging merrily on a pole and an old lady with her nose in a magazine. And on this sunny, hot, lazy afternoon the train trundles on peacefully towards the city.

But back now; back further: back to yours truly sitting hunched up in a battered old Ford Escort, grey and dented and everything I own squeezed in around me, guitar cases and boxes and bags filling the car, sticking out of windows, obliterating every field of vision except the one that points straight ahead. I go to my mum's house and down the garden path of my rollerskating and cricketing youth go those boxes and cases and bags, through doors and up stairs and laid to rest in the room that was once my teenage bedroom, its black wallpaper now fading into charcoal grey, my smudged childhood handprints still visible. And in the doorway my mother leans and looks on, arms folded across her disapproving chest, and she is saying, "put it there," and, "mind the paintwork," and, "so what are you going to do when you get there?"

I put down a box and look up at her and smile.

"I don't know," I say. And I smile some more.

A week before that, though, I am not smiling: I am leaving my girlfriend of the last eighteen months, and all those bags and cases and boxes are being filled with the things that once filled our house in Leeds. It's long past its sell-by date, this relationship, but it isn't making the goodbye any easier, and after all our fights and bitternesses suddenly it's sadness and wanting and sex, and instead of, "it's over, I'm leaving," it's, "I'll be back in a month, we'll see what happens then." She's a lovely girl beneath all her hatefulness and moods. And a great shag too – though I've been rubbish at that for some time.

I've been on the dole and depressed pretty much the whole of the previous year. I've slid slowly into a cocoon of playing computer games, of watching daytime TV, of downing four-packs of lager in front of Eastenders and never

4

leaving the house. I sit in the sagging armchair of my depression surrounded by those half-empty boxes and bags and it seems like something that must have happened to somebody else. Because now I am breaking free. Now I am leaving this room, this town, this girl, and I am moving to London, moving in with my best friend Tim, and seeking something new.

Except, suddenly, I find myself lifted up and out of that chair and heading for the telephone, and there's this thought in my mind: "Rory, my boy," it is saying, "why not take a holiday? You're twenty years old and you've never been out of England; maybe you should go somewhere, take some time out before London, postpone this move a little." And in reply I am nodding my head and thinking, why the hell not? Teletext is scanned and destinations perused; New York presents itself: it's cheap, they speak English, and…and maybe I could get a car, and drive across country, and see and do something cool (John Wayne Texas desert, Route 66, rattlesnakes, Indians, Grand Canyon, Boss Hogg) before I get back into the humdrum of English life. Thought takes hold, fingers push buttons, and then a woman's voice is saying, "where to?" and I am saying, "New York, one month, next week, thank you very much."

And that's how it happened: it was a spur of the moment decision; a total whim. I could so have easily gone to London and moved in with Tim, joined a band and gone down the pub and met a girl and got into shenanigans and japes and who knows where all that might have led? But instead I boarded an Air India flight for New York and went on holiday. After all, what difference could a month make to life? And London wasn't going anywhere.

Eight hours out of Heathrow, then, and I'm in that silver speeding tube as it rocks and races through tunnels and over bridges, past shops and streets and highways, flashing through a piece of the world I've never seen before but which I know is not-England, is America: walk/don't walk signs and enormous old cars, and back in my West Yorkshire coal-mining dogshit village days, when my chief aspiration was to reach drinking-age so I could walk into a supermarket and buy a bottle of something alcoholic because I thought that's what you did when you got older, and pretty much all you did, I met a man who had been to Paris and for a moment my mind had stopped because I could not comprehend that he had left South Elmsall, and left our island, and gone that far. And I knew that it would never happen to me.

But here I am: New York.

I wonder what it was to be that boy? I wonder what he was thinking when he emerged from the bowels of that city and into the bright blue sky of a hot Manhattan afternoon? With what amazement did he look on legions of careening yellow taxis, and towering tall buildings, and rotund, gun-holstering cops? With what trepidation and angst – and, later, surprise – did he tiptoe into Central Park and find not the muggers and rapists and conmen of the films but joggers and children, trees and streams and ducks?

I walked through the park and somehow got chatting to an ex-soldier; he offered to buy me a beer from something called "a liquor store." He gave me the address of his family's farm, saying it was in "Massachewsets, not that far from here" – but then he said it was four hours away and I couldn't work him out. We said goodbye and I went to find the hostel I'd earmarked for my first night out of England – the Banana Bungalow – except the hostel was full. I tried another – full also – and by now I was tired and frustrated and hot. I didn't want to walk anymore. I had a vague sense that maybe I should have booked ahead. Also, that the sensible thing to do now would be to find a phone and call some places, and reserve a bed. But it all just seemed like such a hassle. Instead, I switched to the infinitely more appealing Plan B.

Plan B worked on a simple premise: while America was, for the most part, a complete mystery to me, I did know that Americans were famed for their hospitality – and that they loved to lavish this hospitality on no one more than us Brits. They simply couldn't resist our accents. It was like catnip. All I really had to do for a bed and friends was stroll into a bar and show off my voice.

"Just got here today," I'd say, "don't even have a place to stay" (laughing in my eccentric English way). Three girls swoon and beg for more.

"Oh, I just love your accent," they say in unison, and smile, and play with my fringe, surrounding me with their interest, their affection, their love.

"I like yours too," I mumble shyly, and listen as they tell me I sound just like The Beatles and offer me the spare room and vacant bass player's position in their otherwise all-girl band. Now I'm on my way to celebrity and sex and it's all thanks to the way words sound as they tumble from my mouth and make their way to their delicate American ears.

I take the underground down to the East Village, find a bar, and buy myself a drink. Several hours later, though, closing time comes – four a.m., and nine in the morning for me – and I'm still there, still drinking, and still in need of a place to sleep. Sure, people have been friendly, and I've had more than enough time to show off the gravy on my dulcet Yorkshire tones, but what I've come to realise is, an Englishman in New York is no rare thing. Maybe down Mississippi way, out in the back of beyond, but not here, not in Manhattan. Everybody is from somewhere else – and everybody, it seems, has already met an Englishman, already has their full quota of English friends.

The bartender calls time on my first night out in New York and bolts the door behind me. Beyond tired, and more than a little pished, I stumble into the dark peasant streets of the Lower Eastside and, for lack of anything better to do, I go for a walk.

I walk all night through near-empty, canyon-like streets; beneath endless rows of towering skyscrapers; past unconscious grey-bearded drunks and discarded McDonald's containers. I see Madison Square Gardens and the Empire State Building. I sit on a bench by the East River and watch my first American sunrise. I cross the city and breakfast in an old aluminum-sided diner, and chat with a waitress, and even get given a phone number that I know I'll never have the balls to use. Morning comes and I walk over the Brooklyn Bridge and get lost in decrepit neighbourhoods under train tracks and roads, where tramps in fingerless gloves stand around burning rubbish in oil drums and bad things happen in movies. A car full of black guys honk their horn and shout something about my ivory-white legs, and I get scared and put my jeans back on. I find Prospect Park and Williamsburg, and when darkness comes I take a train back to the Upper Westside, back to the Banana Bungalow, and back once more to the words, "sorry, we're full." I throw myself in desperation at the receptionist, protesting no sleep for forty-two hours, and no idea what the hell I'm doing, and this Australian angel takes one look at my delirious, lobster-burned face and says, "I'm on the night shift, you can have my bed." I thank her with an intense and almost teary-eyed gratitude, and fall promptly and still dressed into her soft Australian sheets, sleeping harder than I ever have, stirred only by the rhythmically creaking springs of the bunk below.

This is my introduction to New York.

Chapter Two

The Banana Bungalow occupies the top five floors of a ten storey building on West 85th Street, the rest of it made up by the tenement apartments I imagine it all once was: one of those hotels that aren't really hotels at all but places where sozzled old men sleep on urine-soaked mattresses in rooms the size and comfort level of prison cells. So in the entrance lobby us youthful foreigners sign in and check out at a reception desk on the left while various drunks and wrinklies and extraordinarily large black women with shelve-like arses shuffle past a similar desk on the right. We merge in the creaking elevators and share the journey with their shopping and their trash; sometimes I get out on those first five floors and walk down dark, bare corridors listening to televisions blare and strange voices in their arguments and self-recriminations. The smell is intensely bad: it's like someone's taken a pile of soiled nappies and cooked them in a big pot with sweat and rotting food and gallons of well-used chip fat and then sprayed the whole foul concoction into the ceilings and the walls and everyone's got strict instructions to keep all the doors and windows shut tight so that not an ounce of stink is lost.

I meet my first travellers – my first fellow travellers – in the lounge and dining area at the very top of the building. They sit around reading guidebooks and watching television and talking in loud voices about how ridiculous the Americans are and how much better it is in South Africa or Australia or wherever they're from. I think I'm expecting adventurers – people who get out there and do all manner of wild and exciting thing – but this bunch are more like stingy tourists. I can't understand why they've come so far to watch TV and moan. Some of them, it seems, are old hands who have been here for years: they're the ones who own the lounge, who know the answers to every question, every query. But the only time they leave the hostel now is to get drunk in local bars trying to pick up cute Japanese girls, no doubt impressing them with their travellers' tales and wisdom.

I take myself off and explore Manhattan. The streets are rammed with people and those brightly-painted taxis are everywhere, swooping through the city, weaving in and out in some madly-choreographed dance. Driving looks like fun, like some insane giant-scale dodgems. Steam even comes up out of the pavements – I thought that was just in the movies. Homeless people are everywhere, begging dimes and spinning yarns – but they're not rubbish like the ones back home, they're wise-cracking and philosophising. They seem to have intelligence. They chat with white-skinned businessmen in their suits and debate things. They play Scrabble and chess in the parks and they're bloody good too.

The buildings are big in New York. South Elmsall's tallest buildings are the pubs, but none of them are over three stories high. We still have half-day closing there on a Wednesday and on Sundays you can walk for miles without seeing a soul or hearing a car. This place, it never stops, and if I want sourdough bagels at three a.m. (whatever they are) then, hey, no problem. Times Square lights shine bright all night – but I can't find no hookers or sex shops there. Ten years ago, they tell me; things were different then.

Central Park is the only respite from the city, a giant rectangle of grass and trees right in the middle of that crowded little island. I follow gurgling streams and find secluded hollows where the city is forgotten and becomes but a distant hum. I fall asleep in meadows with my shirt off and wake up red and raw, a five-fingered white shape where my hand has been splayed across my stomach. I sit in the sun and watch rollerbladers and joggers and think, this isn't scary at all. Where are all the muggers? Where are all the guns and the violence? Central Park isn't what I'd expected; neither is New York. All the bad I'd seen in the movies and heard about, I just couldn't find; all the good – the excitement, the things to see and do, the people – it was all there, and more.

Still, I do manage to meet a few of those fabled New York crazies – like the guy who stopped me in the park one day and asked me if he could dictate a letter he needed to write, but couldn't, for reasons he didn't care to elaborate on. Normal looking guy, grey-haired, dignified, so, "sure," I say.

"Dear Jackie," he begins, as do I, pen in hand, eager to do someone some service, "while you were asleep last night I crept into your apartment using a skeleton key and injected a slow-acting poison into your left breast..."

Or the guy who barked at passers-by all day with his invisible dog. Or the guy who talked to me for hours about the 'mole people' who live in disused tunnels underground and number tens of thousands and have a hierarchy and their own doctors and only come out to murder and rob and rape, and he could take me there to show me but I'd probably never come out alive. Or the fish-faced man who stood gurning at me for hours from the mirror the night I met JoJo the bro' at two a.m. in Central Park and had a hit of his five-dollar acid...

After three days I feel homesick and sit ruefully on the roof of the Banana Bungalow listening to police sirens and traffic and reading a three dollar copy of The Sun. Another three days and I'm just plain bored, on the verge of becoming a part of the crust in the lounge, sick of this building, the smell, the noise of the city. I've seen all the skyscrapers and streets and shops and squares, the Scrabble-playing black guys spelling out insane long words like 'ollamhs' and 'fauteuils' down in Washington Square Park. I'm ready for something new. Either that or, perhaps, I ought to just go home.

It's about then that I see this ad on the hostel wall:

Man with car seeks travel companions for
Maine, Canada and maybe Texas

and soon me and him – a tall, gangly Australian chap called Simon – and Kev from London, and a South African named Roger are riding in Simon's oversized American boat of a car up through the streets of New York and out over the Hudson River and into the open roads of the country and, wow, I'm thinking, wow. The car feels like a cruise liner: it sails, it glides, it simply floats on up the road. I've never been in such luxury. You can move the seats with the touch of a button and everything's covered in leather. Compared to my old Ford Escort – about the only car I've ever spent any time in – it's a limousine. The buildings and pot-holes and traffic are gone and now we're smoothly speeding up this curving wide strip of highway with trees and green and water flashing by, and me there with my head hanging out the window and a great big smile on my face and, man, this is the life.

"Where'd you get the car, Simon?" Roger asks, his accent putting an image of Joss Ackland calling Mel Gibson a kaffa-lover in my head, a flash of some Spitting Image song about never meeting a nice South African.

"Auction," Simon says, "twelve hundred bucks. Pretty nice, eh?"

"It's amazing," I say, "have you seen these seats?" And we all start playing with the buttons that make the seats go up and down and back and forth and probably somewhere in there one that turns the whole thing into a bed or a spaceship and the rockets come out from underneath and jet us up and over the trees.

"It's got a funny name though," I say. "Oldsmobile? Isn't that a bit like calling it a Crapmobile? Or a Rustmobile?"

And on up the road we drive, in our Oldsmobile Eighty-eight.

Several hours later we're somewhere in what they call 'Upstate New York' when lanky, affable Simon pulls to a smooth Australian stop.

"We've got a flat," he says.

And then we're all standing by the car watching him try and get the wheel off, as men are wont to do, but the nuts are all rusty and he's getting nowhere – no matter how intently we stare and shuffle our feet and point.

Meanwhile, everyone's getting bitten by some flying bug-type creature.

"What the fuck is that?" I say, "I'm getting bitten all over."

"Mosquitoes," Roger says, "you never seen a mosquito before?"

But no, we don't have mosquitoes in South Elmsall – I thought they were an Indian jungle type thing. I lift my hand to my eyes and watch one settle. In goes the long bloodsucker and then the thin body begins to swell with blood until it's full and fat and red. Amazing. There are thousands of them and Kev says it's because we're parked by a little river, that they like water. Now my body is itching and I'm starting to go just ever-so-slightly insane.

"It's stuck," Simon says, and Kev takes over while we slap our arms and necks and faces. He lies in the gravel at the side of the road and those nuts just won't budge an inch.

We all stand and gaze at the wheel and the sad, deflated tyre.

Just up the road there's a house and I figure we should see if they can help us. So me and Roger take a walk up there and find this big old guy working on a tractor in a building full of tools and tell him our situation. He listens, and when he's heard enough he wipes his big greasy paws on a rag, arms himself with various weapons and tools and, baseball cap perched precariously on head, follows us back down the road. Pretty soon he's lying by our bug-infested car, sweating and grunting into the rusted-up wheel, and slowly the nuts begin to turn while we four stand around watching and listening and feeling both bad and grateful at the same time. He tells us he's never been to New York City, even though it's only three hours away. He tells us his boy's a truck driver who's been all over the country but he's never been to New York City either. I can't understand it: we've travelled tens of thousands of miles between us to see that fabled place and this guy's lived sixty years right on the doorstep and never bothered to peek inside. He tells us he's never had any reason to go.

Finally, in the darkness, in a cloud of biting bugs, the last wheel nut gives up the fight and we're celebrating and congratulating our saviour. He's been working on that wheel for over an hour. I don't know how the other guys are feeling but personally I'm overwhelmed by his efforts. I want to give him everything I've got. We try to offer him money but he doesn't want any. We say we'll bring him a six-pack on the way back.

"Listen," he says, "you just pass it on. Next time you see someone in trouble, you take the time to help them the way that I've helped you. That's the way it works."

He takes off his baseball cap and wipes the sweat from his forehead. He swishes at one last mosquito and then shakes our hands with his great, greasy paw and leaves with our thank yous and waves trailing up the road behind him.

That night we find a hostel on a farm near a place called Podunk. It's a converted barn, six dollars a night, rustic and quirky and cool. I go outside to take a piss in the perfect silence and all in the blackness of the fields I can see these little floating lights flashing on and off, like some kind of army of tiny flying saucers. I can hardly believe what I'm seeing – and then something in my skull tells me it must be fireflies, like on the nature shows. I stare into the night and watch their blinking lights glowing in the darkness and I feel like I really must have gone somewhere to be seeing this. There are hundreds of them scattered all around. I stare and stare and when one comes near me I try and follow its light and catch it in my hand. I get one and hold it, and it sits in between my palms, little legs crawling on my skin and an intermittent glow rising and swelling and falling through the gaps in my fingers. I want to explode with excitement the way babies do when they see cats or pigeons or squirrels. I want to do this all night. Not once did I imagine in all my growing up days that I'd one day be standing in a field so many thousands of miles away from home and be seeing this spectacular show of these bugs and their lightbulb backsides, and holding one so tenderly in my hands.

And the funny thing is that, despite all the things we did – those days of poker and fishing and plucking leeches in Podunk; the power and roar of Niagara Falls; the lights and streets and bars and girls of Toronto, Ottawa, Montreal, and Quebec City; and all the laughs and fun we had – what I remember most from that trip up into Canada and back down through the endless woods and beautiful lobster coast of Maine is that old guy fixing our tyre and those fireflies flashing their arses in the dark warm night. I remember those two things when so much else has faded – and one more thing besides: being on the phone to my ex right near the end of our trip and telling her all we had seen and done, and her saying, "you keep saying the word 'beautiful,' Rory; I don't think I've ever heard you use that word" – and me being so surprised by that because it seemed only natural that there was all this beauty in the world and, surely, I must have mentioned it before.

Chapter Three

Well then at the end of all that we just about rolled back into New York – and when I say *rolled*, I mean *trundled*, because tall, lovely, nice-guy Simon's Oldsmobile Eighty-eight spluttered its last somewhere up near the Bronx and we left her with some smiling sweaty mechanics by the side of the road with her engine all burned out and took ourselves on buses and trains back to the familiarity and safety of the Upper Westside youth hostels where we said our various goodbyes and I never saw Simon again. Kev I saw some weeks later – and we'll get to that in due course – but me and Roger…well, me and Roger stuck together, because Roger had a plan and it was a plan I liked the sound of.

Somewhere back there on the road Roger and I were hunched down in the backseat of the car and I was asking him what all he was going to do when we got back to the city. Simon and Kev, I knew, were going to have another month or so of travelling before returning to their jobs, but Roger had other ideas: he was going to get some work, he said, find a place to live. He'd done it before, in London and elsewhere in Europe; he knew the way things worked. He knew a guy, too, who'd heard about a furniture moving company run by Israelis and Jews who didn't give a monkey's about work permits or where you came from, who paid in cash and paid pretty good, and he was heading that way just as soon as we got back.

I weighed up my situation. My month was almost up and London and England were expecting me. But what did I have there? I'd left it all behind in Leeds and the only thing I had waiting for me down south was a good friend's floor and some half-baked ideas about joining a band. In America, on the other hand, I'd gotten a taste for those roads, for the freedom and the excitement of it, for the newness and the possibilities. I'd spent the last twelve months drinking four-packs in front of the telly and eating chocolate with a miserable girlfriend and now it seemed like I was actually living. So my money was just about gone – but Roger had a solution to that. So I had no place to stay – but I was sure something would turn up. So I would be illegal – but, so what? So I decided to put my plans for England to one side and give America a try. And that was when New York, for me, really began.

The first thing we did, Roger and I, was find a single room in some flea-bitten tenement between Amsterdam and Broadway and kit it out with an extra mattress stolen from the eighty-eighth street youth hostel. It was two hundred and fifty dollars a week for this bare concrete box not quite big enough for our two beds, and we shared the dingy, paint-peeling bathroom and toilets with a few dozen others. It was cockroach city: a hot, smelly hell that made the Banana Bungalow look like some jacuzzied-out, upmarket, twelve-star hotel. Roger soon got a job as a bartender in a fancy French restaurant just down on Broadway and I got myself a couple of days work at Ben Hur – the Jewish removals company – during which time I managed to steal a rather nice mountain bike from a storeroom below their office and somehow stumbled into a second post as a Manhattan cycle courier.

And, man, what a hoot that was! Me and my red hot bicycle racing all over the city, zooming down through Soho, in and out Wall Street and Midtown, pedalling madly the wrong way up the middle of Fifth Avenue head on into taxis and buses to be the fastest guy there, to get that parcel done. For pure adrenaline rush, that job had it all. For danger too, it had it in spades: at least three or four times a day I'd be floored by blind-eyed pedestrians charging out in front of me, ridiculous immigrant taxi action. The taxi drivers were particularly good at going, say, ten blocks with the left indicator flashing away and then suddenly veering to the right without any warning, directly in front of me, leaving me swerving and sliding, and occasionally denting doors. In a heavy rainstorm, about two weeks into the job, I was floored by yet another crazy madman taxi and took my final bite of asphalt: danger had surpassed buzz and I handed in my pager and satchel and headed back to Ben Hur for a life of hauling pianos up narrow staircases while harsh-voiced Israeli foremen barked orders and hassled customers for impressively massive tips. You really wouldn't believe how many people in New York have pianos.

That courier job wasn't without its benefits though: as well as learning the city better than any other I knew, I got to see so many of those fantastic New York buildings from the inside out, up and down seventy-storey skyscrapers in mad fast elevators that propelled you skywards stomach-first, the rest of you half a second behind. With my insider knowledge I found a fee-free, queue-busting way up the Empire State Building via two or three office-workers' elevators and a dozen or so flights of the fire escape. The only risk was when you got to the very top and had to emerge through a guarded door into the touristed area. I did it several times, though, finding some confused and accented mumblings about the location of the toilet good enough to bluff my way past the security guy there. This insider knowledge also took me up the Mecca of New York's skyscrapers: the Chrysler Building.

The Chrysler Building was built between nineteen twenty-eight and nineteen thirty and was, at the time, the world's tallest building. I'd loved it ever since I was a kid – since I'd seen it in some Alex Cox Moviedrome flick called Q: The Winged Serpent about this prehistoric flying beast that lives up there. It's all that shining silver and those art deco eagle gargoyles, so different from all the other skyscrapers in New York. It always made me smile when I looked up and saw it. And wherever I was in that city, no matter how alone or unhappy I might be, if I could just catch a glimpse of that shimmering sunlit peak I knew there was a friend for me somewhere. I just had to get up it.

The security guard in the foyer was a bit more vigilant than in some of the other places: he stopped me at the elevator and wanted to know who I was going to see, what floor, etcetera, but luckily I'd had the foresight to check out the company directory and had a name picked out already. He took a peek at my courier's clipboard and my backpack and let me through – and then my mission began, for it's not just a case of taking one lift straight to the top; in a tall building like that they often don't go all the way up, but go up in stages, and I knew I'd have to change once or twice part of the way. Also, the lifts don't stop at all floors and some floors would only be accessible to certain key-bearing people. It actually took several trips going up and down between floors to find the interconnecting elevators that would take me into the upper reaches. I had to use the fire escapes too – probably about twenty flights' worth – when the elevators seemed to disappear or dead-end. Eventually, though, after maybe half an hour of stairs and lifts and corridors and wrong-turns I made it to the top two floors and emerged out into splendour.

I remember bursting through that last door and just thinking, wow.

The top two floors, I later found out, had been like the private drinking club for Mr Chrysler and his buddies – but they hadn't been used for decades. So it was all oak-panelled walls and twenties leather couches and enormous picture windows looking out over Manhattan, perfectly framing the taller, uglier sister of the Empire State. There was a long, heavy wooden bar and a wide, richly-carved staircase that lead up to marble toilets (had a pee) and floor-to-ceiling paintings. I explored every nook and cranny of that frozen paradise. It was magnificent. And it was mine.

I moved on up, into the narrows of the summit of the tower; into the dusty, forgotten domain of the chrome-plated eagles and the shining, arched windows – and then I saw that the windows weren't windows at all, just openings, no barrier between the unvisited darkness inside and the world I had left behind. I shimmied my way up the wall and swung myself onto the ledge and there I sat: legs dangling down, heels bumping on thousand feet high metal, and nothing to keep me from sliding down the slope of that roof and out into the void of the city below. I sat looking out at the sky and the horizon beyond those eagles, beyond that glistening chrome, and I was alone in my space: no one to touch me, and no one to bring me down.

Chapter Four

When people ask me about New York and my time there I know it's the excitement and the buzz and the crazy adventures they're looking for, and I'm sure there was some of that – but it's not really what I remember. For me, New York was a depressing, lonely time; a time best forgotten about; a time only to learn from and never live again. It was mad and it was ridiculous, and it was all brought on by my own selfish desire to hoard every single penny I earned.

It started, I guess, with that room of Roger's and mine, and my disgust that I was paying so much for so little. A hundred and twenty-five dollars a week for a curled-up mattress on a cockroachy, concrete floor didn't represent good value in my mind – it was pretty much what I'd been paying for a four-bedroomed house in Leeds – so what I did, after two weeks of this, was take that mattress up onto the roof of the building, get me an extra key cut, 'move out', and then have some rent-free living just as good as I'd had it before, if not better, since the roof was much cooler in those sweltering Manhattan summer nights and the cockroaches didn't seem like they could be arsed to go all that way to do their cockroachy thing. I lived up there for about a week – and then when I discovered the neighbouring, near identical building was completely empty, being in the middle of some stalled renovation, I hopped over the roof, dragged my mattress down into a room there and that was where I dwelled the rest of my New York days. It was pretty good living, having that place all to myself: I even had a telephone line, provided by tapping into the wires that ran across the top of the building with an old two-dollar phone I'd found in a Salvation Army store. I called England, let a few people know I was no longer in Leeds. I bragged about being able to see the Empire State Building from where I sat.

In the meantime, Roger and I had parted ways – he had found a succession of eager women, and a social life, and had moved into a studio somewhere – and at the end of August my three-month tourist visa expired and I became what is known in these parts as 'an illegal alien.' I worked pretty much every day for Ben Hur, often from six in the morning till late at night and my mission was to save as much money as possible, buy a car, and take that mythical drive out west, to Texas and beyond. I'd by now met several people who had done this and returned with their one sunburnt arm and tales of desert driving, of hardly seeing anyone, and that's what I wanted. I wanted it so bad, that promise of a good life in the future, that I put aside any thoughts of a good life in the now. Here's how I lived:

- For accommodation, I've already said – though I haven't mentioned the stress of it all, the worrying at every little sound that somebody was coming to catch me and turf me out slash turn me in. It was cold too, once October came. Occasionally I slept in youth hostel toilets if the building was too risky or I needed a bit of heat. I also snagged a nearby empty penthouse in similar fashion, for a week, but that ended when the superintendent and the two owners found me sunbathing naked on the patio.
- For food, I stole it, apart from my daily treat of a couple of Grey's Papaya's fifty-cent hotdogs. Mostly I'd skank Twixes tucked into my socks, or Diet Cokes and tubs of Ben 'n' Jerry's ice cream. That was pretty much what I lived on. The stealing was easy – though I did once get caught and had to fake some tears in a storeroom full of Mexican shelf-stackers, crying something like, "I'm from England and I've had all my money stolen and I've just got to survive these last two days before I get my plane back home."
- For entertainment, I discovered the Barnes and Noble bookstore and spent my hours in their comfy chairs reading whole books in one sitting, or maybe having a nap. Occasionally, for a real treat, I would go to the two-dollar movie theatre and sneak from film to film and watch at least three.
- For company, I hung every now and then with a few travellers and mainly this mad, incomprehensible Glaswegian, Alan, who I sort of hooked up with. Alan had been in the States about six months, never had any money, but had somehow managed to visit almost the entire country doing auto-driveaways – which are perhaps a North American traveller's best hidden friend, a free car to take you pretty much anywhere and all you have to do is pay the gas and drive. He now earned his bed and board sweeping floors in one of the hostels. Our Sunday afternoon treat was to hit this five dollar all-the-chicken wings-you-can-eat, all-the-beer-you-can-drink bar where fat-necked Americans went to watch 'football' and pump their fists and, I don't know, maybe compare necks. For Alan and I it was an opportunity to get fully loaded on the cheap, leaving mountain-high piles of greasy plates and dozens and dozens of empty pitchers in our sozzled and stumbling wake. I rarely remembered anything after six p.m. those Sundays. The Americans, amazingly, just drank and ate as normal, as though they were totally unaware of the magnitude of the bargain that was available to them: the place didn't even get full. Had it been Leeds or Glasgow they would've been queuing two towns over for a deal like that.

Now you remember Kev, who I travelled with up through Canada and New England, who I didn't really say anything about? Or SuperKev, as we called him, for his uber-Kevness: for his penchant for finicky little gadgets in rollout wallets and wearing white socks with shorts and sandals and being kind of uptight? Well, he came back through town on his way to Blighty and the two of us headed out one night for some beers with a couple of German girls. Things were going well – all getting nice and merry – and we decided to head off to a club downtown somewhere, down on the subway. The three of them bought their dollar twenty-five tokens – but me, as ever, I just hopped over the barriers without paying, feeling cocky and good impressing the girls like that. That was when a couple of guys in jeans and t-shirts came and stood in front of me and flashed their wallets and spun me facing the other way and put something cold and tight and metal around my wrists. Then they handed me off to some other guys who pushed me back through the barriers and lead me upstairs looking sheepishly over my shoulder at SuperKev and the girls. And out into the dark night street we went. And then they pushed me into the back of a van with seven other guys, all their hands cuffed behind their backs too, all sitting on cold metal benches and waiting.

In a nutshell, I got arrested.

Chapter Five

Back in school, back in South Elmsall, getting a girl was hard. Number one, they all fancied Patrick Swayze and Corey Haim, and I wasn't either of them; and number two, there were always loads of twenty-year old guys around who were well into girls six years their junior and who lived far more glamorous lives than I could ever dream of, what with their moustaches and mopeds and criminal records. They'd wait outside the gates for pregnant Shelly and the other dirty girls and talk about how Dazzer or Bazzer or NugHead had just been arrested again for nicking cars and joyriding around the village. From the way people talked I guessed this was supposed to be somehow cool and impressive – but I could never understand that, and could never understand how these girls could even bring themselves to *talk* to guys like that, let alone *touch* them – as well as God knows what else. Getting arrested just seemed like the lowest thing in the world, the thing that only happened to really, really bad people, people elsewhere, people I didn't know and never would. It was beyond me.

At least, that's what I thought back then.

I'm in the back of the van, squeezed up with the other guys, rolling through the night. I'm staring at that locked door and all I can think about is how I've got to get out of there before we get to wherever we're going. Images of TV shows and movies flash through my mind: all the ways I've watched people make their escapes. I'm sure there's some way of looping my arms around my legs to bring those cuffs out in front of me where I can get to work on them. I pull at them with my wrists, glancing around to make sure no one can see what I'm up to. I sneak a look at the door, to try and figure out how the lock works. I wonder how much time I've got and think, I'd better get a move on. And then I realise, this is useless. There is no escape from these cuffs, this van, these cops. And all I can do is wait and wonder what's going to happen to me.

They take us from the van and push us in a sad line through a heavy, steel door. I have no idea where we are. Still I'm squirming in my cuffs and when a cop sees me he squeezes them tighter.

"Ow," I say, "that hurts."

But he just ignores me and I can't believe how little he cares.

We start to move underground, through door after big clunking door, locks and bars and tired and angry-looking men leading us along corridors and into rooms, and all those locks and bars and doors slamming shut behind us, deeper and deeper into the bowels of this labyrinth, lock after lock after lock between me and the far away world above.

A voice says, "hold this and look straight ahead," and a camera flashes and I've just had my first mugshot. Into another room and another tired moustachioed man is holding a clipboard and pen.

"Name?" he says.

"Date of birth?" he says.

"Address?" he says – and that's where we hit a snag, because I keep telling him I'm from Leeds in England – just a simple tourist, you see, not like these other people at all, sir – and this particular example of New York's finest can't quite grasp the fact that there are other places in England apart from London, or that England isn't a place in London, or, perhaps, that anything outside of New York and America exists.

"Leeds," he says, "that's in London, right?"

"No," I say, "it's in England."

"London, England, right?"

"No," I say, "Leeds, England. Leeds, West Yorkshire. LS7 1JB."

He looks at me and writes it down.

"Place of birth?" he says.

"Pontefract," I say. "Pontefract, West Yorkshire."

"Pontefract, West Yorkshire," he says back to me as he writes it on the clipboard in front of him. "That's in London, right?"

"No," I say, "it's not in London, it's at the opposite end of the country from London. London is the capital and Pontefract's a completely different city, in the county of West Yorkshire – which is the same county that Leeds is in. Which is another completely different city to Pontefract or London. England is a country. There are lots of – "

And that's when he tells me to shut up and pulls out his truncheon and says something like, how would you like to feel my nightstick, boy, remember who you're talking to.

They say that Americans are famously ignorant when it comes to the geography of the world and knowledge of countries other than their own. It must be something to do with that 'rugged individualism' that dates back to the Declaration of Independence when Freddy Roosevelt and Jefferson Starship threw that big tea party in Boston. Well I probably can't speak for all Americans but I must say that I came across a surprisingly large number of examples of this fabled lack of knowledge during my first few months there – a lack of knowledge which, now I come to think of it, I haven't really seen anywhere else.

Like the guy who supposed I would be really happy that the New England Patriots were doing so well – because he, a lifelong American football fan, thought they were from England.

Or the otherwise intelligent and very well schooled girl from Virginia who had no idea where the nearly-neighbouring state of Pennsylvania was on a map.

Or the woman in Texas who said, in all earnestness, "Arizona? Is that in England?"

Not to mention all those who had no idea England was actually smaller than America, and so much smaller that it would fit into Texas alone five times over, and who thought we all lived in castles and knew the queen well enough to pop around for a spot of tea whenever we pleased and, say, what language do y'all speak in England anyways?

Another thing many Americans seemed to lack was a non-demented idea of their ancestries and of where they had come from – so that if I was to count the number of Americans who had told me they were from Ireland, for example, it would probably take me until about a quarter past three (it's now just coming up to one thirty). The fact of the matter is, upon further questioning I would invariably discover that they had never been to Ireland, nor were they or their parents born there, and they were as likely to find it on a map as they were to name the entire history of Irish Taoisigh in correct chronological order. Similarly, those of apparent Scottish descent seemed satisfied to name famous old Scotsmen as their clan by mere dint of sharing a surname. I even met a cowboy once who told me he was a direct descendant of the Earl of Dudley. His proof? No, not exhaustive genealogical research or the trawling through of ancient parish registers, but the far more time-efficient method of concluding thus: my name is Dudley, and his name has the word Dudley in it, therefore we must be related. Simple things, they say, please simple minds – and no doubt there are many thousands of Americans who live contented and happy with the entirely imagined belief that they are descended from ancient nobility and greatness.

Not that this has anything to do with my being incarcerated deep in the bowels of some inescapable Manhattan dungeon…

Ah, you can't beat those initial first few hours, the losing of your custodial virginity! All that fear, all that remorse – all that wondering what's going on beyond those steel sullen bars! All the cowering and hiding and whimpering inside, furtive glances at cellmates, ears pricking at everything that is said. All the thinking: when are they coming for me, my God, I'm so hungry, doesn't anybody care? All the discomfort, the bright lights, the hard floors, hour after slowly-ticking hour in that windowless room hundreds of thousands of metres deep inside the earth…

I am sitting there on the floor with my arms inside my figure-hugging short-sleeved shirt trying to find some warmth from the merciless blast of the air-conditioning. The room is a large concrete rectangle with benches around the edges. There are thirty-three inhabitants and I'm the only white: the rest are a mix of blacks and Hispanics and they talk amongst themselves and mostly look as uncertain and miserable as I feel. It's past four a.m. and I've been here about five hours. My belly rumbles and my eyes wish for sleep but I don't think either will be satisfied for some time. I watch as the cell doors open and the cleaners walk in with their translucent rubbish bags and brooms. Several men approach them and when the guards aren't looking money and jewellery are exchanged for cigarettes that are then shared or sold on to others. A pack is ten dollars and an individual fag is a buck, and it looks like the cleaners are making some decent additional income out of these sorry-looking Mexicans and blacks. I huddle deeper into the corner and surreptitiously watch the show. And then I see this tall sinewy black guy sidle up to me and sit in close beside.

"You got a watch?" he says.

I nod.

"I know," he says, "I seen it." He looks at my shirt, at the place where my right wrist is pressed against my chest and his eyes bulge and smile. Once again I rue the decision to wear my tight, Britboy, androgyny-implying top – only this time it's not down to the lack of protection it gives me from the cold.

"Listen," he says, "you wanna make some money? I got a deal for you." He tries to catch my eye. "You see that guy there," he says, "he's a friend of mine. You give me your watch, he'll give us two packets of cigarettes for it. We sell them for forty dollars, we got twenty dollars each." He looks again at the round man holding the broom. "It's a good deal, huh?"

I look at the cleaner and hold my hand over my watch. "I don't like cigarettes," I say. It's true, I've never even tried one, not a single drag. Besides, this guy doesn't look like the kind of business partner I could trust.

"They're to sell," he says, "we can make some money."

"I know," I say, "but I like my watch and I don't need any money."

"You'll need it when we get to the pen," he says.

"The pen?"

"The penitentiary, up on Riker's Island."

I think I smile when he says this – he seems to think that I'm like him, that I'm on my way to big jail too – as if! I'm just a British tourist, just passing through, some mistake. I think about him stuck in there, his days and months in some hopeless little cell while I'm out playing in the sun.

"Listen," he says, and he takes this long, wide fist of big black knuckles and presses them against my face, "you can either give it to me or I can take it."

I feel his bones and skin against mine and I freeze in my seat. In that cell, with those thirty-two non-white prisoners and the cleaners that are indistinguishable from them except for their brooms and their freedom I know I don't stand a chance. I don't know what to do – but before I even think about what it I get up and walk across the room, past the cleaners, and out the open door and into the corridor. I push past a guard and then I'm standing at some window begging to be taken out of that cell, away from the guy who's going to steal my watch and beat me up. I keep on at him – I beg and beg – and eventually he gives in and moves me up the corridor and into a small cell with just one other guy who doesn't look like he'll give me any trouble at all. I settle in and even manage to drift off to sleep for half an hour.

I'm woken from my shallow slumber by the sound of a key turning in the lock. My eyes blink open to the sight of the door swinging shut behind six foot three of muscled arms and clothes and legs, and at the top of it all the smiling head of my would-be associate in the tobacco trade.

Inside of me a voice goes, "oh shit," and I want to cry at the injustice of it all.

"I got a friend," he says, flashing his teeth. He slides himself along the bench and squeezes me tight into the corner. He takes his hand and moves it down to his crotch, and hard in his trousers I see the stiff outline of his erect penis.

"I like you," he says, "and when we go up to the pen I'm gonna make you my bitch." He smiles when he says this and his crotch-stroking hand gets just a little more excited.

"Now gimme your watch," he says, "or I'm gonna beat the living shit out of you. And if you think I give a fuck about these guards it ain't gonna make no difference to me."

His fist is in my face again: his other hand takes a break from stroking his cock and he reaches over to my wrist and makes a grab for my watch. I jump up and I think, man, I don't care that this is just some ten dollar Chinatown fake or that this guy wants to batter me, it's mine, and there's got to be some way out of this. I make for the cell bars and take off my watch and I'm kind of standing there holding it through them out of reach – except his arms are longer than mine and he's reaching through now to try and grab it from me. I'm shouting something – I don't know what – and the other prisoners from across the way are stirring to have a look. And just as he's about to get it from me I toss it into the corridor and then neither of us have it.

A guard comes by and picks it up and wants to know what's going on.

"It's mine," we both say – and then, "it's mine," my shaky voice shouts, "and this guy in here's trying to nick it from me. He keeps saying he's going to beat me up and wants to make me his bitch and, honestly, I swear, you've just got to get me out of here; please, you've got to let me out."

And tiredly and uninterestedly the guard reaches in and gets his keys and open swings the door and out I go. Watch is returned; Rory is intact; all is well. Back to the huddled Mexicans and then at some point in the afternoon – about sixteen hours after my arrest – a whole bunch of us are taken up to this rather nice and quite glamorous courtroom full of heavy carved wood and we stand and listen while the judge chats with his officials and issues bits of paper that basically say, "come back soon," and then it's out into bleary-eyed, blinking sunshine and business-suited New York streets and, to everyone else, it's like nothing's ever happened.

Chapter Six

Before all that, though – before the arrest and the illegal alienship – I'd bought a car. I'd been working at Ben Hur about two weeks and had saved up the rather monstrous sum of five hundred and twelve dollars, and then I'd met these two Swedes who were on their way home after living out in Texas for a year – they actually had Texan accents, too, drawl and all – and they had this little silver Mazda 626 for sale. It was five hundred dollars and probably not the wisest thing I could have done with my money but, the thing was, the car had California license plates on it and when I saw those, with their little palm trees and hints and nods towards Beverly Hills and Baywatch I thought, I'm having that. So I bought the car and that left me with twelve dollars in my pocket.

Now as luck would have it I got chatting one night to this Australian girl who wanted to get out of New York and go up to Niagara and Chicago. She was all set to take the bus but I offered to save her a few quid and take her there if she paid for the gas and maybe enough for a sandwich. I guess I was just itching to get on that road and leave town for a while. We left for Niagara about two a.m. and, apart from getting pulled over once for speeding – the cop left me alone once he saw my pictureless paper UK driver's license, as alien to him as, well, an alien's license – we made it okay. I got to see the falls again – and then I was actually on the make once I'd picked up another Englishman who wanted a ride to Chicago and then Indianapolis to see the racetrack there, and a French guy who just wanted to go anywhere. Probably I could've crossed the whole country like that and returned my 626 to California, still with my twelve dollars intact. As it turned out, though, Eddie the Brit and Michel the Frenchman wanted New York and we pointed ourselves eastwards once again.

It was somewhere in the peaceful flat tree-lined greenness near Wheeling, West Virginia that our trip was cut prematurely short.

I was driving and Eddie was in the passenger seat. Our French friend was in the back sleeping. I'm not really sure what happened next – probably I was too busy digging the trees and the sky or something – but I remember looking up the road and seeing this big white lorry kind of angled across the freeway, and just as I was wondering what that meant I noticed that everyone in front of me had stopped. I slammed on the brakes and braced myself on the steering wheel, and about a millisecond later the car went skidding into the back of this enormous old brown Dodge, some behemoth straight out of the seventies, and then there was this almighty crash and crunch of metal and everything went black. Except instead of going hurtling through the windscreen or looking down puzzled at the strange, syrupy red object protruding from my chest, I was still sitting there, still gripping the steering wheel, and I was okay. Through the windshield I could make out a mass of metal and pipes: the big brown Dodge was actually sitting on top of us. I stumbled out in shock and stared at the crumpled mess of my beautiful California Mazda and wanted to cry, the bonnet and front end totally destroyed, the windshield and roof caved in. I staggered to the boot and pulled out a beer, and took some pictures, and started to drink. Apart from a tiny one-centimetre cut on my little finger I was undamaged. Eddie and the sleeping Frenchman were fine too. I couldn't understand it – none of us had been wearing seatbelts and we must have been going at least sixty before I hit the brakes.

We left the car right there on that West Virginia highway, to be towed away and never seen again. I did salvage one license plate, its California palms speaking hopefully of better days to come. Eddie and Frenchie and I then spent the rest of the day and night riding along darkened Pennsylvania highways with a number of kindly truckers. They'd heard of the accident and our plight and would radio each other trying to arrange connecting rides, trying to get "these three poor boys" back to New York and "back home to their families" – and they did. In the early morning darkness we were deposited once more on the Manhattan streets I knew so well, where we said our goodbyes and each drifted away to our various destinations. I suppose I'd gotten them there one way or another. And I still had my twelve bucks.

Chapter Seven

It's little wonder then, looking back, that I was so miserable in New York. Getting arrested, crashing that car, sleeping semi-rough, and all those lonely days and nights living like a ghost on wet streets, hiding in toilets and bookstores – I mean, crappy things were happening to me, but I was responsible for them all. I had an inability to do things the right way, always searching for some short cut, some way around things, spending as little money as possible. I'm not sure why that was but I guess, in one way, it paid off: by November I had saved over three and a half thousand dollars, thanks to Ben Hur removals and a volunteer drug study I did out in Princeton, New Jersey with Alan, letting nice nurses stick needles in my arms and test untested pharmaceuticals on me, but mostly just lazing around in bed watching movies and playing Risk and eating gelato. When the next cheap car came along I was more than ready to leave my festering New York behind.

There was, however, one last drug study to do, and so crazy Alan and I loaded up my newly-purchased two hundred dollar Chevy Cavalier and took to the Henry Hudson Parkway, heading for Princeton. It was a trip that was doomed from the start. Ten minutes into the journey Alan started yelping and shouting and going on about the "hingme" – I never could understand a word he said – and I looked over to see that his shoes were being melted by some steaming green liquid that was filling up the passenger footwell.

Naturally, all I could do was laugh.

"Hingme! Hingme!" he shouted.

"Well just pick up your feet, man, don't worry about it."

"Hingme!"

"I can see that they're melting but what can I do?" The traffic was chocker and we were moving at a crawl towards the tunnel. The green liquid was sloshing as we stopped and started, going into the back.

Alan spun around and grabbed his by-now soaked bag.

"Hingme," he said, despairingly.

Well, what option was there but to carry on? There was no way to turn around and the car was still running so maybe it wasn't vital. Maybe it was just spare green fluid that I didn't really need anyway. We continued to crawl and eventually we reached the Holland Tunnel. Where I realised we were three lanes from where we needed to be.

"Dinnae," Alan said – but he was too late. Our left turn light turned green and I whizzed across in front of two lanes of traffic to make the right turn we needed. Straight in front of a couple of cops.

They flashed, and I obeyed, and that was the end of our driving for the night.

They asked to see my registration and I told them I'd only just bought it, I didn't have one yet. They asked me for my license, and for all my other documents, and I handed them over. They perused them for a bit and then said, "leave the car there, you can't drive without your registration." I protested, and Alan told me to shut up, and we did as they said. I guess, as an uninsured, unregistered, illegal alien driver they could have done a lot worse.

The thing was, we needed to get to this study: it would be another thousand dollars, worth far more than the car, and it didn't make sense to jeopardise that. We tramped off and took the train, and Alan grumbled about my lousy driving and his molten shoes, and I worried about the car and sort of resigned myself to having lost it, knowing that it was parked in a strictly no parking area, yet another four-wheeled friend down the drain – my fourth in less than three months of actual driving. Worse still, when I got to the study they decided not to use me, and sent me home after three days, barely two hundred and fifty dollars better off than when we'd left.

And, of course, the car was gone. And along with it my dreams of escaping New York and driving across America. I was back to square one: homeless and jobless and cast adrift in Manhattan, and not even an Alan to keep me company. Sure, I had lots more money now than I'd ever had – but what I really wanted was that car. I asked a policeman where it might have gone.

"Probably at the pound on west thirty-eighth street," he said.

"But I only left it for an hour."

He shrugged his shoulders and pointed to the north. "West thirty-eighth and twelfth," he said, "right on the water."

I walked the three miles there and, sure enough, they'd got it, and would be only too pleased to let me have it back once I'd paid the three hundred dollars worth of traffic tickets and storage and release charges – which was obviously out of the question. I protested this and that, and when I said that there wasn't even a no parking sign on the whole street they told me I could take it up with the judge. And I said, "right, I will."

I saw the judge; the judge said there was nothing he could do. He said I'd need evidence, some statement from the police, photographs to show that the sign wasn't there. I said I'd get them. He said it wouldn't guarantee me getting my car back.

"I'll get them," I said, "there definitely wasn't a sign. I wouldn't have parked it there if there was."

I walked back down, three more miles, anger and schemes brewing in my head. I'd turn up at four in the morning and wrench every no parking sign from its pole. I'd forge something from a policeman. I'd beseech every judge in the goddamned city till they gave me my car back, say one had said one thing and

27

one another, tie them up in knots till they were in a daze and gave me the slip of paper I needed. Or I'd distract them one day, lean over their desk and get the slip myself; sign it, Judge Rory; done.

In the end, though, it was much simpler than that. I took dozens of photos of the street, from every angle, snapping everything but the post with the no parking sign on it. And then I crossed over the street, and aligned myself with the no parking post so that the sign itself was hidden behind a pole, and snapped a few of that. Those New York signs, you see, come out of the top of the pole like a flag, and this particular one was at about a forty-five degree angle from the road: from the opposite side it looked just like an empty pole.

In fact, those were almost the exact words uttered by the judge as he looked through my pile of beautifully taken pictures.

"Nothing but an empty pole," he said, about three seconds before signing my release slip.

I pretty much skipped to the pound with that paper in my hand – and with great glee got the people there to release my car and charge up the battery before whizzing on up to the Upper Westside to collect my secreted belongings. And with a greater glee still did I whizz back down to the Holland Tunnel – right-hand lane, right-hand lane – and, green sloshing liquid and all my possessions around me, disappear under old Henry Hudson and escape that city.

Five months of it, then, and suddenly I'm up and out the other side and into the mess of northeastern New Jersey, flying now along the steel and dirt and noise of the Pulaski Skyway high above the billowing industry of chimneys and pipes with the famous and once more beautiful outline of those Manhattan skyscrapers fading into the distance behind me as night falls black in the dark November cold. I want to look back but there's too much going on around me to think about that magnificent silhouette, those streets, my times; all I see are headlights; all I hear is the roar of traffic – ten thousand cars racing from New York, fleeing the city, jostling for position. We strive to survive, to avoid each other, to forge ahead; tyres turning madly over steel and tar; Newark has been and gone; other unnamed shadows of New Jersey cities rise and fall, are swept aside – all I see is the road, my hands feverishly gripping the steering wheel, my foot hard on the accelerator, my gaze straight ahead. We thunder onwards until finally the noise and the lights subside a little and the road is quieter, and my foot eases off the gas. Now I'm alone in the dark in this blue cocooned car and at last there is something other than the drudge and trudge of Manhattan streets, of Ben Hur stairs, of lonely days and lonelier nights sleeping on illegal concrete floors, in toilets, on roofs. Now there is a car and a road, and it's a road that is pointing west.

Chapter Eight

So me and my Chevy Cavalier drove on, down through the battlefields of Gettysburg and the real life Willy Wonkaville of Hershey, Pennsylvania – where the whole town smells of chocolate and the main streets are named Cocoa and Chocolate Avenue (but, like most American chocolate, it still tastes of sick) – and then into the Blue Ridge Mountains of Virginia – my first ever mountains – and down the four hundred and sixty nine-mile long Blue Ridge Parkway, one of America's great scenic highways. That was where the trip began in earnest – that was where I started to have what I'd call these 'fuck me moments', where I'd round some bend and then suddenly be looking out across mountain vistas to rivers and forests below, the blue haze of the sky lining the peaks and not a soul for miles around; where I'd pull over and switch off the engine and stand there looking, wanting to dance, and thinking, oh my God, and, fuck me, and those are the only words that would come because I'd never seen such beauty and I didn't have the capacity to hold it in my tiny little mind.

In Charlottesville, not far from the Parkway, I pulled into town late one night and, sipping a beer at the bar, turned and said to the guy next to me, "I know this sounds like a stupid question but, can you tell me where I am?" – knowing full well exactly where I was – thanks to my shoplifted Rand McNally – but figuring what a great way to start a conversation, provide a bit of interest and, of course, show off my accent and eccentricity. Not too dissimilar to my failed Plan B – except this time it worked. Four hours later, person after person, beer after beer, I'd landed an invite to stay in a house with these five university girls, one of whom had taken more than a bit of a shine to me. Three days I was there, a little kiss and a cuddle, and my first ever experience of marijuana by way of some kindly baked brownies. Sat like a mute and retarded zombie in front of The Dukes of Hazzard for several hours and felt very strange indeed.

And in Tennessee: horror. From the traffic jams in the supposed wilderness of the Great Smoky Mountains, to the sheer, pink-edged insanity of Pigeon Forge and Dolly Parton's very own theme park, Dollywood. Even in Nashville, which I'd long thought this Mecca of musical cool I found madness: men wearing actual genuine cowboy hats and boots and these extravagantly-tassled shirts that I'd never really believed existed; and by their sides, enormously-haired women tottering around like cheap impersonators of the aforementioned big-breasted country crooner, the sidewalks packed with the bizarrely-attired. Surely no one would pay good money to make themselves look this ridiculous.

But they did. Meanwhile, the main road was an endless, circular procession of massive pickup trucks and sports cars parading up and down, up and down, stereos blasting, big-necked young Americans leering out of windows and shouting back and forth at the women. I couldn't understand any of it. I left.

I left for Natchez, Mississippi, by way of another scenic route, the Natchez Trace Parkway, and in Alabama I got my first taste of southern hospitality when I heard the immortal words, "come back y'all." At first I thought she was taking the piss – must be the cynical, untrusting Yorkshireman in me – but when I realised she wasn't, and when I heard it again and again, I started to feel their unabashed friendliness rub off on me. People were saying, "hi" and smiling for no apparent reason, and waving as they passed me in their cars, not because they wanted my money, or wanted anything from me, but because they were human and that's what humans round these parts do. Probably that's the way we were all designed but years of deceit and lies have made us wary – or, at least, they have me. When I come to think of it, I'm not sure I've ever really experienced anyone who was kind just for the sake of it – not since my gran and her hot dogs and chips, her milkman-delivered fizzy lemonade.

I'd started to find Americans so much more trusting than the Brits and I liked it. In England trust had to be earned, and people automatically came from a place of mistrusting, of putting up a barrier and waiting to see what you would do. Here it was the opposite: here it was assumed that you were okay, that you weren't going to do something wrong, and people were friendly and open, perhaps until there was a reason not to be. Down in Alabama there were old-style gas stations where you'd fill up and then have to go on the hunt to find someone to pay, where they had no idea how much you'd put in, they just asked you and assumed you'd tell the truth. And, sure, I thought about lying, or just driving away, knowing I could get away with it, but the sheer decent honesty of it seemed to get to me, to stop me and make me want to do the right thing. I can't imagine that working in Yorkshire, in England – just as I can't imagine people using those newspaper machines they have here without seeking some way to rip them off. Even in the big cities I'd see them, and see people drop in their fifty cents or dollar, open the little door on the front – and then take just one. It was mindblowing that they didn't take the lot. I know for a fact that if they put one of those in South Elmsall there'd be a race every morning to be the one who got the whole day's worth of papers for the price of one. And then they'd stand there trying to sell them – or more likely end up throwing them all away – but, for sure, they'd be gone, because anything that isn't tied down or has even the merest whiff of a bargain about it is snapped up, devoured. Maybe because things aren't as cheap and we don't have the same sense of abundance, or maybe because we remember too clearly the privations of rationing and the war.

Or maybe there is something inherently dishonest about us, something that trusts less, some loss of innocence that the Americans haven't yet suffered – and long may it be.

And back on the road, down through the rolling hills and sleeping grasslands of Alabama and Mississippi, heading for some twenty-four hour casino ship parked up in the river somewhere, I guess I prove the point once again when, driving through Port Gibson I fail to see a stopped car awaiting a left-hand turn into a gas station and slam my eighty-seven Chevy into the back of a van. Suddenly, I've gone from contentedly cruising Highway 61 to sitting shocked in the middle of the road, steam rising up from under the crumpled, glass-covered hood of my seemingly fucked car. I turn the key and I get nothing but the oil warning light and I assume she has gone the way of the Mazda, killed on the road because of my lack of concentration. The van has pulled into the gas station, its back window shattered, and glancing across I know that's where I'm supposed to go too, to await the police and to go through the whole process of documents and recriminations. But I'm sitting in an unregistered, uninsured car and I'm an illegal alien. I'm in Mississippi. I'm fucked. I know the only sensible thing to do is make a run for it.

I plead and I plead with my car to take me away from there, frantically turning the key over and over again, crying into my steering wheel, stamping on the pedals, but all I get is that blinking red light and more and more steam. The beam of my one remaining headlight shines uselessly into the empty black sky and I wonder how long it will be before that same night sky is filled with the lights and sirens of the cops. I turn the key again and when my Chevy miraculously fires up I slam on the accelerator and leave the gas station and my guilt behind. I'm driving wildly, practically blinded by the incessant cloud of steam, searching desperately for a way out, some place to hide. Not far down the road I see a dirt track heading off into darkness to the right and I race down it, skidding like crazy in the mud. All I can think of is getting away, putting some distance between myself and the accident, escaping the cops. I'm swerving all over the place, driving way too fast, until finally the hood of my car – which has come unhooked and has been rising about six inches every time I go above thirty – snaps violently back, crashing into the windshield. I slide to a halt. I'm panting, my fingers tightly gripping the steering wheel, the adrenaline flooding through my veins. I'm so fucking scared and only one thought sounds in my brain: how do I get out of this?

I sit for a while and then I release the steering wheel and slump back into my seat. I feel my breathing calm itself; the night is quiet and humid and all around me I hear the noise of a million chirping crickets. This dirt road has taken me into the middle of nowhere.

I look the car over. She still runs, and there's no oil leak as I'd feared, but the front end is pretty much destroyed, the grill gone and three headlights smashed. The hood won't sit down at all, the front bent upwards, its two catches misaligned now by a number of inches. I take a luminous yellow shoelace from one of my rollerblades and tie it into place, and then I continue slowly down the dirt road, plotting a route to Louisiana. Head for the border, I reckon: that's what the outlaws in the movies always do. I wonder if it still works, the county line, not my jurisdiction and all.

I come out the other end of that dirt road and slowly pick my way through sleeping neighbourhoods and along backcountry roads, amused at the irony of the signs on the lampposts that signify I'm following an evacuation route. Eventually I enter another town – a safe, Louisianan town, I assume – and pull into a place for gas. But as I get out I see some sign on the wall that strikes me as vaguely familiar, and when I look behind me and stare down the road I realise that I have been here before, that I've done some huge, ill-navigated circle and landed myself right back in Port Gibson. Now I'm really scared: it seems like some total fucking nightmare from which there is no escape. I jump back into my car determined to find a way out of this Mississippi Twilight Zone of chirping cricket night, where the innumerable solitary country white churches ooze images of the Ku Klux Klan and torchlit lynchings from creaking old oak trees. Soon I'm back on curséd old Highway 61, back to the last place in the world I want to be, speeding frantically past the gas station of my doom and, later, past three parked police cars, and on and on I go, grey-haired and wrinkled, until I make Louisiana and can finally exhale. The deserted city streets of wherever I am feel friendly and safe and I know that the police of Port Gibson, Mississippi will have no authority here.

Still, that's little comfort when I see the flashing blue and red lights behind me and I'm motioned to pull over into an empty parking lot.

The cop walks over to my window and says hello.

"You know you've got a taillight out," he says.

"No," I say, "I didn't know that."

"Well see if you can get it sorted," he says – and that's all he says. No ticket. No questions about my battered front-end. All he wants to do is let me know I've got a problem and it needs fixing.

Chapter Nine

And from the chilled out jazzy days and nights of New Orleans, the Big Easy; across the whole of hill and desert Texas by way of cool college Austin and Thanksgiving with some cotton-picking Mexican farmers eating turkey off of paper plates; on into the mountains of New Mexico in a blizzard that killed several people, and me sliding off the road into some trees when the other side was a rocky fifty-foot drop – that old two hundred dollar car of mine keeps chugging along, despite various breakdowns, its one headlight struggling valiantly to illuminate the way. I stripped naked and ran around on the dunes at White Sands; checked out the world's largest something or other at Carlsbad; zoomed around the dusty, cactus strewn desert south of Tucson looking for and finding old adobe jailhouses and ghost towns; discovered smalltown magic in funky Bisbee, a town that looked as though it had been built by dropping a load of sheds on a hillside; and dug those Boot Hill, Wyatt Earp, OK Corral, Doc Holliday gunfighting legends in Tombstone; and in the mountains of Arizona one freezing cold no moon night I got out of my car at a scenic viewpoint to ironically stare into the blackness for a laugh and suddenly could have almost bumped my head on the plethora of stars that hung there like a milky soup. Things like that, when you've grown up in South Elmsall and maybe seen the occasional dimly glittering twinkler peeking through the cloudy night but mostly your life has been cigarette butts and beer stains and concrete, they make you want to cry.

I was pulled over by the cops several times and I built up a mighty impressive collection of traffic violation tickets – mostly for speeding and illegal parking, but a few for not having any insurance or registration documentation, blah blah blah. The thing was, they always let me go, despite my lack of paperwork, and despite my non-valid driver's license and expired tourist visa, and as I zipped from county to county, from state to state, I realised it didn't really matter – for what was Arizona going to say about traffic tickets issued in Mississippi? And what did the lawmen of California care for offences committed thousands and thousands of miles away? As far as I was concerned they were all entirely separate entities and by the time the judge in Hicktown, Alabama was calling for my head I'd be off and over the Rockies and there'd be nothing he could do about it. Better still, this pile of tickets and summonses and citations wouldn't mean a thing once I was back in England – and in that there's a great lesson to be learned: commit all your shit overseas and then you can go home scot-free and clean. As long as you don't get into anything major and get busted for drug-running in Thailand, or lose your head in Syria, or get bummed stupid in New York, as I very nearly was...

I did think I was done for once in New Mexico, just after leaving those lovely turkey-sharing cotton farmers. I'd just crossed the border from Texas when my battered, shoelace held-together Chevrolet was spied by some desert highway cops who did the old flashing lights thing and pulled me over. They wanted to know about the damage – standard excuse: I hit a deer – and where I was off to, what I was doing. They said did I mind if they searched my car, sort of implying that it would be worse if I said no. I opened up the boot: my clothes and possessions were scattered all over the place; my money too. Mostly it was in a plastic bag – piles and piles of fives and tens and twenties, a few thousand dollars worth – but a lot of it just in amongst the clothes. Kindly, they collected it all together and put it with the rest. They asked me questions about where it had come from. Then they came across a child's jacket – a tiny little adorable flying jacket I'd bought back in New Orleans for my ex's three year-old daughter – and their eyes sort of narrowed a bit.

"Can you just go and sit in the back of that car there," they said, "while we finish having a look around?" I wandered off and slid into the backseat. I sat and watched them through the window, a meaty shotgun strapped to the other side of the mesh enforcing the powerlessness of the situation: just me and those cops in the middle of all that sand.

Three more cars arrived, and now at least seven or eight cops were going over my stuff. They were lifting more and more money out of the boot, and pulling out my diaries and with latex-gloved hands turning the pages and reading. They read a lot. They must have read page after page of mad, depressed, meandering New York drivel. And my road diaries. And my wrongdoings. What if they came across my mishap in Mississippi? What if they found me gloating about yet another traffic ticket ignored? The cops swarmed over my car, heads underneath the chassis, carpets being lifted, and then –

And then, out of nowhere, this plastic-gloved policeman lifts up his pen and right there dangling on the end of it: a single solitary child's pink shoe. They gather round and stare. I have no idea where it's come from. I realise, with the jacket and the money, and all the damage and the holes in my story, this doesn't look good.

All of a sudden this inescapable police car backseat feels a whole lot more like an actual prison.

They ask me about the shoe and I say I haven't a clue. They ask me about my diaries; ask me if I'm all right in the head, if maybe I shouldn't be having therapy, and I'm embarrassed. But they ask me so sincerely it makes me think that they've never had a real or questioning thought in their lives, never been depressed, never wanted more, as though the things they'd read in there might as well have been written by an alien they were so far removed from their shaven-headed, square-jawed existences. They make me squirm a bit with

34

vague threats and warnings and then issue me with a couple of summonses to appear in court with my insurance and registration documents – which I've told them I have at home – and then they let me go and send me thankful and relieved beyond relief back onto the road, resolved to never pass through that particular township slash county slash jurisdiction again. I add the tickets to the pile and smile a little as I imagine my name repeatedly echoing around some small town courtroom, me by then a thousand miles away and untouchable. I am back on the glorious desert highway, once more free.

I fall head over heels and madly in love with the desert, and quickly declare it my favourite landscape of any on Earth: I love the cactuses and the quiet of it, the way that nothing really grows, that it's just sand and rocks and desolation. I'll be driving along the highway and then off to the side spy some dirt road leading into mountains and emptiness and duck off down it, just bombing along to see what I can see. I find cliffs and hills of dust and stone and want to be at the top of them, and go scrambling up and look out for miles and never see a thing. I find old abandoned houses in the middle of nowhere and wonder. The desert is the perfect playground for a boy like me.

By the sixth of December I'd been on the road nearly four weeks and done just over five thousand miles, and now it was time for the Holy Grail of Route 66, with all its mad Americana and legend. Man, you feel good just *being there*. There's barely a hundred and sixty miles of that road left now but what there is, is stunning, disappearing off into the beautiful nothing of the desert, a lone railroad running alongside, the horn of some mile-long freight sounding hello as you cruise through tiny little towns straight out of the fifties, drive-through diners with girls on rollerskates and crazy, souped-up Cadillacs as long as a swimming pool. You drive across America and you see the wildest things: out of nowhere, a twenty-foot tall concrete duck advertising shotguns or – look! – a dozen cars impaled on a pole reaching towards the sky and it's called Carhenge, would you believe. You can cruise for miles and miles and never see a sign of another living soul, endless highways that plunder ever onwards towards unseen destinations, boards overhead proudly proclaiming Albuquerque: 452 miles...Albuquerque: 371 miles...World's Largest Invisible Gold Mine: 263 miles – things so far away to an Englishman they might as well be in France or Spain. Back home the signs read in quarters of miles and within any given five-mile stretch of road there'll be the names of maybe nine or ten villages. You could never take a road trip there – not a proper one, not the kind you can here: in America it's not just the things you see, it's the space you have, the time in between stop signs and gear changes and corners. In England, even on a long journey, you're doing something every minute or so, something that keeps your mind on your driving and doesn't give it the space to start pondering and realising in the way that you can on those long desert strips of tarmac. In England, you're never more than a few hours away from your destination, and you're always thinking about getting there; in America, it's as though there is no there to get to. You're sitting there, looking down the empty road, looking into the empty vastness of the deserts, the mountains, the forests, and everything's taken care of: no gears to change (it's automatic); no pedals to push (it's got cruise control); no steering wheel to wrestle (the road's long and straight and there's no other cars on it) and all of a sudden there's nothing more to think about, no destination or junction coming up, just the road and the slowly changing scenery as the land unfolds and reveals itself over the course of fifty or a hundred miles. That's when all these thoughts and things start occurring to you; that's when your mind goes wandering off trying to figure stuff out.

What I finally realised, somewhere up in the snow near Flagstaff, broken down and stuck for a couple of days while some backwards mechanic put other jobs ahead of mine and left me sitting in a motel on the outskirts of town, was that I had a real deep feeling of unhappiness down inside of me. It seemed whatever I did, I was never completely satisfied, that I'd never actually been 'properly' happy. I traced a line back to the good times I could remember – and what I found there was that all my best memories were soaked in alcohol and tainted with inebriation and wrongdoing, and were only really half-memories anyway because I was generally blacked-out or unconscious and couldn't remember what I'd gotten up to. But how could there be any real satisfaction in a life like that? And how could it be that a wasted, drunken night equalled a great time? That the more wasted I was, the better the time I'd had? I was waiting there in those cold and wintry Flagstaff days, supposedly en route to the Grand Canyon, just eating Twix after Twix and none of it made any sense. All I wanted was to be happy – it's what I'd always wanted, what I used to tell people I wanted to be when I grew up – but I had no idea how to achieve it. All I could think of was a regular job, a steady girlfriend, and a bunch of friends. The normal life. Except I'd tried that and it hadn't worked. Now I was seeing the world and living the dream, and experiencing things in the mountains and the deserts and the people of America that blew my mind time and time again, and gave me a joy higher than anything I'd ever felt – and still I felt nuts.

That was the day before I said fuck it to the cold and wind of Flagstaff and abandoned my plans to see the Canyon – hell, it wasn't going anywhere – and I headed on back down Route 66, where my misery was soon displaced by a roadside café and a sign for "Dead Chicken" in funky fifties Seligman; that was also the day before my restored good humour got me into a fun race with a young couple up US-93 – the 'loneliest highway' – and a loud pop from under the hood of my poor, semi-destroyed Chevy signalled the beginning of the end. Ninety-five miles an hour was just too much for her, running on two cylinders, perpetually overheating – especially when I ignored the pop and carried on anyway: the pop was the splitting of the pipe that carried the water that cooled the engine. Without water, engines apparently burn up and die.

I slept that night by the side of the road, and in the morning I sold the car for ten bucks to a passing scrapmerchant guy and then stood in the desert and stuck out my thumb. It was my first real hitch.

Chapter Ten

I'm coming now to the end of Part One, the bit that I hadn't really thought I was gonna talk about, though I'm actually kind of glad I did. It's amazing how much I remember, and how things kind of piece themselves together, sentences and paragraphs I hadn't dreamed of appearing out of nowhere, apparently always waiting there but needing to be birthed by the ones that precede. Seems like I remember that time as an unhappy one characterised by loneliness and dissatisfaction – but there must have been fun in there too, for even though episodes like my realisation in Flagstaff were true, they were also fleeting, and it wasn't long before I was back to boozing and living it up in the usual Britboy abroad stylee. Indeed, in Vegas, just a few days later, I'd hooked up with a crew of fellow travellers – Isle of Manners, in fact – and I was beyond drunk and going wild in America's insanest of cities, getting thrown out of casinos and threatened by security guards and rolling around under pool tables with my hands in the knickers of a cutie from Arkansas, all under a sky of a billion crazy lightbulbs and those endless strips of casinos where three in the morning is the same as three in the afternoon and if you don't leave within the first few hours you probably never will.

I also got to see the Grand Canyon with those dudes. Pretty grand, it was, too. Like a big hole in the ground. I told them that I'd come back one day and walk across it and they laughed and said, no you won't.

I wintered in San Diego, working the reception at the Grand Pacific Youth Hostel for my bed 'n' board and spending my days at the beach, rollerblading up and down the promenade, befriending and flirting with cute Japanese girls and living the life of pizza and beer and sun. Christmas Day was blue-skied and hot and as I sat in my shorts and blades looking out over the Pacific Ocean it all seemed such a long way from the grey and wind of Yorkshire. At the same time, though, I knew I had to go back there, if only to clear up the loose-ends I had left behind – guitars, possessions, money, people – and return to America absolutely free. I had a new plan, you see, a plan to get to know America more, away from the tourists and travellers, and away from the road. I wanted to live in a small town – a town with no Brits or South Africans or Australians – and work, and rent a place, and get to know these American people in a normal day-to-day way, to see where that would take me. I wanted to live in Charlottesville, Virginia, the easy-going town just east of the Blue Ridge Mountains, the place with the beer and the girls and the friendly faces I had stumbled into simply because I liked the way its name spoke to me as I read it on my map.

I left San Diego at the beginning of February just after rectifying my visa situation by taking a ten-minute sojourn across the Mexican border and pretending I'd been there for six months. It was a few days after my twenty-first birthday. I made for LA to pick up a driveaway car and ended up stranded at one a.m. in Compton when the last bus suddenly terminated and turfed me out. That wasn't good: I'd heard about Compton – something to do with crips and bloods and drive-by shootings – and there was me and one other white guy trapped in the same boat. We huddled together trying to phone a taxi while big-ass pimpmobiles low-rided around us like circling sharks, black eyes peering out and sizing up their prey. We called taxi after taxi and nobody would come, not there, not at that time of night, until finally we found some one-eyed lunatic from Texas who told us he was the only one that dared enter Compton and the last time he'd been there some nigger had stuck a shotgun in his face – and the time before that too.

I got the driveaway car – a repossessed Honda Civic – and they gave me ten days to take it to Statesville, North Carolina, a twenty-four hundred mile trip. I did it in two – sort of. See, the plan was that I was going to Mardi Gras to meet Erica, this lovely Australian girl I'd snogged in San Diego, and I thought if I made it there as fast as I could I'd then have the car to ferry us around, like a free rental, before doing the final leg and dropping it off. So I left LA at ten a.m. and crossed the entirety of California, Arizona and New Mexico in one long stretch before midnight. Then it was onto Texas, America's largest state and a seemingly impossible expanse that first time coming west, and I just kept on going, hoovering up those deserts and plains like some road-hungry bitch. I stopped only for coffee and pee and gas, and by Austin I was hallucinating like a motherfucker, deer and ghostly tramp-like hitchhikers bouncing all over the road, screeching me to a halt in the middle of pitch-dark nowhere. But morning came and the sun brought some relief from the visions, and across the mad concrete expanse of Houston and the eerie gloom of the Louisiana swamps, I made my goal of New Orleans and the rendezvous with Erica after eighteen hundred miles in twenty-nine hours. But that turned out horribly – we quickly discovered that we hated each other – and Mardi Gras wasn't anything approaching fun – all those boozed up Americans baying for boobs and dropping their pants – and after a pretty shitty week I polished off the remaining miles in one more long shift across Mississippi, Alabama and Georgia, collecting a thirty thousand dollar Chevrolet on arrival to drop off in Connecticut. And, man, was that car a luxury! You could have lived in it – and for the three days I had it, I did. Within two weeks of leaving San Diego I was back at JFK, back awaiting an Air India flight, and back on my way to England.

And England, eh? Weird accents at the airport and I get some money and stare oddly at the bizarreness of a fifty pence piece, its jaunty jagged edges so different to the bland conformity of American money. I feast on Mars Bars and

Dairy Milks, starved of good chocolate, and when I see Hobnobs and Digestives and Bourbon Creams I gorge and put on eight pounds in a week – and then I realise that's about half a stone and it seems so quaint that these people weigh themselves in rocks – and that's even before I've gotten back to Yorkshire and dived headfirst into fish and chips, the greatest meal on Earth, piled high and salted and ketchupped, sitting once more on my grandparents' sofa watching Grandstand and letting my nan bring me Ben Shaws lemonade and some extra bread and butter, and then finishing off hers because there's nothing finer than the leftover fish and chips that someone else can't manage when yours have all gone and you still want more.

I had a pretty awesome time in England, and in a lot of ways it was too awesome, because it made following through with my plans to go back to America all the more difficult. I was happier now, freed from the crippling depression that had hung over me like a stink – and to my friends, I was a hero, full of reams and reams of madcap adventures that they all loved, and loved to tell each other about, and it was impossible for me not to love that too.

I flitted around between Yorkshire and London, larging it up in boozing and shenanigans and moving from one party to the next. I spent a lot of time with Tim – and I loved hanging out with Tim – and also with Tim's brother Ben, down in his university halls at Goldsmiths. Ben was a big boozer; he liked his pints. And given that I liked pints, and he liked pints, and he and I both liked pints, we went out and drank lots and lots of pints. Like, for days on end. Like, twenty in a session. Like, when we once totted up we worked out that was about the only thing we'd ingested in maybe a week, apart from a couple of chickens' legs. We were on a bender, being mad and drunk and doing dares like snorting washing-up liquid and pepper and nicking strangers' chips, or the time I ate a pound of uncooked rice, or the time I offered his horribly shy and tuneless friend a hundred quid to sing Bohemian Rhapsody at a pub karaoke night and she did. And it was one of those dares, I suppose, that got me back to America, when at one of Ben's parties his other brother Richard offered me a fiver to shave my head and I naturally agreed. So they set about it and these four or five guys did me good and proper in a Terry Nutkins stylee – bald on the top, long at the back and sides – hacking away with razors and scissors and knives. And after I'd blacked out, passed out, regained consciousness and looked in the mirror, a sort of creeping sense of horror had come over me. My hair was clinging loosely to the side of my head in messy patches. I hadn't eaten in three days and I'd imbibed enough alcohol to kill a small horse. It was the end. It was the gloom of Flagstaff returned. The rest of the hair went and I slunk off to Spain looking cancerous and grey and taking my mighty hangover and depression with me. Nothing like drinking loads and then not drinking at all to get you in a funk.

I sat on clifftops and reflected. There had to be something more than boozing and getting wasted and all the ups and downs of that. Or, at least, even if there wasn't, I knew that I couldn't really live like that, that it just made me too miserable. I resolved to get back on track and get back to my plan of smalltown America and Charlottesville. I bought a ticket, and now, virtually possessionless and free, with nine hundred dollars in my pocket, I was once more bound for America. I landed in Washington DC sometime in April and, after seeing an enormous tinfoil construction in a museum there that some guy had dedicated his life to, which convinced me once and for all that the world was truly mad, I got on a train and made it Amtrak-style down south. And in an already hot and sticky Virginia May night, under the blackness of the sky and the crickets and the sweat, I arrived in Charlottesville, where the girls were more plentiful than anywhere on Earth, and where my new life awaited.

Part Two

Chapter One

The reasons I moved to Charlottesville were sort of funny, I guess, and if anyone wants to say anything about my time there and try and apportion some of the blame my way they need to go and have a word with Laurel and Hardy, because they're the ones who really started it all. Boy, I loved those guys as a kid! And, still, there's nothing gives me great big belly laughs like Stan Laurel's stupid face and the way they so carelessly demolish everything around them. So back when I was a boy my mum had bought me a couple of their videos and I watched them over and over, and one of them was Way Out West. And in that film there's a song they do in a bar where Stan sings in a silly high voice and Ollie bashes him on the head, and then Stan sings in a silly low voice and Ollie stares perplexed before Stan finally falls over. And the song's all about the Blue Ridge Mountains of Virginia.

I was in the Columbus Circle Barnes and Noble planning my cross-country route when I first flicked to the page of the Rough Guide that mentioned those mountains and the road that runs the length of them, the Blue Ridge Parkway. Those words and their familiarity made me take note. A scenic highway. Beautiful views. Mountains. And, of course, the essence of Laurel and Hardy; I was on my way. I always was a sucker for a name and a connection – that's what took me to San Diego, because I liked the name, and because I used to have this tape of a really great Jimi Hendrix concert that was recorded there. It's also what took me to Charlottesville on my first cross-country drive, sitting in a diner in Front Royal and looking at a map one night, not really tired and wondering where to go en route to the Parkway, and seeing that stately moniker jump out at me from the map, only a hundred miles away. I write that now and, really, it almost seems like destiny, a chain of links and connections too unlikely to be anything but.

So like I say, good people of Charlottesville and America, if you want to blame anyone for what occurred there then perhaps you should be looking a little more close to home, and to two of your more belovéd comedians, a certain Mr Norvell Hardy and a certain Mr Arthur Stanley Jefferson – who, I must hasten to add, was born in Lancashire, England – because if they hadn't recorded that delightful song and released it out into the world, none of this would ever have happened.

Charlottesville, as I was soon to discover, is actually one of the premiere locations to live in America, and has been designated so on several occasions. It's very well to do: it has a grand university, designed by Thomas Jefferson no less, who was a local; and loads of that old style architecture with pillars and balconies and mansions and such. It's a bit like Gone With The Wind, very well-spoken and proper, and very, very white. The people have money, and the students have money, and they all seem very white too. The students are also strikingly conventional, not at all like the goths and alternatives and patchouli oil stinking scruffs in Leeds: these guys are practically in uniform, all baseball caps and khaki shorts; sandals with socks; and girls trying to look like the cast of Friends; and keg parties and frat houses and sororities and convertibles. And once again, it's a far, far cry from my native South Elmsall, where I thought people were rich if they owned their own house and absolutely nobody but nobody of university age could afford a car.

I moved into a thin-walled student apartment up on Ivy Road with a couple of undergrads called Troy and Steve, who were apparently two of the most boring people on the planet. As far as I could work out, they studied, and jogged, and then came home and talked about studying and jogging.

"I really worked my hams today," Troy would say.

"I ran a couple of laps backwards," Steve would say, "really works your calves in a different way."

And on and on and on.

I blagged myself a job at this restaurant, the C&O, borrowing South African Roger's life for the occasion and spinning some lies about having worked at a French place in Manhattan. Truth was, I didn't know the difference between a crêpe and a crouton, as they were soon to find out: my first day there they asked me to make a salad dressing and I set to work on the bewildering list of ingredients. Vinaigrette? Mustard? Olive oil? It was all a mystery to me. Pizza was the most exotic thing I'd ever eaten and I'd only tried that for the first time in San Diego, very reluctantly, and not without some massively irrational fear. Up until that point I was strictly a bread, meat and potatoes kind of guy – and certainly never let anything green touch my lips. I was a quick learner, though, and gamely got stuck in, whacking in two dozen pieces of garlic – garlic? – and some lemon juice and mustard, etcetera, and coming up with what I thought were the goods. It was only when I watched another waitress come in and pour it out for one of her customers that I realised I'd gone wrong somewhere.

"Who's put whole cloves of garlic in the dressing?" she demanded to know of the kitchen, as they plopped out into her salad, one by one.

The chefs and cooks looked at her bemused and I did too, tutting and laughing at such incompetence. And that was how I learned that garlic was added to a salad dressing pressed or chopped, not whole.

I bumbled along and learned about lettuce and carrots julienne. The owner seemed genuinely pleased to have bagged an actual European and the customers couldn't get enough of my accent. The tips were ridiculous: I was easily making at least a hundred dollars a night – probably more than any other waiter – and life was good those early C&O days, buzzing around the tables, meeting people, making friends. I met Tyler the barkeep – who I later shared a house with – and Stuart the posh, experienced waiter who taught me how to tuck my shirt in. I met Charles DuBois, a real old time southern gent whose job it was to greet people and show them to their tables and talk in an incredibly refined accent that put anything I'd ever heard in England to shame. I even met Dave Matthews, the local rock star, late one night at a lock-in talking long and drunk about cockroaches. And I met Nathan Hart, the dishwasher.

Nathan was this sort of cool young guy with a homemade punk hairstyle and soft Southern drawl who washed the plates and glasses and enthused endlessly about Johnny Cash and fishing and a million other things besides in this deliciously intoxicating way. He got excited about everything. He told me about his friends and the things they did. He always had some plan for some trip to somewhere or other, to go jump in a lake or drive up to New York or just fish. After Troy and Steve he was like a rainbow. We became friends and he took me with some poles down the river; took me shooting hoops in the ghetto; took me driving Virginia roads in 'The Vomit Comet' – his beat-up old Escort – where the locks didn't work and the windows wouldn't wind up but nobody cared because nobody stole anything around here anyway and, wow, man, people really did leave their doors unlocked all day and night. At least at his house they did. He lived in this place called Kappa Mutha Fucka, a ramshackle old shack stuck in the middle of all the frat houses with boarded up windows and bottles on the porch and people coming and going, waking up on sofas in the afternoon heat and cooking and sleeping and opening another bottle of beer or vino tinto and drinking. They were gutterpunks, he said, sort of anti-types, and, my word, there were plenty of them.

Nathan had a girlfriend, Lauren: she wore black Doc Martin's with bits of coloured blue glass glued to them; she had her own homemade hairstyle and she was eighteen. They were tight, her and Nathan, and they said, "I love you, baby," and got drunk and cooked together, and sometimes they'd get into fights about music or how much paprika to put in a stir-fry and throw things at each other and scream, but they always made up. The first time I met her she was shouting at some foot-taller mean-looking skinhead and calling him, "a fat ass piece of shit." I think she'd been a lesbian at some point in her past.

Then there were his roommates, Gus and Deya and Monster Boy and this other chap called Zach who sort of dossed on the back porch with his pregnant girlfriend Peggy while he was waiting for something or other to come through.

Then there were the ones that came by, some straight looking guys who didn't really talk, and arty types and musos but mostly goths and punks and sweaty old rednecks with glass eyes leering after girls; a fat performance artist called Joe Christ whose performance piece was showing people the remains of the penis he had hacked off with his own fair hands; a pair of vampiric sisters who would get wrecked and throw things at one another, and the older one always trying to get kisses and sex off her younger sibling; and Johnny Boom-Boom, and Wacky Jen, and Raphael and Nemo, and Jessika the Wig, and dozens and dozens of randoms who would turn up once and never be seen again, or who would turn up after having been missing for two years, or who would zoom in from Philadelphia or New York for no real reason, and all of us drunk, or on the way to getting drunk, or waking up drunk in between drunks and thinking about getting drunk all over again.

So my fortnight or so of clean-living and tennis and TV with Troy and Steve was out the window and I was now rolling in stinking of booze after going missing for three days, leaves in my hair and no sleep, and just a quick shower before getting back to the C&O where I worked pretty much every day turning on the charm for rich Virginian ladies and getting merry on sneaked beers and leftovers and then the practically free bar once the customers had left, emptying the wine fridge and pouring my own beers and lock-ins till five a.m., and all the other waiters and waitresses coming in from their own now-closed restaurants, all us bright young things with pockets full of cash and nothing to do but spend it on parties and drink.

Charlottesville, with its tradition and money, its grand university lawns, and Thomas Jefferson overlooking it all from on-the-back-of-a-nickel Monticello, and old money, and all the fat-necked students living their lives for their parents, all those fees, and, damn straight you're gonna get a proper job at the end of it all, and that kicking restaurant scene, and arts and music and girls.

And towering above it all, those Blue Ridge Mountains, the piedmont, the foothills, Old Crag and the scenery and splendour that had brought me there in the first place, old Laurel and Hardy and their Way Out West song On The Trail Of The Lonesome Pine, and all because I loved it as a boy.

Chapter Two

I was out one day with Nathan Hart on our way to pick up Lauren from her job at Wholefoods on Barracks Road. The windows were down and my bare feet were soaking up the sun, resting on the wing mirror. In the back: fishing poles; an enormous doormat recently stolen from the cinema; empty bottles and cans; some dumpster-dived broken dolls later to be stuck with safety pins and needles; usual stuff. It must have been July by now; we were tight, me and Nathan; we spent all our time in this manner.

"You know," he goes, all southern drawl and nose-ring and hair in his eyes, "we should get you a girlfriend. I know this girl Megan; she's sweet. I think she likes Brits."

Ears prick up and already my mind is dreaming of this unknown beauty and the happiness that awaits us.

"Sure," I say, "sounds good."

"I'll get her over later, get some drinks. I'm sure she'll go for you." He nods to himself as he thinks about it. He's nodding and thinking and then: "I did stuff with her once," he says, "but that's between you and me."

Does stuff; I like the sound of that too.

And he's sure she'll go for me. Nice one.

We get Lauren and in she tumbles, and with her this pair of hairy hippies, a guy and a girl she's befriended that day that she's bringing home. They're a couple. They're living in their car out in the woods somewhere, been coming in everyday to buy organic beans or whatever the hell those people eat. Lauren's decided to cook them something up.

"Ali," the hairy guy says, and pokes out his hand through fishing poles and his hippy girlfriend's hair. The fishing poles are getting in everybody's way; we're all getting tangled up in lines and hooks.

"Rory," I say.

"Fuck! A Brit!" he goes, "man, tell me this: how do I get me one o' them British passports? If I had one of those fuckers I could work anywhere in Europe, right? What kinda passport you got? How'd you get a work visa, man?" He's got these dark eyes that are staring right into me, enthusiastic and into it but a little too much; he could be Rasputin under all that hair.

"Rory's an illegal," says Lauren, "swam over the Rio Grandé from Mexico – wetback limey bastard!" And she snorts, "ha!" and then she snorts again, and that's how she laughs.

"Hey, you guys could get married and then you could live in Europe and Rory could work here," says Nathan, "why don't you guys get married?"

"Suits me," says Ali, grinning through his sweaty hair and mad monk eyes.

"Sure," I says – but what I'm really thinking is, man, his girlfriend's cute, and I'm sure *we're* gonna be very happy together once I steal her away from him. She looks like she'd go for me, this sweet, sensitive Michelle. I've always had a thing for my friends' girlfriends.

And in this manner, a backseat full of poles and hair and skirts and people, and Lauren laughing, "ha!" in her blue glass-coated Doc Martin's, her new friends beaming, and my feet out the window, and Nathan Hart dreaming of flounder, and nobody's wearing any seatbelts: in this manner we speed back to Kappa Mutha Fucka and tumble out and up the stairs and past the front lawn where dreamy Swedish Deya is sitting making a crown out of coathangers while Gus gesticulates and waxes lyrical about chickens and vodka iced tea and spills vino on himself, and inside Monster Boy is there all spiky dog-collared and dressed in an old lady's dress, and with a box full of junk at his feet and a smile on his black-lipsticked lips this is what he's saying:

"Guys, guys: look what I found."

And smiling and grinning through his eyeliner and his nail polish and his studs and pins and chains his hand plunges into his box of presumably dumpster-dived stuff and pulls out a vase.

He holds it up to us.

It's a thin glass vase. That's all it is.

Chapter Three

These guys, they loved their dumpster diving. And for those of you who don't know what that is, dumpster diving is the art of going around the back of some shop or store – usually a charity place – and having a good old root around in their bins to see what you can come up with. It was how I got my mattress for the place I lived in after the student apartment, and also a bicycle and a couch; and it was how they'd found a lot of their records and books and furniture, and occasionally food, as well as the ubiquitous dolls. And it was how Monster Boy had come up with this innocuous looking vase that he was so proudly displaying to us.

"It's like a giant shot glass," he said, and he was right, it was. An eight inch high shot glass.

And then he took out a bottle of rum and poured a monster shot, and downed it in one, and passed it on.

And Nathan did one. And Lauren did one. And I did one. And Ali and his girlfriend passed, and back it came to Monster Boy.

"Let's have a drinking competition," I said, "see how big we can go."

And just then open bursts the door and in falls these two girls, friends of Lauren's just drove down from New York, Sarah the Redhead and Virge, and behind them, slightly more demurely, another redhead, this one Megan, my supposed new girlfriend, and the room is full of bodies and squeals and I'm wondering how we'll all fit in. Deya and Gus come in from outside – Deya now resplendent in her coathanger crown – and I don't know how it happens but suddenly it's just me and Monster Boy pouring out enormous shots of rum into this vase while the girls all shout, "drink, motherfucker, drink!" and Gus is there trying to be sensible and bemoaning the rum – "don't drink all the rum, man, it's a waste!" – and me and Monster Boy are going for it big style. In goes the rum – glug glug glug – and sickly sweet it races down throats and shivers through bodies, bristling along veins, up arms, into brain. "Pour me another!" I shout, and someone says, "this is stupid, you're gonna be sick," and the girls all cheer and chant and, really, that's about the last thing I remember.

Except I get this sort of flash that I'm driving a car that's not really going anywhere and the next thing I know is I'm on their couch in the bright morning sun strapping on my rollerblades and chuckling to myself about where the last sixteen hours went.

I later found out.

But, just to digress, I must mention something about one aspect of life at Kappa Mutha Fucka before I go on, and about its oldest and wisest inhabitant, Gus. Gus had a good ten years on the rest of them and he was a painter and a writer, and the main thing he wrote was an online journal called 'The Musings.' This was back in the day before online journals were called 'blogs' and before everyone had one; back then, when Gus started, I'd say there were only about a hundred in the world and the idea that a person would share online the most intimate details of their lives was a novel and almost universally balked at one. Hard to believe, in this age of myspace and facebook and youporn, but that's how it was. 'The Musings of the Gus,' as he called it, was one of those that paved the way and broke through some of the boundaries of what people thought of as privacy. It was a no holds barred account of all the crazy mad shenanigans that were going on at the time.

Gus wrote everyday and he had readers all over the world. We were its stars, I suppose, our daily lives gobbled up by his followers and fans in the same way that I once devoured my thrice-weekly dose of Eastenders. Some people, of course, protested at having their sex lives, their drug-taking, their semi-criminal activities splashed across the 'net, where parents and partners and vicars could see it, and Gus was frequently being threatened with violence – particularly when he'd write about some of Charlottesville's less savoury characters, the skinheads and the Nazis he inexplicably encountered. Gus, however, somehow always escaped unharmed and full of glee, and carried on writing uninhibited and unhindered by any sort of moral constraint or regard for the privacy and feelings of others.

More than any sense of the negative, though, in that writing, that daily reporting, there was a cohesion and a unison that brought all of us together – Nathan Hart and Lauren, Monster Boy and Deya, Kappa Mutha Fucka and The Brick Mansion In The Hood, Wonderboy Neek and redneck Doctor Steve, Sara the dominatrix, Zach and Peggy, the C&O, Plan 9, Angela the goth and me and Tyler and even Aaron the SHARP, and a hundred thousand other characters and goofballs and innocent bystanders – so that we could have our times, and get all wild and drive three a.m. to the quarry, me swinging drunk on the roof of The Vomit Comet while Nathan Hart speeds swerving through the cricket chirping night and everybody full of howls and giggles, and then stop off to hop in apartment swimming pools and get shouted at by locals and security guards – "of course we live here," shouts Nathan as we pile back into the car, "apartment 11b!" – and not remember a thing. But the next day it would all be there, the arguments and the gossip, and who disappeared into bedrooms with who, and your own name up in lights, read by thousands around the globe, and even when he got it all wrong and talked shit about you and made you want to shout at him and say, "take it down, motherfucker, else there'll be trouble" – even then it was still exciting and good, a certain amount of fame and infamy, people you met in the street talking about you – "hey, I read about that thing in The Musings, that was cool" – and the more you read of yourself and your doings, the more you wanted to read and do. It was just one more ingredient in the pot, the icing on the motherfucking cake in those mad Charlottesville months when all were young and free and whooping it up good time.

According to The Musings this is what I did that night: drank all the rum; annoyed Sarah the Redhead by repeatedly attempting to suck on her toes; went for a walk with Megan during which time we agreed to try the girlfriend/boyfriend thing – but then left her and ran off through some frat boys' garden, emerging with a coat that wasn't mine; tried to suck on Sarah the Redhead's toes some more; disgusted Lauren by going on about wanking for ages; ranted about foreskins and the barbaric and misguided Americans, who I was amazed to find out had hacked all theirs off; ate some glass; ate some money; fell on a bottle of tequila and put a long, deep gash in my hand; cried and said I was dying while everybody cooed around and said what a lovely colour my fountaining blood was; realised I wasn't dying and then sprayed blood everywhere, up the walls, on my friends, on someone's windshield; drank a bottle of Robitussin; and then disappeared.

This I found out later: all I knew that morning was that I couldn't remember anything and apart from the blood-soaked rag wrapped around my hand everything seemed fine.

On my way out the driveway, though, there was this chap who I recognised as Deya's dad pulling up in a van and he was asking me if I knew anything about what had happened to Deya's car.

"They found it in a ditch up on Barracks Road, burned out clutch and a flat tyre, blood everywhere, abandoned. Don't suppose you know anything about that, do you?"

"No," I said, "that's terrible. Maybe somebody in the house. I don't know if anyone's around, though; I think they're all asleep."

"Hm," he said, eyeing me grumpily, switching off the engine and continuing to stare.

And off I go into the morning sun, blading my way, making monkey noises and singing over and over, "God made it easy on me," from some Happy Mondays CD I'd just bought in a fit of wanting some tunes from back home.

Well, sure, it had been me: boozed and 'tussined up I'd decided somewhere in the melee to go chasing after my one true love Megan, who had quickly grown tired of my company, my attempts at toe-sucking other girls, my stupid drunken rants, and gone home in her car. And so I don't know how but I'd gotten Deya's keys and made it all the way out to Barracks Road – nowhere near where Megan lived; not that I knew where she lived anyway – and then plonked it in that ditch, and burned out the clutch, and then jollily walked my way some three miles back to Kappa Mutha Fucka and rejoined the party – or got into arguments with everyone – or simply collapsed, I know not what. But I do know that it cost me four hundred dollars to fix that car, and pissed off a lot of people, and made them somewhat wary of me.

And this was all long before the Ford LTD.

Chapter Four

Well I made it up with my friends, all contrite and abstinent for a week or so, and back in their trust I was. In the meantime I was learning a spot of html from Gus and getting into doing my own online journal, eager for a piece of the action. The original plan was to put up my previous year's travel diaries. Also, Gus was keen to have some sort of stereoscopic vision on what was going on in Charlottesville at the time, in the name of balanced and unbiased journalism, and so I too set to work reporting on our drunken mishaps and late night insanities. Only problem was I was way too busy indulging in drunken mishaps and late night insanities to actually do any of writing, slurred and sporadic forays aside.

I did, however, manage one day to come up with this:

Tue19Aug Rory's got a big ass car. Oh yeah. What this means is that you're all gonna have to wait until I crash it for any real development of this schminternet thing. '72 Ford LTD, five hundred bucks, sorted.

Oh God, that was a beautiful car! A lime green boat of a monster, five litres of rumbling, purring engine, twenty feet long, clean as a whistle and went like the bejeesus. I'd gone down to Belmont to have a look at a sixty-seven Chevy Impala that turned out to be a disappointing, weed-covered wreck and there I'd seen her, sitting on the forecourt at good ol' boy Belmont Motors, an unbelievable six hundred dollar price tag in the window. I chatted with the owner; we took her out for a spin – man, did she float! – and without any real effort on my part I got a hundred dollars knocked off the price. She was for nothing, that car. Cheaper than piss. And the way she was sitting there, the way the Impala had brought me to her, and the way the guy had just handed me that discount…it was like we were meant to be, like we were made for each other. I was in love. And I vowed and I vowed and I vowed, after all my motorvehicular mishaps and misdeeds, that I was gonna take care of this one.

After stopping off to sort out the registration and take out some insurance, which the rednecks at Belmont had insisted on before handing over the keys – my fifth car, but the first one I had actually had put into my name and insured – I took her down to Kappa Mutha Fucka to show her off and celebrate. Lauren and Nathan came out and wowed over her; likewise a couple of their friends. Gus said she was more pea green than lime. Monster Boy and Deya sat uninterested. But we loaded her up and the eight of us sat spaciously and in comfort on her near six feet long seats and the girls struggled with her enormous doors – despite her size, there were only two of them – and, low-riding in the front, I pimped it up good style. And then, after beers and shenanigans and darkness, I drove straight into a pole in a supermarket car park, bent the bumper and smashed a headlight, and wept.

It was only a matter of time, I suppose – hell, I'd even predicted it in my own journal – but this was a new record, a new personal best. Six hours! And, alas, it didn't end there: pretty soon I'd driven her into two walls and three parked cars; run out of gas six times (twice in one day); had two flat tyres, including a blow-out at ninety miles an hour; received three traffic tickets (one for doing eighty-five in a fifty-five zone); and taken to the American fondness for drink-driving like a duck to an abandoned bag of bread crumbs. It was a doomed, destructive relationship and there was nothing I could do about it. She had me in her spell. We were inseparable. I wanted to drive her so badly.

And you can read that anyway you want.

Three weeks in I took to the road one Friday afternoon with Lauren and another in the fine line of goofball C&O dishwashers – the happily- and hippily-named Ocean Tree – to seek out some mysterious, perhaps legendary swimming hole somewhere off in the mountains. We drank and laughed and, naturally, never found it, settling instead for tooling around on the dark forest trails, and downing beer after beer, and me and Lauren, once sufficiently lubricated, almost making out but sufficing with a slipped hand inside her delicate damp knickers on the piggyback ride back to the car. And then, fuzzily and sloppily, almost home, back on that damn Barracks Road again, I somehow conspired to lose concentration (or consciousness), drift out of my lane, and proceeded to wham my beloved LTD right smack bang into a couple of oncoming cars.

It's hard to know how it happened; I really don't remember a thing. I may, perhaps, have fallen asleep, having slept only a few hours the night before. It may also have been a simple case of way too many beers. All I know is that there was a bang, and that I had a flat tyre, and that my arm, which I'd been dangling out of the window, was covered in oil and blood.

Oh, and also that as a drunk, illegal alien crash-causer, I was once more fucked.

My first thoughts were of getaway, much as they had been that night of the mishap in Mississippi, but the mess of twisted, grinding metal and destroyed tyre had other ideas. We limped instead into a nearby parking lot where I leapt from the car and pulled frantically at the bits of bumper and wing that were preventing our escape. I had a chance, I thought, if I could just clear some of this carnage. I yanked and kicked at the steel and still shining chrome, and when I realised the futility of it all I raced to my friends and grabbed them and held them to me, and jumped up and down and babbled.

"Oh God," I said, "I'm so sorry." I left them and rushed back to the bumper, and pulled on the metal some more. I held them again. "It's all done," I said, "I'm so, so sorry, it's been so good to know you. Thank you. Thank you." I wept onto their shoulders and smeared them with oily blood and bloody oil and then I ran away.

I ran to a bush twelve feet from where they stood, and crawled underneath it, and slept.

I dreamed then that I was being sniffed and licked and poked: such a realistic dream. I opened my eyes and looked into some other eyes: I *was* being sniffed and licked and poked. How rude. I closed my eyes and tried to go back to sleep but the poking became more insistent. I rolled over.

The next time I opened my eyes I was staring into the barrel of a gun.

Chapter Five

And so there I was again, getting myself arrested and spending more time in jail – only this time it was much worse than New York, than my one night of hell there. This time I'd been charged with real crimes: driving under the influence of alcohol; failing to stop at the scene of an accident; and failing to stop at the scene of an accident in which the other driver was injured. The first two were misdemeanours, the last one a felony. And I was guilty as hell.

They took me to the county jail, shackled to a policeman and rapidly sobering up. I stripped and bent over, and handed over my clothes and shoelaces in exchange for an ill-fitting bright orange boiler suit. Then we went to a large gymnasium-style room containing about forty men stretched out on blue rubber mattresses. They gave me my own rubber mattress and then slammed the door. My time in Charlottesville and America was over: as soon as they released me I would be leaving it all behind and getting on the next plane home.

I lay down and fell into an exhausted sleep.

By morning, though, a part of me felt that it was time I stood up and took my punishment, to finally learn my lesson and accept that I was not invincible, or above the law, or charmed. I had done wrong, and I knew I had done wrong, and it seemed high time that I learned to face the consequences. I thought that just maybe I could handle the jail time – it was the proper thing to do, after all – and I was feeling some serious pain at the prospect of leaving Charlottesville and all the friends I had made there, of quitting America while there was still so much I wanted to see and do. They could, of course, just deport me after I had served my time but it was a chance I felt willing to take.

I felt resolved and somewhat at peace with this decision. I sat and watched my fellow inmates as they awoke from their respective slumbers. I awaited what I had been told would be my imminent release, itching to get back to the outside world and to see the others. But all I did was sit and sit and sit. The hours pass and slowly I'm starting to go out of my head, stuck in an inescapable room with no idea who's on the other side of the wall pulling the strings of my life, deciding which direction I'm heading in – if they're deigning to decide anything at all.

Eventually news comes that I have a visitor and off I go in my shameful prison outfit to see who it is. Housemate and work colleague Tyler walks in and sits on the other side of the glass. I slump down in my mournful chair and look up at him. There's no smile on his face. There's no good news written on that countenance.

"How are you?" he says.

I sniff and shrug.

"I don't know what's happening," I say, "they told me I'd be out of here this morning but nobody's come to get me."

He looks reluctant to speak. And then he lays out the terms: without someone who is prepared to risk four thousand dollars for my worthless hide there is no way out.

This, I do not want to hear.

"You're kidding me," I say, "they said I'd be out first thing this morning – how can they do that? No one's going to give them four thousand dollars: I'm English!"

"I know," he says, "I'm sorry. Look, I'll do what I can from my end, from out here. I can bring you some books on Monday – "

"Monday?" I moan, horrified at the thought of it.

"And I'll phone your parents and let them know, maybe they can raise some money."

"They'll never do that," I say, "they haven't got a bean. Well, my dad has but he's as tight as a gnat's arse: you'd be lucky to get four quid out of him, never mind four thousand." I slump down in my chair a little more and stare at my shoelaceless shoes.

"I've been in your room," he says, "I've found enough money to cover your rent for the next few months. But if nobody pays your bail you'll probably have to stay in here until your trial, in about six weeks. And then there'll be the sentencing."

These words sink into me and the reality hits. I won't be going anywhere. I'll be in there for weeks. My parents will find out, and go mental, and raise a commotion. And all the money I've worked for and saved, and all the friends I've made and loved, and my beloved car, and my home and my –

"And there's one more thing," he says, looking sheepish, "Dave doesn't want you back in the restaurant. Ever. He knows you don't have a work permit and he can't afford any trouble. You know he's trying to adopt from China?"

"I know."

"He's pretty mad," he says, "about you not having a work permit. About lying to him."

And that's the job gone too.

"I'll call your parents and maybe see you Monday."

He goes, and I slouch back to the gym and fall into my mattress, the will to live sucked and drained right from me. I lie there with my face pressed into the rubber, curled up against the wall. The minutes feel like hours. The bright lights and the noise of the air-conditioning make sleep impossible. Somewhere, some all-too cheerful Rasta is going on and on and on, his unfathomable banter echoing throughout the gym, booming off the walls, into my brain.

54

Later, it gets worse.

I'm taken for a welcome break from the madness of the interminable gymnasium to visit a nurse and have a chat about my arm. It's nice to talk to someone like her – intelligent, pleasant to look at, female – instead of some halfwit prisoner, some meathead of a guard. She asks me questions about my life; asks me if I take drugs or need medication; asks me if I've ever thought about suicide. I talk freely, about England, about my situation, and laugh a little and say, sure, I've thought about suicide, hasn't everyone? and she smiles and listens and I feel like I've actually been heard. I leave her office somewhat relieved and even hopeful that she might do something to help me, and a few minutes later I'm taken to a new part of the prison.

"Take your clothes off," the officer says, "and change into this." He hands me a translucent piece of yellow paper which I stare at confusedly until I realise it's some sort of gown. As far as items of clothing go, it's about as substantial as a tissue.

I do as he says, and put the paper gown on, and wonder what's coming next. He leads me to this bare concrete cell about six and a half feet long and four feet wide.

He opens the cell door and waits.

"Woah," I say, "what's this?"

"Suicide watch."

He just stands there with his hand on the door and points.

"In you go," he says.

I walk in and then I turn around. The door slams shut behind me.

"Why have you put me in here?" I say, "I'm not going to kill myself. Is it 'cos I told that nurse I'd thought about suicide? Jesus, everybody's thought about suicide, haven't they? You've probably thought about suicide."

He turns the key and starts to walk away.

"I'm not going to kill myself," I say. I move forward to the bars and grab a hold of them. "Come on, look at me." I stand there and do my best to look non-suicidal – as non-suicidal as it's possible for a man in a see-through piece of paper to look. "Do I look like I want to kill myself? I love myself! I can't stay in here; I will kill myself if you don't let me out." I look around and wonder just exactly how I'd do that. There are the walls, and the bars, and a ceiling, and that's about it. Short of bashing my head on the walls or ripping out my own heart I'll have to admit, they've made it pretty difficult for a man to indulge in a spot of the old hari-kari. I rethink that line. "Please," I say, "really, I was just being honest. I wish I hadn't been. But I'd never do that."

He takes a step towards me and looks me in my pitiful eye.

"I'm sorry," he says, "but once the decision's been made there's nothing can be done about it. You'll have to stay here at least twenty-four hours before they can consider moving you back." He looks sympathetic. But at the same time, serious. I know I'm there for the duration.

I slide down the wall to the cold hard floor and huddle up in the gown that is already starting to tear and shred. A fan in the ceiling is blowing a gale around me.

"Do you want a book?" he says.

I nod.

He disappears off down the corridor and I hear him talking to a long-termer in one of the other cells. A few seconds later he returns with a yellowed and in pieces copy of C.S. Lewis's Prince Caspian.

I read it twice.

I did manage a few hours sleep that night but awoke for good at three a.m. and resumed the eternal wait. Later, I met a helpful case worker who took pity on me – she dug my accent – and got things moving, arranging a call with a bondsman, a guy who will put up bail for you in return for some sort of deposit. She told me a hearing had been arranged for later that day and around one p.m. I was taken to court, chained at the hands and feet, and linked together with five other guys – a white with a mullet, a non-English speaking Hispanic, and three black guys on drugs charges who were having the time of their life, judging by their whooping and laughter.

We were marched into the courtroom and I shuffled head-bowed in my ankle-cuffs past the waiting Tyler. We were able to talk a little and he told me that I'd probably be out of there later in the day, so long as the bondsman didn't get too scared by my non-USness. The judge saw fit to reduce my bond from four thousand to one thousand, which I thought was very nice of him, and off we went, back to jail, where I waited until a little after five. The bondsman came to pick me up, went over a few legal things, and then deposited me into the company of my friends in the Water Street sunshine.

I'm glad they were there to meet me, even though I was a hive of shame and gloom. They did their best to cheer me up, and talked about the party we were going to have, and told me they'd been thinking of me. I was so woefully sad, though, that all I could think about was how I was never going to see them or this town again. Nothing seemed to matter. But their actions came as close as any to convincing me that some people do actually like me. I didn't want to go but it seemed inevitable, one way or the other. I couldn't believe how stupid I'd been. I only hoped that perhaps this episode would serve as an example, that my friends would look at me and see themselves, and realise that they aren't invincible and that there is no magic spell protecting Charlottesville's drunk drivers. I did a terrible thing – something I vowed never to do again – but even then it could have been a hell of a lot worse. People could have died, been paralysed or disfigured, and maybe instead of felonies and misdemeanours and a six-month spell in prison I could have been facing manslaughter or murder charges, and the veritable end of my life. Thank God nobody was hurt. Thank God all I damaged were a couple of cars and myself.

Chapter Six

There was more to that crash than three trashed cars, a bloodied arm, and all the various felony and misdemeanour charges that Lauren, Ocean and myself found ourselves lumbered with: it was as though the whole thing sent a shockwave through the inhabitants and acquaintances of Kappa Mutha Fucka, a boulder of reality dropped right in the centre of our mad little drunken pond, rippling out across town and touching dozens of people in their various ways.

For one, everybody swore off drink-driving and took long sober looks at themselves, and realised how lucky they'd been, how easily it could have been them.

For another, Ocean's plans to return to his beloved Oregon rainforests were now on hold, as his charge of aiding and abetting – the cops had made out that he was helping me hide evidence by secreting various pieces of the vehicle about his person – forbade him from leaving the state.

And a little closer to home, there was Lauren, somehow touched by the intensity of our experience, and somehow coming around to think and believe something during those three lonesome nights of mine in the Albemarle County Jail...

She was there the day I got out, in the car with Gus and Nathan and Tyler, and while everyone was buzzing and chatting and wanting to know and say everything under the sun, and while I was sinking sorrowfully into the backseat, grateful for them and their company, but woeful beyond woe, she just kept looking over at me, and not saying anything, this sort of intentness on her face.

We went back to mine after picking up some beers and vino and chicken and all the various bodies came over and attempted some sort of party. Except I was mostly on the backporch trying to pick out mournful little tunes on my unwilling guitar; my hands were clumsy and incompetent though. I slung it in the long grass in a fit of frustration and moped into my beer.

Lauren came out and joined me, and told me that she and Nathan Hart were no more – and then Nathan appeared, and she went elsewhere, and he and I sat down to talk.

"Listen, man," I said, "if you love her you've got to fight for her, 'cos love is the only thing that matters, and if you've found someone, if you think you can make it work, for fuck's sake, you've got to try." I was sincere and insistent, filled with the spirit of repentance.

"She doesn't want it," he said, "it's done. I'm gonna get me another woman, take it like a man. As long as they make whiskey I'll be all right."

And Gus joined us, and others, and we gathered around and listened to him in bewilderment at the news that the golden couple among us had ended. In amongst all this arrest stuff and twisted metal it seemed like the end of the world.

"Look at this," I said, "look at it." In my hand I held a wad of notes, ones and fives and tens earned during my now-over C&O table-waiting days. "What is it?" I said. And I took it and tossed it into the garden after my maybe-broken guitar, and all it was to me right then was a bunch of dirty paper and a representation of something I knew not what but cared nothing about.

"Friends is what matters, and the people you love; that's all that counts."

But as a slow-moving freight train sounded its moaning horn and lumbered across the tracks at the bottom of the garden Nathan got up and slunk slowly through the bushes towards it, and we watched as he grabbed hold of a cold metal ladder, jumped aboard, and trundled off into the defeated black night.

I went to the bottom of the garden and watched him go. I wished I could go too. He'd taught me how to do it once and it was magic. I could have used a bit of magic right then.

I went back up the garden and past the sombre crowd on the porch; in through the kitchen, past the piano, up the stairs. I went to my room. Lauren was lying there on my bed.

"Where's Nathan?" she said.

"He's gone," I said, "he hopped on a train."

"I heard it go," she said.

I lay down on the floor next to her and we talked. We talked about her, and her and Nathan Hart, and all the madness surrounding the arrests and what I was going to do about it, and out poured our hearts and souls onto those sheets and blankets, and in the space between us there was feeling. We drank, and the hours melted by unnoticed, and eventually Lauren addressed the subject that was clearly on both our minds.

"Rory," she said, "I want to kiss you."

And she did. And we did.

And we did a little more than kiss.

Chapter Seven

My God, could that girl give great head! Twice that first night, and swallowed and everything – which was something I totally wasn't used to, something I'd probably only experienced about three times in my whole life until then. Truth was, actually, I didn't really like it – or, rather: I didn't really like that I knew stroke imagined that women didn't like it slash didn't want it slash hated it slash it made them sick; I guess that's what I believed. And somewhere in my young head that thought had got stuck and I'd never been comfortable with it; listen:

When I was at school, before I'd really gotten anywhere with a girl – there had been one uncomfortable kiss when I was about fourteen, this strange slug-like object exploring my mouth and me not having a clue even where to begin with it – there were all these horrible boys around, Jerome Byron and Andy Askew – Upton lads – and you'd always hear them talking about how they'd fingered some girl, or how they'd gotten a blowjob and they'd be going, "and she said, 'don't come in my mouth, will you?' and I was like, 'no, of course not' – but then I did," and laughing and laughing about it, and me there in my surprisingly innocent ways just imagining that poor sweet thing gagging and choking and I never wanted to be like that.

I got my first proper girlfriend when I was sixteen – the best friend of the girl that I'd secretly fancied for about two years but always been too tongue-tied and shy to do anything about – and we sort of fell into this relationship together, ending up being in it for exactly one year and three hundred and sixty four days; that is, we broke up the day before our second anniversary. And this is what a good guy I was:

1. We waited five months before we had sex, the both of us virgins, and it was sort of beautiful that way.
2. Before that, though, she'd gone and told her friend that we'd done it – and, if you can believe this: I was actually offended! Talk about a stereotypical role-reversal gender type scenario.
3. It was another four months before she went down on me, at some Christmas party; I was like, you don't have to do this if you don't want to; she said, "don't come, will you?" I said, "no," and I didn't. And every other time after that too. I'd always tell her when I was about to and move her away.
4. Just after we broke up she came over to see me – I'd moved to Leeds by this point, was living in a hovellous little attic room above my dad's guitar shop

– and after long talks and tears we, of course, ended up in bed. She told me that she wanted to give me a blowjob, and wanted to go "all the way," to be the first to do that. I was down with that – but let me tell you this: it was so hard to let her do it, so filled was I with the idea that this was just a pure horrible thing for a woman to experience, and when I could feel myself getting close I was squeezing her arm, trying to move her head away, trying to do everything in my power to let her know that I was about to explode and this was her last chance to save herself from the horrors of 'saltiness' and 'paste' – but she carried on and she didn't mind at all. It was lovely and sweet and I felt happy that I'd done everything I could to warn her.

And so that was me: I was like that for years and years, and probably still am. My next girlfriend, who I was with for eighteen months, wasn't particularly averse to it, but preferred not to, so I always had to let her know with those patented arm squeezes and gentle removements of the head – and on like the three occasions that she wanted to do it, it was sort of a fight for her to keep my dick in her mouth, so sure did I have to be that she knew I was about to come, and so determined was I not to join the ranks of Jerome Byron and Andy Askew and all the other tens of thousands of skanky lads that terrorise the poor, sweet high school girls of England and the world. And so, to be with Lauren, who made it clear that this was what she wanted to do, and that she liked it, and wouldn't take no for an answer…well, that was something of a revelation to me. A really good, hot, sexy, oh my God, this girl actually wants my cum in her mouth, yes please sort of revelation. The kind of revelation that's gonna make a guy want more.

Lauren vacated Kappa Mutha Fucka the next day and moved into my room, and we embarked on a secret relationship. Nathan Hart was still my best friend, after all, and we knew that he wouldn't be happy if he found out. Plus we all shared mutual friends and Charlottesville was a small town where news travelled fast. The only person I let in on it was Tyler, and I only told him because we had to go through his room to get to mine. But he was older than us, a bit more sensible, and a man to be trusted. He had decorum. So, then, it was something of a surprise when I heard our shared door opening behind me one sunny morning about three days in, Lauren and I fooling around on the bed, my hand rushing for the sheet to cover our naked bodies.

"Tyler, man," I said, "don't come in."

"Rory," Lauren said, a look of horror spread across her face, "it's not Tyler."

I turned from her and peered towards the door. Framed there, the shadowy figure of Nathan Hart.

I turned back and buried my face in the covers, a million thoughts in my head only able to express themselves in the muttered words "shit" and "fuck."

And in the doorway, Nathan Hart turns his back and walks away.

Chapter Eight

Listen, if you're ever in a situation where it looks like you're about to nob your best friend's girl, or your best friend's ex-girl – or, let's face it, the girl of anyone – don't. Stop and think about it for a minute. Take some time out. Go and find somebody wise and explain it all to them and see what they say. And then go to that girl and tell her as tactfully as you are able that you just can't do it right now; that you think she's a charming and attractive and most fragrant young lady, and that you're sure it would be awesome and hot but, all things considered, you just don't think it's a good idea. Chat a little. Flirt, even. But, whatever you do, for God's sake don't nob her.

Chapter Nine

Well if the crash was just the start that discovery really was the beginning of the end, the mini-Krakatoa that brought the walls down and blew the doors off the joint, sending the boozy, mindless reign of Kappa Mutha Fucka into freefall. Friendships and relationships lay in tatters; jobs were fired and quit; people moved in and out of houses; babies were born; partners swapped; and lawyers and broken glass and threats and love and hate; and somewhere right in the middle it all, Princess Diana coming to her messy end in the Paris tunnel night, and it all seemed so fitting to that Charlottesville summer chaos that I found myself such a part of. And that's all rather vague and non-specific and doesn't really tell you what it was actually like – but just maybe I can try again...

Oh, Nathan Hart! Oh, sweet, sweet Nathan Hart! How I hurt you, I know – and how you then turned against the friend you once loved so much, and tried to hit me every time we met, and vented so, and fell then into the arms of another woman that you went on to have another equally destructive and drink- and drug-fuelled relationship with, giving her a child, and eventually breaking up so that it was just you and your son, and elsewhere the mother of your child, that gone and crazy goth girl, incapable and unfit, the woman whose arms I drove you into, and irrevocably your life was changed forever.

And you, Gus, creator of The Musings, having now found the villain that you'd always wanted: how steadfastly and with what dedication did you commit yourself to besmirching my good name, gleefully reporting on all my misdemeanours, trouncing mine and Lauren's relationship in the defence of your innocent friend, rubbishing us in your press for the whole world to read. And then, when I retaliated in my own writings, and when some of your own friends came to support me and my view that the days were over, that Kappa Mutha Fucka was an empire waiting to be put to the sword, and that I just happened to be the man holding the torch – nice mixed-metaphor there, I know – how much more did you turn on me, hands over ears, screaming louder and louder, "Rory is bad Bad BAD!" And all the people that read you, and chose their sides, and shunned me because of it, and threatened violence and ass-kickings, and the jobs I lost...

And Lauren and I – my Lauren, now – somehow in the midst of it all forming something of a loving relationship, more adult and tender than I'd ever thought possible, driving out to your parents in my now-recovered and delightfully battered but still-driving Ford LTD, days in the country, and saunas and swims. Peace out there in that Louisa County idyll, walks with the family and dogs, parents and normality. Sex and beauty and talks into the night about all the things in the world and in our hearts, and me waffling endlessly about mad Englishnesses like Vinny Jones grabbing Gazza's nuts and you just listening bright-eyed and loving it, I don't know why. And you and me, together, holding tight against the world, in bars, on hills, in cars and fields and barefoot walks in the rain, and if this is all I have then this is all I need, the wind against my skin, and happiness inside, and a woman's hand in mine.

I thought I'd miss the boozy days and nights of Kappa Mutha Fucka; instead I came to see it as a sort of sickness, and it was on our trips out into the country that I felt most myself: out into those Virginia hills and mountains away from the incesticide and madness that crowded within the Charlottesville city walls. We'd load up the LTD and go creaking the country, and out there there was space, and fresh air, and possibilities. The roads were open and long and small towns that knew us not reached out welcoming hands to meet and greet us, little wooden shops selling fishing bait and ice, decrepit old barns saying, restore me, come live in my fields. The rivers and streams gurgled over smooth shining stones, bridges and water and green, and there the world moved more slowly, the south's beating heart not yet up to speed with the rest of modern society.

There was this one time I remember in particular: her dad had recommended a hike up to the ridge about seventy miles out of town and we liked the sounds of that very much. A spot of camping, off in the wilds, just the two of us: perfect. Not taking into account, of course, the best laid plans of mice and men – and drunken mice, and drunken men.

It was quite possibly the least successful camping trip in history.

Number one, we forgot our sleeping bags, and had to do an extra hundred and forty miles to retrieve them. Number two, we then couldn't find the trailhead, and spent two hours fumbling around in the dark; Lauren said we were being tested, that it was how we handled it that was important – and handle it we did, in mighty fine fashion, swigging on Southern Comfort and laughing at our incompetence. We finally gave up the search and went careening around dark country highways, and found a fun little redneck bar just outside Luray with a hopping bluegrass band and a Twin Peaks vibe, and whooped it up while Lauren, with my blessing, flirted with the musicians and I shouted quotes from Withnail and I to anyone that cared to listen, but mostly to myself. And then we romped in the car park and talked about driving to Las Vegas for a spot of marriage. And then we realised that we'd left all her dad's expensive camping gear back at the trailhead, now some fifty miles away, and back on the three a.m. road we went, both pretty drunk and tired beyond tired, one minor collision with a bridge and a spot of nodding off at the wheel to follow.

But we made the trailhead – for the third time that day, well over three hundred miles under our respective, ludicrous belts – and camped up for the night.

We woke in the crisp morning sunshine and ate a cooked breakfast. And before our all-too-sudden departure for Charlottesville we took a short walk up a hill. It was autumn now, the browns and greens and reds of the falling Virginia foliage in full effect, the scorching heat of the humid summer replaced by a mist and a dew, a crisp, wet chill in the air.

We reached the summit of the hill and sat down in silence, side by side, and looked out. Across fields. Across to valleys and forests and mountains. Across the undulations of the land. The trees burned. The country stood still and quiet.

It was beautiful, of course, but something else was in the air: I felt humbled and intensely grateful to be presented with such a scene of selfless beauty. I felt that the hills and trees were looking into me, even as I gazed out into them. More accurately, though, I felt that they were a mirror, a clear and perfect instrument of reflection. They asked nothing of me. They merely showed me what I was, and what I could be. I knew in that moment that I'd been so wrong.

Chapter Ten

So it wasn't all doom and gloom: some sort of realisation was starting to grow in me, that I'd been looking for happiness in all the wrong places: that it wasn't there in booze and drugs and shallow friendships. Neither was it there in material possessions, in earning money, in being known. To be known, but never to know. There was something else: something that evaded me. But in those moments of beauty and love with Lauren I found something of goodness, and in those moments all I craved were more of the same. To forget desires and temptations. And to develop some kind of understanding of what a human being is actually about.

I say all that and I know it was true – and yet I cringe when I think of what is to come, and wonder how I could have been capable of such insight and such determination to make things better while at the same time sliding so easily back into the life of a reckless drunk. So while Lauren and I were better and more mature on our own – and better than her and Nathan had been – we still found it almost impossibly hard to shake our love of the sauce and of mad stuff. We were mad as fish, to be perfectly honest. Mental. And those lucid and clear days of our fledgling relationship spent in the safety of the country were soon disappeared once I found myself another upscale waiting job, and made a whole new circle of friends, and slunk back into the world of free booze and wild parties. Though, for that, I have to blame John.

John, the bartender there at Escafé, was about twice my age, and sort of loopy in a Vietnam vet-style way. He was hairy. He had these massive sideburns. He looked like a wolf. And he was always going on about how he'd been shot one night, and how he was going to take revenge on the people that had done it. He talked about that a lot. He was also an ex-alcoholic – the sort of ex-alcoholic who knows that drinking would be near-fatal for him, and so would never, ever do it, but who just can't quite stay away from the stuff. Which is why, I guess, he worked in a bar. And why he took me so quickly under his wing as a sort of protégé that he could live through vicariously.

I'd get to work and soon enough he'd call me over. He'd have a sneaky glance around to make sure that Sean and Doug, the gay couple owners of the restaurant weren't around.

"You want a shot, brother?" he'd say, leaning over at me, a huddle of conspirators.

"Sure," I'd say – hey, I'm a Yorkshireman, I'll never turn down a free drink – and up he'd serve me a double or a treble, to be quaffed as quickly as possible, lest anyone discover our secret.

"Down in one," he'd say, watching me gobble it up, always with a strangely pleased look on his face. "You want another?"

And so it went: every hour or so he'd call me to him and serve me a shifty drink – and every mistaken order or wrongly-pulled beer had to go the same way too. Martinis, Long Island Iced Teas, glasses of wine, Margaritas, Black Russians, the last bit of gin in a bottle: all down the hatch and despatched as quickly and surreptitiously as possible. I was getting wasted every night. And crazy wolfman John was loving it.

I soon slid back into my old ways, drunk on the job and following men with bags of white powder into toilets, invariably calling up Lauren to rescue me from the four a.m. mess I'd gotten myself into. Not that she was any better: she was always wasted too. She came home drunk late one night with a bloke who I knew fancied her, and got into my bed and passed out in her knickers: he got in after her while I sat there incredulous. Poor girl didn't know what she was doing. But he did.

"Excuse me, mate," I said, "but I think you'd better go home." He was a fair bit smaller than me; I would've taken him if I'd had to. He looked up at me and got his shoes and left. Then I put a hot lightbulb in her undies and watched her grimace in her sleep and satisfied myself with that.

I decided one day to introduce her to the great British tradition of the pub crawl, a mystery to her young American ears.

"You just start at one end of town, get a drink, drink it, and then move on to the next pub. And then you have a drink there, and then move on again. And so on and so on. Until you've had a drink in every bar in town. Simple."

"Splendid!" she said, "let's do it."

And off we went at twelve noon prompt up the far end of JPA for our first beer of the day, a swift pint in Dürty Nellies before heading into town for the envisaged grand finale at the C&O some fourteen hours and many, many drinks later.

"We're gonna be wrecked," I say with glee.

"You know," she says, "Bukowski said that few people in life have the imagination to simply get piss-assed drunk."

"Marvellous!" I say, "here's to Bukowski." I raise my glass and we cheers.

"Goddamn I love Bukowski," she says, licking her lips, "all that life lesson bullshit just unintentionally spilling out of him, all fucked up but all those little insights and wisdoms and seeds."

"You know what we should do? We should make some notes so we can remember it all later." I reach over and grab a large pile of beer mats and stuff them in my pocket. "Here we go!"

So down JPA and into all the bars of The Corner, and then somehow it's dark and about nine and I'm sitting alone in The Greenskeeper wondering where the last few hours have gone, and wondering where Lauren has gone, and in my pocket I fish out a load of bits of scrawled-upon soggy cardboard that reveal a sad story of about fourteen pints and about the same number of arguments and recriminations, and how odd it is to come around like that. Off then to find my girl; no doubt she's just that little bit further on down the road...

Into Southern Comfort where she works now, and there she is sat at a table with a couple of waitresses, bawling her eyes out and lawks a lawdy if I know why. And up I swagger and before I know it we're snogging over the table, and then the blonde-haired waitress wanders off to the bathroom and I go too – and before I know that as well, we're up there in the bathroom all against the wall, and lips are seeking lips, tongue on tongue, hungry and frantic and all out of nowhere.

And the party's back on, and we're stumbling our way towards the downtown mall and Escafé, and more drinks, and on-the-house margaritas, and Lauren's in fine form – obviously I can't remember what kind of form – but she's probably saying things like, "ha!" and, "you limey bastard!" – and then Miller's, and God knows where else, and finally, amazingly, we make the C&O for closing time just before two, and a careful tally of my beer-soaked beermats reveals seventeen pints and two margaritas and the pubcrawl has been a triumph.

The C&O is hopping; the bar downstairs small and packed full of people, and it's my first time back in there since being fired and it feels like a glorious return. We plonk at a table with Good Looks John and this Dutch girl Kirsten DeGoode, and somewhere around Kathy Buchet, and Stuart my old waiting buddy, and Geoff, luckily, is on the bar, not Tyler, and Geoff's always good for a few free drinks. And then there's Dave Matthews and his girlfriend Ashley, who's always had a thing for me, and she pulls me into the toilet and lays out some white powder on the cistern there, and up nose it goes. And do we snog? She was always trying to, and as far as I remember I was always resisting – even that one night when I went back to theirs when Dave was away and we got all drunk and I vomited pork medallions on the floor and pushed them under the couch – but this night? I don't know; I honestly can't remember. But probably I should have done. She was a rockstar's girlfriend, fer Christ's sake! And that's some sort of claim to fame.

Back in the bar I stumble in on Kirsten teasing Good Looks John about his sexuality. He's a good looking boy, no girlfriend, and no apparent interest in one.

"Ha!" I shout, "come on John, we all know you're gay!"

And, "yes!" they laugh, because it's true, "come on John, come out the closet."

And Good Looks John smiles sweetly and he sure is a good looking boy.

"Come on John, we know you're gay; why're you pretending?"

More sweet smiles.

"Come on John, give us a kiss, don't be afraid."

And cajoling and whoops, and faces gathering around the table, and me and John leaning into each other and the two of us having a right good go at it in the middle of that crowd, cheers and smiles and actually quite nice, that Good Looks John – much better than Larry from Mono Loco, the one who's been chasing me for months, his scratchy beard making me laugh that night in the blood-smeared LTD...

Out we roll into the night, Lauren and Kirsten and John and me, and back to theirs where me and Kirsten suddenly start snogging in the living room in front of Diohji the dog, and then after a bit, realising that Lauren and John are sort of sitting there awkwardly and not really saying anything: "hey, why don't you guys kiss too?"

And so they do, and they look like they're enjoying it, but that's sort of putting me off so I suggest to Kirsten the aptly-named DeGoode that we go upstairs, and up we go, up to her bed, and more rolling around ensues while she laughs at my attempts to infiltrate her unit (her words) and then up comes Lauren, and passes out next to us, so we strip her naked and admire her breasts, and while she sleeps there by our side we get naked ourselves and more attempted unit infiltration goes on, skilfully and Dutchly repelled, and kisses soon turn into four a.m. slumber, and in the morning we wake up covered in blood, two women, a guy and a dog, and me just cracking up at the sight of the blood literally dripping out of her pillow from my re-opened tequila bottle wound that's now spraying everywhere, bleeding all over people and cars and beds and streets, and how funny it looks, the way it squirts, I really should get that looked at...

And back and back and back it was to the days of Kappa Mutha Fucka, only different faces and different names, ones I hadn't alienated yet, ones who didn't care about my chequered past but who somehow liked me for what I was, that rolling British drunk that slotted in so nicely with their rolling drunken ways, so long as I stayed away from their girlfriends, which I rarely did.

I came home one day to find Tyler and Plan 9 Dave and Ocean – who had moved in with us – all sitting there in the living room and Tyler said to me that they didn't want me to live there anymore. I turned to Ocean for some sort of support, for some show of solidarity – I had, after all, only just asked him if they were happy with me there, given the madness I was getting up to, and he was like, "sure, man, I'm right behind you" – but there, in that moment, all he had to give me was his pot-addled smile and one of his dippy hippy shrugs, and I knew it was all over. Dave and Tyler sat there like stones. Inside I was a mass of apologies and tearful proclamations, shame at my ways, realisations that I'd somehow done wrong but could also make it better – but all I could say was, "righty oh," and off I trotted to get my shit, and stuff it in the trunk of the LTD, and not a goodbye in sight.

But why didn't I care? And why was I actually glad to be set free of the shackles of leases and housemates? Why didn't it bother me that I'd managed to turn everyone who could possibly have cared against me? Why, when the only thing left to do was break down and cry did I laugh and laugh and laugh? The rate at which I had been plunged into that self-imposed hell was so extraordinary as to be ridiculous. But did I lack any trace of feeling whatsoever? Or was I simply nuts? Yes, maybe that was it.

So began an interesting stint of evictions: three in six weeks. After that I went and stayed with Lauren, who was living with this crazy old hippy lady and that was pretty nice for a while: she even took me to some Tibetan chanting one night and I sort of dug it in my cynical, devoutly atheistic way. But it wasn't long before our acting up had sufficiently destroyed her peace and she threw the two of us out.

And after that I moved into what I thought would be my saving grace, this place over in Belmont with a bunch of cool, coke-snorting waiters and bartenders sure to be as mad and bad as I was, party central, sorted. But on the first weekend there, about ten days before Christmas, we had this party and somehow I was last man standing, up on the roof in a bath towel at eight in the morning, bottle of tequila, powdered nose and shouts to the redneck neighbours to come up and join me, and here come the cops, at which point I disappear into the streets only to vaguely remember being escorted back home with promises of no arrest if I stay there, only to vaguely remember then appearing on the pedestrianised mall wearing nothing but a pair of jeans – no shoes, no socks, no shirt – and wondering how the hell I'd got there and, oh shit, it's two in the afternoon and I've got to get to work soon – and the next time I saw them they were like: you're out of here.

And so I went and lived in my car.

Chapter Eleven

Well I think that just about covers that period of my life, those seven strange and silly months that saw me go from clean-living student apartment boy to highly-paid and highly-cherished upmarket accented waiter; to friend of gutterpunks and gutterdrunks; to gutterdrunk myself; to drunk-driver and felon; to girlfriend stealer; to alienator and evictee supreme; to, in the end of it, homeless, living in my car, all spun out of control, and troubled and lost and saddened and searching. And, of course, I was out on bail and awaiting trial.

Soon after the arrest and release I got given this court-appointed lawyer called Norman who I went to see every couple of weeks to discuss my case. Except, being free of charge, he was sort of useless and mad, and spent nearly all our meetings going on about the injustices of the system, about how wrong it was that the police could violate you – "that the government can stop you in your own car and jab a NEEDLE into your arm – pierce your SKIN – and take your BLOOD – why it's downright unconstitutional!" – and various things about the Fourth Amendment, whatever that is, and I'd sort of sit there bewildered and bored while this large-eared Southern gent ranted on and on about things that didn't really have much to do with me before finally saying, let's meet again on such and such a date.

Meanwhile, I'd been back to court a few times but nothing much had happened there, apart from setting dates for hearings and preliminary hearings and trials, stretching way out into the following February. And so there I was, in the system, strapped to it and trying my best to pay for my sins, but feeling more and more like a character in a Franz Kafka novel, shepherded to and from court for little apparent purpose other than to be told, come back in two weeks so we can shepherd you some more. And that was pretty much that.

So what does all this mean? What it means is this: that you've got some sort of sense of what life was like for twenty-one year-old Rory, shunned and on bail, but in a job that he quite liked, and variously sleeping in his car or getting evicted from houses, and with his girlfriend in a sort of tempestuous and intoxicated relationship that occasionally threatened to break through into something sensible and lasting and good. And that was where we were when the clock started ticking down towards New Year's Eve and the new (false) dawn of nineteen-ninety-eight.

You're probably thinking I was some sort of major first-class idiot and scumbag, aren't you? Well that's all right; I do too.

But listen: the thing was, after that party where I ended up on the roof, and then semi-naked and barefoot wandering bewildered on the Downtown Mall, it was sort of a last straw for me. Maybe it was the coke, or the tequila, or the coke and the tequila (and the beer and the whiskey and wine), but I was on such a downer that next night at work, practically in tears while serving people their meals, that I knew, once and for all, that I had to change. So I stopped drinking that mid-December night and decided to take a long, hard, sober look at myself and see if I couldn't straighten things up a little. Lauren had plans to move to New York but I knew I couldn't do that again, not after all the toilet-dwelling shit I'd been through there; instead I got into this idea of finding my own place away from the action, somewhere quiet and neighbourly and chill. Somewhere respectable. I looked at one-bedroom houses for about five hundred bucks a month and when I imagined myself in there doing crafty things and strumming my guitar and being gentle I sort of dug it. I thought, man, if I'm gonna be stuck in this town awaiting the machinations of fate I might as well try and make something of it. Mad boozy days were over for me; I wanted more than that. And so, in the cool early-winter Virginia sunlight, this was my resolve.

But fate, as ever, was conspiring against me.

Number one, I lost my job. Tyler was up to his tricks again and called up Sean and Doug and told them, no, it's not that Rory merely can't find his social security card, it's that he doesn't actually have one, and if you don't fire him I'm going to grass you up to the authorities and you'll be in a whole heap of shit. And so, fire me they did.

And, number two, I lost all my savings: I lost the envelope containing all the money I had in the world. It was something like two thousand dollars.

See, what I'd been doing was this: whatever I earned from waiting – and it was usually about a hundred dollars a night – it went straight into this brown envelope that was basically hanging around and buried in the boot of my car. At around the point it went missing – which was just after I got fired, which was just after New Year's, which was just after Lauren left for New York – it had plenty enough in it to see me through for quite a few months, and it was my lifeline. And then it was gone. Which left me with nothing. No money, no home, no job, no girlfriend, no life, no future, no nothing. All I had then was a trunkful of possessions, a battered and highly illegal car, and an insane, jug-eared lawyer who was going to try to defend me against a multitude of charges that looked like adding up to six months behind bars. I couldn't work; I couldn't afford a place to live; and I couldn't leave town and follow my dreams of starting somewhere anew.

It was sort of bad, I guess.

So the net was closing in, and it was a pity because, as I was working one of my last doomed shifts at poor old lovely Escafé, and as the clock chimed its knell on ninety-seven and welcomed in the New Year, I remember standing there at my wait station and looking out into the crowd of revellers and drunks whooping it up and, I swear, I was like my own oasis of calm, so strangely detached from it all. Peace was in me, and it felt good. I remembered how someone had not too long ago told me that the way you saw in the New Year would set your tone for the year to come, and I remembered how the year before I'd spent it back in San Diego at the youth hostel running around like a drunken fool and pissing people off and maybe I shouldn't have been surprised how it'd all turned out. And now this year I was sober and resolved, and there was this sense of optimism and clarity that swept through me, and I sort of knew that everything was going to be okay.

So it was a little bit strange to lose it all within a week, all over again. And to be left practically penniless in a town with no options, sleeping and living in that cold Virginia winter on the backseat of my car.

And down, then, and down I went, until I spoke to nobody, and forgot all about showers and hope and happiness. And then, and only then, when the depths had been reached, did I finally come to my online diary, my sole friend beside my smash-mouthed car, and write.

Part Three

Saturday 10th January, 1998

Factoids, baby! A list of things about me:

- I own over a hundred and fifty Jimi Hendrix vinyls, many identical.
- My brother and I don't speak. No vendetta, we just don't speak.
- I have recurring dreams about being bitten on the hand by dogs.
- The only vegetables I'll eat are potatoes.
- I've never been stung by a bee, wasp or any such creature, although I've twice played host to a leech. I like ladybirds a lot, but am afraid of moths.
- I've been evicted from five of my eight homes, including once by each parent. I've also been fired from four of my six jobs.
- I was named after drunk Irish blues guitarist Rory Gallagher.
- I didn't know that toilets had to be flushed after urinating until I was thirteen; I thought that was just for poos.
- Forrest Gump is the only movie I've cried at on both the first and second viewing. The last movie I cried at was The Ice Storm.
- Like Spike Milligan's dad, I've never killed a tiger.
- Sex: I've had intercourse (don't laugh) with five girls, and kissed sixteen others. I once went to bed with (well, more fingered in the bathroom) a girl who had sat on President Clinton's knee. I've also shaken Prince Charles by the hand.
- I've dreamt of sex with my mother many times, though only once with my dad. I imagine most people have those dreams at some point.

- I'll usually eat at least three bars of chocolate a day, although sometimes I have as many as ten. My favourites are Twix and Rolos.
- I've never paid for marijuana or cocaine – but I did once pay a tenner for a bag of Italian seasoning one night in Chapeltown, Leeds.
- Chicken is my very favourite food.
- I haven't ever told either of my parents that I loved them.
- When I was twelve I destroyed every photo of me I could find. Since then I've probably had my picture taken less than twenty times.
- I believe in reincarnation, and quite a bit of other nonsense besides.
- The last time I wore underwear was February 1997.
- As a small boy I developed a craving for batteries, which I stole from the local supermarket. I was caught and banned until the age of sixteen.
- I've never sworn in front of my dad. Not even "shit." It's because I'm afraid he might hit me. He went mental once when I told him to "bog off."
- My uncles on my mother's side are all train-spotters. I shared their obsession for years until I was about eleven. I still like trains.
- On the night I lost my virginity I became so bored and discouraged by my performance that I began to watch really bad TV. It was Russ Abbot.
- My mother and I once sat for four hours with our arms in cold bathwater over an argument about who should take the plug out. I won.
- The best kissing experience I ever had was with a girl from Sydney.
- I used to bury my mum's cigarettes in the back garden in an effort to get her to quit. It worked. I tried the same idea with my brother's peanut butter, unfortunately unsuccessfully.
- I've kissed four men. My one and only genuine homosexual experience happened about a week after I moved to Charlottesville. And I don't want to talk about it.
- I've killed four cars, and mortally wounded two others.
- I didn't eat pizza or smoke pot until I was twenty.
- I can't sing at all. I think I only have one note and even that's out of tune.
- I don't understand soup.
- So far, there have been no lies.

Thursday 22nd January, 1998

Went to court this morning, for the preliminary hearing – which must mean that my last visit in mid-December was the pre-preliminary hearing, and the one in October the pre-pre-preliminary hearing. And in a radical departure from the previous four appearances, the wheels of justice actually turned a little. Not a lot, but turn they did.

I got to sit up front today – exciting! just like a real criminal! – and listened to my arresting officer describe what an idiot I'd been on September 12th. It was nice to see Officer Cox again – he was just as pleasant as I remembered him, and said (when describing my mood on arrest) that I was, "very co-operative, even friendly." That made me smile.

Meanwhile, my attorney – the incomprehensible Stormin' Norman – kept jumping up and down and almost apologetically mumbling things like, "hearsay," and, "objection." That added even more realism to the proceedings. He's a madman, is Norman – before it was my turn we were sitting there listening to a policeman talk about finding a guy with half his face missing and Norman kept chuckling and nudging me, as though it was the funniest thing he'd ever heard. Then he went on about how I wouldn't be allowed to buy a gun if I got convicted, as though that would be a bad thing. He also told me he'd spent some time behind bars because he once refused to enter through the court metal detector, citing personal infringement. A man of principal, if nothing else.

In the event I sat through it all and awaited the familiar end-game of 'setting a date for the next hearing.' I'm sure if it wasn't so bloody annoying and such a waste of everyone's time (not mine – I'm guilty, remember) and money (again, not mine – the hard-working tax payer; it hasn't cost me a bean) I'd look on all this as a fascinating insight into bureaucracy gone mad. And you know what? I do.

Monday 26th January, 1998

Location: The Exmore Diner, on the Eastern Shore, two hours after nearly driving my car into the sea.

So here's what I think...

...it's not much, is it? That's the problem with me – I'm an all or nothing kind of guy. I want it all but I do nothing about it. And here, day after day, year after year, the same fat arses, bad haircuts, and bad jokes – well, these people don't seem too down at heart – in fact, they look positively content. Is that the answer? Mediocrity? Meaningless, inane conversation? Some day soon I'll stop being such a dreamer and realise that this is all there is. How can a thinking person ever be happy? Won't I always want more? Suppose the highlight of your day was sneezing – or hearing someone sneeze. Here's the bottom line: I'd like to be able to say, "I came to America and learned..." – and learned what, exactly? That there's no point looking for anything, because there isn't anything? Don't bother leaving home, don't chase your dreams – you'll just be disappointed? This life is the most beautifully wrapped Christmas present but underneath all that allure and promise sits an empty box. Leave it where it is. You can touch it; even pick it up and try to guess what's inside, but don't ever, ever open it. Even when the needles have fallen off the tree and the decorations are long since packed away...

What would happen if I sat down next to one of the toothless old fools in here and asked them what they thought about life? What would their barely intelligible answer be? Or, maybe in their youth – maybe four days before their twenty-second birthday – they sat and looked around and wondered what it all meant. Then maybe that feeling gradually left them until eventually the most important thought in their wrinkled old minds concerned not the question, "where are we going? where have we been? and why?" but, "Bob bought a new tyre," or, "I see it's gonna be cold tomorrow" – or what if it's not even that? Jesus, what do we become? Hungry – eat. Thirsty – drink. Poor – get a job. Unhappy – well, I guess if you're not lacking anything, like a TV or a half-decent truck (assuming you have a job) or friends (but what are friends if not like-minded people? and don't we all become the same?) then why would you be unhappy? Happy – watch TV. Basically, if there's nothing wrong, don't fix it – but I'm not looking for the absence of wrong, I'm looking for the presence of right. And there it is in a nutshell: right *is* the absence of wrong – and happiness is not the positive feeling I'm looking for but merely the absence of misery.

But I can't give in – not just yet.

Thursday 29th January, 1998

I'm not depressed. I've been depressed before and I know how it feels. I did all the staying in bed for a month, filling days and weeks solidly with computer games and television and freaking out at the thought of venturing outside stuff. That was in my last year in Leeds, before I first came to America, and that's not how I feel right now. I'm just a little lost, that's all.

Actually, I've come to believe that I'm in the depths of a mid-life crisis which has been going on for the last four years, since I left school. Okay, so I'm not some thirty-seven year-old guy who's suddenly awoken one morning to the realisation that he's spent nearly half his life in a darkened room auditing the sales of chicken livers – but I am nonetheless determined, in true nineties style, to give my predicament a name, and therefore credibility. I'm too old to qualify for teenage angst and too young to claim a bona fide status like middle-aged crisis or male menopause, however I am in mid-life – that is, a point somewhere between birth and death – and this is definitely some sort of crisis. So there.

The thing is, I shouldn't really be out here: I should be tucked up safe and warm in university. Those places are designed so that this transitional period between adolescence and young adulthood can pass as smoothly as possible, three or four years spent getting progressively deeper into the pool instead of the nasty shock of being tossed straight in at the deep-end. It's too hard to leave the world of readymade friends and institutionally-imposed structure. Freedom can be overwhelming. There's a lot to be said for having someone decide the layout of your day. A sense of purpose is a wonderful thing.

Independent (but not alone); responsible (sometimes); an individual (just like everybody else); free to come and go (especially to the folks back home); always a reason to get out of bed; always focused straight ahead (never looking to the sides)

The first time I lost my sense of purpose was after being fired by J. Scheerer & Sons, purveyors of fine musical instruments since 1882. Up until that point life had been a doddle. Though there had been plenty of ups and downs the downs had never lasted long and they were always conquered with relative ease; when my mother threw me out of home I simply took off to Leeds and began working full-time in my Dad's guitar shop, living in a room upstairs – and when he fired and evicted me it was a mere two days before I landed a much better job at a rival shop in town, quickly followed by a house and a girlfriend. These fortunes were nothing new to me. I had led a most charmed life, from buying and selling computers at fourteen to having my own highly successful guitar trading business at eighteen. Managing the guitar department at Scheerer's I increased profits by an average of twenty-five percent; that December profits were up a monstrous seventy percent on the previous year – surely I was like a gift from God to Old Man Scheerer?

Well it seemed I wasn't quite as indispensable as I'd imagined. I'd been doing my own bit of wheeler-dealing on the side and, when they found out, I was gone. I had no idea how to handle this unexpected fall from grace. Suddenly, everything started to go wrong, from car crashes to burglaries to violence in the street. I basically sealed myself inside the house and only pulled myself from the mire by jumping on a plane to New York. I'm now very cynical about jobs, as I am about relationships and education and all the other things we do to cover over the task of finding our purpose. But they can't all be cop-outs, can they?

Friday 30th January, 1998

Well now I'm twenty-two – woo-hoo – and I'm thinking this is probably the first time I won't get to hear anyone wish me a happy birthday. I was trying to think of my worst birthday but nothing leaps to mind – there have been some pretty uneventful and boring ones but nobody's ever died and I haven't lost any limbs or anything so I wouldn't say they were bad. My best ones were probably my nineteenth, when Rachel and I were still in love and she bought me a cake and a rose and a big black sweater – the jumper I'm wearing right now, in fact – and my seventh, when I had my one and only birthday party and we played pin the tale on the donkey and I got a chess set. Another year I got a cake that said 'Everton' on it and I was in heaven. And a few years after that I got a cheque from my mum for thirty pounds – which included money that she owed me – and it bounced.

Saturday 31st January, 1998

So here I am, running around looking for something real, something that I can believe in, and I'm coming up miserably empty handed. If I wasn't just intelligent enough to know how stupid I am, would I be happy – or at least content? I read some magazine article a few days ago pondering the reasons behind this disillusioned generation I find myself a part of. It concluded that we are "desperately looking for something to believe in to save us from our cynicism, yet far too cynical to believe in anything." Everything our predecessors had – religion, government, fixed gender-roles, career-oriented lives – it's all been presented to us as a sham. So what are we supposed to do? I wish I could be a religious nut, never questioning or searching for answers, having someone else do my thinking for me. I wish music was the same for me as it was for my parents, all innocent and exciting and revolutionary: hearing The Beatles for the first time and shaking my head and screaming, and not knowing why, but at least knowing that it was good. All I've ever heard is, "it's not as good as the sixties." I've had those sixties rammed down my throat my whole life and I'm sick of it.

Right now, I'm a little bit nuts. I don't really feel it but the facts speak for themselves: all I've been doing is killing time wandering the streets alone before returning to my cold car to sleep. I have no job, no home, and little money. There are people who I would call friends but I just can't be around them right now. I don't want to be a burden and I don't have anything to offer. I've had plenty of offers of places to stay, too, and I've refused them all. And yet, perversely, I pray for someone to sweep me into their arms, cradle my head, and assure me that everything'll be all right – and then to make it so. I think I want my mummy.

I'm a man with time on his hands and himself on his mind. The most annoying thing is I know that one day soon these feelings will also desert me –

so how can I take them seriously? – and I'm going to look back on all this and think, "God, was I really such a morbid, cynical and bitter arsehole?" And the answer will be "yes."

Monday 2nd February, 1998

Two stark examples of how far I have slipped:

- Last night as I was making my way back to the LTD in the pouring and miserable rain I took a short-cut which involved clambering over broken bottles to reach the dark and dreary railway lines that run the length of Charlottesville. At one point I looked up and saw that I was passing the C&O, my former place of employment, with its warm lights hinting at the cosy scene within. No doubt it was filled with happy revellers, many of whom I would have known.

- This morning I was woken by the familiar and ominous rat-a-tat-tat upon my window. "It's the cops," I thought, "they'll want ID, and a driver's license, and they'll give me a ticket or two, or take me away." I hid myself under my sleeping bag but the knocks were repeated and I emerged to face the music. It turned out to be a guy who has a business in the Ivy Square Shopping Centre. He said it was private and I couldn't park there overnight. Throughout the brief, mostly one-sided conversation I tried to keep my face out of his sight. I'd met the man before, about a month ago, when I had a job and a normal life and hope. I was thinking of renting an apartment from him but decided against it as it wasn't that nice a place.

Thursday 5th February, 1998

Factoids! It's the latest craze:

- The last time I ate something that wasn't a Twix was three days ago.
- I haven't spoken to anyone since Monday.
- The things I miss about England: bacon, Match of the Day, pound-a-pint night, and my grandparents. That's about it.
- Up until four thirty today I had made more cat sounds than human noises.
- In the last year I've remembered less than ten dreams.

In other news, the court situation drags on – and on, and on, and on. I'm starting to think I should just say "fuck it" to the whole thing and leave it all behind. I'd like to think I had it in me to make it up to society – as if my sitting in a room for three months would in any way "make it up to society" – but I'm absolutely terrified of the prospect of jail-time and I just want to run, hit the road, head for Tucson or Savannah or somewhere else far, far away. Would

79

that be okay? Haven't I suffered enough? I really do think that I've learned my lesson and promise not to do it again...

Friday 6th February, 1998

I went down Escafé earlier today to collect some mail from England. Although I like everyone there a great deal and enjoy seeing them I was rather hoping I would be able to sneak in and out unnoticed. But almost all my former workmates were there when I arrived and, of course, it all turned out fine. They didn't hate me because I couldn't make them laugh or talk animatedly about how great everything is – in fact, they all seemed genuinely pleased to see me and were reassuringly nice. Both the owners were there and they too were touchingly warm considering I had repeatedly lied to them about my legal status.

The mail I had gone to collect was a bunch of birthday cards from England which I didn't really want but felt obliged to take possession of. I had spoken to my mum just after she sent them and told her I didn't mind not getting any. She already knew that, she said, but pointed out that they would mind not sending them. I forget – or rather don't understand – how much we mean to our parents and grandparents; the last time I saw my nan and granddad I felt how happy it made them just to sit with someone they'd watched grow out of nothing. Even little bastards like me.

I took delivery of the envelope and on recognising my mother's handwriting I experienced a feeling I can only liken to having a loving arm wrapped around your shoulders in a time of need. For sure, in this brown package with the Queen's head on it would be the answers to all my prayers. Letters of reassurance and advice, words of love and encouragement. People I trust telling me everything's gonna be okay.

I pulled out the first card, from my mum, and opened it with the kind of trepidation I used to have when waiting to see how much money would drop out, only this time I was hoping for a gift of a rather different kind. But nothing came. I opened the card, investigated the envelope, and found sweet FA. No long and heartfelt letter; not even the inside front filled to bursting. All it said was, "Happy Birthday, Rory, love from mum xx." Fuckin' typical.

Now here is where I go on and on about my childhood, about how hard and miserable it all was, and about what a bunch of useless jokers I have for a family. Do you know my mum used to tell me over and over that she should never have had children? That she purposefully denied me attention because she knew that's exactly what I wanted? That she went to bed when I was about nine and didn't get up until I was something like thirteen, and I used to bang and bang on her bedroom floor from our furnitureless living room for hours on end screaming, "wake up!" and all I'd get, eventually, was a tenner handed down to me so I could do my own week's food shop, and later cook my own meals? My God! I mean –she never cooked for me and my brother; we never once ate together; we were like three strangers living more distant and separate lives than roommates. The food would run out on Fridays and all we'd have for the weekend was tomato sauce and maybe some coppers scraped together for a bit of bread – and no TV, and no gas, and no hot water or carpets or chairs – and all through this my dad was absent and avoiding paying maintenance even though we all knew he had a houseful of guitars and plenty of cash to spend down the pub. Jokers, I tell thee!

I don't really remember my parents being together – they divorced when I was six – other than arguments and screaming, cups smashing against walls, windows with cardboard panes where the glass should have been. They say I changed after they split up – went from being this bright, angel little boy to something a little darker, a little more brooding – but I don't remember that either. I do remember that my dad was supposed to come and see us on the weekends, but rarely did, and my mum put a stop to it when I was nine – just as she put a stop to me seeing his parents, purely out of spite. And I really, really loved those guys. And then she went to bed, and I was left to fend for myself, and that was pretty much how it went until I was thirteen and until this one night where my mum and I got into this real big physical fight and I finally got the better of her. She packed me off to my dad's and he, not knowing what to do with this strange little thing called 'child' just sort of slotted me into his own life and took me down the pub. And on our first night together I got drunk, and puked up all the lagers he had fed me, and that was the start of my new life.

Oh, my parents! It's funny really – they just didn't have a clue. And why should they? My mum was sixteen when she got knocked up with me – and still sixteen, I think, when she left her own violent father and hitchhiked pregnant to South Elmsall to be with my dad; what could she have known about life? And what did she have to give, to share, when that had been her own experience of youth? And then pregnant again barely five months after I was born, and divorced and living alone and practically penniless with two small children in a shithole of a town where she knew hardly anyone only a year older than I am now – what a life! Could she have done more? No, not really – and yet, still, I want it. Still I crave the love and attention that I for some reason feel I deserve. Oh, what a world we live in!

And the thing is – have I really any right to complain, to bemoan my lot? Nobody's upbringing is perfect – I know plenty of people around here who grew up in privileged circumstances, in good stable homes, and I can't say they're any less screwed up than I am. People do the best with what they've got and that's just the way it is. No, I guess it's down to me to sort my life out: I can't expect other people to have the answers simply because they happen to have given birth to me. I guess I really am on my own.

And you know what else? I think I'm bored of my crisis. It's starting to piss me off. I think it's about time I did something with the little bleeder. I think I'm gonna skip bail and quit this town, hitch the hell across America hobo-style, do something cool. New challenge and adventure! Yeah!

Saturday 7th February, 1998

I guess if you're in freefall you have to wait until you hit the ground before you can pick yourself up and start again. At one a.m. this morning I sat huddled in the hard stone corner of the university church and wept. Not gushing tears. Not the kind that leave you feeling fresh and new, as though demons have been exorcised: mine were the pathetic sobs of a little boy lost. I looked up at the Christ bloke hanging high on the far wall and asked him to show me something. If you really want me, I said, now is the time.

Of course, nothing happened.

Although, if I'm honest with myself, I don't think I was really looking for salvation: I just wanted to see something spooky.

Sunday 8th February, 1998

Bloke: "Delta s is negative"
Bird: "So t goes up?"
Bloke: "For an exographic solution?"
Bird: "Yes"
Bloke: "Yes...but we're talking about the delta h solution"

Hanging around the UVA campus I hear this kind of thing a lot. The two students sat to the right of me have been talking in this alien language for a good hour or so. Sometimes they get quite excited and exclaim things like: "Yes! I see – the volume of the molecule is dependent on an increasing value of t in relation to delta h." They're scarily serious. A short time ago the guy somewhat patronisingly asked the girl if she'd studied a certain theory in high school. This led her onto an uninteresting anecdote about something that happened to her in a high school chemistry class – the first indication whatsoever that they were human. The male of the species seemed unable to handle this distraction, nervously looking up and down at his books, subliminally imploring the girl to return to the task in hand. "Error. Error. Does not compute," he chirped, steam emitting from his ears. Fortunately he managed to interrupt her before he had a meltdown and they merrily resumed in talking gibberish.

And I wonder why I'm so fucking cynical! I used to talk like that – I used to love maths and physics and couldn't differentiate enough. Sometimes I'd do it for fun, or with friends, or maybe take a book of statistics out to the country and make a day of it. Now that's not real, is it? What must it do to us, spending four years swallowing meaningless equations, being told that $v=dt$, but f is not equal to x, mindlessly accepting and regurgitating the words of others yet learning nothing of love, of what it is to be a human being? That's hardly a decent preparation for life.

Meanwhile, to the left of me, two girls are looking for a movie to watch: Alderman Library has a number of booths with televisions and videos. They have a huge collection of great titles, all of which are free to be enjoyed – even by homeless people such as myself. Last night I watched A Clockwork Orange, which I'd somehow missed over the years. My two friends are pouring over the catalogue, alternately suggesting things like Die Hard and Pretty Woman, to my incredulity. They settle for Beverley Hills Cop II.

Stupid people everywhere. Stupid, stupid people leading stupid and meaningless lives – even dying stupid deaths and leaving stupid legacies to their stupid children, who probably wouldn't be here without an act of stupidity, and for what?

Go and spend some time at your local courthouse if you feel an urge to see stupid people in their natural habitat: you'll find the most pathetic and ridiculous specimens blurting out preposterous tales of stupidity in an effort to explain away non-payments of maintenance, wife-beating, shoplifting and other such stupidity. "Well," says the judge, "can you explain why you had a frozen turkey stuffed inside your coat, Mrs Stupid?"

And of course she can. She doesn't say, "because I'm stupid" – well, not in so few words. No, she'll spin a stupid tale that she and her stupid husband have decided can't possibly be disbelieved, but it will be ('cos the judge ain't that stupid) and off she'll go, handed by a stupid bailiff to the stupid police officer, to be put away with a load more stupid incompetents in a stupid building built by a stupid government because of the stupid system that some stupid people came up with a long time ago.

Tom Wolfe, in Bonfire of the Vanities, was right – we're not criminals: not people committing crimes as though we know what we're doing and it's an act which requires intelligence and planning – the master criminal – the criminal mind – always one step ahead of the law. No, we're just stupid, dumb idiots stumbling around in the dark. The human race isn't being done in by violence or greed or religious intolerance or hate – these are all by-products of the real cause: stupidity.

On a lighter note: death.

I was just thinking about my Princess Diana joke page the other day. I hadn't received any hate mail for ages and thought it might be time to pull the plug; after all, it's been five months – people have probably forgotten who she was. "Diana who?" an old woman said to me the other day when I tried to tell her #22. Thankfully, it seems that this is not the case.

Date: Sun, 8 Feb 1998 13:08:45 +1100
From: "Jones Family"
Subject: Diana Jokes

Dear dickhead,

I don't know who you think you are but your Diana joke pages make me absolutely sick! Someone at one of my brother's parties thought they were amusing by passing them around to everyone but it turned out most people thought the same as I did – that they were disgusting and truly revolting! What I want to know is: what gives you the right to write about such a beautiful lady in such a rude way? She worked tirelessly for numerous good causes and never received any credit for it while she was alive. Now her memory is going to be tarnished by stupid, ignorant people like you! Leave her alone, loser!

I like that. I like being told that "they were disgusting and truly revolting." I like imagining Mr Jones feeling "absolutely sick." I like to picture the amused guy at the party, the smile on his face as he presents Mr Jones with a printout of my page, and I like to envisage Mr Jones lying in bed with his long-suffering wife and going on and on about the idiots trying to tarnish the memory of this "beautiful lady." Well, Mr Jones, not anymore she ain't.

I like that he calls me a "dickhead" and a "loser." In fact, I don't usually mind being insulted by anyone. Sometimes I actively seek to be told what a prick I am – it's far easier to swallow that than a well-intended compliment. At Escafé my workmates were always telling me what a good person I was. The customers got in on the act too, tipping very generously and saying, "oh, you are wonderful," and going out of their way to say hello or seek my service. I liked it at first but it soon started to wear thin. I told my workmates about some of the stuff I'd done, and showed them pictures of the cars I'd crashed, but nothing could change their opinion of me. It wasn't necessarily that I wanted them to dislike me, I just wanted them to know the real me – and, well, isn't the real me a complete and utter shit?

It's all about positives and negatives at the end of the day. There's a reason why most songs are about lost love and sadness and misery. There's a reason why people sit around and gorge themselves on soaps full of tragic characters and hopelessness. The negative is far easier to believe in. It won't promise you better things only to disappoint you. Put your faith in the negative and, although things will be bad, when some good thing does arise every now and again it will come as a welcome surprise. The reason we like the negative so much is because the negative is reality – because it is the truth about the life we live and who we are.

And that, Mr Jones, is why I like being called a dickhead.

Monday 9th February, 1998

Yesterday, as I was taking an early afternoon stroll down Main Street I was accosted by a bartender I know. He was working the Sunday brunch shift at Southern Culture and invited me in. He's always good for a few free drinks and

I happily accepted the first of four cranberry & OJs and settled down with the Washington Post. I was initially unnerved at being around people in a social situation, particularly worried that I might be ponging a bit by now, but I shouldn't have fretted so. A southern-style Sunday brunch is an easy-going affair: happy diners chatted over their omelettes and mimosas; the sound of Gospel singing from the church over the road drifted in through the windows with the warm sunshine. The bartender's lame attempts to sweet-talk the women added to my sense of well-being. In the midst of trying to talk his way out of the, "you don't have a big bottom, it's a nice bottom" mess he'd gotten himself into he tried to give me a beer. A nice cold pint on a beautiful Sunday afternoon: an oasis in the desert providing respite for thirsty and weary travellers – and free! I thought long and hard. It's been twenty-three days since I've had a drink. I refused.

Number of days since:

- Wanking (2)
- Shaving (3)
- Driving (4)
- Eating a vegetable (16)
- Showering (21)
- Having sex (24)
- Getting drunk (52)
- Falling in love (71)
- Vomiting (95)
- Crashing a car (101)
- Being a non-felon (150)
- Having a legal job (647)
- Being a virgin (2016)
- Having a fight (2463)

Here's what the day had in store for me, according to the Washington Post horoscope:

What had been a blank spot will be filled with colour, adventure, romance. An individual who underestimated you will declare "You certainly surprised me, and I love it!"

Given that I hadn't spoken to anyone for more than ten minutes in well over a week, and had every intention of avoiding the possibility for the near future, I didn't put much stock in this forecast. This was actually a comfort to me: I saw that my newly discovered interest in astrology was just as misguided as I had initially hoped.

I left Southern Culture and turned right towards the Corner. I thought I might pick up a couple of forty-nine cent cookies from the Lucky Seven. It was outside there that I bumped into Jay.

I met Jay on the first day at my last job. He was obviously a regular at the restaurant, knowing everyone there, and known to them. He was a bit of a handful to wait on to be honest, full of personal questions and odd demands, though really likeable and friendly – he even sang me a song he'd written which included my name, something about a guy called Rory who speeds around on a motorbike and fucks things up, which was quite sweet. But I didn't quite know how to handle such an extreme extrovert: I tend to get all introverted and British in the company of a person like that. He's also, like, *proper gay* – you know, flamboyantly so – and it wasn't until yesterday that I managed to let go of the idea that he wanted to bum me.

I'm a bit frightened of gays, I don't mind admitting that – and it's probably Charlottesville that has done that to me. My local for a time in Leeds was a gay bar and I used to enjoy the non-hetero atmosphere, the attention and the flirting. Sometimes things might get a bit heavy but there was always a way out and I was never overly concerned. Here though, in my job at Escafé – and in particular on Friday and Saturday nights when it became an out an out gay bar full of people on their way to Charlottesville's one and only club, 216 – things were different: I was a waiter – rather a professional one at that, always determined to be polite and jovial and keep smiling no matter how annoying my beloved clientele became – and there was no escape.

I could handle things like, "mmmm...you're cute," and, "I think you're gorgeous" – these are compliments after all, and I found them very flattering. Even when, later on, the underlying subtext of these compliments became much more blatant I didn't really mind. It was things like having my arse felt by unseen hands. Or attempting to serve customers whose gaze was fixed on my crotch. Or having the first thing a customer say to me be, "you know, I would suck you dry"; having someone tell me they would be "nice and tight" for me; fending off unwanted gropes and attempted kisses; or – how about this – having a guy twice point at and touch my crotch and say, "what's that in your pocket?" while I tried to take a drink order – and then leave a lousy tip!

Maybe it was my own fault. Maybe because I was enjoying a phase of wearing tight seventies-style outfits. Maybe because I was being ambiguous about my sexuality. Or maybe because I never lost my rag when I probably should have done. I guess I was asking for it. But whatever the reason I think it probably damaged my opinion of homosexuals forever. Like all my prejudices, though, I try and confine them to the masses and judge each person on their own individual merits.

So when Jay and I met we hugged and happily began exchanging small talk. The momentum of the conversation changed when he mentioned he was turning forty tomorrow.

"A fellow Aquarius," I said, and with this he erupted.

"I knew it," he said, "I just knew it."

From there, the conversation flowed – we'd found our common thread, our bond, and the floodgates were opened. He talked about his life and listened to me as I talked of mine, and in his words and in his attentive and receptive presence I found comfort. He told me stories of his younger days, of longing and searching and confusion, and it all resonated so profoundly with my current situation, with my deepest wants and desires; it was like he'd been where I was, walked this path long ago, and was able to give me a good idea as to where it leads. And judging by his happiness and enthusiasm, it leads somewhere good.

We talked for a straight five and a half hours – although I only know this because he pointed it out to me in an email last night. I felt excited and drunk and the conversation was a flurry of ideas and realisations and could well be the most exhilarating of my life. I really can't do justice to the power of the words that were spoken and maybe I shouldn't try. I once read an Anne Rice novel in which she describes a conversation between two men, a transcendental meeting of minds. I dismissed her writing as amateurish; firstly because she seemed to be grasping for words – grasping as I am now – and secondly because I didn't believe such a powerful, life-altering conversation could exist. I was wrong. I really feel that Jay may well be the first person who could even comprehend where I'm coming from.

I'm now feeling a sense of hope which has been missing for some time – and not just these last few weeks. It's the sense that I do have something to offer the world, some reason to be here. Jay gave me insight into why I'm doing what I'm doing, a belief that this random wandering isn't as random or directionless as I'd thought. I'm definitely heading somewhere, and I feel it's somewhere pretty cool. I figure even the road to Paradise isn't all blue skies and magnificent vistas – you probably have to go through New Jersey at some point.

Tuesday 10th February, 1998

I don't do in-betweens. This is a fact, and one I rejoice in for the most part. It's what brought me here ("I'm bored, I'm off to New York," instead of, "I'm bored, I think I'll get a job"). It's what makes most of the good things in my life possible. Unfortunately, this extremism is also responsible for most of the bad things too. Sometimes I just wish I could be normal and spend a month or two without daily doses of drama or trouble or ecstasy. I've been riding this rollercoaster for a long time now and I'm starting to feel a little bit sick. Surely a journey of this length would be better suited to Amtrak.

For the biggest part of the day everything was right with the world. Armed with my rediscovered sense of optimism I headed out into the bright sunshine on my rollerblades, enjoying a good skate around town and beginning to tie up the loose ends that have kept me here for far longer than I intended. The weather, the errand-running, the dealings with the pawn store and the prospect of a bright future were very reminiscent of my first few days in Charlottesville. I felt excited and anxious to continue the adventure.

After a successful morning spent whittling down my possessions – the LTD included (sob) – she and I headed west towards the mountains for an afternoon out. I felt childlike and giddy: the world was beautiful; the LTD was flying; the Radiohead was blasting from her six mighty speakers. Sun, blue skies, and hope – you get the picture. It all ended when I decided to hit a country thrift store.

Well, I didn't decide to hit it: I just *hit it*. I was looking right at it, right through the large store-front window as I pulled to a halt, staring at a bunch of used jeans and thinking, "cool, cheap threads," and the next thing I know I've driven straight through it and thousands of pieces of shattered glass are showering down onto the hood of my car.

It's hard to describe how I felt: what had happened was so impossible, so outrageous, that I didn't have a clue what to do. Crashes between cars are an everyday occurrence, and even if you haven't had one you've probably thought about it, probably have an idea about how you might react. But how about if you were pulling into your driveway and were suddenly taken from the side by a couple of monkeys riding bareback on an elephant? Or your car suddenly collapsed Laurel and Hardy style all around you and left you sitting in the road holding nothing but a comedy 1920's steering wheel? Say it slowly: I've just driven into a large building, through an eight by eight foot window, at three miles an hour, in broad daylight. It just doesn't make sense.

And I'll tell you what: I am fucking sick of this. I am sick and tired of these ridiculous incidents which are conspiring to ruin my life. This shouldn't have happened to me – THIS shouldn't happen to anyone. It's too crazy, too much. How can I hope for a normal life when I can't even park my car without bizarre and insane things happening? Am I doomed to this clown-like existence, to stumble through life causing suffering and pain wherever I go, without even trying? God, it's getting so that I'll soon be scared to shake someone by the hand for fear of killing them. I don't mean to do these things, honest – they do just happen...to me...every fucking day. I give up.

I left the scene of the crime and found myself a little creek where I could sit and beat myself to a pulp, get angry at causing yet more trouble for yet more innocent people, wallow in how worthless I truly am. Seems like the ability to shrug off these wrong-doings has left me: I used to just walk away from stuff like this and never look back – except when in need of an amusing anecdote to please a crowd – but now it's like karma has got me by the balls. Being bad just brings me misery and misfortune and I don't know how to find my way out of it. And, as if to prove a point, on the way back, feeling better and resolved to make amends for my latest disaster, I was given to the law once again.

It was one of those where the cop is travelling in the opposite direction. As soon as he passes, my eyes hit the rearview mirror looking for brake lights or a signal, flicking back to the road only to search for a suitable turn-off – a suitable turn-off being one which is taken before the cop gets you in his sights; one that can provide you reasonable cover in a hurry. It has to be perfect, though – there can be no half-hearted attempts at escape; absolutely no chance that he could have seen the exit. Away in the distance behind me I see him execute his own turn-off and head back in my direction. Now I'm scared. I've been incredibly lucky thus far, and I've just signed an acknowledgement that any more driving I do will result in a ten day jail sentence. Since then, I've also acquired a warrant for my arrest.

For a minute or so there's no sign of him; I figure he's been called away to attend to one not quite so lucky as myself – then, all of a sudden he appears and turns on his lights. We pull up in front of a fruit stand and I prepare myself for three months in jail followed by the unceremonious boot of deportation.

He approaches the window after taking a stroll around my vehicle and looks in at the mess of possessions scattered around the interior. He spies my newly acquired camera.

"Is that yours?" he says, "where did you get it? Have you got a receipt?"

"It is mine," I say, "but I don't have a receipt for it." Nor do I have receipts for my guitar or CD player. He asks me a dozen equally bizarre questions, including whether I'm carrying any guns or drugs or blasphemous publications. They reach the peak of their stupidity on a trip to the trunk, which I offer to show him.

He backs away a little and eyes me suspiciously, and I see him finger his weapon. I imagine what he'll do if I open it up and show him a dead body. He stops me.

"What's in the trunk?" he says.

"Stuff," I say.

"What kind of stuff?"

"Stuff stuff. You wanna see?"

"Sure," he says, and then – "hey, what's that in your pocket?" He looks scared.

"What?" I say, incredulously looking at the tiny pockets on my jeans. They're barely big enough to hold a car key, let alone anything that could possibly be of danger to a cop. I'm starting to lose patience with this guy. "My keys," I say.

"Oh," he says, seemingly satisfied. He opens the trunk and looks in. "Hey," he says, "what's in the bag?"

"Clothes," I say.

"Clothes? What kind of clothes?"

What kind of clothes? What does he want me to say? "Well, I've got this stunning flowery big-collared shirt from Italy...come here – see – isn't that nice? It really brings out your cheekbones." What kind of clothes? Illegal ones? Maybe he thinks I've got one of those new jackets, the ones with the genuine crack cocaine lining, or a pair of .38mm Reeboks. I have no idea what to say;

I'm doing all I can to keep a straight face. Stupid people are stupid people, no matter that they're wearing a little badge and are dressed up like toy soldiers at a fat farm.

After a while he adjourns to his seat and I do the same. I can vaguely make him out in the mirror. I can see a clipboard and it looks like he's talking on the radio but there's no way to tell what he's planning to do. The minutes tick by as I sit there worrying, the level of punishment that I'm willing to accept changing dramatically, from no ticket, to just the one, to, "please just let me go, I'll leave the car," right up to a night in jail ("just one night – and then I'm outta here"). I fear the worst when he approaches again and asks me to sit in the back of his car.

I follow him glumly and climb into the back seat. He closes the door behind me – the door that I know only too well is impossible to open from the inside – and slides into the front. I look at him through the thick metal mesh and he turns around.

"It just doesn't add up," he says.

He lays out the evidence. He has a guy with no license who claims to be a John Rory Miller driving a car which is registered to a Rory John Miller. The information provided by base includes a John Miller Jr (red-haired sailor, revoked license), a Rory John Miller (license suspended) but no John Rory Miller. The social security number of RJ differs from that of JR by one digit. He's called Snooky's pawn shop to check out my story of having bought the camera there earlier in the day and they know me – Rory – and said that I was cool, that I bought a lot of stuff from them. He also knows about my earlier accident. He asks me questions about why I don't have a license, about what I'm doing, and I give him a story that has more holes in it than the socks I'm stinking his car out with and pray.

And, somehow, it works.

Friday 13th February, 1998

I've often wondered why I'm such a bad driver – I mean, what is it about me that renders me unable to pilot a car for more than a few hundred miles without totally destroying it? The best explanation I've come up with is that it's down to nature/nurture – in that, in my case, I just don't have any real experience in a motorised vehicle, whereas your Yanks, for example, are practically *born* in them. They've been driving hundreds of thousands of miles in them, generation after generation. They love them more than they love their own children; use them more than their own two feet. It's absolutely in their genes. Until I started learning how to drive I'd probably only spent about a hundred hours or so in a car – neither of my parents knew how to drive – and I can't say I paid much attention to how they worked. Compared to your average American I was about as experienced as a fish is to bicycling – which is not very experienced at all. I didn't even know how to turn one on, never mind what gears and steering wheels were for.

My earliest memories of cars are wrapped around images of my granddad, handing him tools when I was three or four, his legs sticking out from underneath, me insisting that I wear my woolly hat like his and liking the feel and smell of the grease on my skin. Maybe if the years down the pit hadn't destroyed his eyes and lungs and left him a wreck of a man by sixty I might have learned something there, but it did, and the only time I saw him behind the wheel again was put-putting up the hill on his old man's motorised scooter, which I always thought was a real shame for the fine and big strong guy he had once been. In any case, I was nineteen before I really took any notice of our four-wheeled friends, when I thought I might become a travelling guitar dealer, and I set about getting my license. Excited and keen I booked a course of lessons with BSM and applied for a test at the earliest possible date, which would be in a month's time. They warned me that a month may be a bit hasty – two or three was more realistic. A month, I decided, would be plenty of time for such a quick learner as myself: did they think I was one of these idiots who failed seven or eight times, the people you read about in the paper and laugh about as you contemplate the hundreds of pounds already frittered away? I mean…

The test came and went in May; I failed. Re-tests in July and September were similarly unsuccessful, leaving me heartbroken and wishing I'd never started the whole thing in the first place. And it only added to the depression I was sinking into.

At least my instructor and examiners could all come to an agreement on the basic nature of my inability: in a nutshell, I was crap. I drove too fast and I didn't concentrate. I didn't stop in time. I couldn't control the gears properly. I wasn't observant. I was, in all probabilities, a danger to the public and I was in need of many, many more hours behind the wheel before I could realistically expect to pass. I gave up, too despondent for another test, too tight to pay for any more lessons. What I needed, I decided, was a bit of real experience, a chance to get some road hours under my belt. I got my first opportunity in November.

I was down in Sheffield, in the studio with my band-at-the-time. At some point in the proceedings I'd been despatched to the supermarket for refreshments and somehow found myself in possession of the keys to the drummer's mum's car (okay, I'd swindled them). I was kind of sat in there just catching up with the football scores, seeing how Everton were doing, thinking I should get off to the super – and then thinking, oh man, I'd just love to drive this car. I was thinking, it's only around the corner, I can do this. I had this intense longing; I just couldn't leave it alone. Walking, simply put, was out of the question.

I hesitantly set off down the street, unlicensed and uninsured, almost instantly regretting it but not wanting to turn back. The supermarket *was* just around the corner – but I never found it. Nor did I find my way back to the studio for another four exhausting hours, having neglected to pay any attention to my whereabouts. In the meantime I'd become utterly lost in a city I had never been to, piloting a vehicle I had basically no idea how to properly control. Darkness had fallen and it had taken me ten minutes to figure out how to turn the lights on; turning corners had given me grey hairs, unable to work out how the indicators worked, never sure which way I was signalling. I had several near misses, and probably stalled like twenty times. It was a truly horrendous and nerve-racking experience and left me full of remorse and shame. Needless to say, I was evicted from the band.

By February I'd really had as much non-driving as I could take and I got up one day, turned to the used car section in the paper, and went out and bought a 1985 Ford Escort for two hundred and sixty-five quid. I knew I had no license, that I wouldn't be able to get insurance or MOT or tax, but I didn't care. I also knew that despite promising my girlfriend that I wouldn't drive until I'd passed my test there was no way I could keep to that. Within a few days I was on the road and undertaking my maiden voyage, the twenty mile trip to my darling, disgusting South Elmsall, digging the road and the freedom and my nice new ride. The weeks that followed were bliss, my little red Escort and I taking trips to the junkyard, finding bits and pieces to attach, zipping around town with the sunroof open in the unseasonably warm English spring. I cleaned her addictively; in the midst of my otherwise awful life I had found a small oasis of joy. It's hard to believe, then, that it was just a few short weeks before the accident that killed her.

I was returning late one night from Birmingham, sort of lost but enjoying the drive, discovering new roads and towns, plotting my way across Derbyshire with my trusty map. Somewhere near Bakewell I spied a short-cut and took it, and found myself bouncing along rough and tumble roads. I proceeded blindly on, certain that I would soon prevail out the other side, and revelled in the rally-esque conditions, the sound of stone and grit under tyre, the darkness and unexpected turnings. Fantasy took over – Colin McRae at the wheel – and my speed increased, sliding around corners, making it look easy. And just as I was beginning to feel that I was really getting to grips with this driving lark I hit a patch of ice and skidded head-on into this rather large boulder that some idiot had stupidly left by the side of the road. The car was completely fucked – the rock having buried itself about two feet inside the engine – and it took me hours to find help. I really was in the middle of nowhere; I ended up sleeping in another broken-down car in a junkyard, shivering the night away and trying to keep warm under a pile of old telephone directories. I later found out that the twisting country road I had been rallying down was actually the works track in a quarry.

Still, did it stop me? Did it bugger! Within a week I had bought another old Escort and set off once more along the highways of Yorkshire and Britain persisting with my policy of complete lawlessness. So I parked wherever I wanted – safe in the knowledge that tickets would never find their way to me – and generally averaged about a hundred miles an hour on longer journeys, looking at the opportunities and challenges of overtaking as a kind of game, a way to keep things interesting. I got up to a hundred and twenty on one trip down London way, pulling into Wembley with black smoke billowing from underneath the bonnet, filling the interior, making it impossible to see. A couple of guys pulled up next to me and said something about my car being on fire and me, head out the window, eyes crying with burning oil, just said, I know, and revelled in the eccentricity of it. I don't know why I never feared the police or tried to keep a low profile; I guess it just didn't occur to me. And, anyway, I actually did pretty well in that car, apart from losing half the bumper on a backed-into tree, one little side-on collision (not my fault) and a brief liaison with a crash barrier one drunken night racing with my girlfriend's brother which completely trashed the steering. Apart from that – and maybe three or four other things – the six weeks we had together were pretty much problem-free; very little out of the ordinary at all.

I left that car standing outside my mate Tim's house in London when I came to the States, expecting to pick it up again in a month's time when I got back; I found out a few months later that it had been towed and destroyed, the lack of tax, the rusting, crumpled door, the dangling, strung-together bumper somehow making the council think it might have been abandoned. Appearances can be deceptive, I guess. It did get me through my test, though – I passed that in May, got my license through a few days before leaving for America – and so I suppose it was all some sort of means to an end. And apart from a little go in Simon's Oldsmobile in New England – which I was soon forbidden from driving after veering off the road for no apparent reason – I didn't really drive again until August, after purchasing the Mazda 626. The Mazda debacle really was my *piece de resistance* – it was a mere four days out of NYC, after encounters with the police on each day, that I rear-ended that old Dodge on I-76. I wish I could say it was bad luck, that it could have been avoided – the truth, however, is that it's surprising it hadn't happened sooner; there had been plenty of opportunities for a similar catastrophe on each of the days previous.

I wouldn't give up, though, and my two hundred dollar Chevy did take me over five thousand miles, before dying its humble death in Arizona. I hadn't ever dreamed of getting that much mileage out of a car – indeed, I imagine that I'll look at any future purchase and wonder, "how long have we got?" as though any car coming into contact with me would be terminally ill. I'm not sure that's such a healthy frame of mind.

The crunch came with the purchase of my '72 Ford LTD – a beautiful old car which had survived almost entirely unscathed for twenty-five years. But within hours we'd had our first crash; I hadn't ever felt so sick and utterly disappointed with myself as I did that night – a gentle giant idiotically wounded by the irresponsibilities of youth. And then of course, I did much,

much worse. The destruction hasn't stopped there, either. When buying this car I joked that it would take me a lot longer to finish off than some little Japanese effort – well this has proved unfortunately true. I really wish I'd ended this latest stint wrecked on that first night parking lot post.

And now, today, am I a better driver for this sorry tale? Not really. I still have no inclination that laws must be obeyed: I still drive well over the speed limit whenever possible; see no-entry signs as small obstacles to be taken with caution; red-lights as optional; and haven't had a valid license for three months. When driving I feel capable of crashing at any moment and often fantasise about it. What an impact I'd make by smashing headfirst into an oncoming truck! It takes a great deal of will-power not to initiate these kamikaze tactics sometimes; I scare myself to death. I really wish someone could stop me and save the world – and save me – from my driving.

Wednesday 18th February, 1998

Well Lauren's been down from New York the last five days and I've been off sunning myself in Louisa County, havin' it large in a cosy family stylee. Of course, all that swanning about in a nice big house in the country – walking the dogs, taking saunas by the little lake – has left me feeling pretty content and I can't think of anything to write about – oh well, too much doom and gloom can be a bad thing, I suppose. Tomorrow I sell the LTD to a bloke outside town who wants to use the engine and scrap the rest. I'm trying not to think about her sad demise.

After I bid her farewell I'm going to point myself in a south-westerly direction and leave this town, by foot or by thumb or by train, and just see what happens. I've driven across country and that was cool – but also expensive and lonely – and now I want to take it to the next level, see if I can do it old style. That really is about the extent of my plans. I've had quite enough of this moping about and not really doing anything, and quite enough of being tied to this town because of a couple of boxes of possessions and some stupid court case. Five months I've been waiting for the powers that be to throw me in jail, quite prepared to do my bit for society – well I'm sorry, society, but your wheels turn just a little too slowly for my liking. I know it's not supposed to be pleasant but, honestly, I've got better things to do than spend my time aimlessly wandering around the labyrinth of your judicial system. Maybe if it improves I'll come back and serve my time – but, somehow, I doubt it.

Here's what I have in my backpack:

- Two pairs of Levi's 501s
- Four or five shirts and t-shirts
- Five socks (none matching; only one without hole)
- Tent and sleeping bag

- Scrabble dictionary
- Walkman and music (almost exclusively Britpop)
- About three hundred dollars (plus whatever I get for the LTD)
- A Native American good luck charm (doesn't work)

I reckon that'll keep me going for a month or two – and after that, who knows? Really, who knows where this road might take me? Releasing myself into the wild and trying to make it from Virginia to Arizona under my own steam is a mouth-watering prospect. I know I can survive and prosper in strange cities – now it's time to see how I can cope out on the road, without the comforts of an automobile.

We've become pretty soft, it seems. People are often amazed that I came to New York without knowing a single soul in this whole country. People are bemused when I tell them I came to Charlottesville because I liked the name. It's nothing really. Easy. This isn't Africa or Asia – it's nice and civilised and paved.

Everyone's so scared of getting out there and doing it. We're all running to these little cities and screaming, "overcrowding!" and building mausoleums for the living higher and higher. Instead of gathering around drinking fountains we haven't a hope of using shouldn't we set out and dig our own well? Look at the pioneers, the forty-niners, Lewis and Clark. No cars or pipelines or cosy concrete jungles awaiting them, just the guts to go out there and do it using whatever they could. What was Salt Lake City before the Mormons arrived? A whole lotta nothing. All you people rotting away in the projects – why don't you get off your fat lazy arses, saddle up and do something productive? This country is still mostly vacant, there's plenty of room for everyone – and if you're not feeling quite so inspired...well, just shut up moaning and crawl back into your cell.

NOTE: This isn't to say that me, a pleasant-looking European with an accent pissing about in the southwest for a couple of weeks means anything.

BUT, if you'd like to see just how easy it is for a strange man in a strange land to carve a life out of nothing, STAY TUNED.

Friday 20th February, 1998

Sitting in the dark dirty rain by the railroad tracks waiting for a train to take me the hell out of this town and state. It's at times like these I forget why I'm doing what I'm doing – and then I remember: I never knew to begin with. Always the hard way, eh? Nothing satisfying about taking the elevator up a mountain. But the people who do smile big and true and I look on, as I drag myself to the summit, and hate them, and therefore hate myself.

I'm missing Lauren big time. I'm pretty sure that I definitely think there may exist the possibility that I truly do love her. I wish that among all the stationwagons I saw last night was a little Ford Escort with three zees on the

95

plate and a beautiful girl behind the wheel come back for me. It's scary, how I feel, and I wonder why I say that, because what can be scary about discovering this great feeling and having the chance to follow it? I don't know – but I do know that I'm scared.

I sold the LTD yesterday, for a hundred and twenty-five bucks, and I sorted out my two boxes of stuff, leaving them with my mad Brit-rocker friend Robin. Suddenly, after weeks of trying to get rid of those things, they were gone, and there were no more excuses. No more, "I'm just getting my things together." No more, "I'm trying to leave but I can't, I've got the car, I've got my stuff." Suddenly, I was free, to go wherever I wanted. That's scary too. I guess there was a certain amount of comfort in staying lost in this town.

I really don't know what I'm doing and I have no idea why I insist on living like this. If I was to make a list of my favourite things in life – nestled amongst Scrabble, listening to music, laying with Lauren, playing with Lauren – I don't think I'd find walking alone in the rain or sleeping rough in the Tennessee winter night.

Then again, I went to Escafé last night and got talking with Derek the chef. I told him what I was planning and he told me that he had gone hitchhiking around the country, up the west coast, across Mexico. Listening to him I remembered why I've chosen to go on this adventure and I felt that excitement and wonder at the possibilities of life out there, on the road, and in the west. But he did it with two other guys, and I guess they kept each other safe, and always had some company. For some reason I always have to do everything alone. I wonder why I can't meet someone who wants to do this. I mean, not that I'm saying it's a cool place or anything but, is anybody actually in my tree?

In the morning I'll be gone from this town, one way or the other. It's making me want to weep, the thought of all that I've been through here. I can't believe the things I've done, the things I've lived. I can't believe that not so long ago I had a job that made me happy, and more friends than I've ever had, and more fun than I knew what to do with. And, sure, it was all wrapped up in booze and foolishness – but it's nothing but sad the way I've fucked it all up and been reduced to this. Nathan Hart. Poor, poor Nathan Hart, who'll probably never talk to me again, and deservedly so. Gus and Tyler and Lauren. And all the people at Escafé that I can't even bring myself to say goodbye to, even though I know they'd like to see me this one last time. I'll fall asleep by the side of these tracks and maybe I'll be woken by a train and jump aboard, gone under the cover of darkness, unseen, the way it should be. And once more into the unknown, to watch the sun rise somewhere else, somewhere new. I'm scared. I don't know why I'm doing this. I wish I wasn't, but I just don't know what else to do.

Part Four

Chapter One

Up until the morning of the twenty-first of February, nineteen ninety-eight, the sum total of my hitchhiking experience was that one night getting back to New York from West Virginia after totalling the Mazda, an enjoyable afternoon in Arizona and Nevada en route to Las Vegas following the demise of my Chevy, and a short stint in a snowy North Carolina night making the trip between my two driveaway cars, having pardoned myself from the hellish delights of an interminable Greyhound bus ride (trust me, few things on Earth are as insufferable as the Greyhound; least of all standing in the snow by the road at ten p.m. with your thumb out and a hopeful heart). Things had gone pretty well on those three occasions – my last ride into Vegas had in fact been with a Pilipino mom with her kids in the back, and the religious couple that had picked me up in North Carolina had driven about ten miles out of their way – and I figured if you can make a hundred miles by thumb, then why not a thousand, and why not a whole country or a whole continent? No reason, really. I had heard, too, of a chap called Kerouac, who had apparently done it all back in the fifties, and of the hippies and the beatniks and those poor Oklahoma dustbowl farmers thumbing it out west during the Great Depression, standing in line with dozens of others, all hats and trousers and shoes awaiting passing jalopies. To me that sort of thing was a real part of the American travelling legend – but a part that seemed to be dying out. I never once saw a hitchhiker on my own cross-country drives. And apart from hearing about Lauren and Nathan thumbing it once down to New Orleans, and then chef Derek's timely tales that night in Escafé, I wasn't even sure that people still did it.

But I knew the possibility existed, and knowing that something you want to do is actually possible, and meeting others that have done it, means it's only a matter of time and effort before you achieve it yourself.

Likewise, freight-hopping: the long lost art of sprinting alongside freight trains and hurling yourself into boxcars, riding the rails and whooping it up on mile-long metal monsters, thundering across the whole wide country and glancing out as deserts and mountains and roads slide slowly by. Nathan Hart had introduced me to it, encouraging me up the ladder of a lumbering grain wagon on the way home from the C&O one day, and then some months after that I had escaped the back porch a little inebriated and climbed atop a passing chemical tanker. And what an absolute blast that was! She got up to like sixty or seventy miles an hour, and there I was, riding her like some demented cowboy, screaming the lyrics to Blur's 'Song 2' – "I got my head shaved/by a jumbo jet!" – wind in my hair and far, far below my feet, under rickety bridges and miles from anywhere, rivers and creeks and nothing between my sneakers and the ground except a hundred feet of air. I might as well have been flying. Sixty miles I rode that baby, and then another sixty miles back in the pink Virginia morning – this time sat in the spare engine for warmth, among flashing dials and levers – and, I swear, it was easily one of the greatest things I ever did. Those trains they have in America are beasts: so powerful and huge and long. There can be few finer pleasures in life than being one of the two or three humans that pilot and know them. And in being the only one that is free to swing and leap about, and hang over the edge, and stare into chasms. Yes, I certainly wanted a few more slices of that pie. I'd even got a map printed off the internet showing all the freight lines, those great names like Burlington Northern and Santa Fe and Union Pacific fairly making me drool with the visions that they conjured.

That first night, though, there were no trains forthcoming and I woke up late in the gorgeous February sunshine just a few hundred metres from where I had shared that long-ago student apartment with Troy and Steve. And not only was I a hundred metres – if a thousand years – from there, I was also a hundred metres from some of the university's tennis courts, which were already full of bright-eyed and white-teethed students. I really had slept in. And they must have had to walk past me to get to the courts, all hunched down in my sleeping bag, and with my sorry pink backpack with "limey bastard" scrawled across the back in black marker pen. It was all a bit inglorious really. I didn't want anyone I knew to see me. I wanted to crawl out of there like the dog that's been caught doing a shameful, stinking shit in his master's slippers. I slung my pack across my shoulders and took to the tracks, doing all I could to emit a vibe to those students and the world that might make them understand: no, he's not a tramp, he just looks like one. But really he's one of us; this is his vacation. No, not a tramp at all.

Oh God, I think, I'm a tramp.

I stick to the tracks and make my way to the western edge of town. Train notwithstanding, it's US-250 that'll be taking my sorry ass out of there. But I know I'll be standing there with my thumb out and looking glum, and I just know I'll see someone I used to work with, and they'll look out at me pityingly and think, goodness, how far he's fallen. Or, worse still, they'll stop, and I'll sit there awkward and stinking and their sympathy will be too much. Or, worse even than that, it'll be Nathan Hart and Gus, en route to their parents, and they'll whoop and holler as they come past, and pelt me with beer bottles and then whoop and holler some more knowing full well how much I hated their penchant for throwing beer bottles out the window to land with a smash! on that poor American highway, where children could play, where bicycle tyres could puncture and deflate.

I'm at the edge of town now. Charlottesville is behind me but I have yet to fully escape. I decide to leave the tracks and hop on over to the road; should a train come I can just as easily hop back and jump aboard, and take that legendary trip into the mountains via Crozet thrift store shame and Nathan Hart's hometown of Waynesboro, and eventually, if I've got my reckoning right, somewhere into West Virginia. The road, however, will take me back onto that beautiful Blue Ridge Parkway and down into Tennessee. Such is the beauty of this method of travel, where plans bear more resemblance to jelly than concrete, and where almost anything is possible. As long as I'm heading in a vaguely south-westerly direction I honestly don't care. It's not as though I'm in a rush. I get out my thumb and tentatively stick it up in the air. Two cars go by and one of them sticks their thumb out too, and in return I wave. That makes me smile. I decide that I'm going to wave at every car that goes by, no matter what they do.

Another car speeds past, and then another, and then another, and they all get the wave. It's about the fiftieth car, I think, that finally waves back.

I'm starting to loosen up. I haven't seen anyone I know and I'm thinking I probably won't. And even if I do, why should they see me as an embarrassing homeless tramp? A vagabond? A loser? Why shouldn't they see me as an adventurer, a free spirit, a man with the chutzpah to do something maybe thousands would love to but simply don't have the balls? I'm out here doing it, man: I'm on the road. I'm staring out over the horizon and ahead of me I've got three thousand miles of tarmac leading to deserts and mountains and, eventually, right at the other end of this country, that shimmering Pacific Ocean where the San Diego sun shines non-stop and where the stink of this town can't touch me.

It's been forty minutes now and there's no sign of anyone coming to a stop. I am getting a lot of funny hand gestures, though, and it's been interesting trying to decipher what they mean. Like the people that make a sort of chopping motion (something to do with garlic?) or the ones that point frantically at their steering wheel – perhaps trying to indicate a mechanical malfunction that prevents them from pulling over. And the others, who point up and down and left and right, or shrug and look a million times apologetic. Or point to the backseat and the mess on it, as though I'd rather stand there by the road than get a ride in a dirty car. As well as the occasional middle finger and makes-you-jump blast of the horn from the baseball cap-wearing students.

I start to think about going back to town. I don't know what I'll do there but this hitching malarkey doesn't seem to be getting me anywhere, despite my cheery waves and forced smile. I'm starting to get depressed again. I'm starting to feel more and more like a tramp. I don't understand why people won't stop for my friendly face, all those empty seats and they're obviously going my way. The whole thing is just stupid. The whole idea of hitching all the way to Arizona. Like pretty much everything else I've ever done.

And just as I'm getting ready to pick up my bag and about-face, a car pulls in at the side of the road and before I know what I'm doing I'm racing gaily to meet him.

Ah, you can't beat that moment when you first see the brakelights flash into life and watch as the driver steers himself onto the shoulder! It doesn't matter how long you've been waiting, how miserable or angry you've become, how many defeatist and I'm-never-doing-this-again thoughts you've had, as soon as you see that waiting ride it's all banished into nothingness, and all that's left is a big smile, and galloping legs, and the excitement of knowing that you're on your way.

I gallop and smile and pretty soon I'm sitting next to this young, grinning Mexican man. I love the way the car feels underneath and all around me. I love that we're moving. I love the thought of all those Charlottesville months and all that burden just disappearing behind me.

"You like Macarena?" he says in broken English, reaching to put a tape in the machine.

Like the Macarena? Not usually, no. In fact, I hate it.

I nod.

"I love it," I say.

He smiles at me and pops it in, and soon the mariachi sounds of his Mexicanised Macarena are booming from those speakers, all accordions and trumpets and God only knows what else those crazy Mexicans listen to with their crazy music. It sounds like hell – almost as bad as bagpipes – but today I *am* loving it. Today I am bopping along and nodding my head and smiling right there with my gorgeous young non-English speaking friend as the great green trees of Virginia flash by. The road is flooding back into me – all those new experiences and people, the magic of it all – and finally Charlottesville is finished. Ahead, now, ahead: me and my Mexican brother, and suddenly everything is possible, right there in this beat-up car full of nodding heads and oompah sounding tubas and cheesy Mexican beats.

The road is happening and I am on the road. Going somewhere. Gone.

Chapter Two

He drops me off in little redneck Waynesboro and I take a walk through town to pick up a bit of cardboard and steal a marker pen. The blokes there all have moustaches and look sort of like seventies German porno stars. I stop off in a hardware store and ask the milling crowd where a good place to hitch is, simultaneously and surreptitiously fishing for a ride.

"I don't reckon you'll get picked up round these parts," the main man says.

"Been a few killings round here," says another.

"Yup," says one lanky overalled fella, and they nod, "better off taking the bus."

I thank them for their help. They're obviously scared. What do they know about hitchhiking anyway?

I walk to the edge of civilisation and find my spot: and blessèd spot it is too! For right there at that crossroads the railroad has rejoined me and once again I can thumb, all the while readying myself for my sprint to the tracks should I hear the welcoming thunder of a train. There's a fifty-fifty chance that it'll be going my way – namely, to the south – but the way I'm feeling about wanting to get on board one of those babies I'll probably hop one north too. And as I'm standing there wondering about this and licking my lips in anticipation I realise that there's something very odd about this crossroads I'm at: that no matter which direction I head in – north, south or west, as long as it's not back to town – I'll be taken closer to where I ultimately want to go. It's like it doesn't matter what I decide: even if I head in seemingly opposite directions I'll still reach my goal. It's sort of a momentous discovery.

I catch a ride in a minivan with a moustachioed little black man, nice if unremarkable, aside from the fact that he'd been in Vietnam. He told me that but he never elaborated on it and the conversation sort of waned; I got stuck wondering if I should have asked him about it. I was interested but what could I have said? All I could think of were idiotic things like, "so...how was it?" And that was probably a bit like asking someone what it was like to watch their wife die. Or asking a Jew how they'd enjoyed the holocaust. I kept schtum and we rode on in silence.

Until the end of it when I'd hopped out and he leaned over towards me.

"You want to make a few bucks?" he said.

"How's that?" I asked, sort of immediately realising what he meant.

"Let me give you a blowjob?" He said it absolutely matter-of-factly, no trace of desire or persuasiveness in his voice. He might as well have been offering me a bon-bon.

"No thanks, man," I said. For some reason, I was smiling.

"All right," he said. Once again, not an ounce of feeling in it: no disappointment or frustration, just total acceptance. Like it was nothing.

I closed the door and he departed.

I stood there for a while and let it sink in. The whole thing was so unexpected and bizarre. I was in a sort of puzzled shock.

I walked on up the autumn tree road and I thought: what is it about men and testosterone that makes us think like that? How can this guy have been so desperate for a dick in his mouth – and for someone to *come* in his mouth – that he was willing to pay a total stranger for it? And why would he want to give a blowjob rather than receive it? Or maybe he felt his chances of getting something from a straight guy would be better if he offered the less extreme option, 'the inside of a man's mouth being the same as a woman's' and all that. But I couldn't have done it if I'd tried, even if I was desperate. All I can see is this little old black guy leaning over at me and undoing my zip, moving his head down – and me limp and uninterested, staring out the window, pushing him away and running off and feeling dirty and crying. Basically…yuk.

Men are such strange creatures. Back in Leeds one time, having a beer with Tim in The New Penny – a fairly notorious gay boozer with boarded-up windows and red lightbulbs everywhere – I'd been left alone while he'd gone off for a slash. We'd been having a laugh up till that point, sort of titillated by the snogging, groping couples, revelling in the danger of our being there, brave, eccentric and different. But on my own, suddenly, I didn't feel so brave. Suddenly I felt very tender and young and white. Like a filleted, skinless chicken breast. I looked up and all around the room cartoon images of gays were staring down at me – this one here with tight leather trousers on; this one there with the handlebar moustache; another in a peaked-cap; another with bulging biceps – and I swear they were licking their lips. One guy rubbed his crotch and motioned over to me. I felt like I was about to be torn apart by the famished, blood-thirsty wolves.

Tim finally emerged from the men's room, looking sheepish.

"I think we should go," he said. I didn't need no second invitation.

"Fucking hell," I said, once we were outside and breathing easy, "I thought you were never coming back. You should've seen the way those guys were looking at me. It was horrible, man."

"Tell me about it," he said.

I did. I told him about the wolves and the meat and the crotches and the tongues.

"Is that how we look at women?" I said, "Is that how we make them feel? Like meat? I don't want to do that to anyone; it's fucking disgusting."

"They're like dogs," he said, "all they see is arses and want to fuck 'em."

I couldn't be angry or disgusted at this guy, though: not in the way that I had been that night. He hadn't made me feel like a piece of meat: all he'd done was make a proposal for something that he wanted, in a polite and straightforward and easily-rejectable way, and when his proposal had been declined he'd accepted it uncomplainingly. If only every offer of cash in exchange for sex was conducted in such a civilised manner!

I did wonder, though, if that was the only reason he'd stopped to pick me up, and that sort of made me shudder. I also wondered what the trip had in store for me, given that he was only my second ride...

I got back on the road and soon picked up a lift a little ways down I-81 from a guy on his way to work at Wendy's. And at the gas station that he dropped me off at I thought I'd try a more direct approach, asking the various drivers and truckers if they could give me a ride. I really wanted to make Tennessee by nightfall. I really wanted to wake up in a different state to the one I'd dwelled so unceremoniously in those past ten months.

It wasn't too many rejections – and only a few lies about not going my way – before I got accepted by a kindly silver-haired trucker and swept up into the bouncing blue seat of his spacious high cab.

"Bill," he said, and we shook hands, and we were off.

Man, I love riding with truckers! Drivers complain about them but those boys are the salt of the Earth, living unfathomably lonesome and hard-working lives but, in my experience, gentlemen one and all. And they sure can drive. I've met truckers who have driven a thousand miles at a stretch, who have been away from home for weeks at a time, who have gone for days and days without talking to another living soul. They sit up there in that cab and they just keep on trucking, pretty much non-stop, except to sit in always-the-same diners, eating always-the-same food, before climbing into a bunk in the back for a spot of shut-eye. And I guess they get a lot of time to think: almost always I'd find myself in the role of the therapist, listening as all those hours and weeks of solitude formed themselves into long outpourings of ideas and opinions and histories. And this guy was no exception.

He too had been in 'Nam, and though he didn't want to go into detail it was obvious it had affected him: immediately upon his return he'd gone to live in the woods in Maine, miles from anywhere, without electricity or running water. He'd done that for five years, and then he'd found a wife and raised a family, and like all these guys he spoke so proudly of his children. He didn't see them as often as he'd like, though, what with all the trucking. He worked his ass off, and he had a farm too – amazing how many of these truckers also worked farms. His wife had died recently. His tale was so typical of the truckers I rode with, so tinged with sadness and solitude and exceedingly hard-work – and yet he seemed happy. There was something about him that had kept him going. By the end of the ride I felt such a fondness for him. I wished he'd take me to his home and be my dad.

"You're such a nice guy," I said, as I prepared to jump out into the dark night, "it's been a real pleasure."

"It's been a pleasure for me too," he said, reaching out his hand, beaming a smile across his face.

"So what's your secret?" I said, "I mean, how'd you keep yourself so happy?"

He thought about it for a second.

"Be satisfied with what you've got," he said, "and always keep the good Lord with you."

He shook my hand one last time and I made to step down.

"God bless," he said.

"Thanks," I said, "and thanks so much for the ride."

He'd dropped me at a rest area and I figured it would be easy pickings to get a ride, since they were all unavoidably going my way. I spied an old guy with his head under the bonnet of his apparently malfunctioning pickup: a golden opportunity! I could make conversation; I could offer help and sympathise with his problem; I could engage this hearty specimen of American male on their most favourite topic: their vehicle. And then, after all that, I'd tell him I needed a ride south, and how could he refuse? I stepped up to the plate and began my patter – and pretty soon he and I were puttering down the interstate in his spluttering, frequently stalling pickup at a top speed of twenty miles an hour.

"Must be the fuel pump," he says in his barely intelligible, more than a little preposterous Appalachian accent. "Yup," he says again, "it must be the fuel pump."

He must have said those words – "must be the fuel pump; yup, must be the fuel pump; it's the fuel pump, I reckon; yup, def'nitely the fuel pump; fuel pump, yup; I reckon it's the fuel pump" – at least fifty or sixty times. And what could I do but nod in agreement and listen?

Some distance into this painstaking journey, however, he changed his tune and I was soon longing for the simple ways of our earlier time together, his mutterings on the fuel pump and me like a nodding dog pretending that I gave a shit. Soon I was to look back on those exchanges as the golden era in our relationship.

"You been to Florida?" he said, "well I got a house down there, cost me three hundred and seventy-five thousand to build. Beautiful place."

I eye him and think this guy hasn't got three hundred and seventy-five *dollars*; that's probably about what this truck's worth. He's dressed worse than I am. He's a grease monkey, at best; probably lives in a swamp in a shed.

"Got a place up in Roanoke too, cost me four hundred thousand that one. Or had one. That crooked fucker of a cousin of mine burned the fucker down; stole a hundred thousand from my poor old daddy too. He's a cop but he ain't gonna get away with it, no sir, I got his ticket punched." He laughs and hushes his tone a little. "I'll tell you what I'm gonna do: I got me a sniper's rifle and some special untraceable bullets out of a magazine, and he'll be there one day – I don't care whether it's Arbee's or fuckin' McDonald's – and I'll put a bullet in that crooked fucker's head. Him and all his friends. And if you think they'll find me, you're wrong; there ain't no one'll trace those bullets or that gun. It's special. Untraceable. Yup." He nods to himself in agreement. "I know all the cops; I know the mayor; they all love me. That fucker's gonna pay, no doubt about it, he's gonna pay."

The poor, stupid, ignorant hick is obviously deluded. But how in all hell has he managed to survive this long? How has he prospered in the world, to the extent that he has a truck and at least some sort of home, and has met people and maybe even got married and had poor, unfortunate babies? How is it that he's the one living the normal life and I'm the one cast out and lost, a destitute and possessionless wanderer? And, God forbid, but maybe he really does know all the cops and the mayor, and maybe he really does have all these big houses, and friends that love him, and socialisations and get togethers and happy family times. And, if that's so – and I'm seriously worried that it is – then what hope and justice is there in this topsy turvy world where idiots like that are allowed to not only live, but to thrive?

"Oh yes," he says, "that crooked fucker's gonna pay." And on and on he goes about rifles and bent cops and niggers and "the goddamned government" and I swear it's the worst three hours of my life. Why have I chosen this? Why, when I could be in bed with a beautiful woman and knowing love? Why am I sitting here listening to this oaf, eleven p.m. in the February Tennessee night, and soon to sleep shivering in bushes and trees, and more of the same tomorrow, when I could have Lauren and fun and sex?

He drops me off at a truckstop in Marion, still not out of Virginia, and that's the end of my first day's hitch. I sit and gorge myself on greasy chicken and fries and drink endless cups of free coffee – even coffee before bedtime is impossible to say no to, not when it's free – and I contemplate the day. I've come two hundred miles. I've taken rides with seven different people and listened to them talk about their lives. And I've witnessed kindness and stupidity in equal measure, even within the same individual person. Sexism and racism, love and generosity, small-mindedness and paranoia, murder and God. And I've been offered sex in return for money. You just don't get that kind of experience on your average backpackers' vacation.

My final attempt to make ground that night is in asking the eating truckers if they can give me a ride. They're all sitting solitary and not one of them talking with the other – thirteen guys at thirteen separate tables – which I find staggering after their hundreds of miles of aloneness and silence to get there. I guess they're scared, like so many of us are, of crossing these imagined social boundaries, of saying hello to the friend they haven't yet met. I feel like running around those tables and lighting little sparks of conversation, bringing them together. But instead I act just as shy and awkward as they look as I move from table to table quietly asking if I can get a ride. None of them wants to help me out though, and the closest I come is this black trucker heading for New Orleans who ums and ahs about it for a long time before deciding it's too risky.

"These bastards here," he whispers confidentially, "they'll call up head office and shop me in. They've done it to a friend of mine, got him fired from his job for picking someone up. I'd take you but I can't take the chance. They'll do anything to put us out of a job."

And by "us" I take it he means, "us blacks," and it seems that the spirit of racism and segregation is alive and well down south.

I finish my chips, and have another three or four cups of coffee, and then I step out into the cold raining night to find a place to sleep.

I spy some abandoned trucks around the back of the café and I check the doors. They're unlocked, and I climb in. And that's where I spend my first night of freedom on the road, squished up and not really sleeping in the leaking cab of a rusty and stinking construction wagon, shivering a little and dreaming of Lauren, and wondering.

Chapter Three

The sun is shining the next day and it's all winter blue skies and pine trees and open roads. I'm feeling optimistic and good: today is the day I finally escape Virginia. I grab some cardboard from a dumpster and make myself a sign – "SOMEWHERE NICE PLEASE!" – and get out my thumb. Almost immediately a guy who has been filling up with gas comes over and says hi.

"Sorry," he says, "I'm going to Roanoke. But I did some hitching when I was younger; I know what it's like. You need some money?"

And instinctively, I think I know what that means.

"No thanks," I say, "I've got plenty."

"You're sure?" He looks like a nice guy, sincere and straight-looking and clean. He doesn't look gay at all. But then again, neither did the guy yesterday.

"Thanks," I say, "but I'm all right. That's really kind of you though."

And off he goes back to his car and back up that road towards Charlottesville. It's a sad thing to be so suspicious of your fellow man, especially when they're offering to do you an apparent kindness. But I guess the loss of missing out on a few dollars doesn't really compare with the pain of being reminded just how revolting some men can be. I don't want to take the risk. It's too early in the day, and the weather too good, to experience that kind of hurt.

I ask some other drivers, and get turned down, but instead of being upset I instead issue them with a cheery, "thanks anyway, have a good trip," and move on to the next. I'm waving and smiling: happiness is in me. I want them all to see how much I'm loving it, whether they stop or not. And I am loving it. Little by little, the weight of the previous months is dropping off my shoulders.

Now one thing that bugs me about Americans is their blind and mule-headed patriotism, their blinkered and ill-informed belief that, "they're number one" – well, as far as rape and gun crime and theft goes, they are – and their indoctrinated and ignorant insistence that their great nation is the torch-bearer among all nations for this thing called "freedom of speech." I don't understand it because it's blatantly not true – there's far more freedom of speech in England, let alone in even more enlightened and liberal countries like Holland and Sweden – and the only possible way they can believe it is if they've never once stopped for a minute to question it. But what must they have thought when some woman was arrested for calling Bill Clinton an "asshole"? Or, in more recent times, when people have been arrested for wearing anti-American t-shirts or saying things slagging off George Bush? Not exactly freedom of speech, is it? And yet, were they to visit Speakers' Corner in Hyde Park they

107

would see far more threatening and insidious things allowed. They obviously have no idea of what goes on in the rest of the world.

My next ride, however, another Bill – a doctor from Kentucky – was refreshingly informed and critical of his nation: he told me a story about his conversations with four women he had treated who had all grown up in the Nazi Germany of the thirties before moving to America.

"'It must have been such a relief,' I told them, 'coming to America after that.' They agreed it was – but when I tried to say something about our freedom of speech they wouldn't have it; they said they had more freedom of speech back there, even under Hitler. I laughed at them but they said, 'just go and get yourself a box and stand on the street telling people how they should revolt and overthrow the government and see how long you last.' It really made me think. It really changed my opinion."

Like a lot of the single guys I rode with, Bill had a lot to say about the government. He loved his country but he had grave concerns. He talked about Waco and Ruby Ridge and Iraq. He talked about the "heavy-handed bullshit" Clinton and his ilk had repeatedly used to force themselves into war. He went right back to Korea and Vietnam, and he was not a happy man. It was a real eye-opener to find again and again this extreme level of anti-government sentiment among the proud and patriotic citizens of America. Some of them went even further and saw the government as a malevolent force of evil, sticking their noses into everybody's business and gathering files on each and every one of us. Most of those guys were whacked, though. I'd smile to myself when they went on like this, half-expecting them to move on to tinfoil hats and teeth with miniature transmitters in them – and they did. But if the government had a file on me they weren't doing much about it, given my illegal and larcenous status.

Bill was a super nice guy; in fact, aside from that complete endemol of a baskethead that took me to Marion the night before, they all were: all those single working guys driving their hundreds of lonely miles for their jobs and their families. I was enjoying their company, and their niceness was rubbing off on me. Sure, I wanted to meet hip young things – and maybe some women – but for now these jolly American dads and granddads suited me fine. Bill took me right down to the border of Tennessee – dropped me off, in fact, at the Tennessee welcome centre – and there I was, finally in another state, and finally free of Virginia.

And I can't tell you how good that felt.

Chapter Four

I was heading for this place called Summertown, somewhere in the middle of Tennessee not too far from Nashville, and more precisely to a commune Lauren's dad had told me about called The Farm. Some hippy friends of his had settled there. He was a bit of an old hippy himself – they'd bought the land that Lauren grew up on communally with friends back in the sixties, and built their own houses, and shared a large pond for swimming in the middle, where I guess they took all their clothes off and did their beardy, hippy things. He was a top bloke. He spoke fondly of The Farm and of how it had been, all pitching in together, old yellow school buses for homes, campfires and digging the earth. I figured I'd like a piece of that too. I mean, what better place for a lost and wandering soul to perhaps find a little bit of himself than in a circle of peace-loving hippies?

In the meantime, though, I had to get across Tennessee, and I took a ride down to Chattanooga, not because it was the most direct route, but because it was somewhere that I'd heard of, and it had a cool name. Casey Jones and all that. The Chattanooga choo-choo. And I still liked choo-choos, despite being well out of my trainspotting days. I got dropped off there in a Hooters parking lot. Hooters is a restaurant chain where you get served by big-breasted women in tight tops.

Just then, an over-sized pickup full of large-necked students rolled in and spewed out its load.

"Hey man, are you hitchhiking?" a guy in khakis asks incredulous and excited, spilling his beer all over himself. "Hey guys, check this guy out!"

And over they come, and soon I'm surrounded by a keg-load of fratboys.

"No way!" one says.

"Where you from?" goes another.

"That's awesome, man."

"Too cool."

"You rock."

And then: "you should come with us, bro' – we're gonna get some wings and brewskis in here and then we're gonna go down to Georgia for the game. It'll be awesome!"

They're a friendly bunch, sort of infectious in their slurred and simple-minded ways. But I laughingly decline. I'm going into Chattanooga, I say, gonna see the choo-choo.

"You're sure, man?" the first guy goes, "well take this." And into my hand he pushes a twenty dollar note, and off they go as one, their white socks and chiselled calves disappearing through the door and into the chamber of oversized boobies. I could have gone with them, and been then in Georgia and God knows what, but instead I walk another six miles through the dark and desultory Chattanooga night, past hookers and forbidding neighbourhoods where muggings no doubt take place, and me there with my backpack, and as I think about that twenty and all these possibilities, it makes me smile.

I find a bar and order a coffee. It's late and I don't know what I was thinking walking into Chattanooga and making myself so tired. I watch the X-files on the screen and keep to myself. I think back to the places I've passed where I might be able to sleep: underpasses, railway sidings, bushes. I pull out my journal and write.

"What are you doing writing in a bar?" a small blonde next to me goes, "are you writing a book? Are you writing about Chattanooga and all of us?"

She sort of assumes I am and I don't want to disappoint her.

"What's your name?" she says.

"Rory," I say, and close up my notebook.

"Oh my God, are you from England?" She blushes and I can see that I've had an affect on her. "My name's Vaychelle. Oh, I just love your accent."

"I like yours too." I always say that. But in this case it's especially true. She says, "accent," as though it's got an extra syllable and a 'y' in it: *ayaxent*.

"Honey, what in the devil's name are you doing here? You're travelling, right?" She looks down at my backpack.

"Hitchhiking," I say, "all the way to Arizona. I just left Virginia yesterday."

"And people stopped to pick you up? You're kidding?" Her mouth falls open and she gives me a look of exaggerated surprise.

I smile at her. People always say that: as though the fact that I'm sitting there talking to them isn't clue enough that, yes, people had indeed picked me up.

"People are really good," I say, "so kind. A guy yesterday bought me some fries. And I hitchhiked once and the people went ten miles out of their way."

"You want to be careful," she says, "it's not safe out there. People get killed. Why don't you take a bus?"

"It'll be all right," I say, "I've got a guardian angel."

She stops then and puts her beer down on the bar.

"Do you believe in angels?" she goes, suddenly serious, as though she's discovered the only other person in the world that does. Truth is, I don't – I don't think I do – though I've often thought back to that crash in the Mazda and wondered how the hell the three of us walked out of it, not a seatbelt-wearer in sight.

"Because I do; I've got a guardian angel too." She looks fuzzily around me and I worry for a second that she's going to start talking about auras or tell me she can see some Native American warrior perched on my shoulder. Then I realise she's just trying to focus. She's really, really drunk.

"You want a beer?" she says, "I'll buy you one. I'm celebrating my divorce. Nineteen years down the tube. The bastard. Hey, you should carry on writing, don't let me stop you." And she turns around and says something to her friend, before turning back. "Don't write anything bad about me, will you? Put: 'She was decent and loving to the old people...'cos they are the ones that will lead us to our destiny.'" She leans over me and watches while I write it in my book. "That's what I want on my tombstone."

And then she's whirled back around and left me there bewildered, and not a beer in sight. Which is good, because I don't want one anyway.

But word soon gets around that there's an English guy in there who's going to write a book about all of them, and one by one they come up and tell me sweet and pointless anecdotes from their lives in the hope they'll be included in this book I'm supposedly writing. They check that I'm making notes – I dutifully oblige – and then they leave satisfied knowing that they've done their best to try and make it into my posterity. And every now and then Vaychelle spins in her seat, ever more precariously each time, to grab my palm and tell me, "don't ever deceive yourself...it'll be your downfall"; to say I should come and visit the old folks she works with, tell them about the hills and mountains back in England; to say I should go for a free tarot card reading with her sister; to offer me a tour of the town in the morning; to warn me about the perils of hitchhiking, of murderers and thieves. And then, after each spin, to leave me alone so that I can get her words of wisdom down before they go out of my head.

I wonder about them and think, this is all very well, and kind of adventurous and exotic, but would anyone really want to make a book about it? I mean, would it be any different if I were to sit in The Plough in South Elmsall and listen to the pissheads and nobodies in there? Who would want to read that crap? So it's a novelty to me, and the novelty makes it interesting and fun – but were I to move here, pretty soon it'd be just the same as being back home and the novelty would wear off. Everywhere's the same, really: the same mix of good and bad; the same mix of boredom and adventure; the same people, living the same lives, doing the same jobs.

I look around me at the people in the bar, at all the blonde hair and the tight-jeaned men staring into the jukebox and it really is just the same as South Elmsall. But, at the same time, it's different because I'm different. I wouldn't be sat there in a bar in Yorkshire with a pen and paper philosophising and finding metaphors for life in a discarded piece of chewing gum; I wouldn't be pondering and searching and seeking always to find some sort of way to live, to be happy. I'd be watching TV and drinking and, no doubt, life *would* be mundane. But out here, on these roads, in this alien culture, my mind is somehow altered and changed, and I suppose that's why seek these far flung corners.

I think to myself, I'm glad I'm where I am, and the thought of it makes me smile. The bar and the people and the jukebox and the hair and my backpack and the being out there and the not knowing where I'm going to sleep or what the next day or even the next hour will bring.

I'm glad I'm where I am.

I want to keep that feeling with me always.

"Well," says Vaychelle, "may the road always rise up to meet you." She holds out her hand, and focuses on my left ear, and then she's gone, not a phone number or offer of a bed or sister in sight. It's closing time and it looks like I'm sleeping on the street.

I grab one more coffee and then pull on my coat and leave.

And outside a guy I'd talked to earlier calls to me and says, "hey limey, you need a place to stay?" and, damn straight I do. And soon enough me and George are riding in his car, a couple of his friends in the back, and we're all going to his.

Now one thing people always want to ask me about hitchhiking is whether I met any crazy people and whether I ever got scared. "Weren't you ever scared?" they say, incredulous and wide-eyed. And I answer and tell them, "not really; maybe a few times." The truth is, you do something often enough – even something inherently dangerous and fear-inducing – and any trace of being afraid is going to disappear. Back in those early days of hitchhiking, though, I hadn't done it anywhere near enough times to go beyond my fear. Nor had I placed myself in the trust and care of enough strangers to realise that ninety-nine point nine nine percent of people are decent and kind. So when people ask me about being scared this is one of the few occasions that springs to mind.

We got back to George's and him and his friends sat around in the living room drinking some more. I was, by this stage, tired beyond tired and longed only for a bed. Plus, I was stone cold sober and I was just learning how utterly annoying and unattractive drunk people can be when you're not in the same place with them. I really could have fallen asleep in that chair – but then the conversation started getting weird and I perked up a bit. George was on the phone to someone and the others were speaking in hushed tones; I became convinced they were hatching a plan to get some guys over to bum me. I heard George say something about, "he's a decent guy" – and in this moment of warped and exhausted thinking, "decent guy" was their code for, "nice, tight ass." He said some more things and then he put the phone down and said he wanted to show me something outside. I didn't want to leave my backpack but I didn't know what else to do. I followed him into the back garden while he drunkenly wobbled ahead.

The garden was full of Volkswagen campervans in various states of disrepair. He told me he collected them and did them up. He was going on about the different features of the variety of years and models, things that I couldn't have understood on a good day, nevermind on a night when I had at least one eye and one ear keeping a lookout for my impending ambush and bumming. He took me to one van in particular and wiped the dirt off the back window.

"Have a look in there," he said.

I looked at him dubiously.

"Go on," he said, "have a look."

It was obviously going to be filled with dead bodies, and just as I'd get my nose to the glass and realise – a bang on the head, or a grab from behind, and a night having my arsehole torn to pieces by half the male population of Chattanooga would ensue, until sometime around dawn I'd join the pile of rotting corpses stuffed into the vans, the bodies of a thousand hitchhiking fools and all of them as cocksure and stupidly-confident as I had been.

I pushed my face to the glass, waiting.

No dead bodies in this one.

Then George said something about the door handles in the kitchen area, about how they were real rare and you hardly ever saw them at all, and after talking some more about headlamps and split-windscreens he led me back inside. His friends were asleep on the couch, my backpack, undisturbed.

"'Night then," said George.

And in the morning he took me to meet his charming and fragrant girlfriend and we all ate breakfast together. George paid, and then the two of them drove me out to the interstate so that I could more easily catch a ride up to Summertown. The gas, I noticed in Chattanooga, was about eighty cents a gallon – by far the cheapest I'd ever seen. That made me smile. I really enjoyed keeping an eye on the price of gas.

Chapter Five

Challenge, eh? I loves a challenge. And the thing about challenges is, you've got to keep upping the ante, because once you've completed a challenge it's no longer a challenge at all, it's easy. So driving alone across country had been a challenge – but once accomplished, it was nothing. And driving back in one eighteen hundred mile stint had been a challenge too – but where could I take the driving after that? Okay, so I could've tried to make the whole coast-to-coast route without a break, one mad long fifty hour session behind the wheel, but what would that have achieved, bar frying my brain and probably killing me? So instead I took to the roads under the power of my own thumb, a tent and a sleeping bag and a little bit of money all I had to sustain me – and even then there's scope for more. And the first step in that scope is getting off the freeways and hitting the country roads.

You want to travel in America – and that's by car, as well as by thumb – you're far better off taking the back roads and escaping the interstate. Sure, the interstate'll get you there fast – but what will you see? A whole lotta concrete and a whole lotta cars and I just don't see the point in that. Instead, you get on those back roads and suddenly you're lost in a different time and place, moving slower now, out in Tennessee farmers' fields, Mississippi mudflats, tiny little one horse towns straight out of the fifties, fruit stands and welcoming diners and quirky massive erections proudly proclaiming the world's largest something or other. You're discovering hidden gems like Silva, North Carolina, or Belfast, Maine, or Arizona's Strawberry and Pine and Snowflake. You're meeting real people. You're escaping the noise, the generic restaurants, the whole pedal-to-the-metal feeling of, we've just got to get there. That's when the roadtrip becomes a roadtrip.

The interstate had taken me from Charlottesville and for that I was grateful. Now, though, it was time to get out amongst the hicks and see some of the back country, to take the risk factor a little higher. And so from Chattanooga I headed cross-country on little backroads and it took me three days to cover the two hundred and fifty miles to Summertown and The Farm.

As before, all my rides – bar one – were single working guys doing solitary jobs on the road and either in need of a bit of company or picking me up because they'd been there in their youth. The thing about those guys, though – and I'm talking men who had hitched the length and breadth of the country back in their long-haired hippy heyday – was that they all told me, to a man, that I shouldn't be doing it now. Things have changed, they said, people won't stop. People are dangerous and it's not like it used to be, and there are lots of bad stories, drivers killing hitchhikers, hitchhikers killing drivers. They always said this and I'd always think, what stories? I've never heard any. The more they said it, the more I wondered if there really were any stories to begin with, whether it wasn't just something that was unthinkingly repeated and passed on, ad infinitum, as though it were the truth. But it was all fear and media misrepresentation and ignorance – for wasn't I out there and thriving, and getting picked up, and meeting all sorts of lovely people? And wasn't I the one living the experience and getting to see first-hand exactly what my fear was? I.e., nothing. False evidence appearing real. And, upon investigation, it was evidence that fell apart in my hands.

Still, I was glad for their fears and their warnings. They made me feel like I was special and doing something not just anyone could do. And I wouldn't have had it any other way.

Another thing people would tell me was, you're very brave. That I didn't understand either. Bravery is surely doing something you don't want to do but know you have to, and have to steel yourself for, and push beyond your limits. Like going over the top at the Battle of the Somme. Or the bald-headed child that goes through leukaemia with a smile and a happy heart. But not me; I wasn't brave: they were just projecting. I was just doing whatever I felt like doing and not really worrying about it.

So when they'd say, "you're very brave," I knew what they really meant was, "I'm too afraid to do something like that."

Across Tennessee then, through Jasper and White City, Cowan and Winchester, Lynchburg and Fayetteville and Pulaski. I rode with a guy from Alabama who had just shot himself in the hand while teaching his mother how to load a gun; he showed me the hole and then told me stories about working on movies, and said he had just done The Bodyguard with Burt Reynolds. I rode with cool speedboat-hauling Unc, who pretty much immediately asked me, "you smoke pot?" and shared his pipe and talked about flying single-seater planes all over Alaska. And I rode with a guy who had travelled all of South America and sailed the world, and he could have took me home and made me his son too. They were good blokes. They swept me up and we talked like old chums. They fed me and got me high and deposited me back on that road with handshakes and well wishes and all the while I was making ground.

I spent a night in Winchester, hiding my stuff behind a barn about three miles out of town and hiking in to see if I could find a bar. I moseyed on up to a restaurant and chatted with a waitress there, and made her blush with my tones.

"Is there a bar in town you'd recommend?" I said. Already she's clocked that I'm a Brit and started to go red.

"Gosh," she says, "I'm sorry, what do you want?" She's got a sweet smile, this waitress, probably about eighteen. She's fumbling a bit, looks quite nervous.

"A bar," I say, "is there a bar in town?"

"I'm so sorry," she says, "a burr?" She looks puzzled and apologetic. "What's a burr?"

I laugh and apologise back.

"A bar. Like a pub. A place where people drink beer and hang out. Must be my accent."

And she's a million times sorry, and I say, no, no, it's your country, but still she's a million times sorry, and tells me she loves my accent, and is blushing as red now as the red in the Union Jack, and I'm feeling all mighty and superior to be causing such a reaction. This is what I had dreamed of back in New York. Why hadn't I just started my trip down smalltown Mississippi or Tennessee way? No doubt these ladies here would have taken me home in an instant.

"Well there's a sucky bar a few doors down," she goes, "but that one's real sucky. And there's a good one in town."

"Can I walk there?"

"Walk?" She looks at me incredulous; I'm used to this by now. The idea that you can walk places appears to be alien to most Americans: it seems to be one of the traits – along with sarcasm and the ability to properly spell the word 'favourite' – that was dumped in Boston harbour along with all that lovely tea. But we do it a lot back in England. And it's not dangerous or criminal or wrong: in fact, a good walk can be quite invigorating. If only their media and educational systems would allow them an insight into the practices and customs of other cultures.

"No," she says, "you can't walk, it's too far."

"Really? Oh. How far?"

She stops and ponders for a moment. I know from experience that non-walkers have a real problem judging distance.

"Two miles. Maybe three."

"Oh, that's okay," I say.

"It's real cold," she says.

It's about three degrees: warmer than I've seen women stumbling miles and stilettoed miles in bare-thighed, coatless attire in Leeds of a rainy November night.

"That's fine," I say, and off I go along strip mall boulevard, acre and acre of parking lot, and I just know in the daytime these Americans will be driving from one shop to the next, never considering that they could just park up and use their legs. I think I read once that the average American will walk a maximum distance of about five hundred metres; we used to walk two miles just to get to school, and that was nothing. But then, can you really blame them, when you've got seventy mile-wide cities like Houston and Los Angeles unnavigable by anything other than car, and everything so sprawled out, and all that concrete and traffic and drive-through banks and takeaways and post boxes, and no real reason to walk anyway. Unless you're concerned that your legs might one day shrivel up and drop off from lack of use.

I find the bar and sit down and get warm, and a little while later the waitress appears, still blushing and bumbling, and pops her head in to make sure I'd got there all right. I guess she was worried; that's sweet. I think of her later marvelling at this eccentric Englishman who – wait for it – "walks in the cold," and maybe dreaming a little dream of me and sighing.

Back then later to my barn and tent, and on that dark Tennessee road enjoying the silhouette of trees and the silence, a cop car suddenly appears behind me. I step onto the grass to let him pass but, instead of doing that, he puts his lights on and stops. He wants to talk to me.

"Where you going?" he says. He's a sheriff. Got the badge and everything.

"Just walking."

"What do you mean 'walking'? Let me see your ID."

I'm puzzled now: what am I supposed to do? As far as I know, walking isn't an offence, and I'm not sure what right he has to pull me over like this. I wonder if I've heard something about being able to refuse his questions and requests if I haven't done anything wrong.

"I'm just walking," I say, "I'm camping out a few miles down there. Just been into town to have a look around." He's eyeing me more and more suspiciously all the time; he's obviously never heard of such a thing. "I like walking," I say, "I'm English, it's what we do."

"It might be what you do in England," he says, "but not around here. Where's your ID?"

"I haven't got any on me," I say. I'm lying. I've got my passport in my back pocket. But having skipped bail and all that I'd rather not get into things like record checks and names.

He stops for a moment and then talks into his radio. I think he's calling for backup.

"If you haven't got any ID," he says, "I'm going to have to take you in until you can prove who you are. Arrest you."

Arrest me? For walking! What madness is this? What kind of a world is it when a young man can't take a pleasant evening stroll down dark country roads without being hassled and harassed and threatened with jail? And what kind of a world is it when not carrying your passport is a arrestable offence? I can just see myself spending the next twenty years in jail all because I'm unable to prove who I am on a nighttime amble. Welcome to Amerika, my friends. This cop is obviously an ass. And I am once more in the shit. Which is a shame, because I've been so good of late.

He's on the radio and then he gets a call to check out some crime somewhere else. I pray for him to leave me alone, which he's clearly going to have to do, what with having actual real things to investigate, but instead he calls for another car to come and deal with me and waits till it arrives. The new guy takes over and off he goes to harass someone else: maybe a sitter or a stander, or perhaps a whole group of walkers, a gang of them terrorising the world with their shoes and their feet, with the way they put one leg in front of the other.

"I was just walking," I say – and fortunately for me this new guy is something other than a complete and utter tool and quickly realises what a non-event the whole thing is. So instead of booking me in and fingerprinting me and slamming the door he gives me a ride back to my tent and sends me off to bed with a cheery, "goodnight."

The next night I wind up in Fayatteville drinking coffee in a BP station and fantasising about hiking across the Grand Canyon. The woman there starts a conversation and asks me what I'm doing, and out come all my stories and dreams and schemes, and pretty soon she's feeding me the entire contents of her sandwich counter and, I'll you tell what, their steak and cheese ain't half bad.

"So where you staying tonight?" she says.

"Oh, probably off in the fields somewhere. It seems kind of quiet around here. I've got my tent and my sleeping bag."

"No no no," she says, "you can't do that. It's freezing." She stops and ponders. "I'd put you up myself," she says, "but I've got six teenage boys in the house already. Gee, they sure would love to meet you. But I'm afraid we just haven't got the space." She frowns when she says this.

"It's fine," I say, "I'm quite looking forward to camping out."

But, no no no, sweet Cindy won't have any of it, and in between telling me proudly of her family – three her own, three fostered; all good kids; don't do drugs or swear or smoke, thank the Lord; always keep their rooms tidy; and little wonder they're all so good if they're even half as decent as this gas station angel – she's on the phone to various people seeing if she can sort me out with a bed for the night. Eventually she gets on to her priest and a few minutes later he calls her back and we have success.

"Okay," she says, breathless with all the ringing and the effort, "there's a motel just over the road; just you go in there and tell them Brother Johnson's arranged a room for you, they'll tell you what to do." And once more I'm astonished by the kindness and simple humanity of these people. I realise now that I've been perhaps unfair to my American friends, ridiculing them and their ways, and making out on occasion that us Brits are somehow better; but let me just say this: nowhere on Earth have I experienced kindness and generosity like I did in that vast nation. Nowhere did I meet people who were so trusting and endlessly giving, and so refreshing and beautifully innocent with it after the cynicism of England and my upbringing. For the first time in my life I felt like I was seeing something of a goodness in the world and in its people. They gave, and they trusted, and they showed me what it was to be a decent human being. Slowly, it dawned on me: that human beings are good, and since I was a human being too, I could be that also. I'd grown up with my dad and his vaguely-criminal and money-grabbing ways, my mum and her neglect, her disinterest in me, and somewhere down the line I'd lost myself and gone off the rails. But when I was a boy they'd said I was a veritable angel, kind and generous and compassionate and giving, just as these people were now. I could feel a change coming over me – and it was all because of the goodness of the people I met.

I slept that night in one of my favourite places on Earth: a motel room bed. It was only a shame I was too tired to make more of the TV. I love motel rooms, no matter how cheap or nasty: it probably comes from never having taken a holiday as a child. They'll always be little palaces to me.

Chapter Six

When I woke it was late and I was vaguely troubled by some long and intricate dream I'd had involving Nathan Hart, Lauren, Tyler and The LTD. It had started out with me and one of the guys I'd met in Chattanooga sat in a bath having some sort of wanking competition wherein we were wired up to a machine bespattered with dials and knobs. I glanced up and saw that I was registering a nine, which I was pretty happy with – until I realised it wasn't inches, it was volts. My competitor, meanwhile, all muscled and big, was off the scale. I gave up and the next thing I knew I was in a junkyard having sex with my first girlfriend, Kelly, and then David Bowie. Later, Lauren and her mum appeared and that was all jolly and good until Tyler and Nathan Hart came by, and I beat up Tyler and raced off in The LTD. An old school friend tells me that Tyler's in hospital and I get back in The LTD while everyone chases me. Try as I might I can't shake them off, and the brakes fail and I crash. Usual tale of wrongdoing and running away. My dreams are always troubled.

I have a few recurring dreams, aside from the one of getting bitten on the hand by dogs: one is too complex to explain in words, a sort of feeling of falling into the void of infinity, a black hole of ones and zeros and ever increasing numbers, a sense of space and time just too big for my mind to grasp; and the other is about being pursued by unstoppable killing machines: I have that one all the time. It can be horrible kids from school or zombies or murderers, it doesn't really matter, the premise is the same. Often I think I've got clear but then they'll be there again, back on my tail and me out of breath and exhausted but unable to stop. I'd love to know what it means.

I go back to the BP to thank Cindy for her kindness of the night before and, friendly but not overly interested, she says, "you're welcome." I don't know why, I expected her to make more of it – but the way she acts it was as though she'd done no more than give me the time of day. No gloating. No making me aware of what a favour she's done and how grateful I should be. And no expectation of anything in return. Again, it seems exactly how us humans were supposed to be, before we got all bitter and cynical – except this hadn't happened to her. You'll have to forgive me if this is obvious: my own dad would remind me about it for weeks if he'd treated me to so much as a train ticket.

And back on the road to Summertown, and suddenly I get picked up by a woman. I'm not even hitching at the time – just enjoying a walk in the fields, the sun and the quiet – but she stops in front of me and asks me if I need a ride.

"I've never picked up a hitchhiker before," she says, "but something about you said you were safe." She's a smiling, middle-aged soccer mom, all cleancut and conservative looking, and somehow puzzled yet amused with herself for having stopped. I decide to be extra nice to her, to try and show her that it's okay to pick up hitchhikers, that we aren't all crazy axe-murdering freaks. She listens to my stories with a wide-eyed vicarious wonder.

"You're very brave," she says. And when we say goodbye I feel like I've really given her something in return.

My final ride is Kevin, a moustachioed thirty-something Tennessean photographer en route to Nashville. He's a little round guy in sunglasses. He's dressed like someone from the eighties. His moustache sits atop his lip like a hairy brown caterpillar. We'd gotten off to a bit of a bad start when I'd asked him where he was going with perhaps too little attention to diction given our different interpretations of the English language.

"What!?" he'd gone, and leapt away from me, the colour draining from his cheeks.

"Where you heading?" I said again, more slowly.

"Jesus," he said, relaxing a little and sliding back down in his seat, "I thought you'd said, 'can I fire at your head?'" We sort of had a laugh about that. But probably not as much as we should have done, given how amazingly funny it was.

We made some small talk but the conversation soon dried up. That was a bit weird; not really what I was used to. I even tried to get him to talk about his car – a surefire method of keeping the mouth of practically any American male busy for an extended period of time – but it didn't work on this guy. He just sat there sort of twitching his moustache and looking like he wanted to say something.

The caterpillar made a few more shakes of the tail and then he finally got to talking.

"You must do a lot of walking," he says, "and carrying that heavy bag, it's kind of like a workout. You've probably got quite a muscley body" – twitch twitch – "do you work out? You ever thought of modelling?"

I let out a little laugh. No, I've never thought of modelling, I'm not very photogenic, I say; in fact, I think I might be putting on some weight, what with all the Twixes and french fries and that.

He goes quiet for a while. I look him over and he's there with his sunglasses and that moustache, staring straight ahead, and it's almost like I can see something building inside of him.

"Are you into pornography? What about raw sex?"

And suddenly it all clicks: the clothes; the lack of interest in cars; the moustache and the photography. I get a feeling I don't like the way this is going. I try to change the subject. I tell him I'm more the romantic type, and mention my girlfriend as much as possible. I go on about my own fledgling interest in photography, hoping that'll spark his interest.

Instead, he doesn't say anything. And then that caterpillar of a moustache starts a-twitchin'. And then one final flick of the tail and out it comes, a sly and satisfied grin on his lips, an almost visible excitement in his body.

And so on and on he goes: tells me I should get into modelling; talks about my legs, how they must get built up and firm; asks me what kind of sex I like; asks me if I've got a big dick. And in response I'm monosyllabic and uncooperative, answering politely and calmly but clearly uninterested – which has no effect whatsoever on Kevin.

"You ever thought of posing nude?" he says. And then he goes on about my dick some more. And then he asks me if I want to show him.

And – Jesus! – I was such a pussy in that car: all I did was answer him the best I could but not once did I tell him to stop, to shut the fuck up, to let it drop. Can you believe that I told him I didn't have a big dick? That I'd never really thought about it? Can you believe that I sat there and took all that, when I could have got out of that car, could have told him what a disgusting prick he was being, that he was making me feel like shit? But all I did was hope that telling him I ate nothing but chocolate and had a girlfriend would be enough to put him off.

"You want to pull over and take some pictures in that field?" he says. "You want to show me your dick? You want to make a bit of money?" The guy is unrelenting.

He's building to a crescendo now – we're nearing The Farm – and it is such a pathetic and laughable finale that I actually end up pitying the sad little slug of a man.

"Are you uncircumcised?" he asks. I tell him I am. A smile spreads across his lips, the caterpillar going into raptures. "All I want," he says, "is a guy with a really big foreskin." He holds up his thumb and forefinger and indicates to me what he means by that. About two and a half inches. Which seems kind of freaky.

"Have you got a big foreskin?" he says, "you want to show me?"

The guy is obviously mental. I mean, what the hell is a big foreskin anyway? And why on Earth would you want one?

I tell him, no, it's just normal. I tell him I'm not the man he's after, that he should go to England, there are lots of foreskins there. I've lost patience; I've seen him for what he is. A plump, badly dressed Tennessean tells you all he wants in life is a guy with a really big foreskin you've just got to shake your head and laugh. He's pathetic. He's a pathetic and powerless child – and all the power is with me 'cos I've got what he wants: I've got a foreskin.

He ends it with one more request for a naked photo shoot and then gives me his card, "just in case you change your mind." He's taken me to the very gate of The Farm.

So what is it about these guys who think it's okay to make people feel like shit just because they want a bit of action? Seems like they're everywhere, free to roam, picking their victims and inflicting misery without a second's thought.

They say that one in four women have been raped – and that means there's a hell of a lot of rapists out there. Plain and simple, it is fucking disgusting, and I can barely handle the thought of what a man is capable of when his brain falls into his pants and he becomes a slave to his dick. If this is what a libido does to you, you can keep it.

And now: The Farm – that hippy idyll where I would sit night after night around a campfire in a ring of Volkswagen buses learning about myself and the universe; listening to wise old peace-loving heads expound upon the truth of our human existence; pointing me in the right direction and revealing to me all the secrets of happiness and my own purpose in life. And where, perhaps, I would be swept up into a loving extended family and come to find some respite from this wandering existence where nowhere ever felt like home.

Or, perhaps, where some smarmy ex-hippies would look down their noses at me from their modern, detached houses, and work me to the bone, and then ask me to give them some money, in a sort of wishy-washy, non-direct hippy way that leaves me wondering what the hell is going on, and at the end of it all – three days, maybe – I might leave there feeling more disenchanted and alienated than ever, cast aside even by adobe-loving beardies and once-upon-a-time Earth mothers, despite all my hard work and best intentions, dirty paper being the only thing they're interested in these days. Yeah, I might do that.

And I might also sit there in a basement listening to some tie-dyed teenagers talk about the amazing sunrise they all got up especially to see, and how they think everyone's connected by a web of energy, and how sometimes you have to lose yourself and experience suffering if you want to truly find out who you are, and vibes and communication and honesty, and wonder what the hell they're going on about, thinking it all a load of rubbish but at the same time thinking them so much better than I. And then maybe smoke some pot and sit incapacitated in a chair having wild visions and thoughts and realising the truth about reincarnation and destiny and *everything* – and then immediately forgetting it all – while these crazy beautiful Rasta-hatted hippy hemp kids rock out playing incredible juiced up five-string funk bass, and the drummer's arms going wild, and the singer's head is nodding frantically amazing, and the guitarist wails and sails and goes right on through, and all these years I've just been sat in a cellar in Leeds and dreamed the whole damn American thing right from start to finish and soon I'll walk upstairs and there'll be my dad sat behind his shop counter saying, "all right son?" and drinking tea from a dirty chipped cup, the story of a thousand teabags upon it, his cigarette ash falling on the display of effects pedals by his feet, distortions and phasers and wah-wahs, and back somewhere there the old alcoholic drum tutor emerging from those same cellar depths to talk to my seventeen year-old ears about astral projection and getting higher than acid naturally, and it's all seeds isn't it, the way they're sown and then shoot up and sprout and grow months and years down the line; that's what it is.

Oh, it was all just a dream – but, man, that singer's head was great.

Chapter Seven

I'll tell you now about the strangest and oddest and best and worst night of my life: about the time I dropped five tabs of acid at a rave in an old church in London after me and Tim had been out boozing in Soho. I got them off some dreadlocked white crusty; he had them in his shoe. I think I paid him twelve pounds. I had wanted more but he assured me five would be plenty. I'd taken acid once or twice before but nothing had really happened. Well this time, it did.

First off, I freaked, and Tim had to lead me by the hand to lay me down by some wall where I watched my arm leave a trail of colours in the air and listened to him and his girlfriend talk in backwards echoes and say wonderful things about me. And then we went back to his, and I degenerated into being five years old, spitting biscuits all over him and following him into the toilet while he pissed to bump him and make him pee all over the floor, the seat, his shoes. Three thirty in the morning this was not the kind of thing he wanted to be dealing with. Him and his girlfriend went to bed and left me alone in the living room. And then I freaked again.

I felt so absolutely on my own. I got on the telephone and tried to call somebody. I tried to call Tim but he was engaged. I tried to call my girlfriend but I couldn't remember the number; the only person I could get hold of was some unfeeling woman who kept on saying, over and over, "please replace the handset and try again."

"I'm trying to call my friends!" I protested. But she wouldn't listen.

Eventually I did get through to someone: my buddy Brent's sleeping dad. He was no use either.

I thought I'd better go and look for somebody.

I jumped out of the window.

And running then, barefoot and only in my boxers through the pre-dawn streets of Wembley, flashing fire from the palms of my hands, tearing the paint from cars, smashing windows and gutting buildings with my newfound superpower. And in the distance: Wembley Stadium. And inside it: my beloved Everton. Kevin Ratcliffe and Doug Mountfield: they would make everything all right. I headed for it. I negotiated lava; a million biting spiders; a squadron of fiendish nuns. The sun came out and roasted my skin.

"It's too hot!" I cried. "Colder, colder!" And it began to fade and cool – "that's nice, that's nice" – only to keep growing colder and colder and colder, until it was snow and ice and the hairs on my arms froze solid and I was shivering to death.

"Too cold!" I screamed, and back again the heat comes – "that's nice, that's nice" – until that scorching, melting sun is frizzing my hair, my eyes two poached eggs, my flesh afire. "Too hot," I say, and on, and on, and on.

I make Wembley and suddenly it all becomes clear: I have created everything. All things, I see, are my doing, and I put myself there among them, and told myself to forget it, so I could have a look around and enjoy. I marvel: it's amazing! And all the languages in the world, and Tottenham Hotspur, and roses and cats and trees: I made them all. I'm so very clever, I think. I can't believe I've done it. But it all makes perfect sense.

Then I think I'll need to jump into Wembley, what with the doors being locked – and then I'm a thousand feet tall and the map of the country is spread out beneath me and I think, to hell with this, I'll just run to Leeds, my giant's legs taking enormous and glorious strides over the green, green hills. But then something happens and my mind starts to collapse in on itself, its million billion pieces becoming a billion, and then a million – or, more precisely, one million and forty-eight thousand, five hundred and seventy-six – and down and down like cells undividing until my mind is sixty-four, thirty-two...four, two, one.

I can't see anything. I've watched all this happen from the inside and now it's just a black void and a single solitary dot. And then the dot is gone and I am no more.

I wake up later in an ambulance, in the middle of an interrogation from a nurse: she wants to know my name, my address, my date of birth. I tell her I can't remember and every time I fail thorns sprout from her cracked face and she glares at me and I cower.

"Please," I beg, "I honestly can't remember. Just let me breathe out; I really want to breathe out." I haven't exhaled in hours.

They take me to the hospital – it's on a ship somewhere in the Caribbean floating gently upon the waves. I lie in my bed and sultry sexy funk music fills the room, ooze running down the walls, and the nuts and bolts on the bed and in the radiators turn in their sockets, making love, and oozing too. The whole room is swaying and rocking with the music, and everything is sex. Out in the corridors I hear my friends laughing about me and what a card I am. The doctors and the nurses are laughing too. They all think I'm amazing.

Later, they dress me in a shirt that smells of curry and a pair of trousers at least eight inches too big. They tie up the waist with a shoelace and send me on my way, barefoot. My friends aren't there in the corridor waiting for me. They've disappeared, it seems.

I walk then through the deserted Sunday morning hospital and in a room filled with empty chairs I pick up the phone.

Tim's girlfriend answers.

"Hello," I say, "it's Rory." I laugh and smile at the thought of myself, at my predicament, at the comic japes that are sure to have amused them.

"Rory?" she says, "what are you talking about? You're right here."

"What?"

"Your body's still here. You died last night. You're right here."

I drop the phone and look around me. The hospital is empty and it's true, I'm dead. I run and run and soon I'm outside and walking in the bright Caribbean sunshine. All around me, covering everything, a red and green net of dots joined together by thin lines. It's beautiful. I'm smiling. And even though I'm dead, everything's okay. I bounce along and the Jamaicans laugh and smile right there with me, and we're all dead together on this sunny North London morn.

Chapter Eight

Back on the road, and back through big-haired Nashville, where I walk miles and miles and eventually give in and spend some money on a bus, and note that ninety-five percent of the people on it are black. And in the rainy one-degree Tennessee night. And walking more. And New York Mikey, who can't stand all that dark and empty space; and lovely trucker Russ, who fills me full of optimism and restores my faith in humanity after a troubled day that ends with my sleeping content and satisfied in amongst the roadside trees in Jackson, and all the earlier hardships apparently just necessary tests, and the rewards that follow actually dependant on those hardships, so were they even hardships in the first place? Or is it all just pieces in a wonderful puzzle?

Casey Jones, by the way, is a bloody hero. And his choo-choo is simply magnificent.

I make Memphis and spend the night with an old hippy woman and two Dutch guys getting stoned and listening to her tell stories about when she used to hang with Jim Morrison and Janis Joplin. Then we play some records and sit there in silence nodding along, except every so often I whirl around and say, "sorry? what was that?" and they all just keep on nodding. She lets me sleep in her Volkswagen campervan and the next day I walk across the Mississippi, which is incredible.

I'd been hitching in the rain by the roadbridge for an hour and it was hopeless: the traffic was going way too fast and there was nowhere for them to pull over. There was no pedestrian bridge and the next junction was miles away. And since I'd already walked four wet miles as punishment for eating too much chocolate that wasn't really an option. Instead, I looked down that dirty brown river and saw another bridge, and this time one bearing the beautiful load of a freight train. Maybe I could hop one out of there. I sogged on down and met the tracks.

I waited a little while and no train came – and all the while I'd been waiting I'd had this growing thought that I could just walk right on over there to the other side. It stood at least a hundred feet above the river, wide and fast-moving and full of that Mississippi mud. It was a mad thing to do. I'd be an idiot not to.

And so I walked across the Mississippi. I walked on railway sleepers, and in the gaps in between them I stared down at that raging brown torrent below. I could so easily have slipped off and plummeted down into it. My adrenaline was off the chart. It was absolutely one of the best things I ever did.

And on the other side – on Arkansas flats now – that bridge just kept on going. I'm not sure why I hadn't thought of that but, the thing was, the tracks didn't just suddenly dip down to dry land and allow me to get off them on other side of the river: they continued their journey high up in the air, high atop large concrete pillars and posts, and even slimmed themselves down every now and then to a single pair of rails. Which meant I was a hundred feet off the ground, walking on a solitary railroad track, with no means of escape should a train come my way. Very 'Stand By Me.' I walked four miles like that, in the dark and in the rain, until I was able to descend to the brown muddy earth of the Delta and rejoin the road at a West Memphis truckstop. And there I spent the whole night drinking coffee and indulging in convincing fantasies that I'm actually an alien and the whole thing is but a grand show put on for my benefit; let me explain:

Once upon a time, the fantasy goes, I was a pill in a jar on a shelf in a store. I had no mind or memories to speak of, but at some point someone bought me and implanted all these memories into me, and – voila! – I came into existence. Now it's hard to tell exactly when this happened because all my memories, whether they be seconds or years or decades old, all have the same quality: that is, they're just thoughts and images contained within my own head. It could have quite easily been in this truckstop – or it could have been back when I was a boy, or at any point in between. Furthermore – and perhaps most importantly – nothing exists. There is nothing, and there is nobody, until I decide otherwise. The only things that are actually there are those that I can see, hear, taste, smell and touch. But around that corner? White space. And when a person seemingly turns it and pops into view, really they're just popping into my head. I am the creator of everything. We all are.

Sometimes, though, I'll see someone – an apparent stranger – and I'll look them in the eye and feel as though they know me. They do. They're a part of it. I'm getting closer to the truth and that's why they've come to spy, disguised as truckers, sitting at the other end of the counter and occasionally glancing my way. And that's why they're using the tannoy to blast strange numbers into my consciousness – masquerading as announcements about which shower is ready – in an attempt to disrupt my thought process. I must be getting real close now. Things, I feel, are coming to a head.

And all night long I go thinking like this. Boy oh boy, I don't know what they put in their coffee but West Memphis sure is a weird place. I stagger out into the morning sun and I'm seriously in need of escape: ten miles in twenty-four hours is shabby by anyone's standards. I make a sign for Little Rock and stick out my thumb, and the very first truck that comes my way stops and swoops me up. Raving mad Dennis, with the glint in his eye; with the government conspiracy theories; with the, "files on you, me and everyone, boy." And even the tooth-transmitter-tinfoil business. A lunatic. But I love the way he leans over and spiels his mad spiel and – hell's bells! – he's taking me all the way to Dallas. And on we ride in Roswell cover-up wonderland, and once more I'm back in the middle of impossibly enormous Texas.

There's a lake not too far from where he drops me off; I go sit by it and have a banana, look out at the water and think. I'm relaxed, lying with my head on my backpack, sleepless eyes intermittently closing and juddering open again. I'll probably sleep by there tonight, get a good night's rest and an early start in the morning. And then a voice behind me startles me awake.

"Hey," a man says, "you hitchhiking?"

I look down and see my cardboard sign for Little Rock lying beside me.

"Yep," I say, "I just got in from Tennessee."

"You hungry?"

"A little." He's a clean looking guy, smaller than me and pleasant.

"You want to come for dinner? My apartment's just over there. My wife's working till late tonight; it'd be nice to have the company. I'd love to hear your stories." He tells me his name's Paul, he's done a bit of travelling, he knows what it's like. He says I can stay the night.

I go with him. I think it's about time I just relax into letting a man help me and stop worrying that they all want to bum me. I've met so many kind people so far – but I have turned down a few offers of help, of bed, of showers because I was afraid that they wanted more. This guy seems harmless – and he has uttered the magic word, mentioning the wife. He's probably just yet another one of the kind-hearted souls that I appear blessed with the good fortune of meeting.

He's got a tiny apartment. He points out the pictures from his wedding and I notice a few religious sayings on the wall. He says I should take a shower and in I go, and remove my clothes, and in the heat and the steam I let the water rain down upon my body and cleanse me. It's my first proper shower since leaving Charlottesville. The water keeps on pouring and I lose myself in the steam, in their pink and turquoise bathroom. I've been on the road eleven days and in those eleven days I must have been gifted one form of kindness or another dozens and dozens of times. I set out afraid and now here I am, in a stranger's bathroom, about to have dinner and stay the night. The fears I left with have gone. The trauma of Charlottesville. The funk that held me there in a solitary no man's land for one solid month. The water swirls in the plug hole and disappears, and with it all remaining trace of the dirt of Virginia. I haven't even been tipsy in two and a half months.

I step out of the shower and dry myself in the still-steaming room. The towels are clean and soft and pink; my skin is clean and pink too. And with my growing hair still wet I step back into the living room where Paul is waiting with a smile and a plate of steak and beans and potatoes, and the two of us sit at his table and talk until I am too tired to talk anymore, and on their floor, between the wall and the couch, I sleep.

Chapter Nine

I'm rushing through this now, but that's because I know how much there is to come, and because I know how pointless it would be to detail every little instance of when an extraordinarily kind stranger swooped down to scoop me up, to water and feed me, to put me up for the night and make me feel like the world was a place full of goodness and magic; it happened all the time; it would take the rest of my life to do them all justice. Helen and Paul were extraordinary people, in that they took me, a worthless stranger, into their home and treated me like family – and even asked me to stay the weekend, which I was unable to do, because of my fear of being a burden – and yet at the same time it wasn't extraordinary at all, because it was happening over and over and over. Was it just Americans? Is that the way they are? Or would it happen in England too? Well partly that's an unfair comparison, because England just doesn't have that same tradition of travel – it's too small for any journey to really be an odyssey; there's nowhere you can go that you can't reach in the same day – while Americans are used to seeing people who are on trips that last days and weeks, that aren't pressed for time or in a hurry to get anywhere, that are in need of shelter or happy to divert for an hour or a day to encounter somebody or something new. It's impossible to know what a man with a backpack in England is up to – is he homeless? a walker? just doing some shopping? – but a man with a backpack in America is almost always on his way to or from somewhere, an adventurer, a person probably worth taking some time to talk to.

I've talked about this before and I'm convinced it comes down to the trust and openness that the American people carry in their hearts. They just don't have that same level of cynicism, of fear: of batten down the hatches and hold on tight because, this item, this possession, this thing is mine, and this home is my castle, and this little bubble is my sphere of existence and no one and no thing is going to come into it and disturb it because the world is a bad bad place. Americans were almost childlike in their openness and trusting: they seemed so innocent and curious about everything. And if you want to make the analogy the size of a country you could say this: that England was old and bored and tired; that England and the English had seen everything and done it all and realised that it was all just a crock of shit; that England was an old man, and England had had enough of life, and England just wanted to sit in his rocking chair and say, "bah! humbug!" for the rest of his days. And America? America was a babe in arms, barely two hundred years old and still excited and innocent and learning. Sure, America made mistakes and sometimes got petulant and threw its rattle out the pram, like any child would, but America was bright-eyed and hugged strangers and didn't know the first thing about deviousness or trickery, it just welcomed the world with its open arms and kept on welcoming until the world gave it a reason not to. And what it lacked in experience and knowledge, it made up for in exuberance and energy and enthusiasm. I had now spent an almost equal amount of my post-adolescent time in both the land of cynicism and the land of openness and there is no doubt in either my mind or yours as to which one I was coming to prefer. And which quality in myself I now hoped would take root and grow.

My next port of call was Amarillo, a place I'd first caught a glimpse of on an episode of Top Gear, some feature about ten old Cadillacs buried in a field and one of those steak houses that challenge you to eat a monstrous piece of meat within a certain amount of time. I fancied that, and I also had a hankering to spraypaint the name of my website ("Down The Rubadub In A Terry Nutkins Stylee") on one of the Cadillacs. Those two things, and walking across the Grand Canyon – and reaching, eventually, the desert – were about all I had on my list of 'Things To Do While Hitchhiking Across America.' Amarillo was several hundred miles out of my way but I really wanted a crack at that steak.

I caught a ride with a young guy who was beaming from ear to arsehole after just fulfilling his lifelong dream of becoming a truck driver. He dropped me off not too far from Amarillo early in the morning and I hopped into a pickup with a couple of gay Mexicans who had been up all night at either a casino or a gay sex-show slash orgy, I couldn't work out which. They giggled all the way into town and then took me for lunch and a few games of pool and I could probably have hung all day with those crazy cats and their giggles, but I was hungry for the Cadillac Ranch and set off walking. Somewhere there, though, I catch sight of a newspaper that says it's dropping to minus seventeen (though that's with the windchill; those Americans have got to have their windchill, it makes them feel so much more manly) and when the snow starts falling heavily and heavily falling* I wonder if just maybe I might be better off shelling out for a motel and some warmth. People die in temperatures like this, I hear.

I'm thinking about this and getting snowed on when I hear a voice.

"Hey," it says, "do you know where you're going? You don't know where you're going, do you?" It's a guy sat in one of those dodgy eighties Ford Mustangs. I wander on over to him and point towards the Cadillac Ranch. The snow is thick on my eyelashes and hair. He laughs. "There's nothing up that way for miles. Are you crazy? Get in, I'll give you a ride." I don't need telling twice.

He introduces himself as Larry, an AIDS-counsellor. He's a wiry old bloke with a smile and a twinkle in his eye. I tell him I should probably find a cheap motel, ask him if he knows where there is one. He does, and he drives towards it, and then after a few minutes he says, "you can stay at mine if you want."

"You're sure?" I say, incredibly grateful for my good fortune yet again. Especially when it's saving me some much needed dollars.

"It'd be my pleasure," he says, and around turns the car, and back to Larry's it is. And – fiddle my dee – you've never seen a place like Larry's.

We walk in the door and you can only imagine the expression on my face when I take in the panorama of what is quite possibly the world's gayest house: Liberace had nothing on this dude. It's a huge place and every wall and every table and every available surface is decorated with some homage to the naked male body. His lamps are naked men. He's got dozens and dozens of paintings and photographs and sculptures, and it's all nude guys, entwined lovers, erect penises. The throw on his couch is pink and fluffy and gay. Even the kettle is pink and gay, and on the fridge there are Polaroid photos of various guys with their cocks in their hands posing in front of the graffitied hulks of my beloved Cadillacs.

"Welcome," he says.

"Thanks," I say back, and stand there and blink and smile. It's ridiculous, really, the situations I find myself in. It's brilliant too.

"You want a sherry?" he says, this little grinning man with the wrinkles and the cowboy boots, and he holds out a glass of syrupy red liquid.

"Yes please." And down on his couch we go, and up on his gayified Elvis poof go my feet, and in comes his sniffing and investigating poodle, and all you can do is laugh and wonder and enjoy the ride.

"Cheers," he says.

And in it goes, and smacking of lips, and: "ah, that was nice."

And if you think there's anything hidden in those last three sentences I'm sorry to disappoint you but, there isn't.

I stayed with Larry for three days, and though he never grew tired of trying it on or making lewd comments, there was something so utterly inoffensive and charming about him that he put me totally at ease. Furthermore, he was tiny, and nearly three times my age, and I knew that I had nothing to fear from him physically. Okay, so he had a bit of a torture chamber in his basement – "you don't want to see what's down here," he said, me peeking through the hatch and quickly realising that he was right, I didn't – and made me watch gay porn – wrong! – plus he had friends who he told me wouldn't have taken no for an answer, that I would have been drugged and bound and, yes, arse-ravished and left dazed in the snow, but even that didn't stop the time I spent in Amarillo being anything but fun fun fun.

Larry was the host of hosts, bar none. He took me out every day, cruising the streets and elaborating on the colourful and chequered social shenanigans that bubbled beneath Amarillo's seemingly placid surface. He told me story after story that made me think this town surely rivalled any in America for intrigue and dirt, usually involving millionaire ranch-owners who kept getting caught with their hands in young boys' shorts, much to their adulterous wives' disgust. He told me of orgies and scandal, murder and madness. He told me of the town's thriving gay population, and of all the ones in the closet – the respectable businessmen, the old money cowboy-types – and he introduced me to the cream of the mothereffin' crop, a three hundred-pound gay black preacher with the sissiest of voices all resplendent in blue eyeliner and bent as a nine bob note. And then there was Stanley Marsh, a local millionaire who drives around in an enormous pink Cadillac and pays people to put kooky faux-roadsigns in their gardens; the signs say things like, "Strong Drink," "Dinosaur X-ing," "Hot Pepper," and "Legs Up To Her Armpits." You see them everywhere in Amarillo. He's also the guy that half-buried those ten vintage Cadillacs. They're apparently angled at the same alignment as the Great Pyramid in Egypt.

We went out there one afternoon and Larry was kind enough to furnish me with a couple of cans of spray paint for the occasion. It was his tradition to take all his gentlemen visitors there, and to snap them with their trousers round their ankles. He asked me for a pic and I was happy to oblige myself in denying him. We also went to The Big Texan Steak Ranch, where I sat on stage and attempted to eat, in one hour, in front of the whole restaurant, a seventy-two ounce steak – plus a baked potato, a bread roll and a prawn salad. I'm saddened to say that I failed. I do pride myself on being a big eater but, the truth is, I'd barely eaten a thing since I'd left Charlottesville and I'm going to say that my stomach was out of practice. The last twenty minutes were torture, as my ability to chew and swallow deserted me; I eventually resorted to gulping the meat down whole with my Sprite. I had about four ounces left when the timer expired and then I ran immediately to the toilet and vomited it all back up. After which I was hungry. I ate almost nothing but steak during my time in Amarillo: breakfast, dinner and tea. The thing about those Texans, they sure know how to do hospitality, and they sure eat a lot of beef. I wonder if anyone's ever investigated a link between the two?

Chapter Ten

Fifteen days. Twenty-five rides. Two thousand miles. Put up and sheltered by seven people. Befriended by dozens more. It's been a week since I've had to use my tent – in fact, I've only had to use it twice on the whole trip – and it would be another five days before I got it out again, swept up this time by the hippy express that took me all the six hundred miles from Amarillo to Bisbee, Arizona, back down in my beloved desert where the cactus roam free and the rattlesnakes shake. I had wanted to see more of Texas and New Mexico but the offer of the ride was too good to turn down. Also, it was minus fourteen: time for some sun.

The way those hippies picked me up was pretty fantastic; I'd been walking along the highway for a few miles trying to reach a suitable junction when I saw this guy come running over towards me from upstream.

"Hey," he shouted, when he finally got within range, "you need a ride?"

I ran up to him and together we set off walking the road from where he'd come.

"We passed you back there but I couldn't pull over; did the first chance I got. Can't leave a brother in need, eh?" He had a beard. He was enthusiastic and friendly. He tells me he's a rock digger and has a van full of quartz. Turns out he was parked about half a mile away and had walked all the way back to come and get me.

It's staggering to contemplate something like that. I've had plenty of people stop when I wasn't hitching, and many that have driven out of their way; also quite a few that have done the old 'turnaround', got a mile or two up the road and decided that they did like the look of me after all and circled back. But Scott is the one and only, in all my days, that pulled over and *walked* to come and find me.

And into the van we pile for the two day trip down to good old Bisbee, which I happily declare just as funky and freaky as I remember it, and my new favourite town in America. There's just something about that place: it reminds me of fishing villages back home, brightly-painted houses piled on top of each other, impossibly steep slopes and rickety-ass staircases leading you maze like up and down the side of the hill that a group of men were once crazy enough to build their homes on. Bisbee was actually a ghost town for a while, till the hippies moved into those abandoned miners' shacks and reclaimed it to do their art and community thing. Now the tourists come to dig all that but still they can't spoil the vibe. It's magic. And Bisbee has one of the only roundabouts in America.

Scott thinks he might have some work for me digging quartz and so I wait around for three days to see what happens; nothing does. We smoke pot with his friends pretty much non-stop and that quickly gets old. Scott starts to get a little weird too. He tells me he's killed a guy and been inside; he shouts at his girlfriend and I think she should come away with me; and then he goes into a sort of pot-trance and just cackles for hours and hours and hours, surfacing only to say, "ching," and, "bong" and I think I've had enough.

I leave them to climb Mule Mountain and spend my first ever night camping out in the desert. I'm terrified of rattlesnakes and scorpions; all I can think about is them breaking into my tent while I sleep and killing me. But then I think, why would a scorpion go to all that trouble just to sting me? And why would a rattlesnake go out of its way to poison my ass if I wasn't doing it any harm? It doesn't make sense: they do those things for defence, not because they're hungry. In the event, I end up being terrified by a more obscure enemy: the javelina.

Scott had been the one to tell me about them: "they've got these pigs, man – well, they're rodents, but they look like pigs – and they've got these teeth like that" – and he makes some claws with his hands and a snarling face – "like fuckin' razors, I'm telling you. Tusks too. Sharp pointy tusks. And they can kill a man. I heard a story about a guy who got attacked by a whole fuckin' pack of them, tusked at his ankles and taken down, and then they went at him with those teeth." And there's that face again. "I wouldn't be camping out in those hills if I was you. Fuck the rattlesnakes, dude, it's the pigs you've gotta watch out for."

It's a fanciful story and I'm not buying it but in a bar the night I set off for my camp I see on the wall what looks like the head of a boar stuffed with the teeth of a lion. And sharp pointy tusks. And an evil glint in its unseeing eye. And that's when I realise that javelinas are real.

Still, I sleep good up there on that hill, grateful for some solitude and peace after a week of other people. When I wake up it's still dark and I lie there singing a song about how, "the inside of a tent is a wonderful thing," digging that I could be anywhere right now – that I could open the zipper to reveal a city or a mountain or an ancient civilisation and it's all the same to me – and that's when I hear this snuffling sound: a deep, gruff, powerful snuffling, and lots of it too. There are lots of snufflers out there. I peak timidly through my mesh window and I see them: a dozen dark-furred pigs, snuffling and prowling, and getting ever closer to my tent. They'll tear through that fabric in a second. I'm surrounded. I start to panic and wonder what I should do: I think about making a run for it but then I think about the dead, pig-massacred bloke and his ankles and I don't want that. Closer and closer they come, those little killing machines, those tusks, those teeth; soon I'll be chowed down on and every pig everywhere will have their revenge for all the sausages and bacon I've eaten.

I'm going to be a pig's breakfast. All I can think of to try and save myself is blowing on this harmonica some old RVing couple had given me a few days before. I blow and then they look right at me, right into the tent. They move closer. And then I blow and blow and blow and blow, and make an awful din, and they actually start to look startled. I keep on blowing and their little pig trotters begin to scamper away, and when they're all gone I fall on my back in my tent and thank my lucky stars for the expertly-timed gift that has saved me.

It's about a week before I learn that Scott has made the whole thing up and realise that javelinas are about as dangerous as your average Yorkshire Dales sheep. Which is not very dangerous at all. Unless you're allergic to wool.

I don't know what to do next: I feel like I've sort of come to the end of something. Three weeks ago I'd left Virginia with this goal of hitchhiking to Arizona and now there I was. But what to do when I got there? I hadn't thought that far. And I'd gotten there so quickly – about two weeks before I'd planned – it'd taken me completely by surprise. And it was just too goddamned easy, hardly a challenge at all. There's an emptiness about it that leaves me feeling pretty unsatisfied.

I try to up the ante by covering the thirty-five miles to Tombstone on foot; all that does, though, is give me blisters that cover half the soles of my feet and render me practically incapable of walking. I have to give up half-way and go back to the road, where I'm chagrined to be picked up once more by Scott and his girl.

"Couldn't make it then, eh?" he says and smiles, and in the back I will on Tombstone and my freedom from his ways. He wants me to ride to Tucson with him, help them with the quartz; I get out in Tombstone and pass the afternoon watching a high school baseball game and barely moving an inch.

I camp that night behind an empty house and sit there looking over the desert, across the rocky waste of scrub and tumbleweed and spiky, spiny trees. I decide to have a ceremony to say goodbye to my old New York Chinatown watch – the one I had fought so valiantly to keep hold of in jail that night – since she's long since given up the ghost, her face lost somewhere on the road, hands hanging apologetic and loose, strap in tatters. She's been with me through so much, right from before I was any kind of felon, before I'd slept homeless on a roof, before I'd stolen a girlfriend or wrecked anyone's car or destroyed a million friendships or pissed off a town. And she and I had been back and forth across this country three times now, twice by car and once by thumb, and now we were going our separate ways. I dug her a little hole and gave thanks, for her and for all we had seen.

I was patting the earth when I saw something approaching over the horizon: a strange circular light. It had an orange glow. It was enormous and growing bigger all the time.

"Holy shit," I said.

It was the moon.

It was the moon rising: I'd never even heard of such a thing. I sat and watched flabbergasted as it grew and grew, orange and bold and enormous out there at the edge of that empty dark desert. It really was the icing on the cake. And I knew right then that my time was up.

The thing was, when I saw that moon it was like I'd seen everything, like there was nowhere left to go. I'd accomplished everything I wanted to do and the only thing that remained was to go home. There was a sadness in that – the emptiness that comes when you turn the last page in a book – but also an acceptance: it felt like a very natural passing. And as I accepted that sadness I almost immediately became excited at the prospect of being once more in England, and about refinding my Britishness: cricket and tea, canal boats and biscuits; friends that could understand me; afternoons and nights down the pub and some decent comedy on the box for a change. There was so much for me to do there, and so much for me to do if I was to rediscover some semblance of a normal life after two years of wandering here and there and looking for some place to call home. But home was there all along. And, what's more, I still had my plane ticket, departing for London in exactly one month's time. Time enough to see what remained for me to see, and time too to visit Lauren in New York. But a future for us now was out of the question.

I felt resolved and reenergised by all this. I picked myself up and hobbled into town; found a bar and thought some more about my final month in America. Perhaps I still had time to hike the Grand Canyon – and I didn't want to leave there without seeing the Pacific highway and those giant redwood trees they have up there. That, though, was about it. I'd been through thirty-two states by that point. I'd seen enough.

My scribbling in my journal, as ever, attracted the attention of some of the others in the bar. I got talking to an old RVer, Roy; some good-natured banter about America and England, some stories from the road.

"Ah, you think you're tough, Englishman? I know a guy that'll whip you into shape. You think you're tough you should try him on for size." He's pretty drunk by this point. He reminds me of my granddad. I like him. "Ah, but you couldn't handle him, limey." And he laughs, and I laugh too. Not that I have any idea what he's talking about.

And then he gets all conspirational and serious and leans over into me and I take it he wants to tell me something important.

"Listen," he says, "really. If you're up for a challenge I know an old cowboy's got a ranch just down from here; he's looking for some young guys to train up and teach the ropes. He'll kick your ass so hard you won't sit down for a week. But if you think you can handle it he'll make a man out of you."

He tells me to come and see him in the morning and then leans back in his seat and squints at me, arms folded, smirking.

"Tough guy, huh, limey? We'll see about that."

Part Five

Monday 23rd March, 1998

Well I asks ya, what kind of A to Z would get you here? One minute I'm on my way back to England, the next I'm sitting in a knocked together wooden shack not even as big as my granddad's shed – my new home – and all of a sudden I'm a ranch hand and trainee stunt cowboy somewhere off in the scraggy desert just north of Tombstone, Arizona. It's a wild, wild ride…

So I went down to meet Roy that next morning and, sure enough, he gets me an introduction to this grizzled old cowboy with a slack-jawed expression and a complexion that looks like it's been soaked in gin, and I've never been so intimidated in my life. That's Big Gayle, apparently some ex-Hollywood legend of a stunt cowboy, the one who did all the rolls for John Wayne and the like, getting dragged along on ropes, tumbling out of stagecoaches, trampled underfoot. He's the real deal, this guy: he's got the boots, he's got the hat, he's got the belt-buckle. He wears his bright yellow long-sleeved cowboy shirt tucked haphazardly into his Wrangler's and he oozes menace. He looks at me totally disinterested and scathing and suddenly I don't feel like an adventurer at all, I feel very cleancut and English and I half expect him to grab my hands and peer into my too-smooth palms, toss them aside and say something about never having done a day's work in my life. He looks thoroughly disgusted with me. Roy tells him I want to learn the ropes, that I'm a hard worker. He raises his eyebrows.

"I don't want no freeloaders, limey."

I'm too scared to say anything in response.

"You don't pull your weight, you're gone."

And that's how I became a stunt cowboy for an upcoming wild west extravaganza. I've spent the last eight days learning how to fall off horses at speed; doing vaults and standing rides; leapfrogging into the saddle from behind; as well as all manner of mad and hare-brained activity guaranteed to have a man whomping to earth and left covered in cuts and bruises.

Gayle runs the stagecoaches up in Tombstone and he's got a bunch of other young guys who ride those for him and sell tickets. Carey and Chris are two brothers from Virginia; Carey's a big potato-headed guy, a bit gruff but also quite sensitive at times, and Chris seems to fancy himself as a bit of a philosopher. He's always saying stuff like, "listen limey, what you've got to remember is that no one's gonna remember you or anything you did in a hundred years' time," that sort of thing. And then there's Joey and Gilbert, and Gayle's seventeen year-old son, Jimmy, and a couple of girls, Chris's wife Bridget and Nicole, who's supposed to be one hell of a rider but is right now injured. And together we're all gonna put on this big show, doing tricks and riding bulls, and then teach other people the ways of the stunt cowboy; it's like Gayle and the others have this dream to keep these dying arts alive and it's all so exciting to be a part of.

Big Gayle's wife is also called Gail, and we all call her Little Gail or Miss Gail, and they sort of seem to hate one another, scream and shout and curse each other out to whoever the hell will listen. Gayle also has an older brother, Willy, a half-dead old mountainman who drinks more than the rest of the ranch combined and sits around drunkenly muttering to himself, lost somewhere in the Montana wilderness fifty years past, occasionally blurting out things like, "three thousand head of sheep!" and, "I did it all, goddamnit!" The man's a loon. Every now and then, though, something clicks and he starts telling us these stories – about trapping beaver in ten feet of snow and living on woodworm and squirrel; spending his thirteenth summer alone on a mountain with nothing but a flock of sheep; riding broncs and living wild on the range, billion acre ranches the size of a whole English county – and it all sounds so bygone and distant it's hard to believe that it was this same century.

Finally, there's Dave, a scrawny forty-something cowboy who stays back at the ranch and sorts things out here. Mostly I've been hanging out with him; I guess I'm his apprentice. So I follow him around and try to soak it all in, and get confused when he says things like, "go get me an eggbutt snaffle; hey, that ain't no eggbutt snaffle!" He spits and swears and calls the horses things like, "gunzel knotheads," and he's all right, is Dave. He's apparently been done for DUI on a horse once. He likes a drink.

Now I don't know what's come over me but I've been working like a man possessed. Dave's shown me the ropes but, to be honest, he doesn't get much done – what with the working day ending at about lunchtime when the drinking begins, and I really can't be arsed with that. Mostly I'm left to my own devices and so I've got stuck in trying to make this place look habitable: when I arrived there were piles of rubbish and crap and scrap metal and junk cars everywhere.

So I've dragged it all about and tidied the whole of the ranch yard up; and made a table and bench out of an old broken wagon wheel; and built a large porch from scrap wood and a bucket of rusty nails; unearthed the trees from beneath years worth of car parts; and swept and dusted and polished and hauled and, my word, I've got it looking good. I don't think I'll ever forget the glee on Miss Gail's face when I watched her step from the ranch house to take in what I'd done.

"My God," she said, "he's an artist! He's painting a picture! It's beautiful, limey, simply beautiful!" And then she spent the rest of the evening drunkenly grabbing whoever she could to show them.

I'm so glad someone appreciated the carefully considered angle at which I'd positioned my wagon wheel bench under the old mesquite tree.

I can't get enough of this work; I generally end up cursing the sun each day as it dips below the horizon and stops me, mid-stroke, hammer raised in hand atop roof. I go to bed every night tired and aching but enormously satisfied and fulfilled, and look forward to the next morning's sunrise when I can get up and feed the mules and collect the eggs and then get on with my hammering and my sawing. For the first time in my life I'm working without a care for the financial rewards and I feel richer than ever. The other day I heard Big Gayle call me, "the hardworkingest sonofabitch on the ranch" and I can't tell you how happy that made me feel. I think I want it on my tombstone.

Thursday 2nd April, 1998

A rather nice French-Canadian girl has appeared on the scene, her and her dog on a big cross-country trip. We all went out last night and I got my first drunk in over three months – had five bottles of Killian's – and it was all right. Justine and I made it into bed in due course; I loved hearing her accent. "Ooh," she said, "you are keeling me wiz your 'ands." She also had by far the biggest breasts I've ever seen: I think they were each the same size as my head and while I was deep down in them I kept thinking about this line from one of my dad's songs about a woman with "tits as big as the Bismarck's gun turrets" and it got real hard to keep a straight face. Good, though. Joey and Gilbert were a bit sick that I'd gotten in there first; Joey especially, as he doesn't have much luck with the ladies. His level of self-esteem is about as low as any man's I've ever met. I sort of feel sorry for him – and he gets the piss ripped out of him something rotten. Just because he looks like a monkey.

So I'm drinking again but still haven't had any liquor since my December the nineteenth fiasco, despite the enormous quantities that are being consumed all around me. Big Gayle and Willy were drunk by eleven the other morning, sitting on the porch with a bottle of Canadian Club while I sweated in the yard. I made a gutter for the main ranch house out of some old tin but then Little Gail threw a temper tantrum and jumped up and down on it shouting it wouldn't look right. She could have just said no.

Tuesday 7th April, 1998

Goodness, what a curious life I'm living: I never fail to amaze myself. Check this out: I've just returned from a six hundred mile daytrip to Texas, seemingly going nowhere but in a rather large and pointless circle, yet I feel as though I could well have travelled a couple of light years.

See, I never did shake off that feeling I had while looking over the desert the day before I happened upon the ranch. Indeed, despite enjoying all the horse play and hard work I had made up my mind about four or five days into this unexpected adventure that I would still be climbing aboard that plane back to England on the thirteenth of this month. I stayed on at the ranch for a number of reasons: firstly because I really wanted to get that place looking good; secondly, because I was still very happy there and learning a lot from some wonderful people; and thirdly, because I wanted to leave at the last possible minute so as to set up one final challenge on this American adventure – that of hitching the two and a half thousand miles to DC in under six days.

I got a ride with Miss Gail to Tucson and she dropped me off at the I-10 truckstop on that glorious road pointing east. Leaving had been hard – the friends, the piles of scrapwood I hadn't yet transformed – and it had taken a last minute toss of the coin to convince me that it truly was the right thing to do. Still, even as we were pulling out of the ranch my mind was filled with confusion and doubt, and when Miss Gail had said mournfully, "I can't believe you're just leaving," I couldn't believe it either; I joked about how she should order me to stay, her being my boss and all. But the truckstop gave me heart – the promise of the place so full of that feeling of movement I crave so much – and when the first guy I approached offered me a lift all the way to Houston I was on my way.

We set to talking. His name was Dan and he was totally unlike any trucker I'd ever ridden with before: he'd lived such a different and searching and inquisitive life. We talked openly and deeply and over the course of those first few hours he told me of his life full of extreme ups and downs, of many, many relationships, and of so many crazy tangents that had all turned out perfectly. I listened and it seemed to me like it didn't matter what a person did, that it was all just drops in the ocean, that it all worked out in the end. It was as though he'd rolled the whole thing out in front of me, like some magnificent Persian rug, so I could take it all in at once. I'd always imagined life was like a book that you wrote one page at a time, but listening to him it seemed more like a picture, always complete from the very beginning, always the only way it could ever be, but only revealed to us in small sections, only there to fully comprehend at the end.

We talked and we talked and as we rocketed through the Arizona and New Mexico desert I could feel something building inside of me: these realisations about the twists and turns of life; and an almost physical pain at the thought of never seeing those scenes of sagebrush and cactus again, each passing roadside marker like a stake to the heart, the miles signalling the ever-increasing distance between me and my belovéd ranch. Inwardly, I was weeping, anguished. I longed for a way to make everything okay.

Eventually my predicament came spilling out of me and the trucker gave his most welcome opinion.

"Listen," he said, "it doesn't really matter what you do now; at this stage in your life it's not going to make any real difference in the grand scheme of things. So what if you don't go back to England for another year? What's the hurry? And so what if you don't get your degree or start a career or meet a girl until you're twenty-six? There could be hundreds of women in your life. You might still have a lot of living to do before then." I nodded and agreed; and how coolly amazing and perfect it all was to have picked a ride with this guy at this time, right when I needed it the most.

"I'll tell you what," he said, "just make a list of all the reasons you want to go back to England and we'll look at them together."

I did. It was puny. And we laughed. We discounted them all immediately and there it was: I was on my way back to the ranch.

Dan dropped me off in El Paso and I spent the night atop a large sand dune criss-crossed with the tracks of a thousand desert beasties. I slept excited and light, at peace with myself and knowing that I'd made the right decision in turning back – and also the right decision in leaving in the first place. Now I knew for sure exactly where I wanted to be.

Wednesday 8th April, 1998

Breakfast talk: Niggers, coon-hunting dogs, the urinating habits of said animals, and why slavery was a good thing.

Now that I'm back and here to stay I set about making my home my home. I've moved out of that little wooden shack and into the place that Justine/Frenchie was staying in. It's actually about the coolest place on the ranch – half camper, half cabin – and I've already souped it up with a wood fire, electricity, heat, and even a teasmaid. I used to dream of teasmaids back when I was a boy flicking through the Littlewoods catalogue on my way to the shower section. And now I have one all of my own.

I called my mum later: well it has been two and a half months, ample punishment for her sending me such a lousy birthday card. Not that she was in the least bit bothered I'd waited so long to let her know I was still alive; she's pretty cool like that. She told me again she was never cut out to be a mother. Hard to argue with really.

She also told me that my dad had been trying to track me down and had got in touch with some people who knew about my legal case. Apparently they told him I'm no longer wanted and that all the charges have been dropped. I don't want to count my chickens until I get in touch with Stormin' but, I mean, holy fuckin' shit. Life is almost too wonderful for words.

Thursday 9th April, 1998

Breakfast Talk: The ninety-five percent alcohol fruit punch we just put together in preparation for Jimmy's seventeenth birthday bash tomorrow, plus AIDS and queers.

The younger guys on the ranch devote a surprisingly large amount of time to discussing and deriding gays. Why such a bunch of extremely homophobic people are so interested in homosexuality bewilders me, although it's not an exactly uncommon phenomenon. Probably something to do with repressed homosexual urges; that's how the theory usually goes. Back in South Elmsall I was often on the receiving end of gay jibes because of my long hair and unmasculine appearance – usually from some tight-shirted, muscle-bound, moustachioed meathead who looked a thousand times more gay than I ever could, and generally ended the night pretending to bum his friend over the pool table. Funny, that.

New guy Eddie made me laugh with his attempts to get tough and join in the bigotry: "if any of those queers come near me," he said, "they can suck my dick." A comment almost as ridiculous as his own feeble attempts to grow a moustache.

Unsurprisingly, I've landed myself in the position of ranch liberal; it wasn't exactly hard to earn this award. I think anyone who hasn't used the word 'nigger' six times before breakfast would be branded as left-wing here.

Friday 10th April, 1998

Breakfast Talk: Hairing stories and the upcoming Everclear-fuelled carnage.

After saddling up this morning the boys stood around talking about the peculiar practice of 'hairing': the act of restraining a fellow, putting ones hands in his pants, and tugging violently on his pubes. Hairing is a ranch tradition – everyone has to be haired sooner or later – and Jimmy got haired seventeen times for his birthday. I've escaped a hairing a few times by virtue of being the fastest runner here but I know it's just a matter of time. On the way to breakfast they tried again as we were all bunched together passing through the tool shed. Chris shouted, "everybody stop!" as though something serious was going down; I immediately fled. Fat little Eddie wasn't quite so lucky.

In a few hours there's going to be an interesting gathering of old cowboys, young ruffians, and high school kids in celebration of Jimmy's seventeenth. There'll be a bonfire and barbecue, but the main attraction will most likely be Carey's scary fruit punch, which at the time of writing contains five bottles of

Everclear (190 proof), three bottles of rum, and a bottle of Bacardi. Miss Gail ate one piece of fruit out of the barrel yesterday and reported to being "high as a kite" all afternoon. It's going to be quite some party.

Saturday 11th April, 1998

Breakfast Talk: Last night's festivities

Woke up this morning by the still burning fire and no one else around. The last thing I remember was Chris being lowered into the bonfire by Carey and Joey. He was trying to stick his dick in the flames in a bid to top my barefoot firewalk. My soles are covered in blisters.

So the merriment began with a chicken barbecue and some drunken horseplay. Normally we treat stunt practice very seriously; sometimes, with the help of alcohol, it turns into a free-for-all, slurred shouts of, "watch this," closely followed by the sound of someone ingloriously hitting the dirt. Big Gayle decided the time was right to teach Carey and Jimmy how to do a high speed collision. After three aborted attempts at what is obviously a very difficult trick Big Gayle staggered out into the middle of the shit pile, jam jar full of jungle juice clutched in his hand, and shouted that if they didn't get it right this time he'd fetch a two-by-four and beat them over the head. The sun was going down over the mountains to the west, a wonderful assortment of people were having a whale of a time, and an old cowboy was drunkenly shouting hilarious threats as two fantastic looking horses thundered towards each other at high speed, dust and hooves flying. It was one of the most memorable moments of my life.

We all trooped over to the new place for the party proper in an assortment of pickups and bigass cars, and even a semi belonging to a one-eyed trucker named Steve. The fire was lit, the barrel of juice opened, and the rest kind of took care of itself; the next few hours passed in one glorious drunken haze. Carey staggered about carrying a watermelon which contained a fifth of rum; Jimmy was lead into the brush to receive his birthday present from a lovely-looking Mexican girl; Bridget got totally legless for only the third time in her life; Big Gayle bowed out early, complaining that Little Gail was "pump-pumping" on his leg; and Little Gail went marvellously nuts, dancing around demented to the Lynard Skynard that blasted from the semi.

"Drink to Piglet!" someone shouted.

"Here's to Eeyore!"

And on and on it went.

I don't suppose, when I was a lad, I ever expected to find myself standing in the desert with a bunch of cowboys toasting the characters from Winnie the Pooh – but I did last night.

Sunday 12th April, 1998

Breakfast Talk: The multi-coloured bunnies Jimmy and Carey had painted for Easter. The rabbit pen is now full of stripy blue, red and yellow creatures. They also painted one of the doves.

Did the hay run with Eddie today, craftily ensuring that it would be just the two of us: I wanted to see a bit of sweat coming off his fat little face. Found that I probably don't dislike him quite as much as I thought. Either he's not such a bad sort or I'm getting over my usual, linked-to-the-birth-of-my-brother jealousy of being displaced as 'the new guy.'

Had to come through an immigration checkpoint on the way back – lucky for me I don't look Mexican. And that I'm pretty good at saying, "yup, I reckon" in a passable American accent.

Tuesday 14th April, 1998

The Wisdom of Gayle (am): "Goddamn, I thought the sumbitch was crippled but he just had his hair in his eyes…"

It was the kind of day that makes me question exactly why I love this desert so much, my morning task of erecting a greenhouse for Willy rendered comically impractical when a big gusting wind kicked in and blew my frame and plastic sheets all over the place, ripping them out of my hands just as I was putting the last nail in, sand swirling everywhere. I blow my nose and it's full of dust; I wash my hair and bits of cactus fall into the bath; the skin on my arms bear resemblance to the early stages of leprosy and my lips are parched and cracked despite three tubes of lip-balm and five litres of water a day. You've gotta be tough to survive out here: if you come across something that doesn't bite, prick, stick or sting you then it's probably a tourist. Or a pretend cowboy from Leeds.

Ah, but then the sun disappears, the winds die down, and a big fat moon rises slowly behind the mountains, illuminating the cactus-strewn landscape. All is quiet save for a distant coyote. Even a short stroll through this barren land never fails to leave one with the feeling of exploring uncharted terrain. There's a great, humbling comfort in the inhumanity of the desert.

The Wisdom of Gayle (pm): "That man's got mucho bucks; he'd hold onto a nickel until the buffalo shits…"

Wednesday 15th April, 1998

Drunken motherfucker Dave decided to get everyone up at ten past five with cries of, "c'mon people, we're burning daylight." After banging on my door three times he burst in and again told me to get up, and to make sure I wore my cowboy hat. He was having one of his superman drunks and felt that it would be a good time to break the new pair of big-headed mules. Prick. I can't stand Dave when he's arseholed. He doesn't act particularly pissed, he's just crazy. Poor sod reeks of a man desperately trying to prove to the world that he hasn't just let it all pass by. Chris often says that the worst thing you can do to a man is deny him his sense of importance but Dave has done it to himself.

Being around all these pitiful drunks and alcoholics has strengthened my resolve to stay sober enormously. I'm not saying I don't ever want to get drunk again; I just now realise that there is a right way and a wrong way to drink.

Meanwhile, Joey's balls have been swinging mighty big all day: since sunrise he's been joyfully proclaiming, "I'm gonna get laid tonight." Well, all power to the lad – it's been six months and it's nice to see a bit of swagger in his step.

Dinner Talk: Further recollections of Jimmy's seventeenth due to the polishing of off the jungle juice.

Yup, a couple of glasses of that have warmed me up nicely. My plans for the evening revolve around going to the dodgy karaoke place where Joey intends to get his balls wet. I've been rooting for that lad since day one – and now that he's finally going to get some I'm struck with an intense desire to be a complete cunt, swoop down, and take this mystery girl as my own. I'd love to do it, and for it to come across as a mere practical joke, though I shouldn't think it would. But I'm sure it's just a small stirring of the devil inside, letting me know he's still lurking down there. At least I hope that's all it is.

Meanwhile, Dave's on/off half-Cherokee girlfriend Shelley just stirred from an alcohol-induced snooze to burst in on Joey in the shower and scream, "hey Joey! Don't look at my ass; I'm gonna fuckin' piss"; and Justine is two parts plastered and getting that look in her eye; and Big Gayle has long since checked out, a hard day's whiskey behind him; and Little Gail and Nicole are running around like two giggling schoolgirls; and Dave's going on and on about spending twenty dollars on Shelley and getting nothing in return. It's seven p.m. and time for karaoke.

Thursday 16th April, 1998

The talk around the hitch rail this morning mostly concerned last night's sexual activities. Seems like everybody got some. Joey's woman, who I met last night – she was pretty rough, as expected – dropped him off in front of everyone to a great round of applause. Dave also climbed out of the car: he'd taken on the task of dealing with the 'ugly friend.' The last time I'd seen him had been on the dance floor where he was manfully attempting to cope with her substantial bulk. But Dave's not too fussy.

For my own part I'd decided not to sleep with Justine anymore. We were out drinking Jack 'n' Cokes and having a laugh and I told her that I didn't really enjoy sex. I told her I just didn't think I was that good at it and I'd rather play Scrabble – which is true. She obviously didn't believe me though. She made it clear she likes sex a great deal and wants more of it with me. She's still trying to talk me round when we get back to the ranch but I just go off to bed and fall asleep – well, within a minute she's there by my bed looking upset and saying, "I don't want to sleep alone." She looks like she's had a nightmare. I lift the covers and in she climbs – and immediately starts giving me head. Ho hum; it's okay. And then she gets on top and starts fucking me, by which time I'm sober and just lying there thinking, "I'm tired and I'm bored; I wish she'd go to sleep." The expression, 'going through the motions' has never been more apt. I feel cheap and disappointed with myself. Yet again I've compromised what I want and what I think is right to avoid denying someone else.

Friday 17th April, 1998

We roped the two new mules first thing this morning and set about breaking/taming/maiming them. The guys took the most stubborn one and embarked on a 'three legging': a temper control method in which one of the animal's back legs is drawn up towards its belly by a rope harness. The humans then set about tugging, pushing, punching and kicking in an attempt to literally bring the mule to its knees. Luckily I wasn't required to join in. I kinda like that mule.

Breakfast Talk: Joey's woman, who has already strongly indicated that she'd like to get married and have his babies. I'm told this affects most women who share a bed with an Appalachian-American.

Gayle returned from business dealings in Tucson – drunk, of course – with the news that everything regarding the wild west arena had been finalised and things were really going to start flying. This is great news indeed. For all the ambitious talk and grandiose plans the whole thing was balanced on a knife-edge and could quite easily have collapsed in a monstrous pile of horseshit. Funds have been scarily tight, investors have reneged, and green lights turned to red without so much as a whiff of amber. The tough guy exterior of the cowboy prevents these pressures from bubbling over, on the whole – Chris, however, who stands to lose the most, has been noticeably stressed, as has Bridget. Even Big Gayle was showing signs of doubt: too many setbacks, too many bills. It really looked like their dream was going to remain just that. But now…it's damned exciting to be on the inside of all of this; to be a part of this collaborative vision. These people are so good, so deserving of success – I can't think of a richer reward than the chance to help them achieve this dream. To hell with the wretched 'dirty paper.'

Saturday 18th April, 1998

And so it begins. I'm woken around five fifteen by Gayle and Dave, and within half an hour I'm over at the new place digging deep, dark holes so we can erect a billboard, just me and a shovel in the middle of the empty daybreak desert. It looks like Gayle's promise to "work the living dogshit" out of us is about to be fulfilled. Starting tomorrow we have to be ready for work by five.

Tuesday 21st April, 1998

I really hope it's the heat that's to blame for my irritable mood over the last few days: for some reason I seem to have been permanently cross, always angry but never knowing why. The flies, the dust, Little Gail's shrieking voice, Justine's ridiculous naivety and non-stop chatter – they're all conspiring to drive me nuts.

The object of my frustrations thus far today has been the way trash is handled around the ranch – basically, they just burn everything, aluminium cans included. Since I came here I've been making a fair bit of noise about recycling and have set up bins around the place to make it easy for everyone else, but it just seems impossible: nobody cares. Dave, who sympathises more than most, at least uses the bins – yet I've been out driving with him and watched him toss dozens of cans into the desert without even a second thought. I feel like I'm fighting a losing battle. I feel stupid, and I feel sick. I might recycle a hundred cans today but I bet I'll see more than that laying by the side of the road on the way to the depot. I know I can only do my best but, it just doesn't seem like it's enough.

And there's a flip side – there always is – for who am I to tell these people that they should be recycling? I don't know where these cans go, who benefits from it, or whether it's even good for the planet (which I'm convinced is doomed anyway). Really, I'm recycling because I've fallen victim to the media monster that I constantly vilify. And I never asked why.

But I'm gonna go on. I'm gonna try and get the others involved. Fighting through my cynicism I find a shining light. It's a lesson in the selfless, and the seemingly rewardless, and I'd like to learn how to get good at that.

Wednesday 22nd April, 1998

Here's what I did today:

- Awoke still clutching the letter Lauren sent me a few days ago. I must've passed out in the midst of re-reading. She says she loves me. A lot.
- Fed the horses and the chickens and the rabbits and the pigs and the mules, and sang them the theme tune to Scooby Doo, as usual. I love those morning hours, piling hay into the feeders, having little conversations with

the animals, watching the sun rise up over the Dragoon Mountains. It amazes me to see such beauty – and to watch as the mules chow down on their hay with their backs to it. I mean, why don't they appreciate it too?

- Went for a long bike ride and sunned my naked arse in the desert for a couple of hours. Life everywhere. Went looking for rattlesnakes and had fun with a bunch of roadrunners, and chased a javelina too.
- Learned that there's apparently no money for the arena and the whole thing has pretty much fallen through.
- Sat and watched the first truly awesome sunset since I got here. A monstrous mass of cloud hung heavy in the air above me, beautifully painted and re-painted by the departing sun, which, for once, had been allowed the freedom to create by a clear horizon. Justine interrupted my wonderful solitude and, of course, started yakking. I'm going to be really, really rude to her in the very near future.
- Big Gayle discovered that the seeds I've been planting outside my shack were to produce flowers and not food. He told me that I couldn't water my little garden. I told him that I'd piss on it instead.

Thursday 23rd April, 1998

I'm seething. I feel like I'm about to explode. Something is very, very wrong. I can't stand to hear most people talk; even distant voices feel like a drill to the head. Nothing's working – everything I try to do is laborious and pointless and endlessly frustrating. The other day I tried to fix the water in my cabin; after a couple of hours of sweatily wrangling with pipes and tools all I had succeeded in doing was flooding the place and breaking one of the windows.

What the fuck is wrong with me?

I'm hot, and that does seem to have something to do with it. But I'm supposed to like the warmth [I just wanna say, "shut the fuck up! You sound so fuckin' stupid. Stop talking! Waffling alien mumbles like a bee in my ear! Die, you stupid old fuck!] [now I'm laughing, 'cos for sure this is a bad joke. It's noon, Big Gayle and Willy have been on the tequila, and Willy's off on another planet spouting ridiculous streams of bullshit. I want to kill him.]

Yup, I feel like I may be going mad.

Friday 24th April, 1998

Mood excellent. Got back to what I really enjoy about this place – building and cleaning and dreaming. Trying to forget about all the fighting and business worries. Maybe it'll all fall to shit and I'll be on the road again. But s'all cool by me.

Later on, Miss Gail, her nephew Joel, Nicole and I got completely messed up smoking weed – which means I've now been stoned with everyone on the ranch excepting Willy and Big Gayle, who despises the stuff so much that he'll

149

fire anyone he finds partaking. As far as he knows, we're all very clean in that regard. At some point in the evening Gail stripped down to her lingerie and was being very suggestive and flirty – but it was all wasted on me: I was so fucked up I think my only contribution to the evening was to repeatedly bellow, "eat the chicken, man!" and eat a dollar bill when a friend of Joel's annoyed me with his money talk.

Tuesday 28th April, 1998

Money has reared its ugly head once more, despite my greatest efforts to resist. It started when I looked and saw that Dave was getting paid a full day's wage, though he wasn't doing even a fifth of the work I was. Suddenly I was filled with a longing for the green stuff. But why? Why do I need a couple of pieces of paper in my pocket to feel satisfied? I don't know – I just want it.

Do you ever look around and notice just how much importance people put on money? Like, to actually listen to a conversation – even one which is supposedly about an act of generosity; it always comes down to money. How did it happen? How did we come to worship the green god? It makes no sense.

For about an hour this evening I slipped back into my puzzling black mood. I couldn't bear to hear the voices and words of those around me, and spoke only to take issue with whatever bullshit they were spouting. I could feel my face forming vicious snarls as I talked, and fought desperately to subdue my anger. When I snapped at Willy and told him to shut up I knew I had to escape for a while and went for a satisfying run. Most of the people around me are either stupid or drunk.

I sometimes forget just how stupid some people are. Over the past few days I've been spending a fair amount of time with Joey's younger brother, Jake. Jake is a very sweet, kind-hearted guy, but truly as dumb as a box of bricks. Things which I wouldn't ever imagine could cause difficulties simply don't register with the lad; things such as not comprehending exactly how hard it would be for two guys to carry a one tonne bale of hay. Or that I didn't have to learn English when I came to America.

Then again Jake is about as happy as anyone I've ever met. I envy him a great deal. Intelligence is so overrated.

In the evening I indulged in a little escapism and managed to get more stoned than I ever have. It was just what I needed. I laughed like an idiot for hours and then had a very realistic fantasy that I was a fly. When your only concern in life is licking your limbs and going, "bzzzz," everything seems somehow simpler.

Friday 1st May, 1998

Sometimes I think I've come a fair way – then, occasionally, I believe I'm just as dumb and obnoxious as I ever was. Last night I waited tables in Tucson for

Miss Gail's sister; afterwards I smoked a load of pot, got pissed on cheap beer and Carlo Rossi, and then caused a naked nuisance in someone else's swimming pool. Sound familiar?

Oh, but it was fun...wasn't it?

I'm trying very hard to find a reason to live a life of something more than drunkenness – something more than Lauren's Bukowski dream – though there are times when it seems like an awfully good idea. I mean, drinking's fun, and blacking-out is an absolute riot, and having days disappear as though they never existed is surely as good a way as any to fill the time between birth and death, right? I sincerely hope not. But I'm far from sure.

Saturday 2nd May, 1998

Dreamt I angrily told Big Gayle to suck my cock. He tried to attack me but I ran away then spent what seemed like hours hiding from a large variety of people. These dreams are getting way too repetitive.

On the way home from Tucson Justine asked me what I thought of her – what I really thought of her. I told her that I was well impressed with her ability to skin rabbits but that she was arrogant, boring, talked too much without ever really saying anything, and probably knew about one percent of what she actually thought she did. I did warn her not to ask me.

Sunday 3rd May, 1998

Change is afoot. Last night I punched a mule for a relatively minor offence; this morning I did a three-legging and didn't find it an unenjoyable experience. I see this shift happening before my eyes and there's nothing I can do, because I don't feel I have to do anything. But what am I becoming?

Monday 4th May, 1998

Now Scott the scary hippy I rode with from Amarillo to Bisbee had a book. It was a book containing the letters of a remarkable young man, Everett Ruess, who spent the majority of four years exploring the canyons of northern Arizona and southern Utah back in the early thirties. He did this alone, save for a burro or two, and lived largely on his wits. He disappeared in 1934, aged twenty. His letters were inspiring and thought-provoking: there was so much in there that I felt myself, so many parallels and stirring ideas. I'm truly in awe of what this guy did, and at the same time overwhelmingly envious.

See, this kid just *took off*. He bought a burro for eight bucks and started walking. Sometimes he'd hitch rides – him *and* his donkey – and sometimes he'd meet Indians and have a little chinwag and a bite to eat. But mostly he was just free to come and go wherever he pleased, up and down canyons, off and out there in that remarkable wilderness. And I really, really wanna do that too.

But I've been in the desert and these days it's all fenced off: somebody – whether it be a farmer or the Bureau of Land Management – owns all of it and they don't want you or your donkey wandering around. There's probably laws against it. You probably need to have a permit for your donkey, or pay tax on it, and it's just not fair.

Just maybe, though, the fences could be skirted, and the laws could be adhered to, and the bullets of irate idiots who don't even know why they're irate could be avoided; just maybe a cocky young fool with more arrogance than brains could do something similar in these more progressive times.

Carey owns two donkeys. Apparently they're good for nothing, stubborn sumbitches who – though he paid about a hundred dollars apiece for them – are destined for the cooking pot. Unless, that is, I can lead one of them – the jenny – over the three mile road between the new place and the ranch. If I do this – which, according to those in the know, can't be done – then she'll be mine. Carey and I have made a bet. And I'm going to win this bet. And then she and I will be Utah bound.

Wednesday 6th May, 1998

Two beautiful new horses arrived on the ranch today. According to Gayle they're "good, broke stock" – though, as anyone who's been here for longer than a week will know, that's at best optimistic, at worst, a lie. Sure enough, Jimmy was quickly bucked and dumped by the gelding, and I, trying to catch the mare, had a pair of hoofs laid on my arse – one on each bumcheek. That was my first real kicking – though one of the dumbass mules did aim a mighty hoof at my head the other day, fortunately getting caught up in her harness and missing me by inches. That could have been nasty.

Also today I did a slightly naughty thing: I drove one of those wonky-eyed dogs of Dave's about five miles out into the desert and ditched him there. Sonofabitch mauled my camera.

Thursday 7th May, 1998

And so, again, I watched myself fall into a horrid mood born of frustration and confusion and, today, there's no point in trying to deny it – it's the ranch that has been the cause all along. Things aren't the way I expected or hoped they would be. Stunt training has been non-existent and I haven't done any real work since the day Gayle woke us up at five with the promise that from now on in we wouldn't be getting a chance to wipe our arses. In reality, I was wiping my arse about six hours later and I haven't stopped since.

This place...it's like living in a fucking circus – and the supposed ringmaster is the biggest clown of all. The days are an endless mess of chaos: the IRS, the town council, the neighbours – even the local retard – are all baying for blood and money and there isn't a dime to spare. Especially after the daily beer run has been taken care of.

Of course, Big Gayle never really gets too worried. His whole empire has become horribly over-extended and fallen into ridiculous debt and all he can do is sit and watch westerns all day long. I can see no way out, save for a brave or stupid investor, or a massive, unified effort from us lot. At the minute, though, I think it'd be pretty hard for us to agree on the colour of the sky.

See, what I never realised was that nobody really likes anybody. And I mean nobody. Finally, it sunk into me just how widespread and destructive the lack of cohesiveness that exists here is when Chris disclosed, very bravely, that he really couldn't stand Big Gayle at all. This was a huge shock; for all the shit that's talked about supposed-friends, and all the barely-hidden resentment, I never imagined that Chris could feel this way towards his mentor.

Nobody likes anybody. *Nobody* likes *anybody*. Jimmy dismisses Chris's horsemanship and Chris returns the favour; Big Gayle tells Willy, "these boys can't ride for shit" while saying nothing but the opposite to their faces; and Dave plots behind his hero's back and fantasises about taking over the ranch following its inevitable collapse. It's a complete and utter mess.

And me. I sit and watch and say, "oh" as, one after the other, my friends and co-workers tell me just how dumb or drunk or useless everyone else is. I listen and get more and more upset and frustrated and there's really nothing I can do other than to become more upset and frustrated or leave.

I mean, how can I care, when nobody else does?

You know what I really liked about this place? I liked building, and playing with the junk, and riding the horses and jumping on them and falling off; stuff I haven't done in a while. I've had all my enthusiasm sucked out of me by the laissez-faire attitude of those around me. You can only smile in the fat face of despondency for so long.

Also today I found out I'm to lose my home: my beautiful little piece of shit trailer is to be burnt to a cinder because of the two main reasons that this place is doomed to failure – bureaucracy and a worn-out old man.

One of the annoying bastards who lives in the valley decided to bring a county surveyor down here and inspect all our buildings. And, of course, the three trailer homes that sit around the ranch – on private land, harming no-one – were deemed illegal and needed to be brought up to code. Well, despite the fact that they're all perfectly good for our purposes there's no way that that's going to happen – that would take money and effort – and Gayle has stated his intention to, "torch the fuckers." It breaks my heart to see such waste.

Sunday 10th May, 1998

Mood today: Good, exasperated, rotten, disappointed, optimistic, determined, ecstatic, fatigued, okay.

I woke up and things were better. I don't know why, they just were. I suppose the news yesterday that Gayle was simply going to build around my trailer, thus preserving my one salvation had a lot to do with it. As long as I have my place then things can't ever be that bad.

I fed the chickens and took the eggs to the house. Gail and Bridget and Nicole were talking about funny dreams and it was nice. But...

When I emerged from the house I looked across the ranch yard to see EVERYBODY – and that's EVERYBODY – standing around, and looking into, and poking and prodding the trailer half of my home. I ambled across and said, "what's going on?" – though it was clear that someone – obviously Big Gayle – had decided that six thirty on a Sunday morning was the perfect time to demolish my trailer. And, of course, the boys had to join in 'cos they just love to FUCK THINGS UP.

Yes, they do.

They were swarming – infesting – buzzing around my home, like so many flies. So what that all my possessions were still in there? So what that the whole exercise was completely pointless? I just didn't get it. See, it turned out that all they were doing was seeing if there was room to drag the thing out from beneath my porch. And all they succeeded in doing was collapsing the roof and deciding that, "yes, there would be room" when the time is right. Knowing this place, that time is unlikely to come any time soon. Now I've got to try and sleep in a trailer with an unstable roof hovering about eighteen inches above my head.

I still don't get it. No, actually I do. The ones who thought it was a good idea are simply stupid – the rest just tagged along looking for something to hit with a hammer. I'm flabbergasted.

No matter what goes on around here – all the stupid arguments and ridiculous business practice and drunken nonsense – I could always count on being able to retire to my little sanatorium and find peace. I can tend my flower garden (or rather, dirt patch containing seeds which will not grow); I can go around back and listen to the oldies drift through the window as I gently swing in my hammock reading, surrounded by my ever-increasing collection of funky little ornaments which adorn my 'back garden' (formerly a bunch of refrigerators, tyres and crap, crap, CRAP).

No more, motherfuckers, you have crossed the line. You have killed me.

As you may have guessed, I'm drunk.

So now I must dash: yup, it's time – for I have a donkey. Oh yes, for sure I wasn't gonna leave this place without at least trying to catch that little black bitch from across the road. And – oh! This section would be really good if I could remember what I was thinking and feeling at the time; if I could be arsed to be…arsed. Hey!

What?

Nothing.

Me and a donkey, alone in the desert, just like Jaws except with sand for water and a donkey instead of a shark. Oh, and me instead of…mmmm; that's a tough choice – I mean, I suppose Robert Shaw's the coolest, but he gets eaten and I'm not really the type to get eaten by a donkey. Obviously Richard Dreyfuss is out. That leaves old Roy Boy, who did look pretty good in that movie, though his nose is a bit dodgy…oh, I don't know. I think I'll be Mayor Quimby – in a bath.

Have you ever tried to lead a wild donkey? I mean: ho-lee shit, those little bastards are stubborn. I soon realised why Carey and Gayle and all the others laughed at me when I told them I was going to drag that bitch over to the ranch and make her mine. The first two hundred yards were taken one-step-at-a-time; here's how it went: I'd yank on her head for a few minutes until she stumbled forward, before planting herself again like a rock. This was repeated with only minor variations – sometimes she'd take two steps; sometimes she'd recapture four or five; and sometimes she'd suddenly decide that she didn't want any part of this and try and stomp my head into the ground. It was slow – torturously so – but we were making progress.

I'd say it took me at least forty minutes to get her two hundred yards up the road, and though I had another three miles of this shit I felt pretty optimistic. I always figure that if you can do something to the value of x then it shouldn't be too hard to manage x to the power of ten. And why not? If you're able to hitch one mile you can hitch ten thousand miles; if you can make three dollars you ought to able to make three million. In theory, of course (or, more correctly, in the unimportant ramblings of an unimportant rambler). And it was cool – and it *was* a little bit like Jaws – the sun and the endless blue sky and all the other desert stuff I've mentioned a million times before. Yeah, fuck it – it was cool.

Donkeys are cool too; I've gone off mules. Mules are dumb – 'cos the thing with mules – and even horses – is that they're really fucking BIG, and could quite easily say, "fuck you," drop a killer paw on your head and disappear off to a life of frolicking. But they don't 'cos they're stupid. Donkeys are tiny but they do not take any shit, and if they don't want to go somewhere then – by God – you're gonna have to drag 'em. And they will have a go at you too. Big respect for donkeys.

But back to the story. Two hundred yards up the road my donkey, who was beginning to show signs of improvement, took off, and took me with her. I think I must've taken my eye off her for a second, which was just long enough for her to whip my feet out from under me and career off into the sagebrush.

I fought, friends, oh I fought, but she was too strong. Soon I'd been dragged head first through a Mesquite tree and bounced along on some nasty big rocks. Definitely time to let go of the rope. And as I did so I remembered the one that

I had stupidly tied to my jeans in the hope of preventing her running. Thank God my slipknots aren't what they used to be. With a couple of parting shots from her hind-legs my Jenny left me lying there in a bruised and dazed mess.

Damage report: nasty cut on top of foot; large amount of severe grazing of the lower back; bruised right bumcheek; and...(c'mon, there must be more)...

Donkeys are really, really stubborn. And so am I.

I re-caught her and again we headed back on up the road. It was just as painfully slow and frustrating as the first time; this time, however, I was ready for her. And soon enough we progressed from two dragged steps, to six or seven semi-voluntary ones, to a period where I lost count at around fifty. All the time I was offering my best encouragement to my new friend – "c'mon, Jenny, good girl, Jenny, good girl, who's a good girl, then?" – and I really felt we were getting to know one another. At one point she seemed to be scared of something – more scared than usual – and she tucked her head under my arm until the danger had passed. That was really touching. She'd still be rearing up at whatever imagined demons flutter through the empty mind of your average donkey, and still be locking-up every now and then for no apparent reason, but we were on our way.

The last four-hundred yards were almost as painstaking as the first – my Jenny had forgotten all about how good she could be and was playing 'pet rock' once again. But we finally stumbled into the ranch, three miles and four hours after setting off. Oh boy.

Monday 11th May, 1998

Everyone should have a donkey. Everyone should be able to wake up and feel what I felt on this fine mid-May morn.

I have a donkey.

I leave the land of dreams and see those three words emblazoned across the front of the inside of my head and I don't feel any trace of the reluctance usually experienced when re-entering this world. There is no, "ho hum – another bloody day"; only hope, expectation, and pure, unadulterated joy. I'm happy to be alive, and it's all thanks to a mute, unforthcoming, expressionless little animal with a pocketful of promise.

My donkey hates me and with good reason: I stole her away from a life of luxury; a life of aimless wandering and carefree sex. I tore her from her best friend and lover; dragged her from her home and stuck her in a strange, unfriendly place, and she has no idea why. Now I have to earn her trust and friendship and that's not going to be easy. My own instinct is to be as nice as possible and hope that she can return the favour; some of the others reckon my best bet would be to tie up her back legs and yank them from under her whenever she disobeys my desires.

Surprisingly – very surprisingly – Big Gayle has offered his help in training up my jenny. Even more surprisingly he seemed positively taken with my idea of walking with her into the canyon country of the Four Corners. He gave me many tips, offered to show me how to make a pack saddle, and related a tale of how he and Willy were once going to take a similar trip along the Continental Divide, only Willy went and got drunk and lost all their money. It's normally incredibly hard to get Gayle to share his knowledge – it took Carey three years perseverance for him to start teaching stunts – and though he has come out of his fatigue-induced retirement of late it's obvious there is so much more he isn't telling us. I must've got lucky – sitting on the porch with Gayle and a few others I said something like, "well, I'd best go get me a book on donkeys" and Gayle exploded into life, stating that he was the book, by God, and I'd better not forget it. I'm sure if I'd come straight out and asked him I wouldn't have gotten past first base.

Gayle's first exercise used a squaw bridal – a rope halter which runs through the animal's mouth; when you want them to do something, such as follow or turn, a quick tug on the rope – and therefore their lips and gums – is supposed to do the trick. I did it but I didn't like it. I want her to be able to trust me and do the things I ask of her out of love and respect, not fear. I felt so bad for my jenny, to see that thing in her mouth. Sorry, Jenny.

I guess I'm in love with my donkey. I find nothing more exciting than the prospect of patiently working at our friendship. I find nothing more fulfilling than sitting with her for a few hours and seeing – ever so slowly – that first glimmer of trust. I cannot imagine a more mouth-watering prospect than the proposed expedition Jenny and I will soon be embarking upon. This is going to be something really special.

And there's more: Dave is almost certain that my Jenny is expecting! Can't you just see it? The three of us trekking merrily along through the ridiculously beautiful country of the Four Corners like some demented happy family, Jenny and I turning to answer Junior's cries and laughing together as he hurries to catch up, stumbling over his enormous ears and doing somersaults or something equally as cute. Fantasy Island is a wonderful place.

Friday 15th May, 1998

She's coming along – it's just taking a little more time than I thought it would. I'm doing my best though. I take her treats like pancakes and pears for when she's been good and I've adopted a totally non-violent approach, even though she's had a go at kicking me, as well as biting me. The other night I slept in the corral with her for a few hours.

Big Gayle's disgusted with my techniques and has stopped helping me. Now when he sees me he mutters things about me being a, "goddamned know-it-all sonofabitch." Ho hum.

Been reading The Dice Man by Luke Rheinhart.

Saturday 23rd May, 1998

A week. A week. A week.

A weak week.

A lot can happen in seven days.

Sometimes.

Three and six, and I'm freed from one of the self-imposed chains hanging around my neck. Free, but still sick. No happier, no less happy, and certainly not more unhappy. So it's ok.

Yeah, it's ok. A minor detour – an alternate route to here.

And here I am: bored.

I'm bored, I'm bored, I'm bored. I wish it were the sixties, I wish we could be happy, I wish I wish I wish that something would happen. There's nothing to do but listen to the wind tear through my unbuilt house, fight the unwinnable war with the cursed flies, and to look into the deep, dark pits of my Jenny's eyes and plead with her to be just a little nicer.

A hundred people last year, a thousand this. Keep moving, keep grooving – motion is all. Motion is all.

Who says it can't be like this? When was it decided that we have to rush out, invest everything in one outfit and wear it – and nothing else – with a feigned pride, even when the elbows and knees have fallen out and we've become sick at the sight of ourselves in the mirror? A different pair of gloves every week – different hands, even. It's the only logical course of action.

And why am I surprised when I say, "I don't know who I am"? How could I? I don't even exist.

Everybody's schizophrenic. Everybody's got a million different people inside themselves.

I'm sick, I'm sick, I'm sick. Everybody wants to get busy – but counting money makes me fuckin' dizzy. Isn't there some other way we can measure ourselves as men? Where the hell did this thing come from?

Jake, Jake, dear, sweet, stupid, doomed Jake turns to me and tells me – before he took his dear, sweet, stupid, doomed eighteen year-old ass back to Virginia to fight for custody of his doomed daughter – that he believes a man has to better himself wherever he goes, and my face brightened. And then it fell. "I mean," he said, "if you go from six-fifty, you wanna be moving up to seven, seven-fifty…and then to eight." What the hell does this mean? What do these stupid, meaningless numbers have to do with anything? Does anything happen without money in mind anymore?

It's everywhere I turn. It seems there is no escaping it. A few days ago Dave was telling me about battling forest fires in Oregon; it sounded like a pretty interesting, exciting and rewarding job. I told him so. "Yep, that was a good job," he stated, and then proceeded to tell me exactly how good it was – or, more precisely, how good *the pay* was.

I don't get it. I really, truly don't get it at all. I don't think I ever felt so rich as I did during my first month here, when I did honest work for bed and board. God, that felt good – and so what if it all turned to shit – such a tonic to the ridiculous world of the waiter, five or six dollars for delivering a plate, ten bucks for popping a cork, a twenty for smiling inanely and having a nice accent – what the fuck is that all about? This is true: I often used to feel guilty about walking away from an average night's lazing with what millions of people slave away for weeks for. It just didn't make sense.

It makes even less sense now.

Give in. Give in. Shit, it has to happen. The concept of money is ridiculous and misguided – so what? You've got to have it. Your ambitions and goals aren't practical and don't fit in with the guidelines of society? Tough – find some that do; there're plenty out there.

Give in. Give in. Give in.

I'm great, I'm great, I'm great. I live my life for the stars that shine; people say it's just a waste of time.

Well, fuck 'em.

Friday 29th May, 1998

Enough is enough. This is no kind of life for an adventuresome young lad such as myself. It's been almost three weeks since anything out of the ordinary happened and that's just too long. Time to move on.

It's the same old story, really – boy finds place, boy falls in love with place, boy realises he can't stay in one place for more than a month and gets all pissed off and disillusioned and hateful of those around him – and then takes himself off and repeats the whole thing all over again. It's a shame the future's so bright right now otherwise I could quite happily get all self-pitying and depressed.

So what to do? Well, I've pretty much given up on my plan to walk nearly eight-hundred miles with my donkey. Firstly, though I love her dearly, she really isn't the ideal ass to be taking on such a long hiking trip. Way too independent and strong-minded to succumb to my demands, with just enough brain to know that she doesn't have too. The best I've managed from her is a short ride on her back – which I thought was going pretty well until she decided to ignore my directions and walk straight under a spiky, scratch-inducing tree. And then walk around and around it, underneath the branches, just in case there was a part of my face and arms that wasn't bleeding. Suffice it to say, that was that. Ah well, there's plenty more donkeys in the sea.

I'm disappointed that it's not going to happen. I feel like I've let myself down. And now that that's gone I'm not really sure what to do with myself: there are too many options and as I stand at this crossroads trying to figure which road to take I feel hopelessly lost and displaced. And it's not because I find any of the options frightening but rather the opposite – they're all terribly exciting: the world is, quite literally, my lobster. It's indecision born out of choice. And isn't this one of the problems with today's society? That everything is available to us; that we can go anywhere and do anything, and be whatever we want to be? That's a daunting prospect.

So where shall we go? And who shall we be? My grandfather, and probably all his predecessors, wouldn't have faced this problem. They were miners and men; their wives women and mothers – and was it really so horrible? Are we happier now because we're free? My granddad never saw the Grand Canyon, never got to sit atop a mountain overlooking the Pacific, never got to experiment with his self in the way that I can – and yet...I wonder if he ever sank to the depths of despair that I regularly do, simply because I haven't the foggiest idea who I am or why I'm here.

What's the key to happiness? Being satisfied with what you have, I suppose. My granddad grew up knowing that he was destined to be a miner, and he fulfilled that. He grew up knowing that men were men and he knew what that meant: working hard and coming home to a cooked meal and looking after the wife. And what of the woman? She grows up knowing that one day she'll be married and that she'll be taking care of her husband's needs, get bred once in a while, feed the kids, do the housework and maybe get to play out with the girls, if she's lucky. We mock this style of existence and are thankful for the progress that has allowed us to move beyond it – but how many of us would trade this so-called freedom for the comfort of knowing our place.

Pressures. Pressures of society, of upbringing, of self. Pressures to become more than a worker and a half of an okay partnership. I wonder if my former school chums in South Elmsall – the ones who took the nineties equivalent of my grandfather's life – think and hurt and hate as I do. Work, pub, work, pub, work, pub – if that's your expectation of life and you achieve it, can it ever really be a bad thing?

And I thought I was being so clever by rebelling against the Elmsall tradition of marrying your high school sweetheart, moving into a grotty little council house next-door-but-one to your parents, and getting a job on the factory floor. And eating fish 'n' chips on a Friday. And growing a moustache. And having fights down the pub, and looking forty when you're twenty-three, and turning out stupid kids and then shouting at them for a bit before you die.

Oh no, sir, not I.

But hey, what am I gonna do? Move to a shitty little living ghost-town and satisfy myself with alternately staring at a bloated, boring wife and a conveyor belt? I don't think so.

Sunday 31st May, 1998

Mañana is the day; I've just got to mail some stuff back to Robin's for safe-keeping, sell my donkey for seventy-five dollars to a couple in town, and then I'm off. Back on the road. Back to my glorious thumb.

Part Six

Chapter One

And so the first of June I hit the road in some style – a madman in a bright yellow convertible fashioned from a combination of Volkswagen Beetle and vintage BMW motorcycle tearing through the desert in his goggles and handlebar moustache – and everything was different. The monster pack that I'd dragged from Virginia was pared down to the bare minimum, light and easy on my back, no longer blister-inducing or filled with those extraneous items such as walkman and Scrabble dictionary and too many changes of clothes; every time I travelled I found that I could take less and less and yet I always had more than I needed. And the weather was bright and hot and no longer the snows and rains of that in-comparison bleak and weary Virginia slash Tennessee winter. And I was different too: my head refreshed and alive and even though two months previous I had thought I was done with America and ready to return to the normal life in England now all I could think of was that great American west, its open roads and deserts and canyons, a glorious route up through Arizona, across that Grand Canyon by foot, and then into the wonders of Utah and Wyoming and Montana and that great mashed potato mountain scraped out by Richard Dreyfuss's fork. And finally, my dream to cross the Rockies by freight and go all the way into the holy Hendrix city of Seattle before doing that Pacific Highway right on down to San Diego and – who knows who and what I'd be by then? Where was England in my thinking? It was all America and road and thumb.

Ah, what bliss when that first ride dropped me off at the intersection of I-10 and US-191 and once again I was suddenly out there in the middle of nowhere, hiking off up the road and surrounded by three hundred and sixty degree views of the desert and mountains all around, silence looming and a man alone with a backpack containing everything he requires for happiness. I walked those first few miles and let the recent troubles and dirt of the ranch fall from my shoulders and breathed it all in: stunning is the word. They say in London you're never more than fifty feet from a rat; well out here, in my effortlessly gorgeous Arizona, it appears you're never more than fifty feet from breathtaking beauty. And what better way to see it than with the independence of the thumb? I want to walk, I can; I want to hop down to the road, I can; I want to just camp here for the night and soak it all up, I can; I want company, I want solitude, I want exercise, I want speed; I can I can I can.

I spent my first night wrapped in the warmth of an incredibly kind and giving Mormon family of thirteen children – five of them adopted – and they took me in as one of their own. Chris, about nineteen, had picked me up on the dark highway and insisted I come home to meet mom and pop and eat some dinner and stay. They were so good and happy I even actively enjoyed saying grace and started to wonder if maybe this organised religion lark wasn't such a bad idea after all. I left their place in the morning with a dedicated Book of Mormon – "we're all brothers," wrote Chris in the front, which I thought quite sweet – and, man, I was feeling *love*.

And less than twenty-four hours after leaving the ranch, and still rejoicing with the love bestowed upon me by those smiling Mormon faces I sat perched high up on a scrambled cliff overlooking the funky little ex-mining town of Superior far, far below, and, for all intents and purposes, I was king of the world. I could have fit that town in the palm of my hand. I sat and stared out into the world and I knew no man had ever been so free or content; the world and all its goodness was mine and in me. Free.

My next plan was to take a short stroll across one of America's most forbidding wildernesses, the Superstition Mountains. It's a place about as desolate and far away from human life as it's possible to get in the lower forty-eight states. What I had in store for me was forty-three miles of wild canyon and desert terrain, the promise of no people for the next three or four days, temperatures in excess of a hundred degrees, and little or no water. Plus rattlers and scorpions and cactuses, and all the ghosts and legends of the dead prospectors that have wandered in there and met their doom in its labyrinthine and inhospitable ravines. My supplies total a gallon of water, six pieces of fruit, and a couple of packets of ramen. Wicked.

I walk tentatively into the wilderness and leave behind the signs and noise of man, and soon it's just me and the silent expanses of nature. I walk along sandy tracks beneath hillsides of saguaro cactus, their massed, raised-arm ranks towering above me like some invading alien army; I am humbled in their presence, in their land now, and bow down low before them, seeking entry. I walk through the rocky desert in hundred and five degree heat, and worry at the state of my parched throat, and drink out of dirty puddles. I soak my hat and shirt in the infrequent pools I find and they're bone dry within half an hour. I think about dying, and write a little farewell note to my family, and to those who will find my body. I climb mountains and canyons and my stupidly-shod feet scream out in agony, the Reebok sneakers that were always a size too small for me down to mere millimetres of sole. I get exhausted and unable to go on – and I pick myself up and march six miles up a sheer canyon wall having already come some fifteen gruelling miles in the heat of the day, and I am a runaway train, steaming ever onwards, arms pumping and blissed out of my head, beyond my body, beyond any notion of pain. I barely eat a thing and my piss is the colour of the gold that has lured far more able and well-prepared men than I to their doom. And that's just day one.

The next morning I emerge from my tent sheepish and aching into the cool, dewy grass of the Reavis Ranch, a long-abandoned homestead, and I am scared. I'm now fifteen miles and nearly as many hours from the nearest living person or road, a twisted ankle or snakebite away from death, impossibly alone. My trail-guide for the next section – several pages of which I have lost – promises a day far more challenging than the one before, a never-ending series of ascents and descents, a warning that one must be physically and emotionally prepared. I scoff at this – I mean, I don't even have emotions, do I? – but within an hour I fall whimpering into a large, smooth rock, my blistered feet, my stiffened muscles unwilling to travel any further, and lying there until death comes for me seems preferable to the path ahead. I lie there for so long that I become a part of the rock that forms my deathbed, my body sinking into it until I can't tell where it stops and I begin. Lizards run up my arms and legs, across my belly, unable to tell the difference either. It's peaceful there, not another living soul...

I pick myself up, eventually, and stumble on. Up one thousand-foot canyon and down another; up a canyon and down another – and another, and another, and another. It's an endless cycle of climbing and descending, and always I want to give up, and cry out, and always I go on. The trail-guide was right: it's quite easily the most challenging day of my life. But I make it, and at the top of the final climb I spy the cool blue waters of my destination, Lake Roosevelt, just eleven miles ahead. I celebrate by slicing the top off a beer can I've found, make a little fire, and cook up some ramen – and, let me tell you, a beer can full of ramen never tasted so good. And then I collapse into my tent and sleep.

It's the final morning and I'm bouncing along the trail and lapping up the miles, the lake now just three or four hours ahead of me. The feeling of being dangerously far out there has passed, even though it's still very much the middle of nowhere and by no means within the reaches of safety. But heartbreaking rocky canyons have given way to shade-giving cottonwood trees and the sight of the lake has turned this arduous trek into a pleasant and peaceful sunny Sunday stroll.

And just as I'm at my most relaxed, ambling along and enjoying the birds and the sun and the trees, I hear a noise I don't think I'll ever forget and observe myself performing a reverse long jump of record-breaking proportions before I even know why.

"Aaagh! Fuck!" I scream, and my heart is going a million miles a minute, and I'm shaking like a shitting dog, and it's all happened so fast it's only then that I realise exactly why I've leapt and screamed and shook: a rattler. A fucking rattlesnake. A really fucking big one.

He's sat right there in the trail and he's enormous and fat. He's looking at me and that tail of his is going at it, shaking away – *fffrrrfrrfrrrr!* – and the sound is chilling my bones. What a noise! So loud! And he shakes and shakes, and so do I, and I must have been mere inches from standing on him – or, rather, getting myself bitten into by his sharp pointy fangs – and I can't believe how lucky I am.

I calm down and I think I'd better go and investigate. I creep towards him with my backpack held out in front of me and the closer I get, the louder he shakes: he doesn't give a fuck, this snake; he knows who's boss. I reckon he's about four feet long; I can't get over how big he is – or how beautiful. I pass within about six feet of him and he swivels to stare and I stare right back. I think to myself I'd better walk with a little more awareness from now on.

Chapter Two

Ah, the lake: the cool clear waters of this beautiful desert lake, soothing away my forty-three miles of pain, balming my blisters, restoring life to my poor numbed toes. The bliss of lying here with my feet in the water, the sun beating down and all the stupidly satisfying miles of that extraordinary three-day hike behind me. The lake, the lake, the lake...

But, oh, the people: the retarded, noisy people; the boats and the music and the look-at-me Americans; and the old ones, fogeying away in the visitors' centre oohing and aahing at the displays and taking videos and photographs of replicas of things they could be looking at for real outside.

Oh, the people.

And the bliss of the lake.

And the noise of the boats.

And the kiss of the sun.

And the grating loud voices.

And the crystal blue waters.

And the touch of the stones and the rocks on the beach as they dig into my back and caress me, and how wonderful is this thing called nature.

I decide to thumb it to the nearest free camping spot, about six miles up the shoreline – which I'm in no condition to walk – and settle into what I'm ashamed to say is a most frustrating spell of hitching. Frustrating because I can't understand why the dozens and dozens of cars and pickups that pass me by won't stop, when they have room, and when I'm a cleancut young man standing out in the sweltering heat of the desert and I only want to go a few miles in the only possible direction they could be going. And all those tough-looking good ol' boys in their beat-up trucks – well if they're so afraid of me, why don't they just let me hop up on back? I'd rather ride like that anyway. But instead they just leave me standing there and the indifference and lack of kindness of my fellow man is hard to understand, and I wonder how many of them are Christians, and I wonder how many of them really practise what they preach.

At the same time, though, I'm ashamed because my desire for a ride, and my desire for some well-needed rest and sleep and recovery has caused me to temporarily lose my faith in the Holy Road God, who I should know by now is acting always to bring me that perfect ride, at the perfect time. It's not His fault if I've turned up too early: the car is on its way – we're already inextricably bound – and all I have to do is wait and trust. I should have known better than to lose my patience.

And so, as ever, it's not too long before my frustration has been shaken off and I'm joyously galloping up to tail-lights and a waiting window, and into the fun-filled cab of a big white pickup truck I go, where Billy and Eric, two bare-chested fencers, are busy polishing off a six-pack of Bud Ice and I happily accept their invitation to join them.

Billy and Eric sound like, to me, Bill and Ted from Bill and Ted's Excellent Adventure, and even though I know they're not west coast they've got this effortless kind of banter that just smacks of goofball California surfer dudes loving life and enjoying everything in a sort of haphazard and infectious way. They say, "dude" a lot. They smile and they're tanned and their white teeth shine and their bare chests are big and muscled. They're proper blokes, these guys, and I'm loving them and their accents. I know people over here love mine – and it's at times like this that I understand why.

They're going to a town called Payson. They start to try and sell it to me as an alternative to camping by the lake.

"Dude, have you seen the rim?" Billy goes.

"The rim?"

"The Mogollon Rim, dude; you ain't seen the rim? Aw, dude, you gotta see the rim; you will freak."

"You gotta see the rim, dude," Eric goes, "it's like this two hundred mile wide ridge that jumps up across the middle of Arizona three thousand feet high, and below it it's all desert, and on the top it's all pine forests and rivers and waterfalls; that's where we live, dude; you gotta see the rim."

"And the women, dude," says Billy, "we got the women too." And they smile and laugh and white teeth flash behind the dark reflections of their sunglasses and I'm well and truly sold. Eric issues an invitation to spend the weekend at his place and party Bill and Ted stylee, and all thoughts of taking it nice and easy by the lake are left back there along with the stupid mood I'd allowed to take a hold of me. By sunset I was already three parts pissed and having a merry old time watching a delightful array of characters coming in and out of Eric's place. And this was how it went for the next three days. In a nutshell, I met lots of people and drank lots of beer.

There was, however, slightly more to it than that.

Like on the following day when we went down to the East Verde River and spent the whole day drinking, and got busted by the cops on the way back, Eric and two girls arrested for DUI and possession of marijuana paraphernalia, and a whole heap of drama ensuing, what with Eric actually being out on parole and in the shit if he got into any more trouble.

I, meanwhile, escaped, fortunately choosing a false name and date of birth that didn't have any criminal record attached to it.

And on the Sunday – Sunday bloody Sunday – when we celebrated Eric's release from jail with a barbecue and several cases of beer, and at some point in the afternoon Eric sidles on over to me and asks me if I've ever tried ice.

"What's ice?" I say.

"It's a bit like crystal meth."

"Never heard of it. But, sure, I'll give it a try."

And why the hell not? It's a sunny afternoon, the beers are flowing, everyone's having fun, and you've got to do everything once, right? And so up nose it goes, a line of white powder much the same as any other, and before I know it I'm way out of my shell and talking non-stop to the enthralled masses, and what I'm saying sure sounds good to me. And on and on I go and when the party ends at three a.m. I'm still going on and can't for the life of me find the switch that turns off my brain.

"Just try and get some sleep," says Eric, as he retires to his room – but I can't.

It is, in fact, six a.m. on Tuesday morning before I manage to close down my poor brain and sleep. It's by far the worst comedown of my life: not only am I wired and wide awake but, all of a sudden, it's like every joy-producing chemical in my body has been used up and I'm left a dried-out and useless wreck. On Monday I took myself off and escaped to the admittedly awesome Mogollon Rim and walked there by the river among stunningly sculpted rocks. It's some beautiful scenery, all right – but I can't get anything out of it: I can't even smile. All I want to do is cry and I wonder how it's possible to feel so miserable in such incredible surroundings. I'm fighting back the tears and I'm feeling absolutely rock bottom and in despair. I decide to head back to Payson, desperate to try and find someone or something to put a smile on my face. There was, I felt, one person who might be able to help me.

See, back on Friday I'd met Sarah, a beautiful brown-haired girl with the most magical eyes. I also saw her down at the river on Saturday and then again at the barbecue bash on Sunday, where we'd had a pretty intense conversation, and where she'd told me that she wanted to come away with me on the road. That was quite a feeling: I've travelled for so long, always alone, and to have someone with whom I felt such a strong connection tell me they wanted to join me in my wanderings was just wonderful. But also I was scared, because I didn't think I could handle the responsibility of leading another human being on my twisted path: I mean, I know all the things I've done are cool for me but how on Earth could anyone else tolerate them? Walking miles in the rain and mud? Sleeping cold and lonely nights? Being out there and scared and in a seemingly hopeless situation, no food or water and a hundred and five degrees without an inch of shade? Even though it all leads to intense highs and magnificent and unexpected situations, who else could follow me and live like that? Who else could subscribe to my church?

So I ran away, leaving her a little note saying something stupid and drug-induced like, "it was really nice falling in love with you." Yet for that whole miserable Monday I could not get her out of my head. Every time I closed my eyes I saw hers. There was no way I could leave without saying a proper goodbye.

So I found them all, and we all got rip-roaringly drunk, and Sarah and I sat and gazed into each other's eyes and, despite my wanting her before, I suddenly realised it was impossible, that it was all just part of this highly-charged weekend and me wanting to be wanted. Truth was, the whole town was strung out on crystal meth and most of the people I was hanging out with were on parole for drug-related offences, one positive urine sample away from some real jail time. It was all booze and feeling and the emotions of youth, and it had swept me along much as it had done in Charlottesville, but this time I was over it. Somewhere in the middle of it all one of Eric's friends professed his love for Sarah and had to be restrained from attacking me, and right there and then another guy they knew who was supposed to be inside for something like six years appeared out of nowhere and the roof went off the place. It was tears and joy and shrieks and hugs, and me sat there in a chair absolutely exhausted and drained and completely and utterly on the outside of it all. I didn't know these people and I couldn't relate to the way they lived. It was five a.m. and when my trusted Gilligan hat suddenly burst into flames I knew it was time to check out. Not just because things were getting a little too crazy but because I realised that I would have taken back every one of Sarah's sweet kisses in exchange for the non-spontaneous combustion of my hat. That hat and I had been through a hell of a lot over the last few months. It's not cool when your best friend bursts into flames.

I felt pretty good about leaving Payson, a sense of closure and of seeing things through to the end that I rarely found in my relationships on the road. Payson was a mess, and I was desperate for the loss of my hat, but at least I hadn't left there wondering what might have been.

My sign for Pine attracted a gorgeous blonde in a white convertible Pontiac Firebird, and if it hadn't been for her husband in the back, it would have been a hitchhiker's dream. But sooner or later I was going to get picked up by a foxy lady. It was surely just a matter of time.

And so, through the scarily-friendly funky little towns of Pine and Strawberry, and the immense Tonto National Forest, and the smell of the pines and the blue of the sky is overwhelming. I walk on down the highway and not even the fabled Route 66 convertible cross-country roadtrip can compare to the freedom of this. No expenses, no parking, no cops, no insurance, no gas, no hassles, no nothing. It's all right here in my feet and hands and I go as fast or as slow as I like. If I'm not the luckiest man alive I don't know who is.

And via Camp Verde – where an old lady showers me and launders my clothes in return for my chopping her wood – it's on to the legendary red rock country of Sedona, delivered there by a young crew of three fire safety guys who feed me pot and beer and invite me back to theirs for more of the same.

I've had enough of that action in Payson, though, and we settle for a few chilled bevvies in a cool local brew pub. The conversation, however, passes me by: my gaze is out the window and it's the massive red rocks that leap up from a sea of green that demand my attention. I swear, it's the most arresting view I've ever witnessed. I become desperate to get out among them.

We go rolling out into Sedona's bizarre town of conservative and moneyed houses, sort of like San Diego in the desert, and on up to Schnebly Hill, where the four of us say our fond goodbyes. I set up my tent and then sit and watch the sun set behind the huge towers of rock that lie across the valley to the west. I soon see why the locals love Schnebly Hill so much: watching that sunset is one of the most moving experiences of my life. I'm spellbound. I can't take my eyes off those rocks, sculptured and painted more gloriously than man ever could. Their silhouetted outlines resemble enormous sleeping gods. They seem infinitely deep, full of every colour. I'm shaking with the pure, physical emotion of the moment.

"Jesus," I say.

And, "oh God."

I sit and I watch and I wish that everyone could see what I'm seeing, could feel what I'm feeling. No one could fail to be moved by that sight. No one could enter that sacred space and leave there the same person.

There's nothing I can do but bow down before them, humbled, and weep.

Chapter Three

Oh America! Is there a country in the world which possesses such an abundance of natural beauty, and which is so easily and readily available to its citizens? And yet, is there a country more capable of building ugly and hideous cities, of rendering them dull beyond description with their damned adherence to the grid system, of forgetting that its urban centres are there for people and not for cars? Why all that sprawl? Why strip malls and endless parking lots and places so fantastically far apart that it makes the purchase of a motor vehicle practically compulsory? Why not footpaths and bridleways and public transport and town centres? What's so bad about seeing people together outside? And what's so great about spending half the day moving from place to place in a square tin box? America, with its concrete and highways and suburbs, and barely a winding road in sight, or a snicket, or a short cut across some farmer's fields; America with its barbed wire and eight-lane boulevards, its vanished railroad, its drive-through culture. Oh, what a place America would be if only Amsterdam's canals and Edinburgh's gothic spires and Fes's medieval mazes had been built on its empty swathes of land instead of Los Angeles and Houston and Detroit – but, alas, it has been left to New Orleans and San Fran and New York to carry the mantle as America's only architecturally interesting large cities, and left to Europe and beyond to show the gods that man is at least capable of producing something of beauty, if not in the world's most beautiful places.

And so it is with Sedona.

Strange that after such a wonderful and inspirational night I should spend the next morning so frustrated, trekking miles through Sedona's New Age hell and cursing the eyesore that man had plonked there, right in the middle of such beauty. Sedona had tried, I suppose, by painting its houses the same colour as the rocks that towered above it, but beyond all that it was still the same old North American shambles of straight roads and cars and homogeneity, yet another city that lacked a beating heart or character. Even South Elmsall has its market and high street and ever-stopped clock. And even London is walkable.

I sought an antidote and set off to climb an enormous cliff-face, driven by a desire for something more, a new challenge despite the peace of mind and sense of well-being that hitching was bringing me. It was a ridiculous thing to do, really; it was well over a thousand feet high and took me so long to get to the top that I had to sleep up there on a narrow stone ledge just big enough to stretch out on, a sheer drop of hundreds of feet falling away from me on two sides. Here are some of the things I said on the way up:

- "I'm shit scared"
- "You really ought to go down, Rory"
- "I want my mummy"
- "Why the fuck did you come up here!"
- "Just imagine how you'll feel when you reach the top"
- "I can't give up"
- "I'm gonna kill you"

Of all the stupid things I'd ever done, that was right up there. But, my, what a view. And what a fantastic echo as I whimpered into the night.

Down and off the rock the next day, struggling with my pack, cursing myself with even more enthusiasm than on the way up, and still things were not right; still I hadn't shaken that feeling of, "okay, what's next?" I needed something more, and if risking life and limb would not bring it, and if the stupendous beauties of watching the sun set atop an enormous tower of red and white stone would not bring it then what would?

And suddenly it becomes so blindingly obvious that all the pain and suffering of the previous twenty-four hours are tossed into oblivion: like Doctor Rheinhart and his dice all I needed to do was trust my fates to chance and dedicate myself to the Holy Road God, He who has brung me this far, gifted me the best experiences of my life, and who has never let me down.

With this perfect moment of realisation the heaviness I had been feeling was shown for what it truly was: a momentary loss of direction and just a little too much time in my own company. Soon enough I was back to having fun in the sun, waving and smiling at the cars that were never going to stop, and feeling utterly at home. It was so beautiful to know that I was standing there awaiting 'the right ride' – and the 'only ride' – and that the hundreds of cars that whistled by me didn't matter. It made me realise that it shouldn't make any difference what I did in order to attract a lift, because there was nothing I could do to avoid my destiny: in all probability I could run backwards in the opposite direction to where I wasn't going and still end up in the right place. With this in mind I made up a frivolous little sign – "DON'T WORRY, I'M NOT AMERICAN" – and settled into one of the most enjoyable waits ever.

As far as waiting time goes, this was a long one, yet I never began to feel the frustration I usually do after an hour or so. Indeed, I was completely relaxed, knowing that a car was on its way for me. Sometimes I'd sit and write a little; sometimes I'd ignore the road and go for a stroll – soon enough, though, a young woman in a nice Mitsubishi jeep caught my eye, smiled, and waited as I gaily skipped towards her, eager for the next adventure.

Marie was her name – a pretty twenty-three year-old Montessori teacher from New Hampshire – and she told me that she'd once had to hitch this road a whole summer to get to work and back from her home in Flagstaff. Now, of course, she had a car and could repay the favour – something I longed to do if and when I returned to a life where I could afford such things as petrol and cars. We talked about travel and hitching, and the experiences of the road, and the conversation was fun and easy; it was a no-brainer to accept her offer of a quick bite to eat once we reached Flagstaff. When that developed into an invitation to go and watch some music with friends and get nice and beveraged up, I had no problems saying, "yes," again. And later still, after pool and beer with her roommates, when she asked me if I'd be staying the night…

My dear boy, it was good. And, more importantly, so was I.

Saturday and Sunday followed pretty similar patterns – the beer flowed freely and there was lots and lots of very good sex (and every now and then I'd shake my head in wonder that the girl I was enjoying a rather nice shag with had actually picked me up off the side of the road) – and it was almost a pity that she was due to leave for a six week trip to Hawaii on the Monday morning.

"Come back then," she said, "stay with me, it'll be cool."

But I knew I had to keep on moving.

Instead, we drove down to the airport in Phoenix together, and after seeing her off she gave me the keys to her jeep so I could take it the hundred and fifty miles back up to Flagstaff; and there I was, alone on the desert highway, except this time piloting someone else's vehicle – and what better example can I give of the wonders that this life can bring? For I could quite easily have had a place and a girl and a circle of friends in a very cool town – and even a car to share. I mean, God bless America. And God bless the holy divine road spirit that keeps a watch over hitchhikers and leads them down these merry paths of wonder and delight. Amen.

Chapter Four

I became something of a weather god those summer months out west and was never rained on once, always rolling into or out of a town just in time to miss a storm, but not once did it touch me. Good job too, 'cos my twenty dollar tent was far from waterproof – and I often just slept outside in my sleeping bag anyway. The night before I left Flagstaff, though, I did get a bit wet camped out in a park, lying there tentless. The rain came out of nowhere but I figured it was just a shower and so I let it slowly soak me, too tired to move, waiting for it to stop. It doesn't stop, though, and I eventually get up. And that's when I realise I've been sleeping next to a sprinkler.

I rode into the Canyon with a couple of Minnesota girls who were working the summer there, who had just done a hundred and fifty mile round trip to buy groceries. That seemed kind of mental. People in England would freak if they had to drive *fifteen* miles to go shopping. But to them it was just what they had to do. And luckily for me, because they worked in the national park, I got in for free – which was the case for all the many national parks I visited. Yet another of the benefits of hitching.

The thing about hiking the Grand Canyon, though – about my little twenty-two hour stroll across that most famous of holes – was that even as I was doing it I was thinking to myself, "you know, the best thing about this is going to be telling other people, 'I walked across the Grand Canyon'" – and it was. I walked across the Grand Canyon. It was all right. It sounds impressive because it's famous. But it was nothing compared to the Superstitions – and it was nothing compared to what awaited me once I was up and out the other side in Utah.

Canyonlands – now there's a national park to be proud of: my God, that place is like Disneyland for rocks! It's like they've got every kind of rock in the world. It's one big party of buttes and ravines and canyons and crevices and mushrooms and fingers and hoodoos and arches, and you climb out of one canyon and realise you've actually emerged into a much bigger one, and all around you is rock: you're in rock and on rock and going through rock to shimmy up rock, and you get to the top of the big big rock and then you look around and in every direction for fifty miles it's rock rock rock. It's dizzying and bewildering; it's like the apocalypse and it's like everything that's wonderful about the desert rolled into one. I couldn't get enough of that place: I went there with five pieces of fruit in my bag and I stayed for three days, until my supplies ran out. I hiked all over the shop and barely saw a soul, and one night fell ten feet off a rock in the dark, and another night got lost and couldn't find my tent and shivered under a tree until dawn, and I swear it was the time of my life, my favourite place on Earth, beauty incomparable and it made the Grand Canyon look like the boring, bad-jumpered uncle that has absolutely nothing to say.

I left there happier than ever, and was promptly swept up by Andy, a young guy doing much the same as me, only in his battered old car, and quickly he became enamoured with my strange tales from the road and took me under his wing.

"You just tell the stories," he said, "and I'll provide the food." And so everyday he'd buy me burger after burger and I'd regale him with my hitchhiker and pretend cowboy's tales, and love it as he sat there smiling and open-mouthed and wanting more. And together we did some mad climbing in Arches, and splashed around one hot afternoon in a Utah waterpark, and for only the second time in two years travelling in America I had a companion.

Together we cross the mountains into Colorado and there we say goodbye.

And Colorado is two days and three hundred miles of hitching heaven, pure and simple: from the seventy-seven year-old miniscule great-grandma hunched down low behind the wheel of her behemoth of an ancient Cadillac to the gorgeous and fun twin sisters who can't believe I've never eaten beef jerky and drive miles and miles out of their way to *insist* that I try some with them, via all the outdoorsy young snowboarders and skiers and bikers and hikers who typify the Rocky Mountain country of Colorado. It's a stark contrast to back east: great-grandma aside, they're young and free-spirited and always zooming off somewhere or other to do something almost sickeningly healthy and energetic, and at one stage I realise that eight out of my ten rides have been with single girls, and at least half my rides since the ranch have been with women. Everything's wide-open out west – and, no, that's not an innuendo – and that American innocence and lust for life is multiplied ten-fold here in Colorado: these people are as children in a playground, safe and excited and eager to try everything. Yes, they've got the weather and the scenery but, man, they've also got the ethic and the zest to make the most of it and they sure love life. And as I'm winding my way slowly through the mountains and the valleys and the insanely wonderful small towns and all that space and sun and youth in the godblesséd heavenly nature of the American west, I love life too.

In fact, I get so stupidly happy I can barely stand myself. I stand in the road and spin and dance and when the cars come and pass me by I smile and wave and I feel so genuinely happy for the people sitting in them, the children gawping through the back window. I shine on their puzzled expressions and dream of them turning to mommy and daddy and saying, "what's that man doing, mommy?" and mommy and daddy will explain that he's out there, on the road, just a tent and a sleeping bag in his pack, and barely any money, and maybe they'll look back on that vision of me one day in years to come, sitting at their desks and in their jobs and think, you know, that was the happiest man I ever saw.

I'm on the beach in the one-street olde worlde resort town of Grand Lake, Colorado, digging the water and the rocks and killing a few hours before England take on Argentina in the World Cup quarter-finals, and sort of laughing and smiling to myself – and then sort of wondering if anyone has overheard me quietly saying, "I love my life," over and over again. But no, it's just me and the boaters in the sun and somewhere off at the other end of the beach a middle-aged woman sat alone and looking out to water too. I stretch down on my pack and close my eyes a while…

"Excuse me," a voice says. It's the woman that was up the other end of the beach. "You're travelling, right? Do you want to earn a few dollars? We need a dishwasher for the weekend. It's the fourth."

It's the fourth of July; so it is.

"Seven bucks an hour, cash. And I think we've got a spare apartment you can stay in. Probably be about five days' work."

I think about it for a second. I've still got about two hundred dollars and I'm only spending about five a day; I should have enough. Freedom is far more important to me than money right now.

"Not really," I say, "I'm sort of on the move."

"Well come over and check it out, and see what you think; I'll stand you a burger and fries." She's a nice lady. She goes off back to her work.

And by the time I've finished watching England do the same old same old in the penalty shoot-out against the dirty Argie bastards I'm thinking five days' work, and several hundred dollars, and a free place to stay, and a chance to get all funky in this fun little resort town wouldn't actually be a bad idea. It's friendlier than anywhere on Earth: already I've been given free drinks by a sweet bartender and also chocolate fudge cake by a chap from Cuba. It's got mini-golf and the lake and the kids run around happy and free after dark. I'm in.

And for the next five days I'm a dish-washing fool, splish-sploshing in the water and polishing off plate after plate of leftover trout, and then after work partying with a ready-made bunch of friends, all the other hip young things that're working there for the summer, and it's kayaking and meeting friendly souls and one a.m. dips in the icy water, and beers and beers and beers, and taking a cute little Australian girl back to my rather nice pad to indulge in our mutual love of kissing rather than boring old sex, and plate after plate, and pan after pan, and Lord knows I'll never curse the waiters' lot again, not after finally realising what it is to be a dishwasher, my poor sweet Nathan Hart.

But now – some apologies:

First of all, apologies to the owner of the restaurant slash hotel, because even though you were an uptight asshole and nobody liked you, I'll admit it was wrong of me to glug that behind-the-bar Jack straight from the bottle, and I'll admit that could probably be construed as theft. Also, I'd like to confess that when you practically forced me to clean some rooms – not in my contract

175

at all – I instead just watched tennis, and straightened up the beds rather than remaking them. It's just that the sheets looked perfectly fine to me – only used once – and I didn't think that the new people would mind. Also, it was Wimbledon. And I loves Wimbledon, I does.

Apologies too to the owner of the bar that I entered with a smuggled half-gallon bottle of Tequila stuffed down my jeans, thereby denying you revenue. And apologies to anyone who was offended by the sight of me with my trousers down and no underwear on, after I pulled it out and offered shots to everyone. Apologies too to the guy who was caught by the bouncer finishing off the bottle and ejected from the building while I drunkenly and obliviously slid onto the dance floor. And to the woman I elbowed in the back of the head during a game of mercy, and to anyone else I may have injured during what I'm told was a fairly manic display of dancing.

Thanks, though, to the bartender who kindly responded to my night-long requests for, "two free beers, please" in the positive – hope I wasn't too out of order when hitting on you later on.

To Brianna: awfully sorry about the overly passionate cheek-biting and the subsequent passing out (though, as you told me later, I had warned you of its impending arrival and you didn't really mind). Here's hoping that the staff at Grumpy's, where we ate breakfast, wouldn't have been too upset had they caught me drinking a couple of beers from under the table; and here's hoping that nobody minded us finishing off that cooler of beers I found by the lake, remnants of the previous night's party.

And thanks once more to the aforementioned bartender who served up a bunch of free beers when I went in to tip her for the excellent service of the night before.

Apologies, though, to the owner of the restaurant again, who appeared none-too pleased when I turned up for work with eleven beers in me belly, and the high which naturally goes hand-in-hand with such a level of alcohol consumption. Plus, very sincere apologies to the bitch cook who kept on turning down the Dylan, and who subsequently received a couple of unnecessary though well-intended insults from yours truly.

But thanks yet again to the bartender who wasn't at all put out when a friend and I appeared on her doorstep at four in the morning intent on cooking her breakfast – and further thanks to her for treating the pair of us to pancakes and bacon in preference to our offerings of a box of mostly-broken eggs and a bottle of Merlot.

Finally, to the motel manager whose six a.m. canoe we then borrowed, setting sail upon the lake on the hunt for some early morning beverages. Consequently, apologies to the lakeside residents who were woken by our drunken cries of, "we want beer!" and, "ya got any booze?" Sorry about that.

Yeah: sorry, sorry, sorry.

Chapter Five

The morning I left Grand Lake I awoke from my most troubled dream in a long time, endlessly chased and accused by dozens of people, finally snapping and telling Nathan Hart, "get over the fact that I shagged your girlfriend." But still I was hounded. I don't ever remember being so disturbed by a dream: mainly, I suppose, because I had thought that I was a better person now, and that I deserved for my nighttime wanderings to be as pleasant as those of my days. I hadn't been in trouble with the cops, hadn't stolen anything – unless you counted the Wal-Mart Twixes I snagged as often as I could – and certainly hadn't messed with anybody's girlfriend. I took it as a sign to keep on being good – and to be more good, even.

I cross the Rockies on the back of a pickup truck, sat there in the thin mountain air and feeling so, so grateful that they'd made me sit outside so I could make the most of the view. At the top we pass a cyclist chugging along on his bike and I stare at him in wonder; later on, we find out that he's died. It's apparently not uncommon up there, the exertion and all. Another person who has died is Dave, my old mentor from the ranch. He's been stabbed to death by Shelley while they were drunk. She always did have a temper. And it's such a Dave way to go. And finally, my granddad – my dear, sweet granddad, my favourite person in the whole wide world, who saw me through my teenage years with endless hours of televised sport and horror films and shandy – though I wasn't to discover this until about a month after his demise. My folks, of course, had my email address, but they just didn't think to tell me; too much effort or something...

Down the other side and through Estes Park and into the plains, which are, indeed, very plain – and despite myself, and despite knowing that this is what everyone does, I could not help but stand there and stare and go, "boy, it sure is *flat*." And there I seem to have crossed the line between the cool of the west and the dreary of the east. And there, too, in a town called Greeley that smells almost entirely of dead chicken, I almost end up under the wheels of a too-fast train.

There's a right and a wrong way to hop freight trains; this one was the wrong way. The right way is to find a place where you can have a nice run up; a flat area with no nasty surprises; a space where you can work yourself up to a sprint and take the time to board safely and smoothly. You can, I've discovered, mount and dismount trains that are going at a fairly good speed, and though it's best to jump one that isn't going faster than you can run, it's still possible.

Ideally you get yourself up to maximum speed and then grab a hold of the ladder, and then keep on running while you work yourself up to placing your foot on the bottom step – and once you've done that: lift off. If they're going slightly faster you get dragged along a bit but it's not that much more difficult. That time in Greeley, though, the train was going way quick, and I had no space to run: I was between it and another that was parked up and I couldn't get going fast enough; when I reached out my hand the momentum of the train knocked me off balance and threw me into the stationary one, which then bounced me back into the moving one. Luckily I managed to push myself off it and land in a heap in the gravel, mere inches from its great turning silver slashing wheels.

That was enough freight train hopping for one day.

Colorado and Kansas plains give way to pretty Nebraska and South Dakota hill country, and the skies are blue and the people are good, and the vibe that's been in me since leaving the ranch is ever-present and wonderful. I sleep every night somewhere out in the quiet and as I drift off I am smiling and happy, content and at ease in my heart. The country is bathing me in its goodness, washing away all memories of the ranch, of Charlottesville, of what I have been.

A pretty ranger takes me with her into Wind Cave National Park and feeds me pizza and beer. She says, "you ever been spelunking?" I say, "what's spelunking?" She says, "you gotta go spelunking."

And so spelunking I go.

I join a group of about a dozen people and soon we're following our guide into the deep, dark depths of the earth, all overalls and miners' hats, and it's damp and cool and so, so quiet. I love quiet more than any sound – my favourite quiet is the quiet you get out in the desert following a ride, following a crunch of boot on gravel, following the slamming of a car door and the slow and steady disappearance of the noise of the engine as it vanishes out over the horizon and it's then just you and a whole lot of empty land stretching out for miles and miles and miles to the distant peaks – but there's nowhere quite as quiet as being under the ground, pressed between rock. I work my way to the back of the group and every now and then I let them go and switch off my light, and lie there stilling my breath and digging it. It's the most peaceful place I've ever been. Longer and longer I let these moments drag on, wishing I could have them longer still – until one time I don't know how long I've been lying there but when I turn on the light and rejoin the trail there's no sign of the group and I'm alone, under hundreds of metres of earth, surrounded by rock.

I rush through the cave seeking to catch them up but hit a dead-end and realise I've taken the wrong turn. I backtrack to the place where I must have forked and I end up somewhere completely different. I backtrack again and the same thing happens. I have no idea where I am, or how to get back, and that immeasurable mass of rock is weighing down on me immense; I suddenly get a picture of the situation that I'm in: that I'm a man buried alive in a maze of tunnels and that I'm either going to go mad and starve to death or I'm going to be like the people the guide has warned us about, who wander off and they take three days to find. I spin this way and that in a frenzied effort to retrace my steps – but everything looks the same, and every cavern I emerge into has a dozen different tunnels leading from it. There's no quiet anymore: the noise of my panicked breathing and frantically beating heart is deafening.

It's maybe this that leads the ranger to find me. Ten minutes I've been gone. It's perhaps the longest and most terrifying ten minutes of my life.

And not only does Wind Cave scare the living shit out of me, it also offers me yet another unforgettable encounter with nature: for the next morning, after camping on a high hill, I'm merrily bounding my way down the twisting trail, sort of absent-minded and happy-go-lucky, when around one corner I find myself face-to-face with two enormous charging buffalo coming up the other way, about fifteen feet in front of me. I've got a split second to think – but like in all split seconds that occur in moments of crisis, there're a lot of thoughts that can be crammed in there.

I remember something about not running away, about shouting loudly and making yourself look big by raising your pack above your head – and then I wonder if that isn't for bears, or tigers, or maybe dogs. I notice that the buffalo are each about the size of a tank and they don't look like they're stopping for anyone. I marvel at their nostrils and fur and horns and power. I see an image of myself stupidly holding my backpack in the air and still getting trampled underfoot. And I spy out of the corner of my eye a fallen tree just off the side of the trail and I think, that's the place for me. I dive behind it and ready myself for their coming after me, but instead they just stop and stare and the three of us have a sort of face-off right there in the empty South Dakota morning.

Their nostrils are going mad; the breath they're blasting out of them is immense and loud, strong enough to knock a small child off its feet.

They stare and snort and I've never seen anything so wonderful or so big, right out here in the wild, totally unexpected.

They're all head, these buffalo: ninety percent of them, I swear, is head.

They've got these tiny little stick legs. They're a massive head on legs, in a seventies sheepskin coat, with enormous snorting nostrils.

They blast the grass some more and then shuffle off past me. It's a misty hillside morning in the middle of nowhere and there I stand, backpack clutched, half-cowering and half-peering from behind that fallen tree as two gigantic furry heads go wobbling up the path. Fuckin' buffalo, man. Like back in old wild western days. Fuckin' buffalo.

The rattlesnake, the javelinas, the road runners and scorpions and saguaro and now buffalo. The time I was hitching on the prairies in one of the Dakotas and popping out of the ground all around me these yapping little dogs, first one, and then another – and then a dozen, and a hundred, and a thousand: yap yap yap, over and over, driving me jibonkers. Or in Wyoming, on the way up the

Tetons, when that elk came out of nowhere and practically licked my ear. And wild horses and donkeys and mules, and all the birds and lizards and snakes and skunks – and back in England, I maybe saw a fox once, and held a hedgehog, but beyond pondskaters and badgers, what do we have?

Oh, American west, with your abundance of wonders in the natural world! Oh Rockies! Oh Tetons! And, oh, Wyoming! Twice the size of England but with less population in the whole of your grand mountain and desert and prairie state than in that one cramped city of Leeds – and still your people say it's getting too crowded. And Thermopolis, and the world's largest hot spring, and Yellowstone and Wind River Canyon and all those marvellous and scenic miles I hitched on my grand loop around that most wonderful of cowboy states before entering into Montana for my destinous meeting with that Seattle-bound freight in perhaps Havre or Billings and the dream of re-crossing the Rockies riding her steel hulk bareback up from the plains, up and up, climbing granite peaks, and descending again, oh wide-open American west!

Chapter Six

Hi mom!!

Well things have been pretty interesting since last time I wrote you from Thermopolis. I left there on Wednesday afternoon in a hundred and three degree heat after enjoying the waters and got a very cool ride down the Wind River Canyon into mosquito-infested Riverton, swatting and swishing by the side of the road for ages, but couldn't get a ride out before sunset. That was fine by me, though – I ended up in a bar watching foxy boxing and lady wrestling, and saw about a hundred and fifty cowboys spend endless amounts of money on lapdances and the chance to oil down and fight the wrestlers, who were surprisingly tasty. I'm really into women right now.

The next morning, after camping in the park and eating breakfast in a homeless shelter, I made pretty little Lander and then caught a ride on US-287 towards the Tetons with a couple of young Indians. We "smoked a bowl" – though it didn't really do anything for me – and then my next ride from Fort Washakie was a fun couple who were already on their third case of Budweiser. He was Arapaho, she Shoshone. Got nice and merry with them, then had to take over the driving duties as they were way too far gone and ended up back in Lander. We were supposed to go to a Sun Dance and eat puppies – seriously! – but the Arapaho are, apparently, pretty strict about the drinking thing and Joe didn't want to appear pished in front of the elders, so that didn't happen.

I decided to stay in Lander and check out a block party and also the large quantity of tasty birds. Sadly, Lander is another one of those American cities full of fantastic looking high school girls yet completely and mysteriously devoid of an attractive, older stock. Where the hell do they all go? Still, I don't think one can ever grow tired of ogling nubile young fifteen year-olds. [Making that noise Homer Simpson does when he's thinking about yummy food.]

And after that, as I strolled the pleasant main street, I was accosted by a couple of young guys looking for someone of sufficient age to buy them a couple of forties: "oh, and one for yourself too." That was me taken care of for the rest of the night – I ended up hanging with my new, ridiculously young friends, getting plenty wasted, eating some nice pizza, and not spending a dime! I hadn't ever felt so old as I did when the conversation turned to curfews.

One thing does puzzle me though: how come even though I'm now pretty good at pulling older, more mature women, I'm utterly useless when it comes to girls young enough to be my sixteen year-old sister? Odd.

I may stay here today and do more of the same. I hope everything's cool your way. Take care.

Your loving son,
Rory

Hi Mom!!

Let's see...the last time you heard from me I was attempting to molest sixteen year-olds in Lander, Wyoming – well, thankfully nothing happened on that score and I exited there with pride intact (deciding that the reason I couldn't pull was because my usual tactic of being interesting and funny, yet aloof, only works with women, not girls – and, really, the thought of one of those little things taking hairy – *manly* – me into hand was a tad unrealistic, don'tcha think?) On the way out of there I stopped by to browse at a yard sale, hoping to collect a cheap book. One of the vendors asked me if I'd like to purchase a plastic bag for a dollar and then fill it with whatever I wanted. Bargain city! For one dollar I got: a little tranny radio and headphones; a nice big copy of Don Quixote – rather fitting, I think – and a book by a Greek bloke called Herodotus, plus a Sega Genesis (Megadrive) and a Super Nintendo. My plan was to sell them to one of the pawn stores in town for a monstrous profit but unfortunately they all closed at midday and I was scuppered in my greed. Eventually I gave them to a workman I found on the outskirts of town. When I told him how I'd come about them he said, "I can't see you losing your dollar," and gave me two, which was all he had on him. So even though I later gave away the books and the radio I still made me a little money.

Funnily enough my ride out of Lander was the Arapaho, Joe, who I mentioned in my last letter. He was sober this time. Then, after a long, almost uncomfortable wait back in Fort Washakie I was picked up by an interesting geologist slash teacher from Austin, Texas – another one of those 'turnaround rides', which is always nice. She took me all the way to Jackson at the south end of the Tetons, where I was looking to do a bit of the old hiking and camping. The drive was fantastic, passing through deserts and red rocks, into forests and grasslands, and then the Tetons themselves – French for "big tits" – their jagged peaks and ridges shooting almost seven thousand feet straight up out of the plains. The Rockies may be much higher but I'd say those mountains are far more dramatic and beautiful.

I made it into the park before dark, and hiked about three miles up the trail to find a campsite and to avoid the expected crowds by getting a head-start.

The trail I wanted to hike was a nineteen mile loop which, I had been promised at the visitors' centre, was impassable without an ice-axe: challenge! I had also been warned that it would be crowded in summer – though it's fairly obvious to anyone who has ever been hiking in the national parks that ninety-eight percent of Americans and tourists won't (or can't) walk more than two miles.

Sure enough, on the hike the following day I ran into very few people, and even fewer who were attempting to cross over Paintbrush Pass, which – at ten thousand seven hundred feet – was still under two feet of snow. Just before the pass I came to Solitude Lake, still maybe seventy-five percent frozen – in the middle of July! In fact, though I spent the entire day in my shorts I think I saw more snow than at any other time in my life. This truly is some extraordinary country.

On the way down from the peak – naturally experiencing some of the most beautiful scenery of my life – I did a lot of thinking about my next destination, Yellowstone. From what I knew about the place it was obviously something quite magnificent to see, yet horribly crowded with car-loving, traffic-jamming, bear-feeding tourists. Yellowstone also covers an enormous area – about three and a half thousand square miles – which means two things: that there is plenty of country to get lost in, but also enormous distances to be hitched in between the points of interest – and hitching inside the national parks is no easy task. I decided to ditch my original plan of spending five days escaping out in the back-country in favour of doing a cop-out and heading in and out in one or two days; there's definitely a time and a place for being a tourist and it seemed that this would be it. Also, I think that the Tetons are probably more suited to the back-country experience than Yellowstone and I certainly felt plenty satisfied with the two nights I had spent there.

I made Old Faithful about seven and sat with around three thousand others waiting to see my first geyser. As the bubbling began, and the excited masses around me started snapping away, a young Corona-wielding bloke sat down next to me. After a few minutes he turned and asked me if I'd been hitching at the entrance to the park earlier. "Yeah," I replied. "And in Fort Washakie a few days ago?" Again I answered in the affirmative – to which he excitedly turned to call his companions, shouting, "hey, guys! This is the hitchin' dude we keep seeing!" It turns out that they'd passed me twice already and had wanted to pick me up but didn't have the room – this time, he said, they were gonna make room: meeting like that for a third time couldn't be ignored. I found myself being swept up by these four young roadtrippers in the most delightful way. "Don't worry about the booze and food," he said, "you're coming with us."

The next four days and nights were probably the highlight of the trip. We did Yellowstone in style – possibly a completely original and unique style – beginning with one of the guys lifting three bottles of rum, and ending with a ticket from a Park Ranger for me riding atop their four-wheel drive (for which I supplied him with a false name). In between, there was a roaring bonfire and cook-out on Yellowstone Lake, some late night skinny-dipping, an odd, drunken encounter with a couple of old junkies, drink-driving shenanigans, drugs, and a hell of a lot of shoplifting. My Yellowstone experience was about as far removed from my intended plan as was humanly possible – and, God, was it fun.

The boys had somehow landed themselves a night on a fantastical ranch in the Beartooth Mountains and I was invited along for more yummy food and liquor. Following that, there was a further invitation to go on a two-night camping trip that I found hard to resist – of course, the only stumbling block being my fear of becoming unwanted. I am so glad I accepted, and equally glad that I caved in to the boys' style of camping – i.e., lugging about five times as much food as is necessary, plus three and a half bottles of whiskey and rum – rather than my own preference for the bare minimum.

Talk about stylin' it. After a five mile hike to Granite Lake we found ourselves the most ridiculously perfect camping spot imaginable. About fifty feet from where we placed our tents was a lakeside fire-ring that sat on a rock providing a magical view of the lake and surrounding mountains. The spot also had perfectly spaced trees for hammocks – the guys had two – plus plenty of firewood and a relatively high cliff-jump, behind which was a huge rock face ideal for climbing and watching the last of the sunset. For the most part we had no real need to go anywhere – for the most part, we didn't. It was two days of eating and drinking, fishing and laughing – I don't think I stopped smiling or giggling the whole time I was there. There were so many great moments but the one that really stands out is this vision of Steve paddling out into the middle of the lake on our homemade raft to catch us a fish supper. The raft was basically a submersible – we'd made it out of six thin logs roped and taped together – and as soon as he sat down on it it sank just beneath the surface, though still supported his weight. And out he paddled with his frying pan-taped-to-a-branch oar, and the four of us left on the shore wept with laughter at the sight of him basically just *sitting* on the water casting his rod right there in the middle of that grand magnificent lake. It definitely encouraged my ambition to raft down the Mississippi in a nineties Huck Finn stylee someday.

We just said a rather odd and painful goodbye in the diner where I now sit, in Red Lodge, Montana – easily the most uncomfortable and sad of my trip. Next up is Billings and that freight-ride over the Rockies to Seattle, finally.

Talk to you soon!

Love,
Rory

Dear mum,

Well it's only a day later and already I'm in Missoula, crashing at one of Steve's friends' places; it's been a wild, wild ride to get here. I think I'll tell you about the second part first, because...well, I just want to put off the first part for a little while. And the second one's a good one.

So I left Red Lodge and got to the next town of Laurel by about ten thirty, and, for one reason or another, I really, really wanted to get out of there. Hitching at night, of course, is nigh on impossible, so I made my way to the train tracks, not really sure about catching out or where anything is going, just sort of comforted by their familiarity and feeling safe there in the deserted and grimy dark. And as I sat by the rails pondering various shit I saw a couple of guys cross over about a hundred yards up from me, spying their bedrolls as they offered a wave: hoboes! Real live genuine freight-hopping hobo bums of olde – living legends, in my humble opinion. I quickly caught them up and was pleased to find out they were friendly old bums, eager to share a little knowledge and even some food. They too were going west, having just arrived from Casper a few days back. We talked about the bulls – the railroad security – and they gave me advice regarding the job situation (I resisted the urge to tell them, "hey, this is just my vacation, you know"). They had at least a hundred years between them – looking much older, of course – and they seemed like real nice guys, just unable to find a place in society. As we were about to set up camp I spotted a westbound freight rumbling towards us – they opined it was a hot-shot heading straight for Missoula. They said it was going too fast for them but I decided I just had to give it a try. My first effort was a little dicey, to say the least; my second, more well-thought out attempt was not – and I pulled myself aboard. Euphoria. There was the small matter of dodging the security lights, and of jumping across the couplings so that I wouldn't be sitting at the front of the car – essential, in case of a sudden stop – and we were on our way.

Next time: earplugs.

And a torch.

Oh, and some Ibuprofen.

God, those babies are loud! So incredibly, thunderously noisy. Sleep was impossible. But then, why would I want to sleep? Even though it was dark I could still make out the trees and the valleys, and the stars were magical, and – above all – I was riding a fuckin' freight, man! And like so many times on this trip I was five years-old, whooping and shouting, singing and laughing, and embracing this life with a delirious passion. My platform – though only just big enough for me to lie down on – felt safe for the whole trip, and the only remotely scary periods came when we stopped for crew changes in Livingston and Helena, and then a frightening fifteen minute wait inside a tunnel breathing fumes and listening to the engines' deafening roar echo all around me, and hoping beyond hope that we hadn't stopped for the night.

But we rolled on and the sun came up just before we reached Helena, some two hundred and fifty miles in, and with it the most enjoyable stretch of the ride, following the Clarks Fork River towards Missoula. The tracks criss-crossed the river many times, allowing me to indulge in my favourite freight-hopping pastime: that of sitting on the ladder and gazing down at the water below. At one point, as we wound our way up switchbacks towards the five and a half thousand feet high Continental Divide, I looked out across the valley able to see both the front and rear of my train without turning my head – in fact, they were closer to each other, separated by the bowl of the valley, than I was to either of them. An incredible, incredible sight.

We finally rolled into Missoula at around ten o'clock and I hopped off in front of a couple of bemused looking students, issued a cheery, "good morning," and set about exploring this rather nice town – the kind of place I would have wanted to live had I not discovered the joys of nature and become so unable to stand too much time in a town of more than about twelve hundred people. Still, it's cool, and my new friends are pretty nice – Steve had actually given me their number as an afterthought before leaving Red Lodge, even though I had no plans at the time to end up here. And, normally, of course, I'd never do something so brazen as to call up a stranger and say something like, "er, I'm in your town, and your friend gave me your number, and I was wondering if you could entertain me and/or put me up for the night" – it's just not the English way, is it? But today, for some reason, I did. And though Steve's friend Dave wasn't there and his girlfriend answered, she had no hesitation in inviting me over and showing me the couch where I was welcome to crash for as long as I liked. I tells ya, these Americans are bewildering and beautiful in the way they so passionately embrace the concept of hospitality. One day I really hope to have a house with an open-door policy and return the millions of favours I've received.

Now, alas, onto the first part of my story: how I got from Red Lodge to Laurel before catching the train. Do please forgive me this, it's honestly not my fault: it's that blasted Kerouac – and I haven't even read Kerouac yet. But everywhere I go I feel like his spirit haunts me – people that pick me up are always saying, "have you read Kerouac? you should read Kerouac" ("no!" I say, "I want to find my own philosophies!") – and even though he's long dead and bygone and not that I have any idea what he actually got up to anyway I can still see him out there, hitchin' around and roadtrippin' far more rock 'n' roll than I ever could, him and all those other hippies and beatniks living it totally large and putting my exploits and adventures to shame, the bastards.

I was thinking these thoughts by the side of the road in Red Lodge not too long after I'd finished writing my last letter to you. I'd gotten one short ride about three miles out of town but then there I was standing in the twilight in a crappy hitchin' place going nowhere. The cars were going way too fast and there was nowhere to stop. My mind wandered back to one Sunday morning near Kaibito, on the Navajo reservation in Arizona, when a car with two drunken Indians in it stopped and asked me if I needed a ride. Thing is, I was heading east and they were going west.

"Where you going?" I said, sort of curious as to why they'd stopped.

"Aw, we're just cruising," the driver said, "we're gonna get some beers – c'mon, get in."

I thought short and hard and decided there probably wasn't much point in getting wasted with a bunch of people I knew I would neither like nor respect.

But after they had departed I took a few moments to reflect on what I had done: namely, turn down an invitation for an interesting experience that would almost certainly make a good story for the folks back home. But, more than that, there was a bottom line and the bottom line was this: Kerouac would've done it. And right there on that useless stretch of Red Lodge road I thought of this, and I thought of all the other things of roadtripping legend that I wasn't doing: things like getting wasted with dumb Indians; things like finding my way to ridiculous drug- and sex-fuelled orgies; things like robbing gas stations and stealing cars; things like…things like stealing cars.

I must point out, my last ride had given me three or four beers. And it really was a desperate hitchhiking spot. And you know what I'm like when I feel I need to up the ante…

See, right there – right there where I was standing and thinking and being haunted and taunted by the beatnik's ghost – there was a big factory of some sort, and standing outside it, an enormous old truck. And I knew – I just *knew* – that the doors would be unlocked and hidden up inside the sun visor, just like in the movies, the keys would drop out. I twitched on the side of the road, and thumbed and twitched, and every few seconds I'd take a step towards that truck and then turn back, and darker and darker it got, and here was my chance.

The doors were unlocked. The keys were under the visor. The thing was started.

It was big, my God, and it was far too big for someone like me to drive – but drive it I did. Listen: I'm not proud but – I stole a grain truck.

And listen too: it was fuckin' horrible, and I hated every minute of it.

I knew the moment I steered its enormous bulk onto the highway and pointed myself in the direction of Laurel some forty miles to the north that it was a bad idea. It wasn't just the fear of being pulled over by the cops and landing in a whole heap of shit that had me cursing my stupidity with such gusto; it was more the realisation that I'd let myself down and done something that I immediately knew would tarnish the wonderful memories of my travels through this beautiful part of the world. I beat the steering wheel and almost cried with the frustration of what I was doing – yet I was too scared to stop or try and turn around, bewildered and paralysed by the sheer size of the thing, never the best of drivers (as you well know) even in normal circumstances. The entire forty mile journey was one long nightmare, that dark Montana highway too narrow for that truck and my skills, and every set of headlights appearing in front or behind sending me into a panic. Would it be the cops? Would I crash into someone? And all the way I beat and cursed and sweated and cried, and vowed never to do something so stupid again. I haven't ever been so grateful to see a McDonald's sign as I was when we hit the outskirts of Laurel and I was able to pull over and park up and get the hell out of there, fingerprints wiped and skedaddling for all I was worth.

I'll be in touch.

Love,
Rory

Chapter Seven

Missoula, Missoula: hippies in the sun and madcap Dave talking thrilled about Glastonbury in England, and some supposedly magic hill there that could create its own weather system, and a bloke called Piers Anthony whose books revealed the secrets of the Illuminati, a bunch of naughty misters who actually run the world, and the eye on the dollar bill, and he's as crazy as David Icke.

And these hippies with their shorts hanging down under their bellies to reveal their pubes and just not giving a good goddamn, and off to the river to strip off naked and dive in unashamed while the white and uncertain limey looks on timidly and climbs in first and *then* tosses his shorts to the river bank, never having been naked in front of strangers before, still more than a little embarrassed to let even a lover or a girlfriend get a peek of his unextended penis. But not these hippies; no sir. No inhibitions here.

And the hippies say, "let's get some beers!" and the limey smiles but then looks on puzzled when they come back with a six-pack of microbrews and he wonders what's going on 'cos there's four of us and how are we gonna get good and wasted on that? And for that price, he says, you could have got a whole twenty-four pack of Natty Ice – and now it's the hippies turn to look puzzled and confused, for why would they want that?

And out comes Dave with the mountain bikes to take the limey cruising around town, and talks about picking wild berries and wild garlic and all the crazy things you can eat just off the ground if you know what you're looking for; and talks about Mexican hallucinogenic cactuses and the visions they induce; and the spirits of our ancestors, and energy and chakras, and I've got no idea what this bearded little Dave is going on about but he sure seems kind of happy.

I get stung by my first ever wasp in Missoula. And my second. And my third. It's on different days and miles apart and I wonder what the hell is going on. Maybe the wasps of Missoula don't like me. Or maybe the wasps of Missoula are trying to tell me something.

And Dave and chums are sweet, and three days I stay there with them, and in the garden, in the sun, naked chests and pube-declaring shorts, Dave and chums put on a circus show of spinning sticks and balls and ribbons, and Dave has this thing I've never seen before: devil sticks, it's called. He has two straight rubber-coated sticks in his hands, and one longer one with jingling tennis balls on each end, and with his two he sends the one flipping and flying and whizzing around his head and under legs and he's throwing shapes like shapes have gone out of fashion and come back in again all retrofied and groovier than ever. I sit and watch this dancing dude with his dancing sticks and hours and hours pass with me hypnotised; and when I leave them and Missoula a set of those sticks goes with me, and by the road while I wait I drop them and pick them up and tentatively start to put together some spinning hippy moves of my own.

A few days later I wake up in a strange bed in a strange motel and I have no idea how I got there. My mouth tastes of cheap beer; the space behind my eyes is pounding. Someone, it appears, has injected some sort of nasty chemical directly into my brain. The last thing I remember is dancing wildly at a fancy dress party put on by the rangers of Glacier National Park, the remnants of a duct-tape bikini clinging valiantly to my chest. An image of a pretty girl's face looking horrified and askance. A keg. Five dollars, all-you-can-drink. Yes, I think, that might have had something to do with it.

I grab my pack and leg it; I may not know how I've found that bed but I know for goddamned sure I haven't paid for the privilege.

I stumble out into the cool, foggy morning and head on over to the tracks. Today's the day I fulfil my dream. Today's the day I finally board that westbound freight up and over the Rockies and motor on into Seattle. Except that's what I'd said yesterday, and instead I'd ended up spending the entirety of it staked out in the local diner watching mournfully as every single train that had come my way had blasted on through, full speed ahead, and no possibility whatsoever of clambering aboard. It's doubtful whether they ever slow down or stop in East Glacier; those trains really seem to run to a pattern. I decide to head on back into the plains in search of a better place to catch out. I trudge through the sleeping town under a huge grey sky and the chill of the morning reminds me that the end of the summer, and the end of my travels on the magical roads of western America is approaching. Soon I'll be thinking about settling down; soon I'll be in Colorado or Hawaii or Alaska and back to working and living normally. It will be amazing but it's not a prospect I look forward to. The time on these roads has been too good.

I stand alone on US-2, one of America's great coast-to-coast highways, and I stick out my thumb.

I soon pick up a ride and leave the mountains behind, and before me and all around me sits the legendary Big Sky country of Montana. It's everything I've been told it would be: the overwhelming expanse of the heavens crowding almost every part of my vision – just sky and sky and sky, one vast cathedral dome.

And suddenly my head is filled with dreams of hitching all the way back across Montana and North Dakota, right on into Minnesota, in order to catch this train at its source. I imagine the journey from the Great Lakes city of Duluth, sitting astride that hundred-car freight and speeding through the vastness of the plains, rolling on forever, hundreds of miles of nothingness punctuated sporadically by grain silos and blink-and-you'll-miss-'em towns, the glorious monotony finally broken as the Rockies slowly loom on the horizon, dark and ominous and growing ever more enormous. It's tempting – it's so, so tempting – but it's also an extra two and a half thousand miles and I'm just too hungry for the train and for the journey west for that.

My rides are mostly Blackfoot Indians. There's two schools of thought, I've found, regarding American Indians: one, that they are wise and nature loving, the image of the elder talking emotionally yet collectedly of "many buffalo," of the terrible tragedies that befell a noble and proud race at the hands of the pale face; and, two, that the Indians are no better than a bunch of booze-hungry and lazy rednecks, drinking themselves into early graves on government money and gambling their livelihoods away. Personally, I don't know if I've had enough experience to make any kind of informed judgement – although I have to say that pretty much all my experience of Indians back in Arizona and Wyoming confirmed the latter. The Blackfoot, on the other hand, I find kind, intelligent, humorous, and not drunk at all.

I get picked up by one old guy who makes this odd little sojourn into the plains all the more worthwhile: he's hilarious. He tells me extravagant tales of the history of his people; claims that they once numbered fifty million; compares their treatment to that of the Jews in Nazi Germany; re-enacts a supposed conversation between Hitler and Roosevelt.

"'Listen, ya dirty crippled bastard,'" Hitler had apparently said, "'what I'm doin' ain't no worse that what you done to those Indians, ya dirty crippled bastard, you.'"

For some reason he believed 'dirty', 'crippled' and 'bastard' were just the kind of words that the one-balled man with the moustache would have used when speaking to his opposite number – and I was having too much of a good time to argue with him.

Waiting for my rides was just as much fun as having them. The country is just *so* flat, and *so* empty, I couldn't help but be overcome by the sheer ridiculousness of it all, seeing myself standing out there thousands of miles from home surrounded by nothing but the vast expanse of fields of grain stretching away to the distant horizon like a sea, the parallel twin delights of the highway and the railroad shooting arrow straight away from me and out over the curve of the earth. Though there were few cars I couldn't have cared less, completely and utterly fulfilled by the wonder of my situation. I felt high, hopping between the tracks and the road, dancing and spinning and singing customised sections of Nirvana's "On a Plain." By the time the sun came out, around noon, I was in love – and even more so when I was deposited under the shadow of a twenty-seven-foot tall concrete penguin proudly proclaiming: "Cut Bank – Coldest Spot in America!"

Now it could be that the penguin bewitched me but I felt strangely drawn to Cut Bank (population: three thousand one hundred and five) and decided to break my journey there. I visited some funky little stores and strolled the unspoiled streets, seemingly unchanged since the fifties and the days when the two-lane highways were king. The locals were friendly and welcoming. I was charmed.

As I walked back towards the highway a monstrous rainstorm swooped upon the town – the first real rain I'd seen in around four or five months – and I took shelter under the porch of a little visitors' information centre.

"Come in," a voice said behind me. I turned to see the smiling round face of an Indian lady, her long hair in plaits. "Have a look around," she said, "we just opened yesterday."

"Thanks," I said, "I will." I walked over to a display of Blackfoot artefacts, looked at some pictures of the area. The woman asked me where I was from, what I was doing. Soon enough we were talking and laughing; I felt thoroughly happy in her company and twenty minutes had passed before I noticed that the rain had already stopped. I picked up my backpack and made ready to leave.

"Have you had any breakfast?" she asked.

I thought about what to say.

"I've had an apple," I said. The look on her face told me that an apple didn't really constitute a reasonable breakfast in her mind.

"Here," she said, pressing five dollars into my hand, "go to a diner and get yourself something to eat."

I pocketed the money and left. Already I had a plan of what to do: I would use part of the five dollars to buy a few bananas from the grocery store and the rest I would save. I would supplement my diet in the usual way, by stealing Twixes from Wal-Mart. This way, I would be full and fed, and have even more money for later.

But as I approached the grocery store I started to think about my kindly Indian benefactor and her shining round face and I had a change of heart. It wasn't my habit to go blowing that sort of money in one go, when a couple of bananas would have sufficed, but she had given it to me for a reason and I needed to honour her intention. I needed to treat her kindness with the respect it deserved.

Spending that five dollars, however, was far more difficult than I could have ever imagined.

I found a fifties-style diner and settled in at the long Formica counter fairly licking my lips in anticipation of this long overdue taste of the luxurious side of life. Three or four middle-aged waitresses buzzed about me carrying coffee-pots and delivering plates of food. The place was almost entirely populated by old women.

I ordered a coffee, burger and fries, and chatted with the waitress. I told her I was hitching around the west, checking out her beautiful country. She asked me what I'd seen. She listened with interest to my stories.

"You're very brave," she said, "I wish I'd had the courage to do something like that. Don't you ever get scared?"

"Maybe a little," I said, "sometimes. But, you know, ninety-nine percent of people are wonderful, so kind." I sipped some coffee and reminisced, eager to share some of the goodness I'd found in the world. "It's been an amazing experience," I said, "the best thing I ever did."

She smiled at me and filled my cup.

"I think you're very brave," she said, "very brave."

I sat back to enjoy the vibe and await the arrival of my food; tip included, it would come to exactly five dollars. I felt satisfied that I had done the right thing. I thought my little Indian lady would be happy.

Soon enough, a different waitress appears with my meal and places it on the counter in front of me.

"You know your food's paid for, don't you?" she says. And before I have time to answer her, she adds, "and you can have a piece of pie, too – chocolate, cheesecake or strawberry?"

Bemused, I mumble, "chocolate," and she goes to fetch my dessert.

I figured the first waitress had probably decided to let me have it on the house. I was overwhelmed with gratitude, and deeply moved by this second display of Cut Bank generosity. When the second waitress returned with my pie and told me what had actually happened, however, these feelings were multiplied tenfold: it wasn't the waitress at all, it was an elderly couple who had overheard my conversation and asked that the cost of my meal be added to their bill, embellishing it with a pudding.

I don't know why but, when she told me this, I practically burst into tears.

I looked around to thank them and they were nowhere to be seen – they had slipped silently away, not looking for any gratitude or praise, only seeking to show some kindness to a passing stranger.

I sat and stared at my food, and all the thoughts of the goodness I had been shown since stepping onto the road came flooding back to me. People had been so nice: people had fed me and washed my clothes; taken me in and trusted me with their homes and their possessions; listened to me and taught me and gone out of their way to take me to where I needed to be. Hundreds of them. Almost everyone I'd met. And when I thought of the shit I'd pulled in Charlottesville, and of the mess I'd left in England, and of how bad I'd been in my life, I just couldn't take it. Looking around that diner I felt so unworthy, their kind and innocent and accepting faces such a contrast to myself, a history of larceny, a bellyful of stolen Twixes, the scrawled words 'limey bastard' emblazoned upon my backpack. I reached down and turned it over, ashamed that any of them might have seen it, ashamed that I had ever rejoiced in such a moniker. In the mirror of that diner I was nothing but a selfish and arrogant fool. The camel's back was broken. I couldn't take it any more. It was like being beaten over the head with the most wonderful stick. Finally, I had got the message. Finally, I knew for certain that my life had to change. Finally, I gave in.

Chapter Eight

Some days on the road were like a life in themselves, and when I'd look back on them, tucked up in my sleeping bag at night, in the grass somewhere, in a park, under a tree, I'd piece them together and lay puzzled and happily confused that so much had happened in such little time. Some days I'd meet dozens of wildly varied people, get to know several different towns, more than one type of terrain and weather, and have all the ups and downs and emotional experiences of a week or a month in normal life. Some days I'd go to sleep a changed person from the one that had woken up. And my day in Cut Bank was one of those days, and perhaps the most memorable of those days, and the one that had the longest lasting impact. For I never stole a Twix again – nor anything else that did not belong to me. And that was just the most tangible of the transformations that came over me during that Montana burger and fries epiphany.

I caught the train in Havre the next morning and my great Burlington Northern and I plunged ever onwards through the plains and back towards the Rockies, accompanied by the highway, and me there, that mad little Yorkshireboy atop the mighty metal beast, dancing for the passing motorists, waving at every car. Destiny was fulfilled.

A hundred miles in, though, we began to slow down on approach to a town and I didn't like the idea of sitting there in full view of the townsfolk and the railway workers. I disboarded, and once more I was on the earth. I figured I could walk through town and maybe recatch it at the other end once it readied to leave. But she started up again and I climbed back on – this time on the back of a wagon that lacked the stable platforms I was used to, that had an open space that allowed me to drop down between the great spinning wheels and hold myself there, out of sight.

The wheels spun and I knew one slip would see me underneath them.

We picked up speed. We were going through town.

I popped up my head to see what was what.

There was a cop.

I leapt up from my hiding place and grabbed my pack and sprinted off. I looked behind me and the cop was coming over the train and after me. I knew, though, that I could run faster than any American cop. The buildings of Shelby were just ahead and I could lose him in there. I ran and ran and I ran straight up a dead-end alley.

And when I turned to exit the cop was there, gun in hand.

"Against the wall!" he screamed.

Pack went down, hands leapt behind head, body pressed against the wall, just as the nice man had said.

The gun was right there by my head.

Cuffs and threats and muttered anger about me making him risk life and limb by coming over that train after me. Dragged off and dumped in the back of a car, and arrested once more.

Soon I'm chained to a desk in front of a couple of pissed looking cops.

"Name?" they go. "Date of birth?"

"Rory O'Sullivan," I say – it's my crime name, the one I'd used on the ranger back in Yellowstone. Already a plan is hatching in my head – after all, I don't have my passport on me, lost somewhere back in the desert at the ranch – and that Yellowstone ticket may be the only thing that identifies me. Unless they find my plane ticket or drivers' license.

I'm charged with criminal trespass and resisting arrest. I'll be up before a judge and then fined. I'll be released and then back on the road in no time.

Except there's something wrong here: these cops aren't like the ones back in New York or Virginia or New Mexico. They aren't prepared to accept the lies that are coming out of my mouth. They want to know the truth and they know that I'm not giving it to them. They know it because they've been through my pack and looked at every single thing that's in it.

"How long you been here?" they say.

"Two months."

"You've made a lot of friends in two months, been a lot of places."

I shrug and nod my head.

"Who's Rory Miller?" they say. "Don't suppose that's your real name?"

"That's my dad's name," I say, "O'Sullivan's my mum's surname and that's my real name, but sometimes I like to use my dad's name, Miller."

They're not buying any of it: these Shelby cops may be smalltown but they sure ain't dumb. Just my luck: my first non-dumb American cops.

Fingerprints. Mugshot. Cell.

"I think we'd best get Border Patrol in and fax this off to the FBI, see if you're wanted for anything else. If you are, we'll soon find out. In the meantime, how's about you think about telling us the truth? Because you're not going anywhere until you do."

And as I sit there full of sorrow and fear and just about every kind of miserable there is to feel all my indiscretions come flooding back to me, just as they would soon come flooding into the hands of these damn bloodhound Montana police officers. New York subway crimes and New Mexico county court non-appearances; and over two dozen traffic tickets and citations from across the country not once accounted for; and the stolen grain truck, in which I've since realised I've left my fully-fingerprinted replacement Gilligan hat and glasses case; right back to the Ohio Mazda incident and, worst of all, the question of whether they really have dropped those charges against me back in

Virginia – and, even if they have, whether the justice department is fine and dandy with me skipping bail and toddling off into the sunset like that.

They would have it all, the whole rotten mess, and soon I'd be facing a smirking cop and attempting to somehow answer his query about whether I'd ever been in Charlottesville, Virginia, Mr Miller?

Strange, it was, the feeling that then came over me. I sank into my chair and sighed, and with the entire mess right there in front of me I resigned myself to it and accepted the whole thing. In my heart I said, "yes, I did it all," and there was a peace in that. "The key to happiness," I'd often been told, "is acceptance." And making the best of a bad situation, I suppose. Suddenly it didn't seem so bad that I'd be spending six months or more in a strange jail in a strange country; I mean, what was the point in getting upset about this fate that I couldn't possibly avoid? And, on the bright side, what an incredible learning experience. And what a great ending for the book. I swear, I was smiling as I thought all this. Shit happens, and that's just the way it goes – it's what you do with the shit that makes the difference to how you feel.

The Border Patrol guy comes in and sits me down. He rolls out the same questions that the Shelby cops did earlier.

"Name?" he says.

"Rory Miller."

"Miller? What happened to O'Sullivan?"

"I just made that up. I was hoping it would help me avoid trouble."

He shifts his not unsubstantial frame in the chair and makes a note on the paper. He raises an eyebrow at me and behind him I watch the two local cops stand arms folded and frowning.

"So how long have you been in the United States, Mr Miller?"

"Sixteen months," I say, "this time."

More eyebrows and frowns.

"Well, Mr Miller, it's good to see you finally telling the truth. You could have done that earlier and saved yourself a lot of trouble. Did you think that we wouldn't find out? Or maybe you think that American police are stupid?"

I do my best to pretend that, no, I don't think that.

"Fact is, it doesn't matter anyway; we've already decided to deport you. You'll be back in England before you know what's happening."

He says this with a great deal of satisfaction.

And though I conceal it, I greet his words with no small measure of satisfaction of my own. Suddenly, a lifeline. Suddenly there's a chance that I'll be somewhere over the Atlantic before they realise just what a naughty little illegal I am. And I start to pray that the mechanisms of the Immigration Department are in better order than those of the police.

Chapter Nine

It's not so bad being in that jail: it's a damn sight better than New York or Virginia. There are only three other guys in there and they're all cool and, to be honest, the whole thing is a laugh. Trapped in there, with nothing to do, we become like five year-olds, regressed and doolally, and spend all day lying on our mattresses and watching cartoons, or speaking for hours in made up alien languages, or making paper aeroplanes and then eating the quite nice food they bring us before tossing the empty containers into a corner. We have fights with loo roll. We whoop and holler and aim cheeky japes at our jailers. I make a football out of toilet paper and water but I get it confiscated and warned for wasting supplies. I develop a fancy for toothpaste, and become convinced it gets me high, and eat tube after tube of it and get warned for wasting that too. And I pile all my food boxes in my cell and throw banana skins everywhere, and after about three days the warden comes in disgusted and orders me to clean it up like I'm his naughty teenage son. But what can he do to us? I mean, we're already in jail.

I wait and I wait and all the time I'm living with equal amounts of hope and fear; and every time the warden opens the door I wonder what he's got with him: a one-way ticket to Blighty? Or a big fat FBI file on yours truly? But the wheels of justice turn slowly in these parts: one guy has been waiting two months to see a judge and all he did was steal a book of stamps. Another guy – a Canadian law student – has already been in there a week and has been told that he might have to wait another month just to enter his plea; judge is on holiday, you see. And his crime? Coming across the border with some mushroom stems in his car. He didn't even know they were there.

On day four I'm led into a tiny miniature courtroom to see the judge. He's just a guy sat behind a desk, really. He asks me how I plead.

"What happens if I plead not guilty?" I say.

"You'll have to wait for the circuit judge to come around."

"And how long will that take?"

"About three weeks – he's on a golfing holiday."

"Ah. And if I say guilty?" I ask.

He coughs and looks at me wearisome. "You'll be fined," he says, "and released. Although, as I understand it in your case, that means deportation."

"Yes please," I say, "I'll take guilty."

He shuffles some papers and goes through the motions, ticks a couple of boxes and scribbles a few things with a pen.

"For each count," he says, "I fine you a hundred and twenty-five dollars."

I panic. I haven't got enough. If I can't pay will they keep me in there forever?

"I'm sorry, judge, I don't think I can pay that. I've only got two hundred dollars to my name – and I don't see how I could get any more in here."

He looks down at his paper and scribbles some more. I see him draw a couple of lines and cross something out.

"For each count," he says, "I fine you one hundred dollars."

And that's that, all my money gone.

And back to the cell, and back to the wait, and the problem is that because I've lost my passport they can't really prove who I am or put me on a plane, and it's taking a while to bring all that together. But on day nine, they come for me, and into a white van I'm put and soon I'm back on that glorious Montana highway – albeit this time behind a wire mesh screen.

But I am bound for Seattle.

Six hundred miles they drive me, these two bullet proof-jacketed immigration officers, and on the way we chat and have a laugh and they decide to remove my cuffs, such a nice little criminal am I. At a gas station we meander about and I ask one of them, "what will you do if I run off?" – thinking woods and hiding and America once more.

"Shoot you," he says, in a good natured sort of way.

And into Seattle and emergency passport arranged, and plane ticket purchased – nine hundred dollars, it's cost them! British Airways! – and they even buy me a beer and a McDonald's at the airport and try and get me an upgrade into first class.

"We got one for a German guy once," they tell me. But no luck for me.

They're seriously nice, these guys.

And on the plane, and the only way I know how to beat jetlag is to stay up all night drinking, and then stay up all the next day and collapse exhausted at the end of it all. And off I go, boozing it up and watching movies, my first time on BA, saucy stewardesses and wild and crazy me, one day up a mountain, one day on a train, and the next in jail and very nearly incarcerated for a substantial length of time but instead sent back to England in some style for absolutely free.

I roll off that plane drunk as a bastard and there's some vague memory of being shepherded through security by frowning-eyed officials, and a little flash of a nodding and sozzled pink-backpacked tramp on the underground, and the next thing I know I'm at Tim's work and we're off to see Ben. And does the rum flow? And do the stories get told? And am I the returned hero, back from the brink, back among friends, running around crazy and passing out, only to rise up again from the depths to run around crazy some more, half slicing off my toe on the chicken wire fence, blood gushing everywhere on my first night back in England?

I'm up in Yorkshire, spending time with my grandmother and commiserating the passing of my great bear of a granddad. He was such a good man. I can't believe I've missed the funeral. I work out that he died while I was camped up high on a huge red rock somewhere near Mexican Hat in Utah, alone in the desert and loving it. I would have come home if I'd known…

I've been back a month and I'm going crazy: the looming reality of normal life. I've done less living in all that time than in one day on the road. Nothing's happening and I wish it would. Every day should be exciting and interesting – every day should end with my tired head on the pillow looking back content and saying, "well that was cool," and, "I'm glad I'm where I am." But now I'm back I don't know how to find the thing I want. I don't even know what that thing is.

I'm standing outside the cinema in Wakefield and watching all the little tin containers go around the roundabout and I'm thinking, "what is this?" I've just been to see The Truman Show and I can find no more reality out here than in that false, made-for-TV life of his. We move from one box to another as if we were in a trance, just part of the leaderless herd. We carry on with our lives and never really know why. It's ridiculous; I can't live like this. There has to be some meaning

I'm emerging up the top of the stairs at South Elmsall railway station and right smack bang in front of me is one of the most glorious sunsets I've ever seen. It rivals Arizona; it's a beautiful fluffy mix of all the reds and yellows and oranges and blues that Mother Nature has in her pallet. And I thought we didn't get sunsets in Yorkshire. And I thought we didn't get stars too – but the stars here shine brighter than they do on Broadway, and I realise it's all just a matter of perspective. You walk around with your head looking down you see nothing but dirt. Maybe I've just never looked up before. Beauty, they say, is in the eye of the beholder – but you've got to be beholding in the first place.

I'm in a pub in Leeds, sat next to a girl I'm sort of in love with. She's written a poem about me and my travels in the deserts and I think she likes me too. We're watching my dad's band and I can't think of a single word to say to her. I'm locked and I'm blocked and the frustration is killing me. I keep turning to her – she's just so lovely – but all I can do is turn away again. I've been trying to stay sober but finally I buy a drink, and then another, and when I'm drunk I guess I do find things to say. We kiss in the bus stand. She's just the kind of girl I'd want to be with if I was the kind of guy I want to be.

On a beach in the Caribbean, seeking a change. It's okay – but it's no Wyoming.

On a couch in Wakefield, watching Groundhog Day. My God, I think, life can be marvellous – and yet we live it as though the prospect of life is far more terrifying than the spectre of death. We just wait and wait for something to happen, killing time before time kills us. But there is so much that is available to us, so much that we can do, so why aren't we doing it? Or, more precisely, why aren't I?

On the toss of a coin I buy a plane ticket to Vancouver, spurred on by the twin demons of seeking a place to settle down and just never feeling right. I envisage a winter in the Rockies, one of the cool young ski towns I've heard of – Whistler or Banff – now that Telluride has been denied. Indecision follows me all the way there and in the two a.m. airport I wonder what the hell I'm doing, why I've once again left my friends, why I'm in a country where the people don't understand me and my sarcasm, and dryness and references to Vic Reeves go unappreciated. The suspicious immigration officer has declined me a six month visa, offering only two, and all about me people speak in these weird accents that are not quite the American twang I know and love so well, and now speak with myself. And every time I hear them say, "eh," or pronounce "about" as though it rhymes with "boat," I know there's only one thing for it. As day breaks I'm on a bus down to the American border and in the early November chill I'm standing once more face-to-face with a real live U.S. Immigration Officer, new passport in hand, and saying, "can I come in please?"

Fifteen minutes he's gone, running my stuff through the system. And that's not a good sign. But then he comes back and says, "it's six dollars," and even though I know I'm supposed to be banned for five years, and it's only three months since I was last there, there I am again, on American soil, standing in the road with a backpack and a thumb and this time I really am going to Seattle.

Chapter Ten

Why oh why did I go back to America? Why on earth, when all I wanted were relationships that went deeper than a few hours, like-minded souls and people I could grow to love, and who could do the same for me? And dreams of a dear sweet Yorkshire girl, lazy mornings cuddled up in bed talking and laughing and never really wanting to get out? And a place to call home and feel comfortable in?

I'm on the bare-tree autumn roads chugging along through dismal Washington mist and I get the feeling that the whole trip is just going to be one big lousy disappointment. Once more it's single guys in pickup trucks and I just can't be arsed with it. I can't be arsed with America and I can't be arsed to hitch either. I'm tired of the road and of meeting the same people over and over again, having the same conversations. These relationships can only go so far. It's cold and it's grey and I've been a fool to think that I could recreate something of those wildly wonderful summer months. The magic has passed and it can't be the same because I'm not the same. A new challenge is what's needed – and what greater challenge could there be than to learn how to settle down and find magic and happiness in the humdrum sameness of everyday life? I know that's all there is to this trip: I know that I've come six thousand miles just to learn that it really is time to go home.

I do make Seattle, though, and I do finally kneel at Hendrix's grave and issue a heartfelt and surprisingly tearful thank you to my first ever teacher, the man who sang of manic depression and, oh, there ain't no life nowhere, and for ten days I sort of have fun playing cards and watching movies with Lauren's older sister Carrie and her roommates in the ever-grey Seattle gloom. I've heard about the weather in Washington State – about how the sun never shines from October to April; about how the suicide rate goes sky-high; of how it shames the rains and grays of England – and everything I've heard is true: not once in those ten days do I feel even an ounce of sunlight or see the rain abate and it's depressing as hell. I was going to hitch down the Pacific Highway, finish my American odyssey, but if this is what the weather's going to be like I don't think I'll bother. Instead, I ring around for driveaway cars and hope to find one that'll take me back to Virginia, to grab my stuff and see Lauren, and then head back home without a doubt in my mind.

I land a car to Georgia and wait for it to come ready.

There's a strange thing that happens one day in Seattle, though, walking around a lake not too far from Carrie's house. I'm doing a lap of the water

201

huddled up in my big Brit jacket and this guy coming the other way catches my eye and smiles.

"I saw you last time around," he says.

That's all he says – but the way he says it, and the way he smiles…there's something not quite right about it. And he hasn't seen me before anyway. And there are dozens of other people around when he says it – so why has he chosen me?

It's nothing, really, but it puzzles me so severely I feel shaken to my core and I can't let it go. I feel like he knows me. I feel like I did that crazy mad night in the West Memphis truckstop – only this time I'm not sleep deprived and hyped up on coffee.

Who the hell is this guy?

The next day the car falls through and I've had enough of Seattle gloom. I hitch out of there with a seventy year-old granny and spend the night at hers, giving her my best ever game of Scrabble and feeling mighty embarrassed by my margin of victory. The day after that I spend the night at another woman's place getting stoned, and eating the world's finest chicken nuggets, and just as she drops me off she tells me that she likes me.

"If you ever want to settle down," she says, "I'll take you on."

I tell her I'm flattered and that I'll think about it. But, the truth is, she's nowhere near attractive enough for my tastes.

I'm still in Washington and going nowhere fast. The gloom is all encompassing. I'm getting rained on all day and it's hours and hours waiting for each ride, soaked to the skin and freezing, and so much walking. Oregon's the same. This really is the pits.

I call Lauren from a truckstop and pour my frustrated and malcontented heart out to her. I've been there for hours. I've already walked six miles that day. It just won't stop raining. My bones hurt, Lauren, and I'm tired and I'm lonely and I think I've got pneumonia. I can't understand why no one will pick me up. I just want to go home.

I walk back outside and half-heartedly ask the nearest trucker if he'll take me.

"Si," he says, "vamos." He's Mexican. He's dear sweet Alex. He's smiling and he's bouncing and he's driving all the way to San Diego, right down there in the best part of America, because the wester you get, and the souther you go, the better it all becomes. And there's nowhere as southwest as San Diego.

I'm onboard and I'm smiling. I'm up there in that high cab and Alex's simple olive-skinned happiness is infectious. The rain that has hounded me so is outside now and unable to touch me. I fall asleep in the seat and when I open my eyes it's the next day and we're deep down in California and the skies are blue blue blue. It's like I've never seen sky before: two weeks of grey and now the skies are blue. I can't stop saying it: the skies are blue.

Oh, holy beloved road God, how can I ever thank Thee!

Alex and the skies and the goodness of the road have cheered me so thoroughly that I decide to part from him at Stockton and cut across to the coast, and once more I'm gazing out at Pacific Ocean and finally making some of that blesséd US-1, Carmel and Monterey and sweeping bends with far below waves on one side and pine-covered mountains and hills on the other, and not a house in sight, just that thin strip of tarmac zooming over bridges and above rocky beaches, and it's Big Sur, baby, all the way, oh yeah.

I make San Diego almost exactly two years to the day that I first laid eyes on the place. Gus, my old friend stroke enemy from Charlottesville is living out there now and I email him to offer an olive branch over a cup of coffee. Instead, he invites me to stay with him and his new girlfriend, Kat. It's a surprising gesture considering the last time we'd seen each other I'd been plotting his kidnapping and he was calling me a dipshit in The Musings. I guess we're not the kind of people to dwell on such things.

I find their house in Ocean Beach and Gus says I should stay till the weekend, till after this Christmas party they've got planned. We drink beer and have long conversations about fate and the road and when Gus goes to work I go shopping with Kat and we take her miniscule white Schnauzer for walks along the beach. Kat's an attractive girl and we get on well. But I don't want no fuck-ups here; all I'm looking for is a bit of quiet in the sun, and maybe a chance to redeem myself in Gus's eyes. And then it's back to Virginia and my two boxes and home.

On the Wednesday I go out to Pacific Beach and get chatting with these Italians and we smoke some pot. Soon enough I'm marvellously stoned and tunnelling frantically in the sand and mumbling at my feet. I look up and I'm all alone; the Italians have gone and so has the day, the sun now low in the sky and shining golden across the water. Evening walkers are silhouettes against the horizon. I remember then that I've got the keys to the house and I have to get back. I get up slowly and start to walk.

Suddenly I hear this great *whooshing* sound as though some huge and powerful prehistoric bird has come swooping down over my head. I look around the beach and the sand is empty, like it's been swept clean of people. Everything is silence and I become aware of only one thing: a lone dark figure standing by the water about a hundred feet away.

I see the outline of a squat, goblin-like body and a bearded face with hair tied back. It starts dancing and spinning and it's juggling something. It looks familiar. I focus more closely and I realise it looks exactly like Dave Shapiro, the hippy guy I'd stayed with in Montana back in the summer.

"Wow," I say to myself, "cool hallucination, man," and laugh. Of all the things I might expect my subconscious to manifest on a California beach this fleeting figure from my recent past is certainly a surprise. I watch his silhouette perform its strange routine and debate the various pros and cons of approaching my hallucination to see what it has to say for itself. Most likely it's not what I think; most likely it's some completely different guy – or a canoodling couple – or I'll get to it and find that I'm actually sitting on a bus somewhere in a pool of drool and having a deep conversation with my knees, much to the amusement and consternation of my fellow passengers. There's no way it can be Dave – but it sure looks like him. I decide to give it a try.

And, against all odds, it's him.

"Dave," I say, "what the fuck are you doing here?" He stops twirling and grabs his sticks. He stares at me.

"Rory?" he says. "Dude! Is that really you?" A big smile comes across his face. He throws his sticks to the sand and steps towards me. "Oh man," he says, "this is too much." He stretches out his arms and gives me a hug. "Unreal," he says, "I was just thinking about you."

"I thought I was hallucinating," I say. I tell him I'm running late and need to get back to my friends, and he says we can get some bikes and ride together. He's staying with his sister just a few blocks away.

We cycle the smooth San Diego streets and fill each other in on the last few months. I tell him about my arrest and deportation.

"That's rough," he says, "they're such bastards."

"They are," I say, "but I'll tell you the truth, it worked out perfectly. I never liked England before – I fuckin' hated the place and couldn't stand the thought of going back – but things were different this time. I noticed things I'd never seen before, like the stars and the sunset, even in my home town. I used to tell people that we didn't have stars or sunsets – or even sun. But it was beautiful."

"So what brings you back?" he says.

"Not sure," I say, "maybe I got bored; I guess I still thought there was more to life than settling down and having babies and working. I missed the road, too, and it was driving me nuts that I hadn't seen the northwest and the big trees. But I didn't even bother with it when I was up there it was so fuckin' wet and cold. Tell you the truth, I'm a bit bored of travelling now too; I'm on my way back to England to see if I can make it work there. I think I've made my peace with Uncle Sam. I feel done with America."

"Really?" he says, "me too. I'm going down to Mexico."

We pull into Gus and Kat's and I open the door. Thirty seconds later I hear their car in the driveway. Dave and I go out to meet them.

"Perfect timing," I say, and then turn to Dave. "This is Dave; I stayed with him like four months ago in Montana. I just bumped into him on the beach, totally random."

"Really?" Kat says, "that's wonderful!" She shakes Dave's hand and grins at him. "Are you travelling too?"

Dave nods eagerly. Behind us, Gus is walking into the house.

"Are you guys coming in?" Kat says, "I just picked up some beers."

"I'd love a beer," I say, "but I think we'll just sit out and chat for a while – catch up, you know." Kat smiles and hands us a couple of drinks.

"Nice to meet you, Dave," she says, "that's such a great coincidence, you two meeting like that." She disappears inside and Dave and I sit down on the lawn. Dave pulls something out of his backpack and starts to unfold it. He spreads it out on the grass between us and talks. It's a map of Mexico.

"I've been having these dreams," he says, "I've been dreaming for years about the pyramids down there, down in the Yucatan." He points to the map, to a mass of land at the most south-easterly point. "That's where the Mayans were," he says, "before they left the Earth. They learned how to raise their vibration and moved into their light bodies. It's like some energy vortex. I know I'm supposed to go there."

He looks at me with a sort of bright-eyed, excited expression on his face, and I know he wants me to feel it too. Crazy Dave: he thinks this stuff is real. First it was magic hills in Glastonbury and now it's vibrations and pyramids.

"Look," he says, pointing to the map, at San Diego, at the place where we now sit, "what I'm thinking is, I can hitch down here, down Baja California, to La Paz. That's like the world's longest peninsular, a thousand miles of deserts and mountains and beaches. There's just one road straight down the middle, all the way from north to south." He runs his finger down this long sliver of land, tracing the red line of Highway 1. "And then here," he says, stopping at a town on the east, "I can take a ferry over to the mainland, to Mazatlan, and then down the coast to Puerto Vallarta and Acapulco, across to Oaxaca, Chiapas, and then: the Yucatan." He finishes his journey and looks up at me. "It's all jungle down there," he says, "I might even go to Guatemala, to Tikal." He picks up his beer and takes a schwill. "You should come too," he says, "I'm leaving on Monday."

I sit and stare at the entirety of that enormous, sprawling nation. I've never looked at a map of Mexico before and suddenly I realise I know absolutely nothing about the place – except that they speak Spanish and live mad, dirty, dangerous lives. The idea of going to Mexico is terrifying. And yet, as my eyes move from place to place across that great unknown, I feel the first twinges of excitement and the lure of adventure begins to whisper sweet temptations into my heart.

"We could make it down the Baja together, and then, if you wanted, you could head north instead of coming to the pyramids." He points to where the ferry docks and fingers a route heading to the top right hand corner of the page. "That takes you back to Texas," he says, "if you're going that way anyway."

"It looks good," I say. I have to admit, it looks good.

"That's the Copper Canyon," he says, touching a point halfway along this alternative route he has planned for me, "it's like four times bigger than the Grand Canyon. It's supposed to be amazing."

My head is swimming. I'm plunged back into a conflict I thought was won. Suddenly, I'm enthralled by the possibilities of adventures new.

"It looks good, Dave," I say again, "but the thing is I really want to go back to England. As soon as I'm done here I'm gonna make Virginia as fast as I can, pick up my stuff there, and then home."

He lifts his head from the map, and sips his beer.

205

"Are you sure?" he says. He's obviously disappointed. I hate to let him down but I've got to do the right thing.

"God, I've done so much travelling I just don't think I can do anymore. No, really, it's time for me to go home." Now I feel really bad. "But I'm sure you're gonna have a great time, Dave, I mean, good for you, it'll be awesome."

"Yeah," he says, folding the map.

"Listen," I say, "if I change my mind I know where to find you."

The next day Gus goes to work and Kat asks me if I can help her practise her shiatsu.

"What do I have to do?" I say.

"Just relax and let it happen."

We go into the bedroom and I take off my shirt. I lie on the bed and she climbs up beside me. She moves her hands over my back and I let out a little moan. Her touch feels good.

After a while I tell her about Dave's proposal.

"That sounds great," she says, "are you gonna go?"

"I don't know," I say, flinching under her hand.

"Is it too hard?" she says. "Tell me if it's too hard."

"Maybe a little." I hear her squirt some oil onto her hand and feel the moist smoothness as she rubs it into my skin.

"The thing is," I say, "when I was back in England I felt like I was with my own people, like I could communicate more easily. It made me realise I wanted more from my relationships than what I got through travelling. It made me really question the whole hitchhiking thing." She finds a tender spot and I pause to concentrate on my body. "I mean, it was brilliant, don't get me wrong, but it was like having the same conversation over and over again. I never really got to know anyone."

"U-uh," she says, her hands moving up and down my spine.

"I want to learn things," I say, "and I don't need to meet any more people, I just want to know certain people more. I know it's only a few weeks out of life but it's nearly a year since I slept in my own bed and I haven't been truly settled for God knows how long. I think it might have damaged me. I feel like I don't even know how to live a normal life anymore. I mean, when was the last time I had a good friend, one I knew would still be there in six months, or a year – or even a week?"

"Well that's because you keep moving around."

"I know, and that's the point – I need to stop. I don't need to be heading in the opposite direction, going to a place where I can't speak the language. I shouldn't even be *thinking* of crossing borders. *And* I don't have any money." I let out a sigh. "I guess I'm just ready for something familiar, something I can rely on."

She pushes into the small of my back and all the air rushes out of my lungs.

"So you're not going?" she says.

I hold my breath while she works on another tight spot. I squeeze my eyes and then everything lets go.

"I don't know," I say, "I just can't stop thinking about it. It's like – you won't laugh, will you?"

"I don't know," she says, "I might."

"Oh," I say. I don't want her to laugh.

"No," she says, "I won't laugh." She giggles and I wait until she goes quiet.

"It's like something bigger is at work. It's like something wants me to follow him down there."

It's Monday morning and I'm eating breakfast with Gus and Kat and Gus is saying something about last night's Christmas party. As ever the sun is out and the cloudless skies are impossibly blue: it's another perfect day in southern California. I should be relaxed and enjoying it but I'm not. I can't sit still and I know it has something to do with Dave. The thought of him just won't leave me alone – it's like everything I've ever done in my life has led me to that meeting and if even one little thing had been different it would never have happened. The timing had to be immaculately perfect. Even the decisions I've made in the last few weeks, and on that day, could have changed everything. But what if I hadn't met those Italians and hadn't gotten stoned with them? And what if Gus hadn't taken me in, or the driveaway hadn't fallen through, or my rides down the coast had been just that little bit quicker, that little bit slower? Even my first meeting with Dave was the result of strange and random coincidences, what with the Wyoming hitching boys, the grain truck, and freight train ride. It feels like destiny – but how can it be that when it's so flimsy and fragile, and so entirely dependent on apparently pointless and even ludicrous decisions? And yet, there's such a perfection about the whole thing it could almost have been written in stone.

"Fuck it," I say, pushing my chair away from me and leaving the table, "I want you two to witness this." I reach into my pocket and pull out a quarter.

"It's best of three," I say, "heads I go to Mexico, tails I stick with the plan and go back to England."

They stand up and join me in the middle of the room.

"Okay?" I say, "and no changing the rules."

I flip the coin with my thumb and watch it spin deliciously in the air. I catch it in my palm and slap it onto the back of my hand. I lift unveil it and smile, and let out a sigh of relief.

"Tails," I say, "tails never fails."

I toss the coin again and it comes down heads. I'm surprised, but it's okay; it's just for the drama. I know the last toss will be tails and I'll be on my way to England.

I look nervously at Gus and Kat and smile.

I steady myself one last time, and when the coin lands again I slowly lift my hand and stare.

207

Part Seven

Chapter One

Mexico, Mexico: I've never been and I don't want to go...

Mexico is dangerous. Mexico is something different and foreign and they don't speak English. Mexico is where Mexicans slit your bag open from behind, rob your passport, assume your identity. Mexico is dirty poisoned water, parasites and germs, poor begging children and donkey-fucking whores. Mexico is guerrilla warfare; maniacs with machine guns; bodies disappeared into jungles. Bent, bribe-loving cops. Armed soldiers on the highways just itching for trouble. Kidnappings. Terror.

I've hitched the whole way across America. I've been in American jail three times. I've ridden with self-confessed psychopaths and walked rattlesnake deserts, and seen the worst of what New York and Los Angeles and New Orleans has to offer. I've done all these things and watched time and time again as my fears have dissolved into nothingness and still I'm scared.

And judging by the expression on Dave's furtively glancing face, he's bricking it too.

We take the nervous San Diego trolley down to the border and it's my New York subway ride all over again. Only this time it's for real.

"Dave," I say, "I've got some pot in my bag."

"What?"

"That hash you gave me. I forgot it was there." We're about twenty feet from the border, shuffling along in a long line of tourists, surrounded by high barbed-wire fences. It looks like some kind of prison.

"Jesus," he mutters through clenched teeth, "well don't do anything now." He points with his eyes and I notice a bank of staring cameras. Ahead, a Mexican in a green uniform with a dog.

"I should go back."

"I think it'll be okay."

We walk on.

We walk on and on, and soon we're sitting by a stone fountain in Tijuana. American Immigration haven't said a word to us; neither have the Mexicans. I'm confused: we've just walked straight into another country, across a heavily guarded border – carrying drugs, for Christ's sake – and nobody's blinked an eyelid. What's more, this Tijuana hell of hustlers and fake medicine and ping pong-shooting prostitutes is actually quite mellow. It's mellower, in fact, than anywhere I've ever been. Two children play football in the dust against a wall; a couple of women are looking at shoes; and a dog sniffs its paw: that's about the extent of the action here.

We get a bus to set us on our way and soon we're motoring down the desert highway in a windowless old hulk, the breeze rushing through, the Pacific flashing by. I look over at Dave – his now relaxed face, his smiling hippy grin peeking out through beard and hair – and I understand instantly what this trip is about: I'm his shepherd. It's as simple as that.

I realise this and I feel as at peace with it as Dave looks. He's obviously been nervous about the whole thing, procrastinating in San Diego, desperate to find someone to go with him – and yet this is his destiny, his dream. All along I'd thought our meeting was about me – but I was wrong. Now I see that it was for him, that he needed someone to see him safely on his way. And for my part I get to enjoy some cheap living, a bit of tequila and some tacos, and then it's off to Texas to reacquaint myself with my own destiny. Seems like it's time to do someone else a favour and repay a bit of that good karma.

"Check this out," says Dave, and we go leaning out of the window and shielding our eyes against the sun.

It's the burnt-out shell of a car, about twenty feet off the road, down a steep ravine. And right there next to it, six white crosses and flowers.

"You see that all the time down here, apparently," he says. "'Mal kaiyays, bwayna hentay' – it means, 'bad roads, good people.' It's a Mexican saying."

And there again, another white cross, and another.

We sleep that first night in the dirt by a big wall just south of Ensenada. Dave introduces me to another Mexican tradition, a whale of a bottle of beer called, "la Ballena." You can take it back and get a refund, just like we used to do with Ben Shaw's Lemonade.

Dave licks his lips and stretches out on to the dusty ground. The woofs of a thousand dogs come drifting over from the darkness of the town: there's a blackout, a dust storm – just a little something to show that there might be some menace in the mellowness of this first Mexican night after all.

"I was scared to come down here," Dave says.

"Me too."

"I can't believe it" – he chuckles – "I've never been anywhere so laidback. Did you see that old guy with the sombrero in Tijuana? He was like something straight out of a cartoon. Did you see the light in his eyes? Golden, laughing – he knows the score."

"I missed him," I say. "Did you see that dog though? With all the teats?"

"This place is awesome," he says, "I can't wait to get on the road, down into the desert. One thousand miles. One road. And barely anything on it. They have a race down here – the Baja 1000. VW Beetles all the way. They call 'em Baja Bugs. We'll probably see some whales too."

Dave sips on his beer and then closes the top and it looks like he's done for the night. But he's still got half a bottle left. And mine's all gone.

"Don't you want your beer, Dave?" I say. I'm not tired. I've just got a little buzz going.

"Save it for tomorrow, I think, I've had enough. Check out the stars, my brother. Hoowee, sweet mamma!" And off he goes telling me some story about beings from a distant planet and how you can will them to appear before you if you try hard enough. He's seen them, he says; him and his friends. They were like light. Peace and light.

"Were you on acid?" I say.

"Yeah."

"I'd love to see aliens," I say, "I believe in stuff like that."

And with the noise of those thousand and one scraggly yapping dogs, and the gentle roar of the Pacific, and Dave's beer bottle still half-full, and my one eye open, and the blinking Mexican stars above our heads, we drift off, off and away, and all night long I dream I'm on a plane back to England, and when I get there I can't believe what I've just done and I wish I was back in Mexico.

But in this dream, there is no going back.

Chapter Two

And me and Dave, rolling on down the Baja, Highway 1 all the way, and if I thought the deserts in Arizona and Utah were wild, they ain't got nothin' on these babies. There's no sign of man out here: no billboards, no barbed wire, no tourist stops and rest areas and the gas stations are few and far between and sometimes they run out of petrol: if you get stuck you get stuck and you have to settle down until mañana comes – and sometimes mañana doesn't come for two or three days. Now we really are standing in the middle of nowhere, thumbs out and at the mercy of the road.

"This is some wild country out here," I say, "it's nothing but cactuses." There's forests of cactuses as expansive as any pine forest I've ever seen: they stretch right on out to the distant mountains, crowded in together, standing huge and tall – and you just know that on the other side of the next mountain range they'll be even more of them, land that man has never had the audacity to tangle with. This is the desert that I've always longed for, full of danger and possibility and madness.

"There must be a billion of them," I say.

But Dave don't like it: "we should get a bus," he says, "it's only fifty dollars."

Well fifty dollars is a quarter of what I've got, I tell him, and I don't do buses; besides, you've just got to relax, there's a car coming, it's just a matter of time. Dave's presence is making me love the road even more, making all the usual worries and frustrations vanish during the minutes and the hours by that lonely desert highway where the cars are as infrequent as the cactuses are plenty: the more anxious he grows, the more relaxed and loving it I become. I lie down by the road with my head on my pack and I swear I could just sink into that asphalt, that wait. The silence between cars in the beating desert sun is blesséd.

Dave's impatient and uncertain, as I was back in my early days, but when the inevitable ride comes and we race on up to meet our new friend and chauffeur he's as joyous and giddy as I ever was, and on we go, on the backs of pickups, in tourist vans, with RVing snowbirds from BC and Seattle. We pick up a ride with a Christian Arab and an Israeli Jew – "on a mission of love and peace," they tell us – and they talk about Todos Santos and the lazy beach days of swinging in hammocks and that's how you can pass your winter, and we grin at each other and our grins say, that sounds good to us. We ride with a California surfer dude in his half-dead, clapped-out old Beetle and he says, "have you seen the cows down here? You gotta see the cows, man – they're *tiny*" – and when we finally do see them, and he jumps up and down in his seat and goes, "see! see!" I realise that's just what cows look like naturally, before they've been pumped full of hormones and goddamned Frankensteined out of all sense of what evolution intended them to be, and it's little wonder they taste so good down here.

And on the back of an open-to-the-air cattle wagon we realise just why there are so many roadside crosses, standing there with the breeze in our hair and the amazement slowly dawning on us as the driver pulls out on an uphill blind mountain bend to overtake a fifty-foot long semi, a hundred foot drop to the side. There's not a chance in a million we'll survive if anything's coming the other way. We look at each other with the same questioning expression, then simultaneously realise that there's nothing we can do about it and – if your number's up, your number's up, and you might as well just enjoy the ride. We crack into grins and shake our heads.

"Fuckin' hell," says Dave, "he's a lunatic."

And so are we as we laugh and laugh as he crawls right past that long white semi, our hands on the rails, looking down over the edge and staring out across the wide-open expanse of rocky mountain desert.

We break a few days by the beach in Mulegé and in that sand by the quietly lapping waves I lie, and in that sand I feel rested for perhaps the first time in my life. Listen: I've been out there and alone, and chilled out in the desert, but one thing I've never been able to do was just stop. Just stop and not feel the need to move, the urge to go on. In Mulegé, I lie; and I lie so still, and so peacefully, for so long, that I begin to wonder what's happened to me. I remember the times I've hiked myself stupid – across the Grand Canyon; through the Superstitions and Canyonlands – and even though I was beat up and in desperate need of rest, feet blistered to buggery, collapsing at the end of it all thinking, this is me, this piece of ground, for the next few hours or days – always, within five minutes, I'd be up and limping away to my next destination, unable to enjoy even one moment of completion and triumph.

But in Mulegé, I lie.

Mexico was washing over me: the slowly turning days; the peaceful gait of the people; siesta time and mañanasville; lazy dangling dogs in the hot Baja afternoon; and the hours and hours by the quiet desert road sipping Ballenas with Dave and sharing our most recent discoveries of tacos and two-dollar potato tequila and signs on the buses that read, "don't be a pig, throw your trash out the window." The people talk slow and are cheerful and good humoured: the only anger or stress I ever see is written on the faces of gringos. They're patient with my lack of Spanish and teach me, and even though I've gone there not even able to say uno dos tres, within a few weeks I'm already onto talking about how the weather there in el invierno is like el tiempo in England en el verano; how even though it's muy frio for them it's muy caliente para mi; and how, si, esta muy triste that Princess Dee-ana has died. They taught me all that – they adapted themselves to what I knew and then took me to the next level – and pretty soon I was even agreeing that, si, que el mundo necesita es amor, dulce amor, and getting into conversations about la familia, el corazón, y even Dios. They seemed to prefer that sort of thing to talking about dinero.

By Christmas Eve we'd neared the tip of the Baja and found our way to that lazy Todos Santos beach, Los Cerritos, where a ragbag mix of surfers and campers whiled away the hours eating tacos in the sun and watching the waves. Dave and I bought a bottle of red wine for Christmas Day and hiked on over a rocky hill to camp in a deserted cove. The waves battered the jagged rocks and there wasn't a soul in sight. I pulled out the potato tequila and drank the whole thing in celebration. Not that Dave wanted any anyway.

At some point in the night I woke up to go for a piss and then I couldn't find my tent. "Dave! Dave!" I shouted, "I can't find my tent. Dave! Dave! Where am I, Dave? Where am I?" I stumbled onto his, half-collapsing the roof and treading on his fingers. He woke up and shouted something, and then I saw my tent. Little wonder I couldn't find it; I couldn't even remember putting it up. That potato tequila may have been cheap and tasted like gout but it sure did the job.

I woke up late the next morning and joined Dave for breakfast.

"What happened to you last night?" he said, "that was a side of you I've never seen." From the look on his face he was obviously less than impressed with my comical behaviour. "You were like a retard."

"A retard? Really? What did I do?"

"You don't remember?"

"No, not really. I remember not being able to find my tent" – I giggle – "but before that it's all a bit of a blank. What'd I get up to?"

Dave just sort of shrugs. He's not mad at me, he just seems a little bit confused by my behaviour.

I go for a swim to clear my head. You're not supposed to swim here – something about undercurrents – but it looks okay to me. Not that I'm much of a swimmer – about three strokes is usually my limit. The waves are big and loud and I like the way they tug at my ankles, like it's a game.

I wade out up to my chest and stand there looking back at the beach and back at Dave tending the fire. Something about his response to my shenanigans has bothered me; it's like...I am a retard. Suddenly, in the face of someone who doesn't get messed up, who doesn't want to, and who doesn't understand anyone who would want to, I don't understand it either.

I test out my fledgling swimming skills and ponder. I manage two strokes before the water hits my eyes and I rush to a stop to thrash my head about and spit and snort. I hate getting water in my eyes; that's probably why I've never learned to swim. I try it on my back instead. I'm quite good at that.

A little while later I look up and orientate myself; I've been swimming towards shore but, much to my surprise, I'm actually further away from it. I get back on my back and swim in towards Dave. After a minute or so I look up and the same thing has happened: I'm getting further and further away. A wave crashes on me and I swallow water. I gasp and throw my head and I decide it's time for action. I take a deep breath and launch into a front crawl: a blast of everything I've got just to get me close enough to relax. I give it my all and when I breathlessly come to a halt I see that I've just gone sideways. My arms are aching now and I don't like this one bit. I don't know how to tread water. I don't know how to float. All my energy has gone and I'm still no nearer the shore.

I summon up my reserves and give it another blast on my back: the same thing happens. Over and over I reach exhaustion point, and over and over I find a little bit more – but it's all to no avail. The waves are pounding me, filling my eyes and mouth with the salt of the Pacific Ocean; my arms are dead. I try again and I can barely lift them out of the water.

And there I am, bobbing uselessly immobile, a lull in the ocean's activity granting me a temporary reprieve from the waves. I take stock and look back at the beach, and make out Dave sitting there in his shorts, the red can of a Tecate beer plainly visible in his hand. I'm going to die, I think, and there's my friend drinking beer and catching some rays. Further up the coast I can see people queuing at the taco stand; they're all out enjoying the sun, being tranquilo and happy on this Mexican Christmas morn, no hay problemas aqui. I shake my head in amazement at my checking out in such surreal and unexpected circumstances; I really am a card, I think, and a smile comes to my lips. It's not so bad, this dying malarkey. It's weird, I'll give you that, but it ain't so bad. I feel at peace. I feel absolutely ready to accept my fate.

And just as I'm preparing to slide into the water one last time and swallow and suffocate and drown an enormous wave comes crashing down on me; hits me in the back of the head; sends me spinning around and around under the water, like a sock in a tumble dryer, until I don't know which way is up anymore – and somewhere in there my toe catches solid, sandy ground and I sniff a chance at life.

My head is above water: that wave has barrelled me right towards shore. The ground has gone and I'm being pulled back out again, but suddenly I have energy and zest, and I give it everything I've got before the next wave reaches me and finishes it for good. I pound and I pound and I don't care about salt in my eyes or water in my mouth, and I reach that blesséd sandy bottom and know that salvation is at hand.

I stumble up and out of the water and stagger on up the beach. I fall on my back next to Dave and breathe the sweet, sweet Mexican air.

Out of the corner of my eye I see that red glint of his beer can still resting against his knee.

"Good swim?" he says.

But all I can do is breathe.

We go hitching later that Mexican Christmas Day across the southern tip of the Baja on the back of pickup trucks full of families, and sometimes with the families in the back there with us. I love that they just let you jump aboard and don't give a figgy monkey about seatbelts or health and safety or if you want to dance on the roof at forty miles an hour. It's like the only law in Mexico is don't hurt anyone else and be good, and it's a law that makes sense. Would I be arrested here for hopping a freight train? Doubtful. Unless the cop wanted me to grease his palm. Here, it seems, anything goes.

Across the tourist hell of Cabo San Lucas – America's Benidorm, all golf courses and tacky nightclubs and ugly concrete hotels, and I weep for those poor sweet Mexicans having these Yanks inflicted upon them – and then into the more pleasing resort town of San José del Cabo, where we eat some Christmas tacos and decide to camp the night on the beach.

We set up our tents and then wander into the nearest bar – but it's a gringo bar with no other customers, and the owner in there is a loud-mouthed American who's got the football on the TV and is spouting off about everything under the sun: usual American bullshit.

"These goddamned Mexicans," he's saying, "you gotta light a match under their goddamned lazy asses if you wanna get anything done." And on and on he goes, mañana culture, can't stand the taxes, can't make a living, nothing's as good as the States, these robbing bastards down here – and I don't know what comes over me but when Dave's not looking I sidle up to him and whisper in his ear.

"Don't tell anyone," I say, "but I'm the new Messiah."

I expect him to explode at me, and rant and rave, and then we can get gloriously kicked out and have a good old laugh about it in the street. Except he just looks sort of stunned. And scared. And he doesn't say a word. In fact, he looks so taken aback that I start to get scared myself.

I wonder what on Earth I've just said.

Chapter Three

We're walking up the beach the next day with our packs and wondering about where to go next. We've done the Baja and the only bit left is the loop back around to La Paz, and back to where our respective ferries will depart from: me, across to Topolobampo and on to the Barranca del Cobre and then Texas, and Dave down to Mazatlan and those pyramids of his. It's been a good time, these few weeks together; nice to have a friend and companion and to dig the chilled-out Mexican beaches and eat a million piled-high beef tacos.

We're on our way for yet more tacos when we see these two girls carrying backpacks. They're sort of hippy looking. They're coming up the beach directly towards us. We're two guys – sort of hippy looking too – and the four of us are smiling. I'm smiling at Dave and the girls are smiling at us and each other and it all just seems sort of obvious really. We walk and smile and eventually we meet and the four of us drop our packs and pretty much instantly decide to team up. The girls are Becky and Jen, a couple of Jewish San Fran hippy mommas fresh off the bus.

We lay on the beach and talk; they're just like Dave, and Dave takes to them and loves them and they talk their crazy hippy talk about pyramids and energies and one of the girls tells a story about being down in Costa Rica where a guy thought he was Jesus and they too saw alien beings from another world – though they too were on acid. I tell them about my trip in London, seeing those nuns and spiders and thinking I'd created the world.

"You were shown a window," Jen says, "a glimpse of reality. Drugs can give you a taste but you can't stay there, you've got to try and achieve it naturally."

I kind of think about it and I remember the next morning when I'd finally made it back to Tim's and I'd been sat there in his living room and the room was full of these spheres made up of swirling red and green threads of light. They were so perfect and beautiful and amazing I just couldn't believe that my own mind had come up with them.

"It was like they were always there," I say, "only I just couldn't see them normally."

And they all nod and I wonder just what kind of crazy people they are.

Jen and Becky are lying with their arms wrapped around each other, even though they're not lesbians. They look so totally at ease. They call themselves "raging women" and I get a blast of sadness that I'm a guy and I'll never be able to lie there like that with my arms so effortlessly wrapped around another man's body and not even the merest whiff of sex or being gay. I always wanted to be a lesbian. Girls have it so easy sometimes.

I look at Dave, but he's not my type.

I want to be a raging man.

The girls have plans to check out this hot springs about fifty miles north of town and Dave wants to go there too. I'm not so sure, though: I'm feeling like maybe it's time to get back to being alone; Dave's on his way anyway and I really want to get back to England. And more than any of that, they want to take the bus, and I don't do the bus, unless it's dire circumstances. Like saving a walk across Nashville. Or being stuck in LA. It's only three dollars for thirty miles but I've already done something like five thousand for less than that. I try and convince them but they won't listen. They don't know how tight money can be. I tromp silently and sullenly to the bus station and all the way I'm thinking about how I'm going to ditch them there. I really don't want to take that bus.

The bus isn't for ages and Dave settles down with his head on his pack to wait. I'm starting to feel incredibly anxious, and actually physically sick, and it's bizarre how much I don't want to take that bus. My mind is in turmoil, a thousand arguments about why I shouldn't go their way – but it's just a stupid three dollar bus, for Christ's sake! I flail about for ages and then I finally think, fuck it, okay, have your way. The moment I give in and stop fighting all the anxiety and nausea disappears.

We make the funky little town square town of Santiago and bag a ride on the back of a pickup down sandy dirt-track roads out towards the seven thousand feet high Sierra de la Laguna Mountains, and suddenly we're in beauty. Everything's so green and alive: cactuses and grapefruit trees, oranges and jasmines and hibiscus. I'm freaking out in the back of that truck it's so stunning, and all around me the smiles of my flowing skirt and much-haired friends, and we really can't believe where we're going. The sun is setting and it's the middle of nowhere and, yet again, I swear it's the most incredible scenery of my life.

And on and on we go, bouncing down these sandy, nowhere roads, until we reach the wide open mouth of the canyon, and nestled there, the hot springs: two natural rock tubs under a tree. The water in them is caliente: agua caliente! The girls and Dave are happy, and me and Dave go rushing up the canyon to explore and find a place to camp.

And – oh God! – it's beautiful! It's amazing! It's making me weep just thinking about it. It's palm trees and sheer rock cliffs, grey and black and patterned like marble. It's boulders nestled in the clear green waters, boulders that we go leaping over like sprites, happy and ecstatic at the views of stunnery that are greeting us at every corner. Dave goes ahead and shouts, "oh, you've got to see this!" and I take him over and shout back, "Dave, Dave, this is amazing!" We clamber and bounce and each new turn is something magical. There's a beach by a swimming hole; there's a secluded sandy area surrounded by palms, perfect for a tent; there's a massive cliff jump into a deep, dark pool; and there's a rushing waterfall, rushing over that striped and speckled great grey granite rock, seams of black and white and gold running through it all the way from the mouth of the canyon and up and up and up.

We stop at the waterfall and as we do I look up to see two guys coming the other way: a tall, muscular man in tight cut-off shorts, and by his side, leaping with intense grace and ease, what looks like a golden-haired goblin in pyjamas. He's got these pink pyjamas on, I swear. And the way he moves, landing barefoot on those rocks, is staggering, like he just floats down onto them. He looks at me and smiles and there's this glow in his eyes that takes me back.

"Hello boyos," he says, "welcome to paradise." And then he starts singing this song and laughing, and it's weird but he sounds like he's got a Welsh accent. Him and the tall guy go bouncing off back down the canyon and I'm left flabbergasted by what I've just seen.

"Blimey, did you see the way he was jumping from those rocks?"

But Dave's already leapt from the cliff, and dove in, with a splash.

The golden-eyed goblin is Lindsay, and he is indeed from Wales; his friend is David, an Italian (pronounced: *da-veed*) and they also met on the beach in San José. Lindsay tells me they've been there five days.

"Five days?" I exclaim, "what on Earth have you been doing in here for five days?" I really can't imagine how they've stayed there that long.

Lindsay laughs. "Cooking, singing, dancing, enjoying the nature – I'm off to be an air-steward in Houston, Texas, boys, need to breath in a bit of good air before I go back to the city. Been out in India and Nepal the last four years in the monasteries." He picks up his little toy guitar and starts singing 'Boxcar Willy' and I feel like he's aiming it directly at me. He's thirty-six and he seems like a child.

"What's with the pyjamas, Lindsay?" I ask.

And he just laughs and laughs and laughs.

And then he's singing, "all you need is love, love," and we all join in.

The six of us hang out all night around a roaring fire and Lindsay cooks up a feast right there on that little beach, honey jars for teacups and chopped-in-half milk cartons for bowls and plates. It's the best food I've ever tasted. I even let him persuade me into some avocados, my first ever green and exotic thing; they're delicious. And to top it all off Lindsay pulls out a bag of flour and declares we're going to make bread, boys.

"Bread? Here?" Now this I've got to see.

"Indian bread, boys: chapatis. You can be rolling man; you're the Miller" – and a quick blast of Roger Miller's 'King of the Road' – "bring that bit of cardboard. Becky, you knead."

And soon he's got us all working, and on a scrap of cardboard, with a honey jar for a rolling pin, I'm rolling out little circles of the dough that Becky is handing me, and I still can't believe we're going to make bread right out here in the middle of nowhere, with barely a kitchen utensil in sight.

"Buddha said fast, Jesus said feast," Lindsay says, "I prefer Jesus's way myself; I'm fast enough already. Right, time for the magic."

He takes one of my circles and pops it in a pan – "to seal it, boys" – and then he clears away a bit of the fire to reveal the red hot coals and drops the circle of dough right there on it.

"It'll get covered in ash, Lindsay," I say.

"Good for you," he says, "puts hairs on your chest."

Dave claps his hands in glee and I look down as that little circle of dough puffs up and it's now almost a sphere – and then sinking back down, just as Lindsay flips it over with his fingertips.

"There you go," he says, and tosses it to Jen. Honey on, and licking her lips, and the next bread in the fire, and – poof! – up and down it goes, flip and toss, next and next and next. And we're all there mixing and kneading and rolling and producing, tossing and flipping and eating and mmmming on a beach in a canyon in the sweet smelling Mexican night.

"I can't fucking believe it," I say, "we're making bread!"

And Lindsay laughs, this strange little Welshman who grew up in a deprived little coal-mining community just as I did, and it makes it all the more wonderful that he's come from the same place, trod the same path, hasn't grown up privileged or rich or with some wise and enlightened parents. It's almost like he's found the something I've always been looking for, right there in the gold of his eyes, the flash and the ease of his smile, the way he sings and leaps and dances and plays. I swear he's the happiest person I've ever met – and, quite possibly, the only happy person I've ever met.

"Bath time, boys!" he hollers into the ribbiting bullfrog echo of the canyon, and off go those pyjamas, and out comes the song – "totally naked, baby, totally nude!" – and down the path of boulders he leads us back through the palms, and in the darkness there we six slide into the hot, hot water for my first ever natural hot spring bath and it's heaven.

"Aaaaah," we all say, bare naked knees and hips pressed together, the sound of crickets in the air, the scent of pine and juniper. Nobody speaks for a long time and then Italian David starts asking Lindsay questions about Nepal and meditation and Lindsay talks a lot about his heart and the tears he's cried and I really haven't a clue what he's talking about but I sure want to learn.

Later, Becky and I kiss, and it's pretty awesome and frantic.

"You're a lot more passionate than you look," she says, "you've got a tongue like a snake."

I smile. It's a compliment, I think.

"That was fun," she says, "but I think we should stop."

I look at her puzzled.

"Sometimes that's all you need to take it to the next level."

219

Chapter Four

When Lindsay said we were in paradise, he wasn't joking. And when Becky and Jen left two days later on the back of a pickup and we four boys stood there waving them goodbye, I felt like I was waving them from my own back doorstep. Five days Lindsay had told me he'd been there. Five days. I didn't leave for another six and a half weeks.

We cooked and sang and danced, and every meal was the greatest meal I'd ever had, and with Lindsay's jovial nudge I was soon eating garlic and tomatoes and lettuces and dates, and twenty-odd years of being a neurotically fearful food-freak was out of the window. Another thing that went out the window was my fear of nudity – because those three boys just didn't give a shit, and hanging out on that little beach there really wasn't much need for clothes: Lindsay and Dave leaping from rocks into the water, and Italian David standing there gesticulating wildly, his proud Italian balls swinging from side to side, and it was like they didn't even know they were naked. I wasn't quite so brazen, but I tried and tried, and little by little I realised it didn't matter that my flaccid penis was flaccid, or that Lindsay had a hairy back, or that Dave had a bit of a belly.

By the end of my six and a half weeks there I was doing pretty good.

I was sunbathing one day on my rock in the middle of the pool, lying there starkers on my back, and I hadn't seen anyone for about three days. I was totally digging the bliss of the sun on my body – the quiet of the canyon washing over me, the peace of that accumulated solitude – when I heard a group of voices coming up the trail. Americans – you could always hear them a mile away: every now and then you'd get a party of loud-ass Californians coming through, blasting like foghorns about their stocks and shares, obliviously charging up and down as fast as they could. I tensed up a bit and thought I'd better get dressed. And then I thought, what the hell, this is my canyon and I'm enjoying this too much to be disturbed.

I heard them come, one and two, and then three and four, until it sounded like there were dozens of them. I took a little peak out of the corner of my eye and there they were, crowded on the beach, about thirty white Americans in their high-waisted shorts and knee socks and visors. They were trying to figure out which way to go. I just smiled and closed my eyes.

Then I heard one of them say, "excuse me," and I looked up to see a middle-aged woman with a camera swinging around her neck.

"Excuse me," she said again, "but you just look so good there, can I take your picture?"

God, I had to laugh! But, sure, I said, why not?

And off she snapped.

And the next time I looked there were about fifteen of them – men and women – snapping away, my naked fluffy penis and torso stretched out on that rock, and not an ounce of inhibition in my heart. And where those pictures ended up, I have no idea.

This was, of course, later, after the 'lovely boys' – as Lindsay called us – had departed and I was left alone. In the meantime, it was six days of us four, fires and camping and hours and hours just lazing in the hot springs, Lindsay always singing and talking with Daveed about love and going deeper and deeper inside yourself, and me there asking questions occasionally – but more like picking holes.

"What about Bob Dylan?" I'd say, "he seems pretty deep. But he's not happy."

"Probably needs to go deeper inside."

"What about philosophers? They don't seem happy either."

But Lindsay would just laugh, and call me Boxcar Willy, and sing a song that said my mind was like a monkey – not in a malicious way but still I'd feel stupid – or this song, over and over: "and now/a quarter of my life has passed me by…" and everything he sung just sort of hit me. I couldn't pin anything on him – nothing fazed him – and much as I loved him and wanted what he had, I began to hate him too, for always being so jolly and happy and clever. He'd talk about the need for purity and how he didn't drink or smoke pot because it dulled awareness, and I'd go and get drunk right in front of him, and laugh and show him what a good time I was having, just to piss him off. But he'd just leave me alone and go and have fun with the other guys or whoever was coming through, and that made me feel worse. And then one day some ropey looking Mexican kids came and sat on the beach and started smoking some joints. I went elsewhere but Lindsay, to my incredulation, just sat there right with them and shared some jokes and got stoned too. And poor, poor Lindsay: right in front of my eyes I watched the light leave him, that golden glow dimmed, his smile fade into something altogether darker, unattractive, and it put me off pot for life. I couldn't believe he'd done it to himself. I couldn't believe he'd gone back on his words like that.

But the thing was: everybody adored him. And when the Americans and the Canadians came through he'd regale them and they'd gather round and he'd sing his songs while I sat off to the side and wonder how he did it and why they didn't love me too. And when the Mexicans came through he'd shout them a warning – "un momento, chicas bonitas, estamos sin ropa!" – and then he'd sit right down and regale them too, and they'd all roll around laughing, and God knows where he'd picked up his Spanish but it didn't seem to matter what language anybody spoke, they all adored him and he always made them laugh.

Down at the mouth of the canyon, just before the hot springs, there were cleared areas where people could park up and camp. And just before the end of the month a load of Mexicans rolled in and filled up the spaces, and I guessed it was some sort of tradition of theirs to head out here, bring their babies and their grandmothers and see in the dawn of the New Year. Lindsay landed us a plum gig with a wonderfully friendly family – about eight generations of them, it seemed – and for three days we were watered and fed and sat around their campfire laughing and singing, and truly they were la familia bonita.

"Ay ay ay ay," we'd go, "canta y no llores/por que cantando se alegran/cielito lindo/los corazones!" And they called Lindsay, "Lucio," and they called me, "Lorenzo," and Dave and David they just called David and Dave, because they could pronounce David and Dave, and it was all good light-hearted fun.

Until, that is, midnight approached on the thirty-first, and out of nowhere they all stood up and formed a circle and held hands, and with us in there with them started saying things I couldn't really understand – things about todos los pobres en el mundo – but understood well enough to know that they were praying.

Round and round they went: the upstanding father with tears in his eyes; the ancient great-grandmother; the tiny little Mexican boy-child with surely no more than a bean to his name weeping for los niños en Africa; prayers for us four guys; and Lindsay there on his knees, floods of Spanish flowing from his mouth, sobbing uncontrollably. Round and round, everybody speaking in turn, speaking more than once, this energy building like a vortex, and me and Dave and David looking on, and me wondering what I would say if I could speak the language, who I would pray for. And when I looked into my heart to see what was there it was like is was totally empty.

Devoid.

And then it sort of hit me, like a lightning bolt flashing in the panic of my mind: "holy shit: there is a God" – and that was about the most confusing thing that could have happened to me.

They stopped and it was as though someone had thrown a switch. The circle was broken and everybody was walking around the campsite smiling and hugging each other and shaking hands. They were jolly and back to how they had been before. But not me. I felt this kind of dirtiness, this shame, like I didn't want them to touch me. I had seen my own essence and I knew that I was unworthy of their kindness, their embraces, their smiles. But Lindsay sought me out and drew me into his arms.

"We're all brothers," he whispered in my ear.

And then it was like this electricity went through me – literally, physically – and I was bound to him, shaking, vibrating, never wanting to let go.

I could have stood there clinging to his hairy back forever.

The time of the lovely boys was almost over: three days later they all left and set sail for their various destinations and I never saw them again. For them, it was three more days of sun and hot springs and playing in the sand; for me, it was a total mind-fuck, because what had happened on New Year's Eve was simply too big, too real for me to ignore. But how could it possibly be real? My whole life I'd been a devout atheist, rubbishing religion, arguing with my teachers at school that The Bible and everything in it was just a made-up myth; telling people that if I went anywhere near a church my head would start spinning around on my shoulders; loving The Exorcist and The Omen and anything with lots of blood and zombies and upside down crucifixes in it. To become religious was incomprehensible, but what could I do? What I had felt was definitely 'God': I don't know how I knew, I just knew.

So what then? Become a Catholic? Get down on my knees and say "hail Mary" and "our Father"? Go to church and believe in sin and give up women and booze and whatever all else these Catholics do? But then, was God the sole preserve of Catholicism or was it just happenstance that I was with a bunch of Catholics when it came? For sure, Lindsay wasn't a Catholic *or* a Christian – he was some sort of Buddhist or something – and he seemed to know the score. And I don't know what Dave was but I knew believed in something too.

Luckily, my questions were answered in a couple of books the others left with me: Tom Robbins' Another Roadside Attraction courtesy of Dave, and a book of discourses on Buddhism by some beardy Indian Baghwan from Lindsay. So I didn't have to become a Catholic, because Catholicism was evil and messed-up. And I didn't have to become anything specific, either, because it was all much of a muchness anyway: many paths up the same mountain and all that. So that was a relief.

And once those questions were answered I sort of settled into my newfound awareness with an open and inquisitive mind – and also a little sadness. It was like my whole world had been shaken up and I was left as a newborn baby, uncertain and fresh. I'd been crying out for something new and I'd got it. Hitching had been a wonderful experience but I guess I'd always known that it wasn't *it*. In hitching America I'd climbed a mountain, and reached previously undreamt of heights, and when I'd hit the top I'd looked back on the less lofty peaks I'd ascended from and it had felt good. Then I guess I'd got bored – and that's when Lindsay had stepped into the void to tap me on the shoulder and say, "look over there," and point out higher and higher peaks still. I had thought I'd gone as high as I could; now I saw there was a lot more climbing still to be done.

223

Chapter Five

That canyon was magic. I lived most days sitting on the beach, and sometimes I'd see a few people and sometimes I'd go a whole week without seeing anyone. I practised my devil sticks and I got into balancing rocks, one on top of the other on their tiniest points, as precarious as I could make it. When night came I'd walk barefoot and naked up to the hot springs and take a long bath looking up at the stars. I got better and better at moving over the boulders, till I could sprint full speed over them, my legs racing out in front of me as though they knew exactly what they were doing, how they were going to land. Every night for a week I dreamed I'd gone back to England and hated it, and when I woke up I'd rush from my tent and feel so grateful to be in Mexico, and finally I said, okay, I'll stay, and I never had those dreams again. I wore a dirty yellow blanket someone had left or I wore nothing at all. I ate mostly what people gave me, plus the oranges and grapefruit and avocados I picked myself. Lindsay and the boys had left a cardboard box with some food in it and it never seemed to empty; some days I'd come back to my camp and it would just be full of all kinds of stuff and I never knew where it came from. One day there was a frozen chicken and I thought, what the hell am I going to do with a frozen chicken? But I wrapped it in tinfoil and buried it in the ashes of the previous night's fire and let it sit there all day, and when I dug it out at sunset it was the juiciest, sweetest smelling chicken this world has ever known. And as luck would have it some cool people had come hiking through and we all shared it together, and even a vegetarian failed to resist, that's how good and magic that poor dead bird was. Another time my devil sticks broke and three days later some young guys from California came through and gifted me a new set. It was like everything I ever wanted and needed came that way and all I had to do was sit there and dig.

More than devil sticks and food, though, it was the people that appeared: they were lovely and open and good, and whenever I had a new question someone would come through and just start yabbering away and there I'd find my answer. Or whenever I thought like I knew something and felt my ego start to grow another person would come and tell me a tale that rendered everything I'd ever done insignificant. Then there was a period when all these guys randomly appeared – Shawn from California, Mark from Australia, Dutch Barry and more – and it was as though the lovely boys had been resurrected and reunited, and we'd all go running around throwing off our shorts and jumping in the pools and playing as children, and suddenly I realised, here they are, the raging men that I'd hoped and prayed for back on that Boxing Day beach. Everything came. And no doubt if I sat there long enough I'd probably meet my soulmate too.

I was balancing rocks one day when I noticed a young guy sat on the opposite side of the river watching me. I'd been doing it for hours so God knows how long he'd been there. When he saw me look up he waved and started out to hop on over the boulders to meet me.

"That's awesome," he said. He was a skinny blue-eyed guy, blonde dreadlocks and a little goatee beard. He blinked and his eyes shone so clear and light. "I find that so inspirational," he said, "may I?"

And he indicated towards the rocks and I said, sure, go ahead. And together we spent the rest of the day balancing, even putting some big ones on points just under the surface of the river so that they looked like they were floating on water.

His name was Shane and he was from Virginia. He was a funny guy with some strange ways: he kept taking these deep breaths and throwing his arms out wide, and then just laughing and saying, sheesh. But he thought I was cool and that was all right by me.

One time he stopped and he just stood there looking out into the canyon.

"Thank you," he said, in a whisper.

I looked up.

"Uh? Oh, you're welcome." It was nothing, really, letting him hang out with me like that on the beach.

And then I realised that it wasn't me he was talking to.

It got dark and he made out to go. And then he turned back as though he'd remembered something, sort of like Columbo used to when he was about to give the suspect the first hint that his days were numbered.

"Sometimes," he said, "my friends and I, we sit down together and we just tell each what we're feeling, about ourselves and about each other, both good and bad. It's like an exercise in truth. It's like a way to go deeper inside yourself."

And there it was again.

"I was wondering if you'd be interested in doing it?" he said. He looks at me bright-eyed and calm, expectant but not wanting.

I feel sort of giddy standing there in my yellow blanket.

"Sure," I say.

"For instance, I might tell you that I think the way you're living here is really inspirational, and, truly, I respect you for that" – I gush – "but...but I wouldn't want to be around you when you're drunk."

That makes me smile too; sure, I can be an obnoxious arsehole when I'm pissed.

"Fair enough," I say, and nod. "I'm game."

We're both grinning at each other. This sounds like fun.

"I'll come back tomorrow night then," he says, and back down the canyon he goes, leaving me strangely excited and looking forward.

The next night Shane returns and we're joined by Dutch Barry, who's also keen. There's a big fire going and we all lounge around it in our various shorts and dhotis and blankets. Shane explains the rules.

"What you have to do," he says, "is, when I say, 'how do you feel?' you bring your awareness into your body, and observe any sensations you have going on – it's a way to bring yourself into the present moment – and then you say how you feel, just trying your best to avoid projection and intellectualising."

"I don't understand that," I say. Barry looks perplexed too.

"Well, okay, how about you just tell me how you feel in your body?"

"I feel fine," I say, still confused. I do. I'm not sick or anything.

"Okay, but how about deep inside, in your back, in your heart, for instance?" He sort of sways from side to side when he says this, like a snake, gesticulates and puts his palms on his chest.

"I feel fine," I say.

"Okay, try this – and pay attention to your mouth and heart" – and then he takes a deep breath before lunging towards me and shouting, "motherfucker! what the fuck's wrong with you! Now" – calm again – "how do you feel?"

"Woah," I say, "like, what's wrong with *you*?" I'm laughing, but at the same time I'm shaken.

"And in your lips? And in your heart?"

And I check it out.

"My lips feel tight," I say, "and my heart is beating fast."

"Good," he says, "and how do you feel?"

And suddenly I do feel something, and I do know how I feel, and it's sort of surprising.

"Sad," I say, "like, why are you shouting at me? Like I could cry. Like I don't know why you did that."

Shane's smiling and I don't like it that he's smiling.

Barry claps his hands and says, "ha!"

"And how do you feel now?" says Shane.

And even more to my surprise, I'm not sad anymore, I feel amused.

"Happy," I say, "and confused. What just happened? Where'd that sadness go?"

But Shane's just smiling and shaking his head to himself, and Barry's laughing and enjoying the show.

"I'd say we're ready to begin."

And round and round we go, our faces illuminated by the campfire in the otherwise dark night, circles of words and feeling and emotion, laughter and sadness, and it's probably the most bizarre night of my life: one moment Barry's talking about the death of his mother, the next he's laughing about something completely different; one moment I'm the happiest I've ever been, and feeling a joy I think will last forever; the next Shane's cut in with his damned slash blesséd, "how do you feel?" and I'm suddenly back to an intense and bleak depression, which is gone just as quickly, and on and on and on. It's like these feelings aren't real – or they're only real for as long as it takes to acknowledge and express and discard them, like peeling away the layers of an onion and tossing them in the bin. And the closer you get to the heart of the onion, the harder it becomes to express what you find there, but express it you must – "I feel like I can't go on"; "I've had enough"; "I'm tired"; "I'm sick of this bullshit" – and on and on it goes.

"How do you feel?" Shane would say, and I'd answer with ecstasy and longing and anger and sadness and frustration and anxiety and fear and self-loathing and blissfulness and peacefulness and love – and right there in my heart, a whole universe of emotion.

We talked on into the early morning, those three pink bodies of ours around that endless fire, the sweet smell of softly burning pine filling the air of the pitch black canyon night, our little beach, the rocks, the sky, wrapped around us like a blanket, and when I looked back on it smilingly the next day I could only feel amazement that I had somehow managed to reach such heights and feel such a variety of emotion without being on some sort of drug. It just didn't seem possible.

Chapter Six

But what goes up must come down; two steps forward and all that. So for every elevation in consciousness and awareness I was gifted by the people who came through that canyon – and by the canyon itself, that shining mirror of perfection endlessly reflecting gorgeous what I was and was not and could be – there also came a test, and it was a test I frequently failed. I was sitting one night with Shane and Shawn, and Shane was like a being of light, and Shawn was peace and tranquillity embodified, and the two of them soon got around to talking matters spiritual, mantras and such.

Shane was talking about this one time he'd been chatting with a friend in her bedroom and she'd asked him if he believed in God.

"I said, 'yes,'" he said, "and then when I did that I felt like this beam of light come down right through me, down through the top of my head. I closed my eyes and there was light *everywhere*, and it was like I was transported, like I didn't know where I was. It was euphoria" – and he laughs – "and I don't know how long I was like that but when I opened my eyes my friend was just sat there staring at me with, like, wonder in her eyes and she goes, 'where did you go?' and I was like, 'I don't know.' She said I'd been sitting there completely still for an hour." He shakes his head and smiles in recollection. "Whew."

"That's beautiful, man." Shawn's nodding and stroking his beard, and then he says: "I went to see this Indian lady once with some friends of mine, like a guru. I went up to say hello and next thing I know I'm kneeling before her, I don't even know why. She touched me on my back and I just started bawling and bawling like a baby, I couldn't stop. And I don't cry *ever*, nevermind in a room full of people. So I went running outside crying and crying – and then I started laughing and laughing, and it was suddenly like…imagine a million bubbles of air the size of basketballs trapped on the ocean floor and then released, and how fast they'd come to the surface – it was like that, bubbles of bliss rushing up from the base of my spine to the top of my head, popping over and over and filling me with ecstasy. I don't know how anyone could contain that, if that's what these gurus are feeling *all the time*. Eventually it sort of subsided and I was just there with a pebble in my hand looking at it and loving it and – it was like the whole universe was right there in that pebble."

"Yes," says Shane, slowly nodding too, "I felt like that once with a blade of grass." He laughs like it's the maddest thing in the world. "Just sat there with my hands cupped around it and feeling totally connected and full of love – for a blade of grass!"

They both laugh, and they're smiling at each other, lost in their reminiscing.

I think, these guys are fucking crazy. Kissing pebbles? Hugging blades of grass? What the fuck are they talking about?

"Those mantras you have," I say, "they're not in English are they?"

"Sanskrit," Shawn answers, "it's the language of ancient India."

"Well how do you even know what they mean? How can you understand them?"

"It's not so much about understanding, it's about what they do for you. Each syllable has a sacred vibration, and the more you repeat them, the more they help you focus and purify your mind."

"That's stupid," I say, "if you don't even know what they mean. You might be saying something like, 'I love cowshit' or something." I think about it for a minute and then I say, "I think I'll have 'All You Need Is Love' as my mantra – at least I can understand that one."

"That would be a good one," says Shane, and I feel sort of satisfied with that.

And then they go on talking some more about various things, the mind and meditation, and how you create your own reality and all you have to do is follow your heart and all will be revealed, and I'm sitting there looking at them yapping away in my canyon and I'm thinking, bullshit, bullshit, bullshit!

Eventually, I've had enough.

"All you have to do is follow your heart, is it?" I stand up and look down at them. "Fine."

And I walk away and stride purposefully and proud back to my tent on the playita and leave them to their nonsense.

Idiots.

Except it doesn't take long for that feeling to subside, and I'm probably not even half-way back to my tent when I realise that all their chatter has left me deeply troubled and more than a little confused. Because it's not bullshit they've been spouting, it's just stuff that I can't understand. And they're not idiots, these two shining beacons of light, they're just people who have experienced things that I haven't, and things that lie outside my sphere of knowledge. I want to dismiss it as nonsense – but there's just something so very real about it, as though it's an undeniable truth that has resonated within my being even as my mind tries to deny it.

Shawn stays a whole week in the canyon, cooking up monstrous pots of beans, carving bone necklaces, building furniture out of the shells of cacti. One night he guides me and Barry in building a sweat lodge and the three of us sit in there naked and sweating and pouring water on the red glowing rocks that have been cooking all day in the fire. We sweat our asses off and dive in the river, and go back for more. It's a Native American thing, he says. We drink pan after pan of chamomile tea and talk…

229

...more...

        ...slowly...

    ...than...

     ...I...

  ...ever...

 ...knew...

...it...

       ...was...

...poss...

  ...i...

   ...ble...

...to...

...talk. He's a real good guy, is Shawn.

But he leaves, and with Shane long gone I'm once more king of the canyon, balancing my rocks and chatting with the folk that come through, some of whom have heard of me by now – "the British guy in the blanket who lives at the hot springs" – and we swap our stories and food and the outside world seems like such a very long way away: it's almost impossible to comprehend that people are out there in it, going to work and shopping and maybe making ready for World War III and stuff.

And just as I start to think I don't ever want to go – why would I? I have everything I need; I've spent about twenty dollars in a month and a half; I've still got a box full of food – fate steps in and decides that my time is up: breaking wood barefoot one day I get a large splinter lodged in my sole and there's no getting it out. I live with it for three days but when a passing nurse spies my bandage and asks me to show her what's underneath, she and her angel husband insist on taking me to the hospital in San José, even paying for my stitches and antibiotics. I've been in the canyon forty-five days. It's time to hand that magical magnetic mirror over to the next lucky wanderer.

Chapter Seven

And where is there to go? Forty-five days in heaven; tranquillity and beauty beyond compare; the palms and the soothing waters of the hot springs; eight-hour baths; cliff-jumps and waterfalls; swimming in the cool clear pools; night after night of fire-cooked feasts; sweet potatoes for breakfast in the still-warm ashes; guacamole and dates; solitude and friends; rocks and cows and those massively ribbiting frogs; and in the middle of it all, me, a boy alone on a beach wrapped in a blanket, cooking in the sun. Where indeed?

I was back in Los Cabos, back to skirting the concrete in pickup trucks and campervans – "look," says my ride, a couple of young Americans, "there's Sammy Hagar's club" – and back once more to movement, to the road. The answer is: there is nowhere left to go. I realise that all I want now is to see a whale and then my Baja experience will be complete. I land up once more in dusty little Todos Santos and then I remember that's where Shane lives, down at some B&B, and I think I'll pop in and say hello.

I wander on down their narrow little dirt road and it's much like that magical journey with the hippy mommas and Dave en route to the hot springs: everything's so green and beautiful and alive, jumping out at me and making me feel incredible, flowering cacti and guava and lemons. And at the dead-end of the road, the bed and breakfast, The Way of Nature. It's a large building but most of it is open to the elements, a huge central area with a circular palm frond roof. There's no one around. I walk through the palapa and at the back there's a large circle of dusty earth surrounded by prickly pear cactuses. And in the middle of the circle, a girl, sitting and meditating.

I sit on the patio and rest for a moment. I think, I'll wait five minutes and if no one comes I'll leave. I don't know what I'm doing there anyway; truth is, Shane's kind of weird; he scares me a little. A quick hello and then I'll be gone.

A woman with long grey hair down her back appears.

"Hello," she says, "I'm Patti, Shane's mom." She reaches out her hand and I take it. Her skin is so soft. She looks right into my eyes with her own piercing blue peepers.

I stand up.

"I'm afraid of – I'm a friend of Shane's," I say, "well, I met him a few weeks ago in the hot springs, over on the other side of the mountains. I was camping there. He said I should come by and say hello; I was just passing through and…"

"Are you Rory?" she says. I nod. "Oh yes, Shane told us all about you; I'm so glad you came." She's smiling enthusiastically and marvellous now. "Are you going to stay for a while? Would you like some tea?"

She gives me a hug and leads me to the kitchen. She puts the kettle on the gas stove and asks me about the hot springs.

"I really want to go there," she says.

"You should," I say, "it's beautiful."

Shane comes back later with a girl, Rani, and later still two guys turn up, Rob and Rani's boyfriend, David. The girl from the circle is Emily. They're all about my age and they glow with health and happiness and smiles. Nobody's actually staying there, though – well, not as paying guests – they just camp out and eat, and in return do a bit of work around the place. Shane says that I should stay there too, just do a bit of what he calls, "energy exchange" – but the thought of that, and of free camping and free food at a bed and breakfast is sort of messing with my normal-world upbringing.

"So what jobs do you have?" I say.

"What I would say," he says, "is look around and do whatever you feel would make things more beautiful. Put in as much energy as you think is fair. But don't feel any obligation; there's never any obligation to do anything. Remember," he says, smiling, "we're human beings, not human doings."

Sheesh, it's not easy getting an answer from the guy. I decide to stay the night, at least, and settle for an afternoon of painting walls with big strong handsome Rob. He tells me about his recent travels in Columbia and El Salvador. He's super nice.

Later, after an organic vegetarian dinner, Shane's dad Craig says they're all going upstairs for a satsang, would I like to join them.

"What's a satsang?" I say.

"It's like a spiritual reading, inspirational words. And then we'll do some Sufi dancing."

"No thanks," I say, "I don't think that's really my kind of thing." I'm starting to think they're just a bit too weird for my liking, what with all this talk of energy and love. I want out.

"Come on," says Rob, "join the cult" – and he sort of makes these mad eyes and hands – "whoooo, join us, join us – you'll get to sleep with loads of women." And then we're just laughing and I think, what the hell, why not? I really can't imagine a more laidback and friendly bunch of people. And up the stairs we trot, where Craig reads unintelligible words from a tatty old book, coughing and spluttering his way through it, and then we all stand up and hold hands in a circle to do this mad crazy thing called Sufi dancing – which is basically line dancing except you're looking other people in the eye and saying soppy things over and over and it really isn't my cup of tea at all.

Or rather, it wasn't.

Oh, man, was it ever beautiful! We're all there holding hands in the circle in a boy-girl-boy-girl stylee, and the dances are so simple, just moving in and out, sort of like the hokey cokey, and then you break off in twos and sing things like, "how could anyone ever tell you you're anything less than beautiful?" to your partner, and they say it to you, and after a while it's like this magic kicks in and you get all giddy and happy and loving it. The words were so cheesy! But I just couldn't help it. Spinning and spinning and by the end of it delirious with joy. The final dance we all took turns in the middle while the circle revolved around us, and I stood there while everybody said how much they loved and adored me, and right there in the middle of them all, surrounded by their smiling, glowing faces, I gushed and gushed and I couldn't have gushed more if I'd just been voted greatest person ever. It was almost too much to bear.

I spent that night in Emily's tent, talking about my heart and my sadnesses and my upbringing. I stroked her hair while she fell asleep, and platonically and in our separate sleeping bags we drifted off content. I didn't leave The Way of Nature for nearly two months.

Chapter Eight

Ah, those heady days of discovering the truth about myself, sitting in circles with the others for hours on end exploring our feelings; sitting there in the shining nature of their essences and seeing all the blackness and badness inside of me; revealing my misdeeds, my errors, my shocking actions of the past, and expecting horror and revulsion and getting nothing but love and understanding and acceptance; crying for how little I knew; and going back again and again with questions and searchings, and striving over and over to grasp the words that I was hearing, to reach the heart of the onion, Shane the ever patient teacher, even as I sought to bring him down in my bitterness.

We got into doing tai-chi and chi-gung in the dirt circle out back. Shane and Craig would come around and adjust us as we went through the moves and say bewildering things like, "bring your awareness into your dan-tien," and, "feel a golden strand of light lifting your head from the crown," and much as I'd want to dismiss it all as bullshit I'd instead try to get it right and sit there envious as the others talked about feeling the chi, gorgeous Rob coming on in leaps and bounds, tingling and vibrating in his palms and limbs, energy bursting from his heart. So much about that place made me miserable.

I was sitting there one morning watching the others do tai-chi and scribbling in my journal about how worthless and stupid I felt – how inferior in comparison to the bigger and faster and funnier Rob – when Rani drifted on by and casually asked how I was doing. Normally I would have said, "fine" or "good," but something about all that sharing and talking in unedited truths had apparently made me brave. I swallowed hard and decided to go for honesty. "I feel...troubled," I said.

Rani sat down and we got to talking; it was five hours before we stopped. Everything came spilling out of me – my insecurities, thoughts about my brother, my mum, my confusion – and the whole time she was right there for me, her beautiful eyes and smile, her patience and honesty. I felt like she cared for me – that she was willing to give me so much of her time. She listened and she made me feel human, and by the end of it I was drunk and weightless and dizzy, intoxicated by the truth. I had probably never felt so good in my life. And it may have been this that was the catalyst for what occurred later that night.

I was standing in the kitchen with Shane and Rani and David and we were saying our goodbyes, the latter two about to head back to their home in northern California. As was the custom at The Way of Nature, the farewells were long and full of hugs and truths and gratitudes. I had said my goodbye to Rani, talking some more in the manner of the special connection we had made, and now I was hugging David, and he was saying something about being thankful and appreciative for me, but I wasn't really digging it, suspecting him of not liking me at all because of the time I had spent with his girlfriend. I told him I felt disconnected. And then I noticed that I felt really, really odd inside.

My head was full of space, an empty vastness that filled the palapa, that made me momentarily worried that I was going to bump on the high roof some ten feet above me. I felt incredibly peaceful and calm. I was in some enormous expanse of blackness.

I stepped back from David, eyes still closed, and tried to speak.

"I feel…weird," I said.

I was getting lost now in the space, overwhelmed and enveloped by it – and deep inside there appeared a dancing blue flame, swaying slowly from side to side. The feeling of peace and quietness grew and grew and grew as I felt myself being drawn towards it.

I thought I heard Shane somewhere off in the distance say something to Rani, something like, "his spirit has left his body," and that sort of freaked me out. I snapped open my eyes and looked about me. I looked at the knives and forks and plates and glasses on the kitchen surface. They were the most beautiful things I'd ever seen. My eyes darted over the surface, hungrily devouring everything they saw, everything alive and sparkling with shining colour and light. The only thing I could liken it to were the few moments of euphoria and shifted sense of reality I'd felt during my manic London acid trip. But this was natural. And a thousand times better. This was heaven.

I grabbed my friends and tried to say something but nothing could express the enormity of the bliss I was feeling. The cups, the forks, the table cloth, the cracks in the floor…it was too much for words; too incredible to hold in this finite container of the mind. I was exploding with joy, overflowing with it, completely given over to this beautiful new world. I cried out in ecstasy and went running into the cold, dark night.

The trees! The earth! The stars! The sky! I went racing around and around, hugging the palms, kissing and caressing their leaves, grabbing handfuls of pebbles and stones and holding them to my face. Intermittently, I'd race back to the palapa and beam at my friends, and hold them and shout, "oh my God, this is fucking INCREDIBLE!" – and then I'd be off again, unable to stay with them, unable to contain it. Around and around I'd go, back and forth, loving everything, absolutely at one with the nature, feeling the trees and the plants and the dirt from the inside out, and everything was love: everything was love.

Eventually I settled on a step on the patio and sat wide-eyed looking into the night, grinning, unblinking, the world entering into me with each inhalation, me holding it there and then breathing it back out. Ecstasy ran up and down my body in waves, filling me with warmth and a shuddering magnificence. I could not move; I just sat and stared and grinned.

I don't know how long I was like that before Rani came and put her arm around me and I turned to greet her beaming, happy face.

"Your eyes," she said, "they're full of stars."

And all I could do was smile.

So that was bliss – the bliss of liberation and the bliss of truthfulness: I guess I must have peeled sufficient layers off and gone down to my core – to the heart of the onion – experiencing the love and the ecstasy that Craig's stumbling satsangs told us resided there. It was a high far, far greater than anything I'd experienced with sex or drink or drugs.

I tried to talk with Shane about it later but it was almost comically impossible. I was out of my head. Whenever I looked at him I saw shapes and colours; watched his face morph into those of goats and pigs, children and ancient Greeks, deformed, ugly demons; saw the world fade from sight and disappear though I stood there open-eyed.

He held my gaze and asked me how I felt.

"Man," I said, "I feel like fuckin' Zebedee, like my feet are on springs, like I could just bounce all over the world, and run a marathon – run TEN marathons – and never, ever stop, and just go go go and...and...and – "

"Yeah," he said, "but how do you feel in your body?" And I could tell that he was trying to bring me back to Earth.

"Oh, right," I said, "I feel..." – and I closed my eyes – "I feel warm in my knees, and my chest feels open and huge and..."

We rejoined the others and I tried to reassure David that everything was all right, thinking it must have been a little weird for him when I broke off from our hug and went leaping and bounding into the night. He was uncertain, confused, and it was obvious that he had never experienced anything like it. Shane, I already knew, had, and I was pretty sure Rani had too, judging by the smile on her face. Now I was one of them. Now I knew what it felt like to fall in love with a pebble.

Chapter Nine

Now, not only was Shane a being of light – the living embodiment of a peace and wisdom that defied the logic of his twenty-two years on Earth – he was also a student. But not a student in the sense that he had spent three years drinking copious amounts of alcohol and vomiting in bushes (and talking loudly enough about drinking and vomiting so that all the world could hear) – no, Shane was a student in a sort of Buddhist-Taoist-Eastern-Zen-Japanese-whatever kind of way. Shane had a master, you see, and the master's name was John. And John was on his way to Todos Santos.

John Milton was about sixty when I met him, a big bear of a man who breezed his way into The Way of Nature and soon had everyone eating out of the palm of his hand: he sat at the head of the table and told story after story and all ears were his. But his stories were ridiculous – tales of men meeting forty-foot long rattlesnakes while on what he called 'vision quests'; centegenarian Chinese tai-chi masters kicking kung-fu hotheads' asses; Tibetan monks vanishing into fountains of rainbow-coloured light – and I couldn't believe that my lovely new friends were taking him seriously. He couldn't get enough of himself. And nobody paid any attention to me. I couldn't stand the guy.

A few things happened, though, that began to change my opinion of John – such as when, near the end of that first, torturous dinner, he decided to give a demonstration of what years and years of tai-chi could do for a man. He got David up from his chair and took him with him into the middle of the room.

"On the soles of the feet," he said, "are two points, called the bubbling well points, which connect with the earth. When you practise tai-chi or chi-gung chi flows from the earth into your body – and vice versa – and you begin to develop a root. The more you practise, the deeper the root will go. Developing the root can have all kinds of benefits on the body and the mind: imagine a tree with shallow roots and one whose roots go deep into the Earth. Imagine what would happen to those trees should a storm come."

He took David by the shoulders and positioned him so that he was facing us.

"Okay," he said, "I'm going to give you a gentle push and I want you to try and resist me knocking you off balance."

David readied himself and then nodded, and John began to push on his shoulder. Within a few seconds, he was stumbling to the side.

"Now do it without using your muscles; just relax, try and let yourself sink down into the Earth. Here," he said, "take off your shoes: it helps the chi flow more easily."

He pushed again on David's shoulder and this time it took six or seven seconds.

"Do you feel the difference? Now try me."

He stood facing us wearing a satisfied smile. David pushed – gently at first – and then with more and more force, until he was pushing with all his might.

John stood looking more relaxed than any man I'd ever seen.

"If I'd tried to use my muscles," he said, "you would have pushed me over straight away. But because I didn't resist and allowed the chi to do the job, you couldn't move me."

David shook his head and giggled. Shane was laughing quietly to himself; he'd evidently seen this before.

"Now you and you," John said, and Rob and I joined David in shoving on his shoulder. Nothing. Not an inch. He was exactly as a tree trunk. Craig joined in too and John continued to talk while we strained against him.

"I once saw a Chinese master take a line of twenty students; I think my best is about twelve."

"Okay Rob, now come and stand over here, and you two get behind him and be ready to catch him" – nervous chuckles; David and I do as we're told – "there are also points on the palms," he says, "and you can use these to eject chi. Now just relax. This won't hurt. Much." He grins and chortles a bit. He takes a step back and builds. Rob looks excited and a little petrified.

"Hnh," he says, and lunges forward, and pushes his palm towards Rob's chest. He stops about six inches short. And immediately as he stops Rob is jetted backwards and into our waiting arms. More gasps of amazement and laughter.

"Want a try?" he says to David. And David does, and he gets knocked down too. John's evidently satisfied with that and starts to return to his seat. But what about me?

"Can I feel that too?" I shyly ask, now starting to warm to this John character.

"Maybe some other time," he says – and it's with a shoulder so cold I think I may have a touch of frostbite.

The next morning I see him sitting alone eating breakfast and I hover around the kitchen trying to think of something to say. All I can come up with is a question about those dreams I keep having, about being chased and never really getting away. I tell him all about them – tell him that I've just had a terrible one a few nights before, the three bullying Thacker brothers from school – and ask him if he can tell me what they mean.

He pauses a moment in between bites of croissant.

"Stop being a victim," he says, disinterested, before going back to his food. I know immediately that I've been summarily dismissed.

238

I storm off with his words ringing in my ears. Stop being a victim? Stop being a victim! What the hell is he talking about? How am I a victim? A victim of what? I haven't got a clue what he means. More effin' bullshit.

I return to the palapa and he's out in the circle doing tai-chi. I sit down to watch and I've got to admit, he moves pretty smooth. And then I'm watching him float and pivot and turn, and all of a sudden I can see right through him – right through to the shrubs and cactuses behind him – and he's practically invisible. And then he's gone. Disappeared. Okay, I think, I'm staring right at where he should be, but there's nothing there. I rub my eyes and look around, and he comes back. But as soon as I start to focus on him again, he's gone. I just don't get this guy.

All of this is before the night I exploded into bliss and I sometimes wonder whether John didn't perhaps have something to do with it. Certainly, the morning after it happened, something had changed; I saw him in the kitchen and, after all his indifference and ignoring, he held my gaze and returned my smile, and in that moment of connection I knew that he knew what I'd been through. He smiled right into me and there was all this love, and in his smile he was saying, you got it.

John had come down the Baja to teach a wilderness solo slash vision quest to a bunch of five guys from the States and Rob and I were invited to join in and listen to the training. So all day long, for five days, we sat there around the dining table with our notepads and pens and listened as he talked about awareness and meditation, about focus and relaxation, about service and surrender and bliss. He'd distilled all his many decades of training under Indian gurus, Native American shamans, and Taoist and Buddhist masters down into twelve principles, and these he passed on to the people that came to do his 'Sacred Passages' before sending them off to sit alone in a wild place for a prolonged period of time, absolutely free from distraction. Shane had done several of them – including one of twenty-eight days – and he said they'd changed his life. Patti had done them too. And I don't know how it happened but suddenly Rob was doing not only the training but also the wilderness solo, and Rob was pretty pleased with that. Meanwhile, John was back to ignoring me, and making me feel stupid, my questions apparently unworthy of an answer, while the questions of the others – especially Rob – were greeted with a patient and kindly smile. And, as a result, I was back to hating him.

The morning of departure for the wilderness solos came and I lay squirming in my tent, desperate to go on the Passage. I'd imbibed all the discourses and done my best with the exercises that John had given us, and I simply couldn't believe that he had allowed Rob to go but not asked me. Something in me was crying out for those six days of solitude on the beach – and it was breaking my heart that I was going to be denied. After what felt like hours and hours of squirming and going crazy and being near tears, Craig came to my tent see if I was going to see them off, and I spilled the beans to him.

239

"I really really want to go," I said, "I can't bear it that they're going without me."

"Have you asked John?" he said.

"I can't! He hates me."

"You should ask him," Craig said, "he's not a bad guy."

And so off I slunk, weary and bedraggled, shoulders hunched and head down, to where the guys were excitedly gathered around water canisters and backpacks.

"John," I said quietly, when I'd managed to get him alone for a second, "I really, really want to do this solo. Please can I do it?"

And with a smile on his face, "sure," he said – and that's all he said – and I was on my way.

Chapter Ten

On the beach, on the beach, miles from the next living soul and – que chulada! – this is the life. It's just me and the ocean and the sun is readying to set and I'm all alone for the next six days and, suddenly, I'm absolutely shitting myself. I mean, I've been alone before – hell, I've just spent the best part of six *weeks* alone – but this is something different: there I had fire and rocks and cooking and wood and swimming and waterfalls and reading and a journal, and it's not until you're plonked in the middle of nowhere with literally nothing on the agenda for the foreseeable future that you realise what alone actually means.

I make my imaginary circle – about fifty feet in diameter – and I settle into my spot. I've got my sleeping bag. I've got my tent. I've got a canister of water and a couple of bags of raw food. And I've got a whole cupboard full of chi-gung moves and breathing exercises and Native American ceremonies to help me through the days. For the first hour I'm fine – and then I start to run out of thoughts. I've been training myself to ignore memories of the past, dreams of the future, things that don't matter – and without all that there's really not much left. Suddenly, it's like: oh shit. Suddenly, it's like: here we go. I remember Craig's words that, "all this stuff John tells you is all well and good but, once you're out there it's more a case of hanging on for dear life," and I understand exactly what he means. Suddenly, there is nowhere to go but in.

I try to meditate – and then I start to whimper. I slide down to the sand and my body curls itself into the foetal position. And, más o menos, that's exactly how I stay for the next three days.

You have no idea how slowly the sun moves across an open blue sky when you know your only salvation comes with its setting.

I was in pain; I was in hell. It was as though every single thing that had been pushed down and hidden within me since the birth of my body was now fighting to reach the surface, desperate to see the light of day, uncorked and unhindered by distraction and busyness and the thoughts and stories of my mind. There was nothing to contain it any longer, nothing to keep it suppressed down in there, and out it came, all my heartaches and traumas, rushing in a torrent, nailing me to that beach, immobile and crushed. All day long I lay there ravaged by emotion, the minutes as hours, the hours as days, longing for the infinite blue of the sky and the sea to turn golden and then dark and release me into sleep. I crave beer and think about the ten emergency dollars I have in my pack, and of how there's a store just over those mountains there, and if I walk ten miles I can come back with a Ballena and have some respite – but

John will know, John will know; he has these powers. I eat all my food within the first few hours of the second day and now I really have no distraction. I thrash the sand and scream at the crashing sea to shut the fuck up, and every time I drag myself up from the depths to try a little chi-gung or do a ceremony I quickly fall back in a heap on the sand in sobs and frustration and moans. But I can't cry. I can't release. I can't do nada. I'm as crippled and impotent as a flailing beached whale.

Three days: but the sunset does bring some respite, as the light of the day turns less harsh, as the noise of the wind and the waves abates, a quality of stillness in the air. Sunset, those first three days, I do manage to sit up and sit in meditation, and as I do my body is filled with a joyous tingling sensation, pinpricks all over. And also as I do, on each of these three days, just at the same time, I have a visitor.

A fly comes and settles on my hand – and in the moment that he lands I know that he is there for me, that he has come to ease me of my torment. Love and gratitude pour from my heart and into the fly. I feel an incredible affection for him, an absolute connection. I say, thank you, thank you, and I reach out to touch him and he doesn't move an inch. He turns to face me, and with my fingers barely centimetres from his wings and back, I think, I could stroke this fly. I stroke him. My finger is on his back, gently nudging his wings; he has no fear; he knows my intention. I feel love for him – I feel love for a fly.

A fly!

And every day he returns to console me after my tribulations and torments, to show me that I am not alone.

The fourth day I am woken by the sea, by an enormous freak wave that charges up the beach and blasts me from my sleeping bag. And when I stagger upright, soaked and amazed, I am laughing: the storm has now passed. Three solid days of supreme emotional anguish is behind me; now I feel peace, and a quiet sense of joy, and instead of doubt and shame, optimism. I know now what I have to do to become the man I want to be. I have to be brave, and give of myself, and not be afraid of appearing vulnerable. I have to be real, and to find and feel my truth, and to live it. I have to not be so goddamned aloof, to ask for the things I want, to make the effort. I have to be honest, and good.

I'm upright and I'm laughing. Everything is so beautiful: and everything is covered in a web of tiny green and red dots, making it all the more shining and alive. I feel like I've been down at the bottom of the ocean and emerged now into the sunny day. My fly is with me constantly, no matter where I go or how I move, sitting there on my hand. I stroke him and I talk to him and, I swear, he listens. Three days, then: three days of peace and happiness and joy.

When they come to collect me, I don't want to leave.

It's impossible to do justice to the power of that wilderness solo, but if I look back at my life I know that it changed me, perhaps, more than anything I ever did. At the time, though, I had no idea what had happened, and while I left that blesséd place happy and content I was also a little saddened by the thought that I probably hadn't gotten as much out of it as the other guys, who had surely had meetings with angels and visions of God, journeys into mystical realities that would render my little tale of falling in love with a fly laughable. It was only when I rejoined them that I realised what a shift had taken place.

Everybody was so beautiful! Everyone was so shining and happy – and I knew that the change wasn't just in them, that the change was in me also; their beauty mirrored in me. John was smiling and joking and gave me this big bear hug, and there wasn't a negative thought in my body towards him. All I felt was gratitude and love, and I understood that all his harshness and ignoring was his way of rocketing me to the place I needed to go, to find and experience and release all the darkness inside of me. He had made me feel so hateful towards him! But because of who he was I had found it impossible to pass that hate onto him and I had had to own it, and see it for what it was: mine. And because I had owned it, and acknowledged and held it, I had also been able to let it go. All my alienation and resentment was gone, all my insecurities and neuroses. Rob and I hugged and laughed and shone bright in the van there together, and when we arrived back at The Way of Nature I saw even more how much I had changed, reflected in the faces of those who hadn't been on the solos, Shane and Patti and Craig.

"You look totally different," Patti said, "more calm, more centred – you're even standing more upright."

And all I could do was smile and laugh and hug and feel my heart surge out to them with love and it was heaven. We stayed up late into the night talking and I was so hyper and happy I couldn't sleep. When the others had gone to bed I decided to try a technique I'd heard John talking about, called mirror meditation.

I went into the bathroom and stood on the hard concrete floor and relaxed. I let my gaze settle on my own eyes, and waited. Ever since that night seeing Shane as a goat and an ancient Greek I'd been seeing other people's faces changing too – and the weird thing was that everything I told them I saw (a monk, a nun, an old Egyptian, for example) they always said, oh, someone told me that was my past life. But I'd never tried it on myself.

After a while, the room began to fade into a haze; I started to lose comprehension of where I was exactly, of which side of the mirror I was on. I could see my face but I couldn't tell who was looking at who. And then the face disappeared, and out of the mist that replaced it, other faces began to appear: faces I didn't recognise. There was an old Chinese man; an Arab; animals and children. I saw something deformed, and then I saw a face that I did recognise: Michael Thacker, one of the bullies from high school and my dreams. I looked at him and he seemed so sad. I remembered meeting his dad one day and thinking what an ogre he was. And poor, poor Michael, despite the torment he had caused me, the fear of not knowing what his fist was going to do next: I felt nothing but a sorrowful compassion for him – because he was sadder himself than any amount of sadness he had put on others. I gave him my love and he faded away.

Another procession of faces, and then a haze, and two hours I've been at it now, standing in the same position in the bathroom, standing relaxed in the mist. The haze continues and I start to think there is nothing left to look at – and then another face begins to appear and I find myself troubled.

The hair comes, the beard, the calm and placid countenance – and I look away. I think I know what's coming – and my mind doesn't want me to see it. I try again, and emerging from the haze, the same face, and my first glimpse of those eyes. And again my mind flinches, like it can't accept, and I see myself again, as I am. I keep at it, and we keep going from me to haze to the first tentative building of the face that my mind revolts at the sight of, and it keeps on flinching and looking away, but little by little we're easing our way into it. Until finally, there it is, and all I can think is: Jesus Christ.

Me there, standing in a red-walled bathroom in my shorts and t-shirt, barefoot on the floor, one glowing lightbulb. The shower off to my right. The toilet to my left. And in front, above the sink, a mirror. And in the mirror, the face of Jesus, calmly looking back.

Oh, those eyes! They were such sorrowful eyes, and in those eyes the burdens and pains of the entire world – and yet they were not burdened themselves. They were as deep and as wide as the ocean, two vast containers untroubled by their load, just as the vastness of the ocean is untroubled by the waves that crash upon its surface, the monsters that dwell in its depths. They were infinite and infinitely peaceful. Accepting. Tranquil. And sad. The sadness of the whole world was in there with him. Everything.

We looked at each other for a long time, and then that face began to fade too, back into the mists. I expected that to be the end of it – but once more features started to form in the mirror. A face of tight, fuzzy fur. Shining, dancing eyes. Two little horns peeping out at either side of the forehead. A smile. It was Pan, and in his eyes, joy and laughter and mirth, the energy of a wild violin and a jig. But no evil, not in this devil's heart.

Chapter Eleven

We shared all our stories the next day and nobody laughed at my tale of the fly. The guys had all had incredible and moving experiences, and all had come back lighter and changed, but I didn't feel inferior anymore; not now that I'd come to realise the extent of the change in me. We sat around that table and laughed and talked and listened as John told us ever more fantastical tales, and suddenly this world of ours was a world full of magic, where levitating monks and disappearing yogis and miraculous little Chinamen and Tibetans were real and out there, doing it all now and not just two thousand years ago. My mind had been stretched and opened. I felt like one of them, no longer different, no longer separate.

Everybody left – the Passagers and Rob and Emily and John – and pretty soon it was just Shane and I, and we'd sit and talk and share and watch each other disappear and get lost in colours and visions. We watered the plants and went to the beach and built up our tai-chi roots to the extent that neither of us could push the other over and we were one another's spirit buddy. We did everything together. We even talked for hours and hours about our feelings on sex, and right there at the exact same moment, sitting under the lemon tree, we were both bitten on the ends of our penises by ants and, laughing, we said, okay, maybe we do need to look at things down there, no coincidences and all.

We went one night to an open-aired disco in town and there was nobody there except some totally wasted Argentinean guys. Shane got on the dance floor and busted some frankly incredible moves, all Michael Jacksonified, and when he'd had his fun the Argentineans came over and started slurring and asking us where all the girls were. And Shane and I just looked at each other and laughed, and realised that we hadn't even thought about girls in the three weeks since Rani and Emily had left. And we both nodded and said, "yeah, we should meet some girls."

There's this thing called 'putting your intention out to the universe,' or, 'manifestation,' and it's sort of like prayer, and it's sort of like bringing the things you want to you, using the power of the mind. Shawn, back in the canyon, had said that I was a master at this but I didn't have a clue what he was on about – except when I had learned a little and looked back later, I understood what he meant: after all, wasn't it kind of funny that every time I needed food or a friend or an answer it'd appear almost immediately? And, really, hadn't this been going on for ages, all across my hitchhiking trip, the perfection of the rides that picked me up and the places that they led me to? It was like, you attract what you are. It was like the lilies in the fields. It was magic.

We left our wobbling and intoxicated friends back there in the disco and stepped out into the street – where we were immediately joined by three young women in a very sort of natural, no need for introductions, we've always known you kind of way. Shane sat down with two of them, and me and the third: well, we just sort of stood there together gazing at each other, and smiling and not saying anything because there didn't seem anything that needed saying. There was this connection between us, and love.

The girls were Sophie, Chelsea and Lisa. They were two Canadians and a Californian. They were travelling together in Lisa's van. And they became a big part of our lives at The Way of Nature over the coming weeks.

In the meantime, something wild was going on in my body: I'd become filled with this electricity – not quite two hundred and forty volts (or even the punier American equivalent) – but a tangible and even painful sensation of current, nonetheless. I felt it mostly in my palms and in my feet, and I kept getting these jolts and zaps, and I'd leap and yelp and curse. It was maddening, a constant sensation of being wired up to a car battery. I had it for three days, until I found a solution. Or rather, a solution found me.

I was in the kitchen giving Patti a head massage; she'd told me she had a nasty headache and thought that might help. After a while she said to me, "I can feel all this energy coming from your hands."

"Really?" I said, "I can feel it too." The tingling in my palms was going mental. But it also felt like it was moving.

"My headache's gone!" she said, "you've got healing hands!"

"Cool," I said, and giggled. Seemed like a good thing to have. Except I had no clue what she was talking about.

Patti, though, knew all about this stuff, and soon enough other people were coming down to The Way of Nature to get me to put my hands on them. Augustine, the farmer from next door, who still used a manual plough, came one day with a knee the size of a melon and Patti told me that he was in so much pain he hadn't been able to walk much for weeks. And walking was sort of important to his job. So I sat him down in a chair and stuck my hands on him and meditated, and after a bit he fell asleep. I was feeling nice and high and I left him like that and went off to enjoy my buzz, and when I came back he had gone. But when I saw him the next day and said, "como estas?" he answered by jumping up and down and doing a crazy little jig, laughing and slapping his knee and rolling up his trouser leg to show me his totally transformed joint. It was ridiculous. It couldn't possibly have been the same leg.

But everyone that came to see me got the same effects, and they all went away happy: the big American guy who cried and cried in his chair and told me that I'd "given him back to himself"; the lady who barely said a word but smilingly pressed fifty dollars into my hand and then later told Patti I'd cured her of IBS; and the old French grandma who had had polio, and not that she was cured of that, but she was no longer wracked with pain nor needed her tranquilisers. They came and went – knees and headaches especially – and all I had to do was sit there with my hands on them and feel good. I even did a sort of exorcism once, on this horrible guy who shouted insults at everyone he met: I offered him a healing and when I put my hands on him I felt his chest *and* his back expand dramatically outwards, at the same time, and bizarre, guttural noises stream from his mouth. When I was done he looked like a baby, sweet and demure, and he was a picture of politeness after that.

And I never suffered that mad electricity again.

Meanwhile, we had girls, and we all hung out and played music and watched the sun set, and Shane got them into his, "how do you feel?" lark, and I was in love with Sophie. I was smitten in love. I had it so bad at times I could barely talk to her. And though I was convinced she felt something for me too – because other times we did talk and talk, and talk for hours, and share and deeply connect, and hold one another – she never did anything about it, and seemed kind of afraid, and me being Mister Chivalrous and all I didn't want to press the issue, despite the magnetic force which was constantly trying to pull my lips towards hers. And then she and Lisa said they were leaving and I was thrown into turmoil. So the only sensible thing to do seemed to be to ride the thousand miles up the Baja with them, to give Sophie a chance to want me too, and then hitch back down again either with or without her. Like I say, the only sensible thing to do.

We hit the road and back up that glorious Highway 1, and back into the deserts and mountains and coast line and wilderness, and the weather was stupidly perfect, and the scenery was almost more than I could handle, and most of the way I had my head out the window feeling the wind in my hair and almost exploding with ecstasy so overwhelmed was I by the beauty of everything. I whooped and I grinned and if the girls would've let me I would've done the whole trip dancing on the roof with my arms around myself and lost in and abandoned to love.

We camped in so-chill Mulegé and in the water that night: phosphorescence! And again my mind was blown. Bioluminescent plankton – on top of whales and buffalos and dolphins and fireflies and snakes – and it was all too much for this Yorkshireboy to take, the wonders of this world, those shimmering, glowing lights in the water as my hands swept from side to side under the Mexican full moon that shone on the peacefully lapping waves of that most beautiful of bays.

And the next day, stopped for a snack break in Santa Rosalia – aware that we were leaving the water behind us – I raced in to swim again, and tossed off my shorts, even though I knew I shouldn't have, and swam in beautiful naked ecstasy, the girls on the shore eating their tortillas and looking on. And when I went back to join them, and sat smiling and contented and wet, I felt a tap on my shoulder. I turned and saw the face of a man in uniform, and three other men in uniforms around him, and the words, "arresto," y, "vienes con nosotros," gently floated down towards my ears.

I've been arrested before, and it's always been the same: I fight and I squirm and I tell lies and I struggle – deny what's going on and deny that I've done anything wrong – and I get angry and frustrated and depressed and eventually, after several hours or days, accept it all and say, "what's the worst that can happen here?" and find peace. In all times of crisis there's a procession of emotions and feelings that have to be worked through before we reach resolution, and that takes time. That is exactly what happened here – I saw the thoughts and feelings come and go, one after the other – except, because of the work that I'd been doing, it had all happened in an instant, and all I was aware of was a total calmness and acceptance, and the knowledge that everything was going to be all right.

"No problema," I said, and got up to go with him. My happiness had not left me for a second: everything in the world was perfect and as it should be, and all things were occurring for the benefit of the evolution of my soul. I went with them to their van and I was just getting happier and happier. Bliss was bubbling in my veins. I was readying to explode. I had realised the truth of what John had taught: that absolute surrender leads to absolute bliss, and that bliss is fantastic.

They drove me around and we laughed and joked and talked about football and, after some time, they let me go. And then it was back in the van with the disapproving girls and only there, away from those cops, could I really give in to the elation that was threatening to sweep me away.

Oh God, how can I even put into words the wonder of what I was feeling? That energy that raced inside of me like a pack of wild dogs? All I wanted to do was grab my friends and share it with them – the magic – the splendour – the ecstasy – but I knew anything I said or did wouldn't make a tiny bit of sense. After all, hadn't I just been arrested? By the Mexican police? I could not, however, in a million years contain it: and so I once more threw myself at the wonders of nature, my head and body out the window, whooping it up, singing and laughing and crying with joy for everything around me – the mountains, the rocks, the sky and sun and birds and road and life – and I was filled with love – incredible love – *true* love – and I gave it and gave it and gave it to all things everywhere.

After a while of exploding out that window I was able to return to the inside of the van and contemplate this love, this ecstasy with a more sober mind. I thought about how I was splashing it all around, and how good I was at giving it away to nature and to others, but I wondered if maybe there wasn't more I could be doing with it. I decided to try a little experiment.

I closed my eyes and felt all the love coursing through me, and I silently said, "Rory, can you apply these feelings to yourself?"

The answer came like a bolt of lightning – "YESSSSSS!" – and my heart exploded as I felt true love for myself for the first time in my life. There was a brief flash of pain when I realised just how hard I'd been on myself over the years, and how I'd denied love the opportunity to flow, but once that passed it was incredible – a real explosion of feelings and releases, and an altogether new level of joy. I felt like a little boy finally receiving the acknowledgement of a parent. I felt like I was being forgiven for the past, and forgiving too. I felt a whole lot closer to becoming whole.

The afternoon passed in blissful silence, the wheels of the van turning ever onwards across the desert under the immense blue sky as we neared our destination and points of separation. Goodbyes were imminent, and it may have been that – or it may have been my most recent awakening – that brought about what was to follow; as ever, it's impossible to say, But everything is perfect...

Darkness had fallen and I was back on Earth, back in my body, sitting up front with the girls and staring out into the night. Somehow we'd gotten into a fairly heavy conversation about men, and about sleazy guys in particular, the evils that they do, and I was trying to tell the others about how we could help things if we only told them what effect they had on us. They'd be able to learn, I said, and the world would be a better place. It was our responsibility to show them where they were going wrong. And we owed it to all the others who might suffer at their hands in the future.

The girls, however, were having none of it.

"I'm sorry, but I don't have any responsibility to try and educate some sleazy guy about what a dick he's being," Sophie said.

"But you could tell him how you feel," I said, "you could tell him that when he gets all sleazy and says shitty things you felt degraded and upset, and at least he'd know what he'd done; he might be a dick about it in the moment but maybe one day he'd realise."

"You don't know what it's like," Lisa said – and no matter what I tried to say, that's all she'd come back with: "you don't know what it's like."

Except I did know what it was like, and every time she said it I felt like I was being stabbed with a hot knife, each thrust stirring up a seething cauldron of anger, something bubbling away deep inside of me. My face was a mass of tension; I was struggling to keep it together. It was futile.

One last time she said it – "you don't know what it's like" – and the bubbling, boiling volcano blew its top, and I could hold on no longer: howling floods of tears gushed from me, as if from every part of my body. I cried and cried and cried, totally lost to the feelings of pain and release, pain and release.

They pulled the van over and I wailed and wept and they held me and stroked my hair and everything came out: my friends who had been abused as children; the girlfriend I'd had who had come home one night, raped; my disgust at watching men on the prowl, preying on and using women for sex;

and my own first hand experience working at the restaurant and being poked and prodded and treated like meat. And more than that, right back to a Friday night about a week after I'd moved to Charlottesville now nearly two years previous.

But, oh God, how can I say this? How can I burden you with these words? I don't know how to do this and I don't know if I can. It's like…nobody knows, that's how it feels: nobody knows. I've never heard anyone talk about it and I've never been in a place where I felt I could talk about it – and, no, I don't know how it feels to be a woman but…I do know what it feels like to be used and abused, to be reduced to nothing by the unthinking, unfeeling acts of another who can't see beyond the end of his own dick, because I was raped too. I was at 216, and I got bought a drink, and the next thing I know it's the morning after and I'm in some black guy's bed with a sore asshole and his dick in my mouth and I don't have a clue how I got there, and when I go home all bemused and falling about I cry in the mirror and it's two days before my head gets over whatever he had spiked me with and I realise something really, really wrong had happened. And the kicker? Months later he was there in my restaurant, ordering drinks and being a total sleazebag, reminding me of things I had thought were long since forgotten. But forgotten only to my mind, because deep down inside it was always there, waiting in the depths of my body, my heart, carried with me wherever I went, and on this night it came out.

Chapter Twelve

Back on my wilderness solo, on something like the fifth or sixth day, I'd thought back to that night in Charlottesville and tried to find some forgiveness for the guy, some deeper understanding of the experience. Intellectually I understood that he was probably a troubled and messed-up soul lost to ignorance and misery and therefore I ought to feel pity and compassion for him. Intellectually, too, I knew to say things like, "everything's perfect," and, "everything happens for a reason," and to try and accept it as an experience, a part of my past. I did a little ceremony, and I said, "I forgive you," and I thought that I was over it. I thought that exploring all my thoughts and feelings around it would be enough. Crying all my tears in the van that night, though, I realised it wasn't enough to simply bring these long-buried traumas into the conscious awareness of the mind: they had to be sought out in the physical memory of the body and truly re-experienced and relived if they were to be properly released. Saying, "I let it go," isn't enough – although it is, perhaps, a start.

We said goodbye the next morning in a dusty parking lot in Rosarito: Sophie and I were practically nose to nose, the magnets pulling us stronger than ever, and it was everything I could do to stop myself from kissing her. There was something deep between us, a connection beyond what we had shared in those few weeks; we even had the same surname. But she left me there, sad beyond sad, and I was on my own at the top of the world's longest peninsular with a thousand miles of dusty, arid desert between me and my spiritual home.

I'd been afraid to leave The Way of Nature; afraid that I'd never find people like them again, because I never had before in my life. Shane and Patti told me not to worry about it, that I was a good guy, that I should trust the laws of attraction, and I had tried to believe them, but I couldn't. Except, on that hitch back down the Baja I got a taste of what they'd been trying to tell me: because instead of the drunks and the pot-smokers that I was used to, I found myself in cars with people talking about Buddhism and energy and love and healing, and in all the hitching I did in the days and months that followed I never once got offered weed or booze again. It really did seem that, as I had changed, so too had the world.

I returned a different man, stronger and more solid, and emboldened for having tried out my new self in the outside world. I soon felt ready to leave – and when I woke one morning from a good dream of England – woke to find myself singing these words: "I'm going home" – I knew it was time. I packed my bags. I said my goodbyes. I left Shane and Patti and Craig and all my memories and transformations and trials and ecstasies behind and I hit the road to La Paz, and got on a ferry, and soon enough I was on the mainland and riding a five dollar train some four hundred miles along possibly the wildest railroad this world has ever seen: eighty-six tunnels; thirty-seven bridges; Tarahumara Indians appearing out of nowhere to flag it down like a local bus and hop aboard; and right smack bang in the middle of it, the Copper Canyon – that Barranca del Cobre – some four times larger and twice as deep as the not quite so spectacular Grand Canyon of Arizona.

I rode down to Batopilas, deep down at the bottom of the canyon, on the back of a police pickup truck, the cops inside it having a whale of a time racing around narrow hairpin corners with skyscraper-sized drops off to the side, me bouncing around on back and loving it too. I think they thought they could scare me: little did they know.

And down in Batopilas, sleeping by the river, I dreamed of an insect such a vivid shade of red, and such a strange looking thing, with these wild feelers coming off its head, and it really struck me, I don't know why. Or, rather, I didn't know why – until I hopped in the back of a pickup the next day to go back to the top and there, along with a Mexican family, and two Mexican hoboes and an American dude, sat this Irish girl wearing a scarf the exact same colour as that crazy insect and she told me about being in the bathroom the night before and seeing this bug with these mad feelers, and described the bug of my dream, and I thought, I'd better stick with her.

So Reina and I travelled up to Chihuahua together – along with the American – and there we were to part, her going south and me destined for the border. Except, inspired by my talk of how spontaneous and free I was, she decided to issue me with a challenge.

"Okay, Mister Free Spirit," she said, "if you're so trusting of this fate thing you're always talking about, why don't you come with me?" She was cute as a button, this girl; she had that twinkle in her eye.

"Ah, well, I would," I said, "except my visa's about to run out and I really don't want any bother, what with having been deported from America already: somehow I don't think the Mexicans would buy me a plane ticket home."

"But everything's perfect, right? And everything happens for a reason? Well what about meeting me? What about your dream? Don't you trust?" She was enjoying this, I could tell.

"I trust," I said, "but..."

"Toss that coin you're so fond of then: tails, you come with me; heads, on to America. The coin's always right, right?"

I nodded. The American guy crowded round closer, intrigued; his destiny was in there too; he was supposed to be coming to Ojinaga with me.

I tossed. It was tails. I went with her.

We rode a whole day on the back of an open-aired cattle truck and then when night fell the driver came out and asked us if we wanted to join him: turns out the poor guy's radio was broken and he'd been going mad up front with nothing to listen to while we were having a ball outside. He asked us to sing him some songs. Reina sang Let It Be and he loved it.

"Más," he said, this poor, cowboy-hatted, radio-deprived madman.

I only knew one song all the way through – Ta-Ta-Ta-Ta-Ta-Ta-Touch Me from the Rocky Horror Picture Show – and I sang him that. I figured he wouldn't understand the words so what difference did it make? I especially enjoyed singing, "I'll oil you up and rub you down (down down down)."

And fifteen hours after we hopped in that truck we were deep down in the body of Mexico, in the stupendously attractive city of Zacatecas, whose architecture and sophistication was right up there with the great cities of France and Spain – and I thought this country was supposed to be ramshackle. We shared a hotel room. We tickled on the bed. And I got to explore some of my sexual issues in a manner way beyond the purely aural.

I left her then; our time was up. I went back up the country and slept my last night near a Monterey truckstop, dodging transvestite prostitutes and thinking back. I mean, hoowee, what a time I'd had: I'd gone there expecting seven days of tacos and tequila, a tired and unwilling drunk, and I'd ended up finding God and becoming a traveller now in mystical realms, all baby-eyed and new. And I'd only spent about a hundred dollars the whole time I was there.

My last night in Mexico I dreamed once more of the bullies: the Thackers and the zombies and the cops. The Thackers had me cornered in a bookstore and something in me said, enough, I don't want to run anymore. I turned to face them and I said, I don't want to fight you. We fell into one another's arms and we cried, and our peace was made. And if everyone in a dream is an aspect of yourself, and if those bullying dreams had been symbols of my victim complex, then what did this new twist say about me? And what of the fact that I never dreamed of them again?

I made Texas. I made Charlottesville. And my last ride to Charlottesville was with this family, and just as I was getting into the car the woman said to me, "listen, I'm a Christian prophet and if you don't want to be preached to, don't get in the car" – but I figured I had something to learn from everyone and it didn't faze me one bit. And on and on she went and eventually she said, "you might think it's a coincidence you getting in this car but it's not – and if you think about it you'll know that it's not. And I want to tell you something: go to Israel. Walk the paths that Jesus walked. And don't worry about money, God will provide." And I was thinking, hoowee again, for this sure is a wild ride, the people I've been meeting, the things that they've been saying and, honestly, who up there is pulling these strings? I think, sure, okay, I'll go.

I'm back in Charlottesville. I'm down at Fridays After Five – the open-air music thing – and there's a free raffle for the chance to win a thousand dollars. I enter, and I'm nervous, and I think, shit, I'm going to win, and it'll be a sign from God, and I'll be on my way to Israel. I'm convinced, and I'm all set for it – but I don't win, some other guy does. Well I guess he needed it more than me. And in any case, I've still got my plane ticket back to England. And, oh yeah, I'm back in Charlottesville.

I'd gone back to Charlottesville with absolutely no intention of seeing anyone, so mortified was I by the shame of my time there, convinced that the whole town hated me. I had two intentions: to get my stuff, and to write lots and lots about Mexico – I hadn't been on a computer in four months – and I figured it would be mission accomplished within a week. I spent my days in UVA computer labs typing away, and at night I crept out to camp behind some bushes on campus. That was number two; my boxes had been dealt with far more easily than that.

I was over at Robin's tearing into them and it suddenly dawned on me: it was all just a bunch of crap. All the CDs that I'd lovingly hoarded – all my Radiohead and Happy Mondays and Britpop – I couldn't even listen to it, they were so bleak and depressing. And all my clothes and books and souvenirs: none of it meant anything to me. All the time that I'd been away I'd thought of those boxes and known that some day I'd have to go back and get them – but all they were weights that chained me like an anchor to the Earth. It was all so pointless. I wanted to be free. I gave or threw the whole stupid lot away. I didn't want anything so mundane as possessions to have a bearing on the destination of my life ever again.

I settled into typing but, slowly but surely, Charlottesville began to reel me in. I bumped into Jay one day – life-changing Jay – and he was so goddamned pleased to see me I could barely believe it. And, whaddya know, he totally understood everything I told him and had been there too, and was just grateful and amazed that I was still alive.

"Look at you, Rory," he said, grinning massively all sparkling eyes and wonder, "I mean, just look at you."

And so it went on, over the course of that first week, bumping into old acquaintances and making new friends, and everybody being so lovely and receptive (except Aaron the SHARP, who always had a flair for the dramatic: "you know," he said, "a lot of people would have liked to put a bullet in your head for the shit you pulled in this town") and soon I was going places with people and people were going places with me, and it was like putting a seal and a cap on my whole Mexican transformation, to be back in the town where I had been so dark and to now be treated as light.

People kept asking me to come and live with them. An Indian yoga teacher I met on the Downtown Mall said, "you're glowing; I can see it." Laila, my old Britpop friend, had found a Sufi master. One night outside Escafé I danced so wild and free to the mighty bluegrass of The Hogwaller Ramblers that when I stopped and opened my eyes a crowd were gathered beneath me, watching, and a guy said, "whatever he's on, I want three." I went inside and everybody wanted a piece of me, and I saw Kathy Buchet, a girl I vaguely knew from back before, and I said, "I've got something for you," and I pressed my hands onto her stomach and she was blown away by whatever energy went into her and the next day spontaneously bought a plane ticket to Peru to pursue her own spiritual adventure. And before she left I went round hers and we fell into this gazing silence, and after a while she stopped a little scared and said, "I saw the devil – and before that, Jesus," and described them exactly as I had seen them in the mirror down in Mexico. And finally, when it became obvious that this was where I was meant to be, and England – yet again – was going to have to wait – I accepted one of those offers of accommodation and moved in with a sweet, sweet couple in an enormous house just a bit further up from where I had dwelled with Tyler and Ocean and Plan 9 Dave, and in exchange for a bit of gardening and some babysitting I had a whole basement apartment to myself. And I got into Kundalini Yoga, and I had spirit buddies everywhere, and everywhere I went I had random magical adventures, and me and beautiful friendly Charlottesville were tight tight tighter than we'd ever been before.

One day after yoga, about six weeks in, Saram the teacher told me about a festival he was going to out in New Mexico.

"It's three days around the solstice," he said, "but I'll be going there a week early to help set up the site. You don't have to pay for the festival if you do the set-up. But also it's better that way: you get to be on the land and meet Yogi Bhajan, and the people are just wonderful. It's like a yoga in itself. You should come."

I was tickled that he'd invited me. It sounded great.

"Saram," I said, "I'd love to, but you know I haven't got a bean to my name. I think I've only got about thirty dollars."

"Don't worry about that," he said, "I'll buy you a plane ticket. But you'll have to let me know tomorrow: I'm leaving for Baltimore and flying out to Saint Louis the day after. Oh, and I can only afford one-way."

This was unreal. This young guy – a year or two younger than me – was offering to buy me a plane ticket so I could go to a free festival and meet a real-life white-bearded yogi.

It was almost too much.

I went home and thought about it. I'd just that day finished writing up my much-delayed Mexican adventure for my website and without the yoga, once Saram was away, I wasn't sure what else there was for me to do there. I switched on the computer and went to write an email to California Shawn. He'd gotten into healing and angel channelling and was studying with an apparently amazing healer called Momma: every now and then I was getting these amazing readings from him that answered my every question, even when what I'd asked was purposefully vague; he said something came over him and his fingers just typed and all he did was get out of the way and let it happen. He'd know what to do.

When my inbox came up, though, there was already one from him:

Date: Wed, 9 Jun 1999 15:04:23 -0700
From: "Shawn"
Subject: Wonderful ~ Full of Wonder
To: "Rory Miller"

Hey crazy man, I had a dream about you last night. I was sitting in a circle with Patrick and George (two of Momma's students) and there was space left for one more. I asked Momma whose it was and she said, "Rory's coming." Amma's in San Fran this month – you know, the Indian hugging lady. Are you coming West?

Love you!
Shawn

And I guess I had my answer.

Part Eight

Chapter One

You want to know how to make God laugh? Tell Her your plans. That's a New Age joke and we like it because it's true. Man makes plans and God smiles; that's another way of putting it. I mean, how many times had I said, I'm going back to England? How many times had I felt it in my bones that I was done with America? Right back to week one in New York. But something had always come up, at just the right time, and forced me to change my mind. And it was madness – for when else did I meet someone who offered me a job as a stunt cowboy? Or when else did I bump into someone I had already met on the road, in eerie and unignorable circumstances, except right when I needed something unreal and totally new to make me change my mind and regrab my interest? The only thing that made any sense was to accept that something larger than myself was at work and that I had to trust it and do as Lindsay had tried to tell me: go with the flow.

So what was this thing? Was it me, creating my own reality, as Shawn had said in the canyon, to my head-shaking disgust? Was it 'The Universe', that mysterious force of energy that did things for New Agers: "the universe provides" and all that? Or was it God – whatever that was – up there on high, pulling strings and levers, making it all happen for some unknown higher purpose? Or perhaps a combination of all three – or perhaps, all three were one...

I was in Charlottesville one day doing chi-gung on the campus at the University of Virginia. I was in a standing still posture and had been like that for some time. The chi was flowing good; I was really feeling it, colours swimming and vibrantly alive, the tingling of energy in my crown chakra immense. I held my hands out in front of me and stood there powerful – and

257

directly ahead of me, about thirty feet away, from the top of an enormous tree, I heard this crunching, cracking, splitting sound. A branch was coming off. It split with a roar and came crashing down through the tree – fell some fifty feet or so – and bounced and settled on the earth, tree-sized itself. All the time I just stood there and breathed, letting everything be. An enormous branch has fallen; that's okay; I'm just observing. I stood and stood and my heart and chest were open and huge and the energy buzzed in me like a generator.

Eventually, I went over to the tree to investigate.

Wow, the vibes coming off that branch were intense! It was like a field of radiation, tangible in the antennae of my palms: if there were such a thing as a Geiger counter for cosmic energy it would have been off the scale. It was magnificent and a privilege to witness. And there was something about it that struck me as significant, thinking nothing is coincidence…

I emailed Shawn and asked his 'Kind Angel' for a reading; he got back to me and told me that the tree was the mind, the ego, and that the goal was to uproot the whole thing. Wicked! I was gonna be uprooting trees. And sure, it was just a symbol – but that was a pretty big branch, and surely a sign that I had made some progress on the path. All these amazing things kept happening to me and it truly felt like I was on some sort of fast-track to enlightenment.

And now I was being spirited out west once more, for more of the same.

I had said yes, of course, to Saram, and we landed in Saint Louis and picked up a ride with a bunch of strong-looking blokes in turbans with beards. They were all called Khalsa or Singh and they all wore white; these were the Sikhs. We ate some rice and lentils at their ashram and then loaded into a couple of trucks, towing trailers, and off we went the thousand miles down to New Mexico.

"Can you drive?" they said.

"I sure can," I answered.

And I did, all the way, and I never crashed once.

We were heading for a place called Española, not too far north of Santa Fe. We stopped off in Santa Fe for some groceries and in they all trooped to this enormous organic supermarket.

"You coming?" they said.

"Nah, I'll stay here." What need had I of supermarkets and all those bright artificial lights and fakery? Truth is, I'd been having a really hard time with supermarkets ever since Mexico, and ever since my wilderness solo on the beach: they just bewildered me. The woman I'd moved in with in Charlottesville had taken me shopping one day and said, get what you need for the week – and, honestly, I couldn't handle it. I mean, I'd been on the road for over a year, and never bought more than a handful of things at a time – and certainly nothing that required cooking; the thought of anything beyond a bunch of bananas and a couple of tins of beans freaked me out. So I avoided supermarkets like the plaque that says, "you'll get the plague if you touch this plaque." Plus, I didn't have any money. What little I'd had, I'd given to Saram as a contribution towards my plane ticket.

So it was surprising, then, when I found myself walking across the parking lot to the supermarket, and entering its smoothly sliding doors, and standing there amongst the cans and bottles and boxes of cereals. I hadn't a clue what I was doing there.

I wandered over to a demonstration table: a couple of pretty girls with a computer offering to do a free reading, something to do with the heart. I thought I might as well get it done, since it was free, and since they were pretty, and thinking it might tell me something about myself – three of my favourite things in the world right there. One of the girls came over with a clipboard and asked if I minded sharing my information – and that's when things got weird.

She asked me my name, but when I tried to answer her, I couldn't, my mouth wasn't working. I started smiling, and then I started giggling. We were looking at each other and she was giggling too. The giggles grew and grew, until we were both howling with hysterics, the tears streaming down our faces, and all the while our eyes locked into each other's and not saying a word. How long did it go on for? Two minutes? Ten? I have no way of knowing: time was elsewhere and so were we. We laughed and laughed and all around her I saw these colours – these reds and golds and greens– and it was the most vibrant display of light I'd ever seen.

Finally, it stopped, and we calmed down, and still not having said a word we threw our arms around each other and hugged with huge open-hearts and joy.

"I love you," I said, squeezing her tight.

"I love you too," she answered.

And we hugged and giggled and then when it was done I smiled at her one last time and made to leave – and then I turned back and asked her for her number, which was something I'd never done before. She gave it to me, and we smiled some more, and then I did leave, back through those sliding doors and back out into the bright and sunny world of an American west supermarket parking lot. The Sikhs were just loading up the shopping. I got in the truck and started the engine and thought, I'd better turn the radio on, get a bit of insight into what just happened there. I clicked the switch and out blasted, "if you wanna be happy for the rest of your life/never make a pretty woman your wife," and I just smiled. So that's all it was: one more incredible and strange meeting on this incredible and strange journey I had found myself on – and not the woman I was going to be spending the rest of my life with. Marvellous.

Chapter Two

The yoga festival was put on by an organisation called 3HO – the three aitches stood for, "healthy, happy and holy" – and the head dude was on old Indian called Yogi Bhajan. He had come to the States back in the sixties with nothing but his turban and his loin cloth and started teaching yoga and meditation classes to all the hippies and peace-lovers out in San Fran. The classes had grown, and after a while he'd decided they needed a little bit more than just getting high and having long hair and he'd smartened them up, got them off drugs, and put them to work. He believed people had to work hard as well as lose themselves in divine bliss. He'd gotten them to start companies: companies like Yogi Tea and Peace Cereal. His organisation had grown and now they had ashrams and did lots of good things for charity, and every year they'd have this massive festival and all the Sikhs and turbans and dhotis and beards would gather in the desert and do yoga, and there were about three thousand of them that came. It was all love and light and goodness – although, as far as Yogi Bhajan himself was concerned, that hadn't always been the case.

"He was a bit of a naughty boy back in India," Saram told me in our tent one night, "he got into black tantra and developed many siddhis – yogic powers. He could make people wet themselves just by looking at them. Apparently he made someone go blind once."

"Wow. Cool." Those sounded like good powers to have.

"He met an enlightened master one day who showed him what power really was. He's never talked about it, I don't think, but he does say that he was shamed into renouncing black tantra and shown the error of his ways. The master told him to do penance and he spent years and years cleaning the steps of the Golden Temple in Amritsar, burning away all his negative karma. You'll do tantra here, but only white tantra – the good kind." Saram smiled. I think he could tell I was intrigued by the black stuff.

"How would polishing steps with a toothbrush help someone stop being evil?" I said. I couldn't quite see the connection.

"There are many ways to burn karma," Saram said, "but roughly speaking you do it either through meditation or service, which is called karma yoga. No doubt he meditated as well. But he believes in selfless service and that's what we're doing now, getting this thing set up."

"What is karma?" I'd been trying to figure this one out for a while.

"Karma is like when a mother tries to show her biting, pinching child what it's like to be bitten – the Universal Mother teaching Her children by letting them know what the results of their actions feel like, for better or for worse.

It's, 'what goes around, comes around' and, 'you reap what you sow.' Concentrate here," he said – and he touched a finger to a spot between my eyebrows – "on the third eye; all will be revealed."

I closed my eyes and breathed, and in that tent, next to a young turbaned yoga teacher, right out in the middle of the desert, I fell soundly asleep.

The next day we got to work.

"This is a great place to see the one-doer in action," Saram told me, hammer in hand, about to head off with some of the guys to put up a marquee. "God is the one-doer," he said, "but normally we try and do everything ourselves, with our minds, with our egos. Try and step aside and let go – let God – and I think you'll see what I mean."

There were about forty of us on work duty that year, spread out over acres and acres of land with our various tools and tractors and tasks. I went for hours without seeing anyone sometimes – but just when I needed to, I would. I'd be thinking about hunger and someone would appear with a snack. I'd be wondering about how to do a certain job and right at that moment a guy would come around the corner asking if I needed a hand. I'd finish my own job and think, what next? – and then get a sense to wander in a particular direction and after a few hundred metres I'd happen upon three guys in need of a fourth, a heavy load to shift. Over and over it happened like this and it was like there was just one body doing the whole thing and we were its parts, forty individuals working together as the fingers and the hands and the limbs of one great unified organism.

"I get what you say about the one-doer," I told Saram over rice. He smiled. "Hey, it sounds a bit like 'wonder,' doesn't it?"

"There's a lot of truth in some of these words of ours," he said, "take God, for example, add nothing" – and he holds up his fingers to make a zero – "and what do you get?"

I shook my head.

"You get good. Or: G-O-D. Generator – Organiser – Destroyer. Like in Hinduism: Brahma, Vishnu and Shiva, the creative, sustaining and destructive aspects of nature and the universe. The eternal circle." He stopped and thought for a moment. "But just remember," he said, "de fun comes before de mental," and he laughed, and did a silly little dance, and rolled his eyes. He clapped me on the back. "We wouldn't be doing all this if it wasn't fun, eh?"

And, oh, was it fun! Working our asses off all day and it never feels like work. And little Indian ladies cooking chapatis and rice and eating the feasts of kings. And crazy Dutch Siridharma barrelling around on his tractor, his mad waxed moustache twirling away like something from the past, his booming laugh echoing out across the desert. And all the girls and guys, those young Americans, so decent and kind and happy to be there, and hugs wherever and whenever you want them, and poor little Rory being bashed again and again with that wonderful stick of all the goodness and kindness in the people of the world, and struggling and striving to accept that this was the nature of things,

261

that this was my nature too, and there was nothing to do but realise it and give in.

The festival began and I moved from workshop to workshop tasting little bits of Sikh philosophy and yoga. There was numerology and healing. There was stuff to do with sex. There were talks on the path, and on meditation and astrology. There was massage and breathing and chai, and everywhere I looked hundreds of people dressed in white, flowing robes and turbans and headscarves. I got a healing from a couple of Sikh ladies and, I swear, I felt my entire head shift from one side to the other, and I remembered how back in Mexico, when I'd first tried to meditate, I'd had a habit of letting my head fall over to one side and John had said that that was going to be a problem. Little by little, though, it stopped, and my posture improved, and I learned to be aware of what my head was doing at all times. Still, though, I hadn't felt entirely 'centred' – but that healing seemed to put me smack bang in the middle, once and for all.

So I was happy and I was healthy – but was I holy? And was I whole? Questions and longing burned within me: I wanted to know why I was here, what was the purpose of my life? I wandered off one night and I stood beseeching the desert, tears of frustration in my eyes. There had to be a reason that I had been put on this path, a reason for my existence. I cried and begged and the next day all these people came up to me at random saying, "you should be a teacher"; "you'd make a really good teacher"; "you're a teacher, you're a teacher, you're a teacher." My heart found peace in these words. They felt right.

The culmination of the festival was three solid days of white tantric yoga, sitting in pairs from morning till night, eye to eye, and chanting and holding hour-long poses and pushing it to the limit. It was apparently capable of removing forty years' worth of impurities and was so powerful that people would cry for hours and hours while all their shit came out, or laugh and laugh and go off into ecstasies, or fall madly in love with their partners and want to marry them. For my own part I mostly just saw colours and faces and had a good time – but some others on the work crew *did* announce they were getting married. And there were plenty of tears and laughter too. We saw Yogi Bhajan and he was funny and odd, and when he spoke about God and purity and kindness his words rocketed into my heart and made me want to burst into tears of desperation and longing and give everything I had to find the truth of whatever that was.

Now my plans for what to do after the festival, such as they were, amounted to going to see Shawn's Indian spiritual lady down in Santa Fe and that was about it. I had no money and nowhere I wanted to be, and I'd been transported back west so unexpectedly that I hadn't even had time to think beyond the festival and the trip to see Amma. I felt no need, though; I felt that things would reveal themselves as and when they were required, one day at a time.

As if to prove a point, the first email that I opened upon my emergence from the twelve-day long cocoon of Española was from John, my Mexican coyote of a teacher stroke shaman.

"I hear you're coming to Crestone," he said, "I'll be there in a week."

And if he'd heard it he'd heard it in some other realm, or in the future, because it was news to me and as far as I knew he thought I was back in England. I looked up Crestone and saw that it was just up the road from Santa Fe. That was where John had his main American base. His other one was in Bisbee, Arizona.

So I guess that took care of the plans, post-Amma.

Back at the festival, as all us work-crewers were swapping addresses and saying goodbyes and giving our long farewell hugs I'd been asking if anyone wanted to join me in going to see Amma.

"There's this Indian lady," I said, "she's like a saint. She gives you a hug and takes away all your pain and suffering. My friend saw her. He said she was amazing."

Siridharma was up for it; he had some time to kill before going back to Holland.

"Well why didn't you say so before?" he laughed, "I wouldn't have had to bother with those three days of white tantra." He rubbed his back and made out he was in pain. He wasn't, of course; he was a yoga teacher. He was as bendy and limber as a sapling.

"I'll come," a girl's voice said. It was Donna, from Texas. "I've got a rental car. We can drive."

And so off we went, down into the desert, Donna with her accent driving – her sweet, sweet accent – and Siridharma with his turban and moustache, and the way he insisted on saying, "Sat Nam" to everyone we met, even if we were just asking for directions or buying tacos.

"Why do you keep saying 'Sat Nam'?" I said, "they can't understand you. You're scaring people."

"'Sat Nam' means, 'truth is my identity'," he said, "those words are charged with the divine vibration. When you say it to people they get blessed. You bless people enough, you can change lives."

"Well it's just a bit weird, that's all," I said, "they probably think you're mad."

"God is mad," he said, and laughed under his glorious moustache, "and you have to be out of your mind to find Him." And he laughed and laughed again.

"Aah," I said, and I clapped him on the shoulder, and nudged him a few times, and in the backseat we started pretend fighting like a couple of girls.

Donna's eyes flashed in the rearview mirror.

"Will you two stop it," she said, "I'm feeling left out."

And: "aw," we said, as we reached over the seat and put our arms around her, and she made out to hate it but loved it really, and we hugged her some more, and in this manner did the three of us careen around the desert, stopping off at some holy healing Catholic church, and doing a spot of gets-you-high Sikh Siridharma-led chanting high up in an ancient Native American cliff-dwelling kiva, and discovering beautiful hillside hot springs where Siridharma taught yoga to naked early morning strangers, and on and on until Santa Fe and our date with the Indian hugging saint.

We found Amma in a marquee outside town with several hundred people crowded around. She hadn't yet arrived for the evening session and, as first timers, we were ushered to the front and took our places. People chatted and ambled about – and then some chanting broke out and all eyes turned towards the back of the tent. I stood looking but I couldn't see anything; that was all right, though, she would be coming right past me. It was sort of exciting: my heart started beating faster. And the closer she got, the faster it beat. She swept past me – this tiny little white-saried lady with her hands reaching up to brush those who stood to line her path, orange-robed Indian men following behind her with strange umbrellas and bells – and as her hand touched mine I sort of swooned and melted inside, and swivelled around to follow her journey almost automatically, my hand rushing to my nostrils and inhaling the deep, strong scent of roses. She was on the stage now, and looking back at us, and as I gazed up at her – at four feet something of her, plump and chubby-cheeked and Indian, and not my type at all – I knew she was the most beautiful woman I'd ever seen.

We sat and the music began, and suddenly the room was filled with tablas and harmoniums and finger cymbals, and the singers sang, and the large, round, orange-robed Indian men with the funny umbrellas had the voices of angels, and Amma sang and moved more freely than I've ever seen anyone move before, and when the first song was over I wanted to clap my bloody hands off, so amazing was this Indian tabla music. But instead there was silence. And then somebody announced the page number for the next song. And they did the whole thing all over again.

The music stopped and we started shuffling on our knees towards her to get our hug. They call it 'darshan' and it's supposed to be like some sort of transmission of divine energy, a glimpse of the guru's reality, as much as the huggee is able to handle. We are like vessels for the divine, and we can only hold so much depending on the level of our realisation. So meditation and yoga and all that stuff is a way of increasing the size of the vessel and allowing more stuff to come in. And sometimes you have to smash the vessel that you currently are to get a new one. It's a constant cycle of growth and ego-demolishing and filling up and emptying. And meeting someone like Amma was supposed to speed the cycle. Shawn reckoned that we were lucky: that in ancient times you'd have had to search for years to meet a guru like Amma. John, too, told stories about would-be apprentices who sat waiting outside their masters' caves for weeks and weeks and weeks without food or shelter just to prove their worth. And I'd stumbled on it without any real effort on my part at all.

Unless I counted all the years of striving and longing and endlessly searching for a better way to live.

"See if you can look her in the eye," said Siridharma, a childlike glee painted plainly across his face as he scooted lotus-style towards her, "I heard someone say it's really hard."

I looked up at her and already I could tell it would be. I started to feel like I didn't want a hug at all. The closer I got the faster my heart beat and fear was growing inside of me. I bowed my head down and shuffled some more; I was finding it difficult to move by now, somehow not in control of my body. My tear ducts were twitching wildly. I didn't know what was going on. Up ahead I saw Donna raised up from her hug, a look of beatific happiness on her face. There were people everywhere, bodies moving all over the place, and it was chaos – except that when I got within about ten feet of Amma suddenly everything was calm, and it was the most tranquil place on Earth. People surrounded me but I barely noticed them. I floated towards her; watched Siridharma in her arms; saw them face to face, and his enormous grin, and her smile as she tweaked his moustache.

And then it was my turn. And I was in.

Next thing I know I'm standing outside with Donna and Siridharma and wearing a smile that is actually *wider* than my face. I feel twenty miles high.

"Wow," said Siridharma, and in his eyes, tears. "Wow wow wow."

We all hugged and held each other there for the longest time, and love was in my veins more strongly than ever.

Later, I took a walk around the ashram and learned something of her story: of how she had grown up poor and uneducated, abused and turfed out by her family, and still she had loved them. I learned of the charities she had set up – hospitals and orphanages, schools and universities and widows' pension funds – and all around there were these folders showing pictures of the work that she and her followers do, and it seems that whenever India is hit by a hurricane or an earthquake or a flood, they are there, distributing food, rebuilding homes, offering solace and comfort and lessons in how to deal with the tragedies and hardships of life. Every time I pick one up I burst into tears, utterly moved in equal parts by both the suffering and the goodness in the world, and I long to do something to help.

We camp that night out in the desert and all night long I can feel these things going on in my body, energy and movement and popping, especially in my chest. It feels like open-heart surgery.

Chapter Three

We dropped goofy, waxed-moustache Siridharma off at the airport in Santa Fe to go Sat Namming his way back to Holland, and Donna and I went into town for a few hours to check out crystals and turquoise and t-shirts with Krishna and his flute on them. I still had the number of that girl from the supermarket and every ten minutes I'd slip off to find a payphone and drop her a line, but there was never any answer. I tried one last time at a gas station on the way out of town and then I gave up. We were on the road to Albuquerque and to another meeting with Amma.

I was gazing contentedly out of the window at the empty sand of the desert when I felt Donna slow the car.

"I really need a diet coke," she said, "I'm gonna go back and get one."

"What are you talking about?" I said, "you don't need a diet coke, you just want one. And where will you get one anyway?"

"That gas station."

"That's like ten miles back."

"That's okay," she said, and – fine – it was crazy but, her car, her money.

We pulled in and I sat there waiting for her while she disappeared inside. I flicked through the free Santa Fe paper and glanced at the horoscopes. Good old Rob Brezsny, what with his pronoia and all: he'd been scarily accurate for me week after week all through my original Charlottesville days and pretty much ever since. Today he was saying something about Adam and Eve, and that I should bite into the apple I would be presented with. Well fat chance of that! I hadn't had sex in nearly a year – not since Marie had picked me up at the side of the road – and though I'd kissed a couple of girls since then I wasn't really sure I wanted to be doing even that. I wanted to devote my energies to spiritual matters and sex things just seemed to bring me headaches.

I chucked the paper in the back and buckled up my seatbelt as Donna climbed in behind the wheel. She put her diet coke down and then just sat there, not moving. Next thing I know, the pair of us have whirled around to stare out of my open window at the car that's just pulled in beside us. And just as it's stopped the person in the driver's seat has done the same, and now she's hanging out of her own window and staring right back at us.

Or, rather, at me.

It's the girl. It's Chaley. It's the one from the supermarket who I've been calling and who I've just given up on. Only…here she is.

I can't take my eyes off her. We look at each other and grin – but this time it's not hysterics and laughter, this time it's something altogether deeper and more peaceful and terrifying. She's beautiful, this girl; I'm totally lost in her eyes – and in my head, all these thoughts: wondering who she is; wondering why I feel this way; wondering why I want to marry her. It's madness – I've only said ten words to the girl and I can't be thinking this.

But I am.

I break off and ask her to say something.

"The answer to all your questions," she says, a gorgeous smile on her lips, "is 'yes.'"

This is not what I want to hear.

I get out of the car and she does the same. We hold each other, tenderly and with love. She's a lot smaller than me, and her head rests under my chin, and she feels good right there in my arms, pressed in against me. I keep thinking I want to kiss her: or, rather, I can see a vision of our mouths coming together to find each other and I feel like I'm being beckoned to bring it into reality. I resist – and then I remember always-right mystic Rob's words about biting into the apple and I move my head back a bit and down, and she looks up, and right there in that Santa Fe gas station parking lot, with Donna somewhere behind me, and God knows who all else coming and going with their Mountain Dews and Sprites, we put our mouth together and kiss. And we kiss for a really long time, and it's like we've been doing it forever, our mouths fit and know each other so well. And then we hold each other some more, and laugh a little, and sigh. And I feel absolutely at peace.

Finally, we speak.

"I'm on my way to Colorado," she says, "to see my teacher."

"Me too," I say, "in Crestone, next week."

I look at the empty backseat in her car and I see an image of my pack sitting there, and me in the passenger seat up front, and the two of us going to Colorado to meet our respective teachers together. It would be so easy, I know. She would accept it with barely a word, this smiling, shining girl with the face and the heart and the kiss.

"What shall we do?" I say. I'm nervous; I'm afraid. It's just too much of a leap into the unknown. And I've got my plans for Albuquerque and Amma. And I couldn't stand to be a burden. And it reminds me of a situation from before, with Erica back in New Orleans, when it all went horribly wrong.

"I don't know," she says, "what do you get?"

I close my eyes and in there there's a quote from The Alchemist about, "what happens once will never happen again, but what happens twice will surely happen a third time."

I relay it to her and she nods.

We hug once more and then back to Donna I go, and again we're on that same stretch of desert highway, less than forty minutes later.

"Why didn't you go with her?" she asks, "I wouldn't have minded."

"No," I say, "it's perfect like this." I'm smiling in my seat and gleeful with the wonder of it all.

"You should have gone," she says, "she could have been the one."

"Maybe," I say, "but if it's meant to be, it'll happen. I can go and see her when I'm done with John."

"I can't believe you didn't go," she says, "and I can't believe that that just happened. I mean, what if I hadn't turned back for a coke? I don't even want it now." She laughs. "You ever have anything normal happen to you? You're one crazy guy, you know that?"

"I know it," I say.

And she laughs again, and I laugh too. I read in a book once that you call an Aquarius crazy they take it as a compliment. And I absolutely do.

Chapter Four

Now Crestone, Colorado (population: seventy-three) must be one of America's strangest and quirkiest small towns, and I think it's a place hardly anyone has heard of, which makes it all the more cool. It's out in the middle of nowhere, at the end of a thirteen-mile road that dead-ends in the foothills of the mountains, and it really is a one horse town – if 'horse' in this case means, 'store' or 'street.' Except there are like a million things to do there because, for some strange reason representatives from more than a dozen different sects and religions have built temples there and it's become something of a Mecca of spirituality for the earnest, Sedona-avoiding seeker. So there's Zen gardens and Hindu temples; seven Buddhist centres and a Carmelite Monastery; pyramids and geodesic domes; a Sri Aurobindo community; and then all the strange and various flavours of New Ageism and communal living. There are also masses of ruins of Native American temples and kivas and, according to John, this was where it all happened, back in the day: this was the sacred ground where the shamans gathered to do their training and vision quests and they knew there was something special about the Earth around here. John was well into rocks and he said the rocks around Crestone had special properties, channelling energy across the land and leading it into stone meditation seats that the ancient Americans had used to further their own spiritual growth: one of his favourite pastimes was taking walks along these routes and getting 'stoned.' I'll testify to the power of walking those rocks in getting a man high. Crestone was also a hotspot for UFO sightings, and on almost any night bizarre and inexplicable lights would appear from behind the nearby Sangre de Cristo Mountains. All in all, it was a pretty weird and wonderful place to be.

Patti and Shane were there, and Shane and I were spirit buddies once more, seeking ever higher teachings. John gave us a transmission of Dzogchen – a blast of uncorrupted spiritual energy passed on from Tibetan master to disciple for hundreds and hundreds of years – and it was so powerful that I was knocked out for the whole rest of the day. We went on our rock walks and I began to practically see the energy as it flowed over the land and into the stone meditation seats. I learned how the different rocks worked and felt their diverse properties: some were heavy and dark; some gave a blast of joy and light when you sat in them. I sat in one early one morning and all through my right arm energy flowed like a current into my body, tangible and blissful – but my left arm was somehow blocked. A mosquito landed on it and stuck in its proboscis – I decided to let it, practising surrender and relaxation, and the energy began to flow there too. The mosquito had unblocked me! Free acupuncture! And so, I had now been helped by God's two most annoying and pointless creatures – the mosquito and the fly – and in those two fair swoops I became incapable of hurting either them or any other creature. Vegetarianism kicked in; and despite meat forming the greater part of my previous life's diet, I missed it not a bit.

John was teaching a six-day course, as he had done in Baja, and Shane and I helped in all the preparations and arrangements for that, answering the questions of the Passagers and seeing them on their way – and then seeing them back again six-days later, when they were done. They all came in glowing with light, shining eyes shed of years' worth of burdens and anxieties, the joy of spiritual connection within them. To see the changes from the other side was almost as affirming as doing it myself.

For my own next stage of growth John had something else in mind: the twenty-eight day solo. Six days had been hell, and absolutely life-changing; I could only imagine what twenty-eight days would do to me. And as the moment of departure approached, I started to become seriously worried. Would I disappear? Would I leave this reality behind and ascend into an altogether different dimension, as the Mayans and the characters in The Celestine Prophecy had done? Would the illusion of the world collapse around me, leaving only the light that I had occasionally glimpsed shining behind everything and everyone? What about my grandma? I hadn't even said goodbye. Or was this the enlightenment that I had craved so much? The final breakthrough into realms Nirvanic, where the truth and bliss of oneness with the all would be revealed and I would emerge resplendent in my Buddhahood, destiny fulfilled?

The night before my solo I dreamed that I was in my tent sleeping when I was woken by a bear. It came in and started to eat me, from the feet up. At first I wanted to panic but then I remembered the golden principles of relaxation and acceptance and I just let it happen. When I woke I felt fresh and happy and I skipped on over to John's to tell him.

"Excellent," he said, "that's a close totemic encounter of the highest kind! The first is encountering an animal in an unusual way; the second is communing with one; the third is having one present its life to you; and the fourth is being eaten." He smiled proudly. "And well done for arranging it to take place in the dreamtime rather than in consensus reality – far less messy!"

There was a story about John that the locals in Todos Santos used to tell, about how he'd been bitten by a rattlesnake and instead of seeking medical advice he'd just gone into his room and meditated. "Juan Meel-ton," they'd say, "el es muy poderoso" – and they'd make this sort of impression of a snake with their faces and hands and hiss.

John told it to us one night in Crestone as we sat around the fire.

"I had been studying with Vasudeva in India for many years," he said, all ears attentive, "a truly great siddha who could control the weather with his words. At this stage in my practise he had been transmitting the teachings of tantra, in which he was a master. After some months he decided that I was ready for the final stage. He told me that I would have to take a deadly poison into my body and transmute it into positive energy."

We around the fire laughed and gasped and shook our heads.

"I told him I wasn't quite ready for that," he smiled. "Years later, I was walking through some long grass near The Way of Nature with a student of mine. We were talking about various disciplines and she said to me, 'John, what's tantra?' I was about to answer her when I was bitten on the calf by a rattlesnake; I knew then that the time had come to complete my training.

"I came back to the palapa and told the student what had happened; I hadn't said anything earlier as I didn't want to frighten her. I told her I would be up in my room and probably wouldn't be down for a while. It took me a week to work that poison out."

Patti laughed and said, "John," as though he was a naughty child, and John laughed and shrugged as though he was one too. He was mostly quite serious – but when he wanted to be he could be as soft and daft as a bearcub.

"And the moral of the story is?" he said.

"Don't tread on snakes?" I said, "or maybe…you can only teach what you know from experience?"

And John looked down on me proudly and he really was so wonderfully good.

I went then up into the mountains, ten thousand feet high and just me and a small rushing stream and nobody else for the next twenty-eight days. We did have a buddy system, in case of emergencies, which involved walking to a point midway between camps and tying a knot in a rope, one person in the morning and the other before dark; should someone have a problem, then, the knot would be missing and help would be at hand – within the next thirty-six hours, at least. My buddy was a sprightly little forty-something lady camped in her own circle about a mile away from mine. I later found out that she had bears come nearly every single day, trying to steal her food and scaring her half to death; I didn't have a single one, despite soon getting lax with the old foodbag-up-the-tree malarkey and leaving it all night long right there beside my tent. I wondered if it wasn't perhaps something to do with my dream, fears overcome not needing to be faced again, that sort of thing.

I settled in and for nigh on a month, that daily knot-tying walk aside, I dwelled within a fifty-foot circle, drinking water from the stream and eating hardly anything at all, and it was just me and the birds and the trees and the sky, and almost from minute one to the very end I bathed in an oasis of bliss and love and light, the appearance of a butterfly sending me into raptures; gratitude to nature and to life pouring almost constantly from my heart, peace supreme in my mind. The agony of Mexico was long behind me. I was quite literally in heaven.

I sat meditating one day on a rock in the stream, naked in the cool September air, indifferent to the cold by now after sitting daily for hours in the rushing snowmelt water. I had closed my eyes and within me I saw golden light, and in the middle of my consciousness a glowing Star of David, the Melchizedek, which had started to appear whenever I felt connected and high. Suddenly, an understanding of the tapestry of my life fell into me as a drop of crystal clear water and everything made sense. All I had been through, the many roads I had walked – literally and otherwise – and all my hardships and trials and deportations and mistakes: nothing had been out of place; everything was as it should be. I wept with gratitude for the perfection of my confused and complex existence. I could not believe that something so seemingly impossible could be true. But in that moment, I knew it was, and my past was signed, sealed and delivered from me right there on that rock.

I opened my eyes and for hours I stared into the water as the tears rolled down my cheeks and I gave thanks. Thankfulness spilled from me; I felt gratitude for everything. Before I had gone in there I had been hoping to receive a mantra – now I felt I had it: thank you.

Except what I really needed was a way to express a million thank yous in one word. And so I danced, and I sang, and I poured my heart out into the nature, and I gave my vow that I would live my life for the benefit of others: I would seek enlightenment, and share myself unremittingly, and leave no stone unturned in my quest to seek and to know the truth experientially, for real, in the depths of my heart. I would give my all, for the benefit of all, and I would never stop. I had tried and lived so many things in my years and only spirituality and God had felt satisfying and true.

About half-way through my solo I started to hear this singing: it was like a massive choir of Native Americans, drums banging and this one word repeated over and over again to a rhythmic tune. It was coming from all around me, and from inside me as well. I didn't know the word but I sang along anyway, and when I sang with them I felt better and better still. I could sing for hours. I loved it.

When I got out I told John about it and he asked me what the word was.

"It was like: yah-way," I said, "over and over: yah-wayyy, yah-wayyy."

"Yahweh?" he said, "that's an old Hebrew word for 'God.'"

Chapter Five

I left that circle changed, I suppose, but it was nowhere near as dramatic as it had been in Mexico, where every few days saw me rocketed into an altogether new reality, everything I had been blasted from me like an old skin, over and over and over. Now I was firmly in this reality and it was more of a slow and steady progression upwards, the long hike to the top of the mountain. Shawn's Kind Angel had told me that my faith was in the testing ground so as to make it unshakeable; I liked the sound of that, and saw the reality of it in action as my mind became less and less doubtful, more established in the undeniability of my new experiences. No longer did I wake up frantic and search panicked for some proof that spirituality was real; it was right there with me all the time. And, sure, sometimes when I thought about it I doubted the existence of God – it just seemed too crazy to be real – but that was all right too, just the wanderings of my doubting mind, nothing to get excited about. My mind wondered about a lot of things and I learned to just observe and laugh at it: it seemed so silly at times, the things it would try and tell me. But my mind was no longer in charge, and little by little, it was being put in its rightful place.

My last night with John I sat with him and Shane and two of his other students and we ate macaroni and cheese and watched The Horse Whisperer: that meal and a movie were sort of his post-Passage tradition. When it was done he switched off the solar-powered TV and we all moved on to the porch and sat in the still, quiet night and told stories. He told us about battling demons in Bali – one of the other students had been there, and laughed as they said they'd seen his body blow up to twice its normal size – and about his time with the Dalai Lama. And he told us more about Vasudeva, the weather god, and those strange times out in India with the gurus and the holy men, still living lives of Biblical proportions, right there at the dawn of the twenty-first century.

"Right back when I first met him," John said, "I asked Vasudeva, 'who are you?' and he replied, 'I am nothing.'" He looked at me then and smiled – and then he was gone. I was sitting there not more than five feet from him and he had totally vanished; my mind stopped, thudded to a dull, confused halt, and all I could do was laugh and wonder in bemusement. Just who was this guy that could make himself disappear at will? And right there and then I saw that I still had so much more to learn.

A crash of thunder, and the rain pouring down, and John was back. He looked out into the night, and just as suddenly the rain was gone. He turned back to us and shrugged his shoulders, and on his face the expression of an impish little child, the coyote trickster, the unfathomable ways of a modern-day shaman. And I dreamed that night that I was sitting cross-legged beside him, as though we were meditating together, and at some point he reached over and pulled all the teeth from my mouth, and rearranged them, and then put them back in. They felt better, but not quite right. Teeth, I knew, were a symbol of the ego.

Two months I'd been in Crestone, and I'd arrived without a bean and still I was beanless, but I'd slept and lived and eaten, and what more could I want than that? Whenever I'd needed a few dollars for food I'd just juggled in the street or grabbed a shovel and dug someone a hole and everything was right there. Everything I needed, I had. And everything I had, I wanted. And everything I wanted, I needed. And so on and so on and so on, an eternal circle of needs provided for, even before I had asked: Crestone even had a free clothes bin where people put what they didn't want and others could help themselves. I got an awesome pair of hospital pants and a groovy red t-shirt that said, 'Property of the Nut Factory' across the chest. One day Shane said to me, "you know, everything you're wearing says property of somebody else on it." We had to laugh at that: even the few things I owned didn't really belong to me. But freedom from possessions was a wonderful feeling – and freedom from the need for them, even better.

Back in Mexico, back at The Way of Nature, we'd been sitting around the dinner table one night and somebody had said something about that quote from the Bible, the one where Jesus says people should trust more, look at the birds in their trees and the lilies in the field, and how God takes care of them so surely He'll take care of you. They'd said it, and then they'd moved on, but something about it had stuck with me, dropped into my consciousness much like Shane and Shawn's stories about falling in love with pebbles and grass: something in me knew that there was truth in those words, and even though it was a truth that I hadn't experienced, it was a truth I felt I could. Travelling and living on trust seemed like the next logical progression for me.

I lived pretty much the whole of ninety-nine on trust – on my "trust fund," I used to tell people when they asked me how I survived – and it worked, and it worked in often miraculous ways. After Crestone, for instance – and after I'd gone back to Santa Fe for Chaley, and found her totally changed, and with another man, and me left there heartbroken by the side of the road wondering exactly what had happened (all prophesied by Life during my last ride to hers: a guy telling me a story about hitching to see some girl he was in love with and how she was already with somebody else, and all the while The Zombies' "She's Not There" blasting out on his radio) – I went and visited a friend, Kate, in Albuquerque, and she invited me to stay. It was a magical time, and Kate and I became super close – and became lovers; and my broken heart was healed – but after a few weeks her roommate decided that I ought to be

274

contributing to the house, and in that she meant money. Kate said she was happy paying for me but I didn't want that, and so I went away for a few days to think about what to do. A day later, though, I returned to Albuquerque with just under a hundred dollars in my pocket: it had been gifted to me out of the blue by four different strangers and people that had picked me up – including sixty dollars from an old lady who had been standing in her garden next to where I was dropped off by a guy who had taken me completely out of my way. I had told nobody I had no money, nor that I needed any, yet in one day I'd been given nearly four times as much as I'd received in nearly ten thousand miles of previous hitchhiking, right when I needed it the most.

And down in Tucson, after a few weeks with John in Bisbee later in the year, I was standing in the middle of a truckstop by the interstate when I realised I'd left my toothbrush behind: now that was a real bummer. My toothbrush and my passport were pretty much the only things I cared about, because everything else I knew I could either find or be gifted, but these two things would require money to replace. And now my toothbrush was gone, left some sixty miles behind me, and that really was frustrating 'cos I sure liked brushing my teeth. And standing there, thinking these thoughts, up comes a man on a bicycle, and into my hand he presses a small plastic bag, and off he goes again, across the massive concrete expanse of the truckstop. A man on a bicycle in a truckstop on the interstate? Weird. But not as weird as opening that bag to find inside it a brand new toothbrush and toothpaste.

Or down in LA, sitting on a bench and waiting for a bus to go and visit Tim – having quickly devil-sticked myself a dollar fifty – and just thinking to myself, you know, I'm a little bit hungry – and within a minute a smartly-dressed lady presses a container of takeaway food into my hand and with a confused look on her face says, "this is for you," and off she goes and leaves me to the delights of a freshly-bought Thai meal and not an ounce of meat in sight. And it's bizarre because, I don't look hungry or homeless and there's nothing about me that says I'm anything other than just another normally-attired young guy sat waiting for a bus. It makes no sense and yet, because of what I know, it makes absolute perfect sense too.

These things happened all the time – the above are but my favourite three examples – and it only took so many days of this before I stopped thinking about where my sustenance was going to come from and devoted my mind wholly to other matters. Another time in LA a woman I got talking to gave me twenty dollars and I just thought, what on Earth am I going to do with this? I popped it straight into the nearest charity box. There just wasn't any point in thinking about it; it was always there.

And through this I learned that the highest form of trust is not having to.

Back in Albuquerque, Kate and I were in love, and intoxicated with each other – people said it was like fairy dust following us down the road as we buzzed about on her bike – but we always knew that it was a love that would have to come to an end at some point; that point came on a little trip I took back to Santa Fe. I'd been sitting all day in the plaza reading Illusions by Richard Bach when, around sunset, I felt this tree sort of beckon me. It's hard to explain, really – it didn't move or make a sound or do anything particularly un-tree like but, it definitely called me to it. I walked over and I felt an overwhelming urge to give it a hug. And right there in that plaza, barefoot and resplendent in my light blue hospital pants and nut factory t-shirt I put my arms around it and squeezed tight, and in my heart, joy and love.

And in my ears, these words: "Shasta. It's time."

Chapter Six

But what was Shasta? Well, Shasta was a TV show – Shasta McNasty, though I'd never seen it – and Shasta was also a soft drink that I'd first noticed in vending machines back in Charlottesville, now four months previous. In fact, I'd noticed that cola and advertisements for that TV show with a surprising regularity, and there was always something about the word Shasta that stuck in my mind. There was also a vague recollection of it as a mountain somewhere out in California or Oregon: Ocean Tree had probably mentioned it one day, although I knew his favourite mountain – being the kind of guy that would have a favourite mountain – was Mount Hood. But now a very different kind of tree was talking to me about it, and while I suppose it could have been telling me to watch the TV show or buy some cola I was pretty sure that it was the mountain it had in mind. So back to Albuquerque I went, and after sad goodbyes with Kate I was once more on the road, making LA in one long ride and I swear the whole eight hundred-mile journey took only twenty minutes, so peaceful was the meditation I did the whole way there.

I met up with Tim in LA and stayed the night with him and his band in Santa Monica; they'd by now been signed to Universal Records and were doing pretty well. It was great to see him and despite my changes we talked easily and fluidly and I guess that's always the way with your true old friends, the ones you've grown up with, no matter the years and miles that pass between meets. He was a little bit shocked by my barefoot, two stone less appearance, though – and by my unblinking eyes and unrelenting smile.

"You know," he said, as we sat drinking smoothies outside the Hustler café on Santa Monica Boulevard, "I don't think I've seen you blink once since you got here. You remind me of this guy I knew in uni; he became a born again Christian. You're not gonna try and convert me are you?"

I laughed. "Convert you to what?"

"I don't know," he said, "Buddhism? Noshoeism? What the hell are you anyway?"

"Nothing," I said, "I'm nothing" – and I glared at him for a second and wondered if I'd disappeared.

"You keep staring at me," he said, "it's weird."

"Sorry," I said. I remembered how Jay had said he really liked the way I maintained eye contact, how a lot of people were afraid to do that.

"So you're a healer now," he said, "can you fix my finger? The doctor says my joint's worn out, it keeps making all these weird clicking sounds."

"Give us your hand," I said, and I wrapped my hands around it and breathed. And after a while he said he could feel all this heat. And after a few minutes more I felt like I was done.

He took his hand back and moved the finger.

"Hey," he said, "it's not clicking! It feels better! How'd you do that?"

And I smiled a cheeky smile and pointed up to the heavens.

"Ha!" he said. He rubbed his finger and looked confused. "That was so weird," he said, "I was like, 'this is just Miller with my finger in his hand' but…it worked. It was sort of…emotional."

We went inside to pay for our drinks, Tim in his cool LA threads, me in my bare feet and hospital pants. And right there behind the counter two beautiful blondes with boobies and smiles and it's plain to see that they're all over me and good old Tim is sadly pushed to one side. Outside he tells me I should have got their numbers.

"They wanted you, man," he says. He can't believe it. "They wanted to sex you up."

"It's not me they want, Tim, it's what's inside of me." And all I can do is love this real-world demonstration of what a bit of God can do for a man, right there in front of my image-conscious brother.

"Well I quite fancied a bit of what was inside of them: you should have got those numbers for me."

And off we go rolling back to his apartment, him telling me stories about people in the neighbourhood getting shot and all the black guys riding around in their pimpmobiles and how he'd chased some on his bike one day because they'd cut him up – Tim! the living embodiment of all that is English and southern and soft, chasing gangsters on a racer! – and also how he's had eggs thrown at him on like five separate occasions, in totally different places, and he's getting a bit sick of it by now.

"Maybe it's a sign," I say.

"A sign of what?"

"Eat more protein?" And now we're laughing and joking and he's calling me a northern tool, and it's just like old times except I haven't got any shoes on and it's LA and not London or Leeds, and what better confirmation of how far you've come than to see your new self in the presence of your old muckers and not get mocked or looked on as crazy and realise just how okay you are. And back there in his apartment, in the dark of his room, lying there in our respective sleeping bags and dropping off to sleep he says my name.

"Are you awake?" he says.

"Yes."

"You've really changed," he says, "it's like you're not the same person anymore – I mean, I know it's you but…everything's changed. I can't believe you're the same guy that used to rip people off in Leeds."

"I guess I'm not the same guy, really," I say, "I feel like...there was me before Mexico, and then there's who I am now. Before seems like a past life – if it's possible to have a past life in the same body."

"You always looked like you were looking for something," he says – and this is news to me.

"Really?" I say, "you could tell? Blimey" – and I laugh – "you might have let me know: I just thought I was miserable."

"Thing is," he says, "you look like you've found it. I thought you might have been brainwashed or something. But you just seem really, really happy."

I smile and let his words echo around my brain – my washed and cleansed brain. The room is peaceful and silent: just our rising and falling breaths sounding quietly in the darkness.

"Rory?" he says.

"Yes."

"Is there really a God?"

"Yes," I say, smiling with the joy of my certainty, half hoping for one of Shane's tunnels of divine light to come and sweep me away.

"What is it?" he says.

"I don't know," I say, "that's what I'm trying to find out. Right now God is like this big invisible friend that takes care of me and fills me with joy and makes cool and miraculous things happen. God is like the wind that blows in the trees: you can't see it but you can see the effects, you can feel it. God is an experience. And more: union with the soul; enlightenment; nirvana – that's what I'm after. I want to be the first enlightened Yorkshireman! But, really, I haven't a clue; I just know that it's real, and it's nothing like I ever thought it was. Definitely not this grey-haired old bloke with a beard up in the clouds saying, 'you're bad! you're doomed!' Hell and damnation and fire and brimstone and all that rubbish. I think heaven and hell are right here, states of mind: even the pope says that. I don't think God goes in for that punishment business; I think that's just man. And it's not boring or serious or sad, it's cool and happy and fun. Spirituality's the new rock 'n' roll, man!"

And then I stop. I suddenly feel like I've said too much. He who knows does not speak and all that.

"Tim?" I say.

But good old buddy o' mine Tim is fast asleep.

Chapter Seven

I figured I'd stop in and see Shawn on the way up to the mountain – he was living in Clearlake, just north of San Fran – but he was away for a while so I killed some time in Berkeley. I stayed with Becky and Jen, the San Fran hippy mammas, and did a whole three days of the Sabbath with them and their Jewish friends: no electricity, no cooking, a great massive feast at the end of it all. It was like I was being taken on a grand tour of all the world's religions and given a little taste of each. I also met up with beautiful shining Rani on her travels in her van and she stayed a night there too. We shared a makeshift bed on the floor and held each other as we prepared to sleep. And then Rani said, "I normally sleep naked. Do you mind?"

"I don't mind," I said, "I do too. Do you mind?"

But she didn't mind either and we cuddled all night, arms around each other, platonic and nude, and not once did the thought of sex enter my brain. She was my friend and we were two pure and innocent children of light with better things to think about than that.

I got an email from a friend linking to a story about an Australian guy that had gone wandering off into the outback with just a Bible for company, wanting God or death. That sounded like the kind of thing I wanted to do – forty days and forty nights and all that. It was the next level of wilderness solo. I was sure I would survive. I'd by now met a few breatharians and people who had done ridiculously long fasts and they'd told me about being able to see energy in the air and watch it enter into their bodies and nourish them: it reminded me of that story where Jesus said he had things to eat that other men couldn't see. Was it prana? Manna? The universal energy? Chi? Across all religions and beliefs, the same stories cropping up again and again, and in them, so much truth.

I longed to know the truth of Jesus and I became obsessed for a few weeks reading everything about him: the Dead Sea Scrolls and the Nag Hammadi library and all the alternative gospels like those of Thomas and Mary Magdalene; the history of the Bible and of how the Romans had twisted it to suit their own needs, the fakery of the letters of the apostles; modern, channelled gospels that talked of him going to India and Tibet and Egypt to learn his stuff; legends of him having lived his life out in Kashmir and a tomb there; legends of him going to Glastonbury as a boy; and insights into his being by more recent-day Indian masters and gurus such as Paramahansa Yogananda and Ram Dass's beautifully eccentric teacher, Maharaj-ji – and in these guys I found my greatest understanding of the man we call 'the Christ' ('the anointed one' – the *enlightened* one; i.e., another Buddha, another Krishna), my rationale being that, while the person and feats of the historical Jesus are impossible to prove and will be debated until the end of time, if modern-day holy people can do it then what's to say that he couldn't too? People like Amma, for instance, had healed apparently incurable diseases and even raised herself and others from the dead – and Autobiography of a Yogi was filled with page after page of such Christ-like miracles. I had seen enough with my own eyes, and through my own hands, to believe that anything was possible – and now I was on my way to meet a real genuine Christian faith healer and mystic and I was sure she would have some answers. The call had come through from Shawn: he was home, and he had Momma with him.

I made Clearlake thanks to some fairly miraculous rides into the gorgeous hippy and redwood country north of San Francisco, picking up a free first level attunement in Reiki on the way and again being fed and sheltered and meeting more and more likeminded souls. People kept saying they recognised me: they swore they'd met me before. I wondered if perhaps it was a past life thing. Or maybe we were all part of the same 'soul family' or something. Northern California felt like home to me: all those little towns and the community feel of it and everybody being so friendly and the nature of the trees and hills and vineyards and coast. It was like I'd saved the best of America till last.

I found Shawn's house the evening after leaving Berkeley and joined a group of people sitting on the porch: Momma was in there doing her healings and they were all waiting outside to see her. I waited with them and eventually Shawn came out in between visitors.

"Rory!" he said, "you made it!"

We hugged and laughed and his eyes were shining more golden than anyone's I'd ever seen. I was getting high just standing there talking to him.

"Listen, I've got to go and help Momma – I'm her assistant, man!" he giggled, "but she'll be done soon. Then you can meet her. You're gonna stay, right?"

I told him I was. And I stayed the whole week right there in his little house by the lake with him and Momma, watching her heal and learning so, so much.

The first time I met Momma, sitting in Shawn's living room saying goodbye to the last of her healees, I swear, I could barely see her. It was like there was this fog all around her, this misty red and green soup. It filled the room. It gave me a headache. I felt like I was getting *too* high. She stood up and came and gave me a kiss right on the lips and said something like, "hello honey," and I was giggling like a five year-old. Shawn was giggling too, and there we were, giggling in his living room, two grown men acting as children in the presence of this woman who instantly felt like everybody's favourite grandmother, the Reverend Delorise 'Momma' Lucas.

Through Shawn and Momma and a couple of homemade information booklets I learned something of her story. She was about seventy, and had been healing practically since birth: her parents had found that just laying her on sick friends and family seemed to cure them of their ailments. Later, she had worked as a nurse, and studied and practised healing in her spare time, working with a healer called Ruthie. Ruthie had told her, "God wants you full-time," but Momma had felt that she couldn't sacrifice her work as she was paying to feed some fifty poor children in her own home. At some point she had gone into hospital, during which time she experienced ten clinical deaths over a period of about seven years, two of which she spent in a coma.

"The last time," she told me, "I went down a tunnel of light and met some angels who told me that I could do so much more good work for God if I wanted to. They said, 'do you want to go back?' and I said, 'yes' – and then I was doing cartwheels and backflips and went like that – wheeeeee! – right back into my body." She clapped her hands and laughed like a child at the thought of the memory.

She left hospital in perfect health two weeks later and had worked constantly as a healer and teacher ever since.

"She's totally surrendered," said Shawn, "she has no idea what she's doing tomorrow or next week; I don't think she even has a concept of the future. She's just totally in the moment."

Shawn told me stories about the things he had seen during his time studying with her: people healed of cancer and tumours; a man almost instantly cured of the cerebral palsy that had rendered him practically unable to speak; exorcisms and battles with demons. I looked over at Momma sitting on the couch and she seemed so innocent and sweet.

"There was this lady this afternoon," Shawn said, "you wouldn't believe it: she looked so business-like and normal but she'd been having a lot of problems with anger and depression and stuff. Momma started the healing and suddenly this enormous deep voice came out of the woman and her eyes were popping out and she was singing this mad song about being a demon in hell and how she was gonna kill Momma and rape her and stuff. I was freaking out and wondering what the hell must Momma be thinking but Momma just sat there and listened and when the lady was done she said, 'that's sweet, honey, would you like to hear one of my songs?' and then sang her some soppy hymn about Jesus and just held her hand and carried on like it was nothing. She did the healing and all the time this woman was writhing about and swearing and stuff and then eventually she stopped and when she opened her eyes she didn't have a clue what had just happened. But she was totally changed. She was so sweet and gentle and clear. She just sat there blinking and smiling and saying, 'gosh.' We didn't tell her what she'd been like."

The week I spent with Momma was a blur of people coming and going, Shawn and I assisting with all the ins and outs, and right there in that chair, hour after hour, I watched as they entered bent and broken and dispirited and left healed and made whole and with smiles of joy on their faces, bones and tissues and hearts freshly mended. A woman came with her husband and told him, "I'm sorry, honey, but that feels better than sex"; big strong guys cried in her lap and were as babies; everybody adored her and she adored them all right back. And in the evening Shawn and Momma and I sat and talked, or watched TV with our dinners on our laps, and when it was time for bed Momma would give us a kiss on our lips and say, "night, honey," and off we'd go like good little boys.

One night we were all eating Chinese and Shawn and I were listening to Momma tell us these stories, about doing healings for Elvis back in the sixties, and how one time she'd got a message through that some beings from another planet wanted to come and visit her but instead she got a visit and a warning from some high-ranking army official and then another message that they'd crash-landed. Honestly, the things that came out of that sweet little septuagenarian's mouth! But whether she was talking about aliens or her love of spring rolls she really was the embodiment of joyfulness and innocence.

"Did Shawn tell you that he's going to be ordained?" she asked me.

"Yes," I said, "that's so awesome. He can come and do my wedding." And I grinned at Shawn and he nodded in agreement.

I sat and thought about it for a moment.

"Momma?" I said, "what am I here for? I mean, what's my purpose?"

She put down her fork and looked at me with a smile.

"You're a prophet, honey," she said.

"Really? Wow." I was strangely tickled by this: it made me smile and want to giggle and filled my body with a fuzzy warm feeling. And then I realised I had absolutely no idea what that meant.

"Momma?" I said, "what's a prophet?"

"A master teacher," she said – and that sure felt good too.

I got a reading one night from Shawn; it was the first time I'd seen him do it in person, after a dozen or so over the internet. He sat in his chair on the other side of the room and started to go into a trance. His thumb twitched madly from side to side and the room became filled with that red and green fog. I could barely see him. The energy was making me super high.

"Good light, dear soul," he said, "how may we be of service?"

I sank into my chair and grew more and more relaxed and spaced out by the second. My mind was a blank – and then a thought popped into my head.

"I wonder sometimes about sex," I said, "I want it but…I know it's supposed to be bad for you, on the path and all that…"

I trail off. Shawn takes a deep breath – but what it looks like is something breathing him – and his thumb starts twitching again.

He talks, and it is Shawn and it isn't Shawn. He speaks much more properly and fluently than I'm used to.

"Even as you ask," he says, "you know that there is no answer to be conveniently provided for you; what would be the point otherwise? The point is to follow your heart where it leads you, not so much to where you are led by others. Understand that the entire creation is at your disposal: do with it as you please, follow your own choices. You are here to learn and you may give yourself permission to enjoy without guilt or worry: it is better to commit a perceived sin out of love than to abstain and yet think upon it constantly. He who does so is a hypocrite; it is not recommended to give up things before you are ready. When you are truly ready, giving up will be effortless. Your path is yours alone to walk but that does not mean that you must walk it alone. Make your choices. Enjoy this life, this creation, simply do not be attached to it as the only reality: enjoy yet do not cling."

I breathe it all in and nod. The top of my head – my crown chakra – is going wild. It's as though the information is coming in through there too: the feeling is one of understanding and knowing exactly what I have to do.

I let it all sink into me and then another thought arises.

"What's the truth about Jesus?" I say, "what was he like? Is he coming back? Will I get to meet him?"

He takes another deep breath. Through the fog I see his bearded face, his eyes closed, peaceful.

"You are blessed, dear soul," he says, calm and loving, "but God has not smiled favourably on you alone, God smiles constantly on all that is and illuminates all with love. Keep walking forward, that's all you need concentrate on. Learn to let go of the future by concentrating on perfecting the moment and walk through the murky swamp as swiftly and cheerfully as the field of flowers. You do not know what lies around the next corner. Endure always remembering that God is the ultimate reality and that this is all a drama set up by the divinity within you in order to reach the ultimate truth. Why speculate endlessly about things that don't matter or cannot be proved or experienced? Aim for the source of all things and for that direct experience of truth and like a well-guided arrow you will hit your target. But for an archer who is gazing dreamily into the sky or watching the drama down the way there is no telling where his arrow may hit."

He pauses for a moment; I think of the Buddhist parable of the poisoned arrow – the point being that too much thought and philosophy can be a waste of time and certainly won't lead to enlightenment.

Again the words sink into me and I sit there in peace, breathing slowly, softly melting into the chair. My mind is devoid of thought: bliss washes over me – and then suddenly I feel a frustration and a desire to cry, and out of nowhere I'm flooded with the thoughts of all my mistakes, the pain and suffering I've caused others. God knows, I'm a better person now, and I wouldn't dream of doing anything to hurt another – and in my heart I feel cleansed and forgiven – yet in my mind the memory of what I was remains and haunts me still. Even if God and the soul forgive, it's so hard for the human to forget. Sometimes I wish I could die and be reborn again, with the heart and love I have now, but with a brain free from the remembrances of my earlier life.

"I've done so many wrong things," I say, "I don't even know where to begin..." Tears come to my eyes; I feel an almost unbearable pain at the thought of how bad I've been.

"We are none of us perfect," he says, "and we all make mistakes. If you accept that you have some dark along with the light only then can you focus upon the light and begin to let go of your lower tendencies. You have sought energy for your journey in the form of other people's love or hate; whether it be positive or negative energy is often of little importance to your astral body: it craves energy and causes situations in which to bring it out of people. Simply to be aware of this and seek your power from within, the source, is enough to curb this tendency. You have 'flaws' only because you have chosen to take on a body and to take on those flaws for your own voluntary growth as well as the growth of others. You have brought with you many trials and lessons. You think yourself a bad person, but who is it that decides this? Who are you? You as Rory are what you believe yourself to be; your ego is this belief bevelled in your brain and brought forth into matter. Recognise your mind for what it is, passing thoughts associated with a body people call Rory; make peace with it and give it thanks then go beyond it. What lies underneath this phantom of thought forms and memories and ideas and self-judgement is that which IS. You have a desire to realise God, which means unrealising everything you think you are. Deconstructing the framework of the mind is a tremendous task and can only be fully accomplished with the grace of God.

"You are now sufficiently purified to be in touch with the truth that, as all things are, thoughts are connected. You have already begun to heal the people you believe yourself to have wronged in the past with the thought vibrations you send forth consciously as well as unconsciously. You are one with a constitution of healing, for you have seen the storm yet chosen the sun. Shine like the sun with your every thought, your very being. In your earthly existence you accumulate actions, all of which have a reaction. You now have the opportunity to neutralize all ill effects of past actions by burning these karmas with your divine brilliance. Remember that which you have already learned, lest your lessons be repeated. Have no worries and have no fear for you are being bathed in perfection and every circumstance which falls before you or which you seek out is arranged that it may bring you closer to the next truth. Continue your service in living and in writing for it is a link to the divine. Not a moment of your existence is wasted. You are blessed and it is with great joy we give you this guidance which you have called forth by your most loving nature, the depth of which you have yet to realise. You shine so brightly you are joy itself. Your goal is inevitable, dear one, you are on the right track. Never doubt it again."

And what could I say to that? There were no more thoughts in my mind; I was as still as the chair I sat in, my arms on the rests, a quiet smile and a relaxed and empty gaze into the fog.

"We see that you have a blockage in your digestive system," Shawn continued. I looked up and saw him sitting eyes closed in his chair, that thumb starting up again. "The blockage," he said, "is the result of sporadic and irregular fasting. Your body has become uncertain of where the next meal is coming from and has developed a pattern of holding onto its nourishment for as long as possible."

So they know about this too: it's absolutely true that I've been pretty much constantly constipated since Crestone and my solo, where I barely ate a thing the last two weeks.

"The body has its own intelligence," he said, "and also its own fears and doubts. Your body has become afraid for its survival and ceased to trust that you will look after it properly. Would you like us to remove this fear?"

"Yes, please," I answered – and in that instant a bolt of energy hit me in my abdomen, invisible hands fairly squeezing my stomach and intestines. It was hot and pleasant.

It stopped, and I felt somehow lighter.

"Thank you," I whispered.

"It is a pleasure to serve," he said, "if you need more illumination you may ask. Good light."

"Good light," I said. 'Good light' is angelspeak for 'good night' or 'good morning' – there being no night or day where they come from.

"Hoowee," said Shawn, "that was a good one." He blinked open his eyes and stretched out his arms. "Hope you liked it."

"Hoowee is the word," I said, "how on Earth do you do that? That was awesome."

"It's all Momma's doing," he said, "I couldn't have done anything without her. She gave me a healing the other day to take out every negativity I'd accumulated since the day I was born. I felt totally new. Everything was like it was for the first time. Tasting macaroni and cheese was like I'd never tasted food before. It was just so good!"

And right there looking at Shawn I had a vision of him as a colander or a sieve, little by little his multitude of holes and openings unblocked and the divine light that poured from above flowing freely through him and into the world, and the sieves of Momma and Amma and the others like them vast and enormous, and barely blocked at all, and my own small and fledgling filter slowly and steadily letting through more and more of that stream of light, and all throughout the world, over lifetimes and millennia, the same thing happening in each and every one of us as we gradually grow in capacity and openness, and journey towards the moment when the blockages are no more, and the sieve is no more, and all that exists is light.

Chapter Eight

Shawn was coming to Shasta with me. He said he'd been getting little messages about it since the summer – probably about as long as I had – but he'd never quite gotten around to it. Now he felt it was time. We loaded up his car with our sleeping bags and tents and up the winding northern California roads we went, thick woods and little towns where I just knew hippy communities would be peacefully happening. We were getting up into the Cascade mountains and it was all grey and mist and rain. It was November now. We were spirit buddies *most excellent* and the miles passed in blesséd silence, no need for words, the two of us just silent pools of energy.

Eventually, Shawn spoke.

"We're going to experience joy," he said, "that's one thing they've told me."

"Who's they?" I said.

"The beings in the back of the car. They've been watching us." I whirled around. "Their minds are so calm," he said, "so still..."

"A bit of joy would be good," I said – and we laughed. Ever since the canyon both our lives had been filled with almost constant and unbridled bliss: walking down the street; breathing; going into ecstasy at the sight of a falling leaf. I wanted to hug strangers and I did, and whatever it was that was in me allowed it to happen, made people receptive. I borrowed a guitar once and walked slowly through town playing, 'All You Need Is Love,' and when I turned around people were following me, their eyes glowing, looking up. I hugged them one after the other and saw them almost knocked off their feet by whatever they'd got from it. Certainly, I was no stranger to joy.

We stopped off at a hot springs on the way and lay naked in the pools talking about how we wanted to be Buddha and Jesus, and who would be Buddha and who would be Jesus? And then when we got to Mount Shasta City, the town at the foot of the mountain, so very X-files was it with its quiet red-brick porches and autumnal dampness and mist, and what with us being on the case and following the clues and all, we decided we'd be Mulder and Scully, and who would be who there? And since we couldn't choose we both decided to be Scully.

The clues and trees and vending machines had taken us this far: but once we were there, what was there to do? We walked the streets looking for answers. We saw a shop slash meditation room full of pictures of some crazy mad-hatted white guy who claimed to be the Buddha of the Ages. There were places devoted to pyramid power and tachyon energy, healing rooms and meditation centres, workshops in wizardry and channelling and all manner of bizarre and wonderful thing. It was like Disneyland for the New Age – but no clues here.

"All I've got," I said, "is I keep seeing the name Lazarus, like on Star Trek the other day; keep thinking that it means something but I don't know what."

Shawn nodded. It wasn't much to go by. There was only one place we hadn't looked.

And up the mountain it was.

We drove as far as we could go and then Shawn said we should walk a bit further and camp. There was about a foot of snow and it was raining hard, little spears of ice. Neither of us had dressed for winter. But off we went with our tent and sleeping bags, and in the encroaching gloom I saw a fiery golden light surrounding all the trees. I'd been seeing this golden light around people and objects in nature ever since Charlottesville, when I'd first noticed it around a visiting Tibetan teacher who was giving a talk at the library. It was like an aura, I suppose. But I'd never seen it like this.

"The energy up here is amazing," I shouted across to Shawn as we tramped up through the snow, through the frozen, biting rain. It was practically a whiteout.

"Damn straight!" he shouted back. We were both laughing and loving it; I felt transported and energised and full of glee, like the child I never was, abandoned to delight. We were on a snow-covered mountain getting soaked to the skin and I was feeling nothing but ecstasy. I could have gone racing off into that whiteness and never come back.

We put up our tent on a bit of a slope and climbed in, giggling at our madness and shivering. But almost as soon as we had snuggled up in our sleeping bags, the tent started sliding down the slope, rolling over on itself: we were both on our way to sleeping on the ceiling. The wind-bashed sides then collapsed and water began to seep in – and all we could do was laugh our bloody heads off. We were lost to hysterics. We went outside to try and rectify the situation and Shawn struggled manfully against the elements, pulling the tent back up the slope and tying it to a tree, seriously hindered not only by the treacherous conditions but by his cracking up the whole time he was doing it. Meanwhile, I stood on a tarp in a pair of wet socks and some long johns and enjoyed the spectacle, my own uproarious laughter making balance all the more difficult.

Eventually we clambered back inside and Shawn got his warm healer's hands out and clasped them around my frozen feet.

"My sleeping bag is soaking," I laughed, "this is lunacy." And he was laughing too. And everything was funny. The way the wind and the beating rain quickly caused our tent to lose all semblance of its proper shape. The way the water came leaking in through the sides and the bottom. The fact of our already soaked sleeping bags and clothes, rendered practically useless before we'd even got in the tent. And Shawn and I lying there in bliss composing stupidly hysterical Scott of the Antarctic style diary entries and giggling our sodden little socks off.

We fell asleep with big grins on our faces but I was too cold to sleep properly, sort of awake and not awake for hours on end. And then I noticed that my feet and legs were no longer cold but that they were actually uncommonly warm. It was nice but I couldn't understand how they'd become so hot.

I sat up and looked at my legs.

My legs were missing.

I nudged Shawn and his legs were missing too: he sat up and looked and what we realised was, we'd started to slide down the mountain in our sleep, and our feet, right up to our knees, had gone through the mysteriously-opened door of our tent and were now buried in the snow outside. We sat there in our sleeping bags looking at this bewildering sight and we just roared with laughter. We pointed and cried and slapped each other's shoulders, and the howls of laughter and tears of joy were so much we couldn't even bring ourselves to drag our legs back in. I laughed so much I laughed till I could no longer make a sound, just pointing at my feet and lost to the moment, and on and on it went, joy unparalleled, bliss beyond bliss, hysterically pissing ourselves beyond all sense of thought. It was joy: oh my God, was it joy! We laughed and we laughed and for maybe thirty minutes we were simply incapacitated by this joydom sitting there in our sleeping bags. Finally, from somewhere we managed to summon up enough sobriety to reclaim our missing limbs and bring them back inside the tent.

And all night long we lay there giggling in our little bags, and every now and then the giggles would break out into shrieks and howls, and explosions of laughter, and that moment sitting frozen and soaked and seeing my feet poking out of the tent and buried in the snow was just the most extraordinarily blissful experience of my life.

So that was joy.

In the morning we went back down the mountain to town – to dry our socks and clothes in the laundromat – and to look for clues. The night had been extraordinary but we knew that was not the end of it. So we wandered around, and found a lovely little crusty café, The Light of Love, and checked out the bookstores to read some more of the mountain and the magical stories that were associated with it: stories of ascended masters and seventh-dimensional beings that supposedly dwelled within the mountain itself; stories of people called from all over the globe to Shasta and having the wildest of times. It all served to increase our longing to experience yet more of what mystical Mount Shasta had to offer. And then, strangely drawn by an ad in the local paper, we went to a store selling alternative health products, and were served tea by the owner, and were then treated to a long discourse about the mountain and those ascended masters. But it was not him that spoke, it was something else that spoke through him: an energy in his words that bore straight into my heart, that

I could only liken to hearing Shawn's channelling; it felt like The Supreme Being Himself was talking to me. And as he spoke, little by little, everything I had learned and seen and done along this path was erased and I was shown once more how little I truly knew, how far I had to go towards knowing. By the time he had finished speaking I was left emotionally breathless and absolutely empty, save for a frustrated and passionate longing to know the truth of this divine mystery once and for all.

We woke the next day to blue skies: for the first time since we'd left Clearlake the grey clouds of winter had cleared and the sun was out, and there was the mountain, that great expanse of rock and snow filling the sky, and she was beyond words. And looking up at her magnificence and beauty, I knew that I knew nothing and that all I had been was gone. The joy of two nights previous was a long distant memory; the joys of that whole year of soul-searching may as well never have been. Dejection and resignation were all I knew. Emptiness overwhelmed me. I had nothing left to give: not one iota of a thought or an idea, no inspiration or direction. I looked to Shawn and I could see that Shawn was feeling otherwise, though.

"We should go up there," he said, "right now." He seemed to know what to do. I turned my will over to him.

We climbed in the car and drove back up the steep mountain road and not a word between us. But no longer the silence of peacefulness and quiet expectation that had characterised our drive up there: now it was defeat and surrender on my part – and steely-eyed determination on his.

We got to the parking area and he took his keys and his wallet and pushed them into the glove box.

"I'm going up there," he said, "and either I find God or die."

And I knew that he meant it.

Thoughts passed through my brain: thoughts of him and his girlfriend; thoughts of what I would tell her; and thoughts of my own quest, and the realisation that there was nothing left for me in this world save my longing for the divine and the truth.

"Me too," I said. And I meant it as well.

We began tromping up the snow-covered mountainside. Up and up we went, Shawn marching on ahead. After an hour or so he stopped and I had the urge to take over. I heard a voice say, "use your knowledge of the stones." I looked around and I saw how the energy was being channelled in a certain way, down towards a pair of stone meditation seats. I led the way and Shawn followed, and when we reached the stones we sat down.

He beckoned me to sit in front of him.

He put his hands on my shoulders and started to speak.

The voice that came through him was not his.

"What we say is not by words and ears," it said, "open your minds and open your hearts."

This was it. This was the moment we had been led to. This was the reason for the whole thing. The reason for my *entire life*.

I prayed with everything I had that my heart would be open, that the bleakness of the emptiness that overwhelmed me would not get in the way of what I was about to receive. I prayed and I prayed, and I surrendered myself to whatever was coming.

I felt myself guided by unseen hands. I knelt down in front of Shawn – in front of that which was in him – and everything inside of me wanted to bow down before him; to go as low as I could; to kiss his shoes. I wanted to give him everything I had

"Follow," he said, and he began moving his hands through the air in a pattern, tracing shapes. I felt energy being shifted and electricity coursing through my body. I was shaking uncontrollably. Tears were in my eyes. I prayed that I was doing it right.

We repeated the pattern three times, and then he stopped.

"This is why we have brought you here," the voice said, "what do you want?"

The words sprang automatically from my being.

"To know God," I said. "To know the truth."

"And what are you willing to give?"

"Whatever it takes," I said – and meant it.

Almost immediately the voice spoke again.

"You will both die on this mountain today," it said. The words hit me and something inside my body whimpered and cried. I saw myself standing and taking my leave from Shawn, walking off into the snowy wilderness alone and finding a tree to sit against and await my demise. I saw myself freezing to death in the whiteness, on the mountain, all to show how much I wanted this and how I was no longer willing to live without it. I thought of my mother and watched as all the ties to my family and my loved ones were dissolved. And then I saw myself dead. I saw my faith and my trust and I knew that I was ready to bring the images in my head into the reality of my life.

There were more hand movements and more electrical surges through my body. I vibrated wildly, and tears longed to explode from me – but now, also, rising up like a bubbling well, laughter. Joy was flowing through my veins; I started to giggle. And somewhere in there it was conveyed to us that the death we would be experiencing would not be a physical one.

"From this day on," the voice said, "your lives are Mine – you are children of God. Wherever you go you will hold a light out in front of you, a lantern."

"It's done," Shawn said.

I fell in the snow and sobbed and laughed. I prostrated myself, desperate to find a way to demonstrate the immense appreciation I felt for all that had happened. If I was not going to be allowed to die the least I could do was lie there in the snow and freeze a little.

Shawn laughed and said, "they say you don't have to freeze your knees for them."

I sat up and looked up at him with tears of joy in my eyes. I felt like I was looking at another human being for the first time in my life. His face was totally changed – wrinkles where there weren't any before, and where there wouldn't be in a few hours time – and his eyes seemed ancient and full of power and light. I told him what I saw and he said he saw the same thing in me. We were changed, and we had died, and yet we were still there, the same as ever.

Had I got it? Had I got it as much as him? Was this the end that I had been so desperate to get to? And if it was, why did I still feel normal?

"There is no end," he said, out of the blue, "there is no there to get to. You just keep on going."

And there was a comfort in that.

We went back to town and sat in The Light of Love and ordered some fries. I felt like I was floating through everything, intrigued and astounded by everything I saw. The waiter laid the food down on the table and I watched his arm with an almost vampiric intensity. He was serving me but I wanted to serve him so badly it was almost painful.

Someone came rushing in from outside.

"Check out the mountain," they said.

We stood at the back door of the restaurant with a small group of people gazing up. The mountain towered alone and magnificent over the green black forest, and above its snow-capped summit, two perfect white circles of cloud: the flying saucer-shaped formations for which Shasta is famous. Shawn and I looked at each other and we knew they were for us. We looked and we looked and when everyone else had gone back inside we just kept on looking. The white and grey of the mountain became a glow of purple and gold, the colours shifting and changing, a huge aura of energy and light shining from its ridges and peaks. I thought then about the words of Jesus: about if we only had the faith of a mustard seed we could move mountains, and I wondered about his saying, "I am the truth and the life and the way" – and then it dawned on me that, yes, it's true, he was right: I *am* the truth and the life and the way. I watched and the giant glowing mountain shifted several hundred metres to the east, and remained there for a second, and then moved smoothly back into place. It was like a wink. God was winking at me. God winking at God. I stood there silently smiling, and breathed it all in, and breathed it all out. My peace was immense.

Epilogue

And so down the mountain we go, Shawn and I, and back on that dark green strip of California highway silently cruising into the night, the motor purring, the headlights steadily revealing the ever onwards black ribbon of tarmac – and then there in those headlights, there is an owl, and time comes to a stop as the owl slowly turns its big white head to meet us, and nods an acknowledgement, and shining pure and white and huge then spreads its wings and flies purposefully and head-on straight into the front of our car. Normally it's a tragedy to hit such a beautiful creature – but this owl is different, close totemic encounters and all, and as its body smashes into the front grill two streams of energy shoot up into the soles of our feet and race through our bodies, and settle there in the centres of our being. And Shawn and I, in our by-now telepathic ways, both smile and nod and accept with quiet gratitude this gift, for owl, we know, signifies liberation, and owl signifies death, and this owl is there for a reason.

And in the morning, there is no trace.

I left Shawn a few days later and hitched on up to the Vipassana meditation centre near Yosemite. All my rides were lovely and spiritual and I even did a healing for one of them, as she drove. And while we were bathing in the afterglow of that, a big truck had slowly drifted on by with the word, "ENGLAND" massively printed on the back.

The lady points at it and laughs.

"Oh look," she says, "maybe it's a sign for you. Maybe it's time for you to go home."

She says it as a joke but, at the same time, I feel something stir inside.

We watch the truck move away from us and I sit and wonder about those seven familiar letters, red on white. I do feel something – feel it after all the times I've longed for England and then been denied; feel it now that England is practically absent from my thinking, now that I'm perfectly happy doing exactly what I'm doing – but feel it all the same.

Except, if it is time, I have absolutely no way of getting there.

293

I do Vipassana; do ten days of sitting on a cushion in a room full of women and men watching my breath come slowly in, go slowly out, eyes closed, awareness focused entirely on my respiration, on the physical sensations as they arise within my body. I bring my attention to my nostrils, to the muscles of my face; right shoulder, left shoulder; back and chest, stomach and legs and feet. A thought appears and then I notice it, accept it, and return to my breathing. Up and down my body I go and slowly thoughts subside, that mad monkey chatter of the mind becoming quiet and still, and peace grows within. Peace and joy. Peace and love and joy. There's a whole universe inside this body of mine: a universe full of subtle vibrations and sensations and light. And the deeper and deeper I go into this universe the greater my happiness becomes.

Ten days we have sat on our various cushions, wrapped in our various blankets from dawn till night – and for ten days we have maintained total silence and avoided interaction of any kind. No eye contact, no gestures, no smiles or acknowledgements: totally within. For ten days I have slept in a room full of men and heard nothing from them but the occasional fart and snore – and then when the ten days are over, and the silence is lifted, the roar of their conversation is deafening.

I slide off into the corner and sit quietly. I don't want to come back into this world; I don't want to talk about all I've just experienced. But I hear them and I can't help but listen as they tell of their trials, their pains, their sexual fantasies; the time when someone let rip and the whole place slowly got the giggles and the teachers told us off and how wonderfully funny it was. About how good the food has been. About hating it at first but already wanting to come back. About, even, peace and love and joy.

But the return, it seems, is inevitable.

A man in glasses comes over and introduces himself as Brad.

"Pretty intense, huh?" he says, smiling and glowing and pleased. "Had some real rough days in there myself – but, you know what, I just gotta tell you that whenever I saw you, and whenever I saw that t-shirt that you're wearing – what's it say? 'Property of the Nut Factory'? – it just made me smile, sort of gave me the strength to go on. You seem like a real peaceful kind of guy. Like, you got the light."

"Thanks Brad," I say, my voice more quiet and smoother than I remember it, a tentative reacquaintance with myself, "looks like you got the light too."

"Listen," he says, "I can see that you want to be alone right now but – I was just thinking, if you ever need a plane ticket to anywhere, you just let me know. I got all these frequent flyer miles. I'm sure I could sort you something out."

He disappears then to find paper and a pen and leaves me standing there in an amazed and grateful stupor. Once again, I have been provided for. Once again, even before I have asked, I have been answered.

He returns and hands me his email address.

And a few weeks later, I am home.

Rory Miller currently lives on the roads of Mexico, where he is en route to a magical little canyon in Baja California Sur. This is his first book. Previously he has worked as a guitar salesman, furniture moving man, bicycle courier, waiter, stunt cowboy/ranch hand, dishwasher, faith healer, receptionist, meditation centre cook, postman, cake salesman, student mentor, administration assistant, high school teacher, charity shop manager, professional gambler, and landscape gardener. He almost got married once, to a girl that features within these pages. But that, perhaps, is a whole other story.